ABERDI
AND THE
HIGHLAND CHURCH
(1785-1900)

*

Ian R. MacDonald.

ABERDEEN
AND THE
HIGHLAND CHURCH

(1785-1900)

*

Ian R MacDonald

SAINT ANDREW PRESS

EDINBURGH

First published in 2000 by
SAINT ANDREW PRESS
121 George Street, Edinburgh EH2 4YN

Copyright © Ian R MacDonald 2000

ISBN 0 7152 0768 7

British Library Cataloguing in Publication Data
 A catalogue record for
 this book is available
 from the British Library

 ISBN 0715207687

The Publisher acknowledges financial assistance from
The Drummond Trust
The Hope Trust
Catherine McCaig's Trust
and the Council of the Highland Fund Ltd
towards the publication of this volume.

This book has been set in Bembo and Charlemagne.

Cover design by Mark Blackadder.
Typesetting by Lesley A Taylor.
Printed and **bound** by Athenaeum Press Ltd, Gateshead, Tyne and Wear.

*
CONTENTS

Part III: FORSAKING THE PAST

To FRASER
whose filial enthusiasm
to teach me new skills
gave me new heart

*

FOREWORD

DR Ian MacDonald has already gained a considerable reputation
as an historian of Scotland's Gaelic chapels – those fundamentally
important institutions which, in such places as Glasgow, Greenock,
Edinburgh, Dundee, Aberdeen, and also Cromarty, catered for the
spiritual and cultural needs of Highlanders who had left their native
heath in search of employment, whether as shipyard workers in
Glasgow, or hewers of granite in Aberdeen. The chapels were central
to the maintenance of Gaelic identity among the migrant communities; as Christian, and predominantly evangelical, institutions, they
complemented the range of secular societies which brought Highlanders together to maintain the songs, stories and general ambience
of their places of origin. In the Gaelic chapels scriptures, sermons and
psalms linked heaven and earth, people and homeland, in cultural
harmony.

Despite their location outside the Highlands and Islands, the chapels
were a potent element in the wider networks of Highland spirituality.
Young men who were to become key leaders of the Highland evangelical world sometimes spent their formative years as pastors of
Gaelic chapels; this was true of the great itinerant evangelist, Dr
John MacDonald of Ferintosh (1779-1849), who served as minister of
Edinburgh's Gaelic chapel (1807-13), and of Alexander MacLeod
(1786-1869), reputedly the first evangelical minister in Lewis when
settled in Uig in 1824, who had previously graced the pulpit of the
Gaelic chapels in Dundee (1819-21) and Cromarty (1821-24). Men
who served acceptably in chapel charges were often eagerly desired in
the pulpits of their homeland, and, as this book shows, their ministries
in Gaelic chapels were frequently frustratingly short. Competitive
tendering for ministers was evidently not unknown.

Gaelic chapels not only enhanced the quality of Highland ministerial leadership; it is equally evident that evangelical spirituality was
strengthened and even intensified in a context in which a proportion of
the Gaelic population became 'strangers and pilgrims' by the streams
of the Clyde, or by the banks of the Dee. The Gaelic chapels enabled
them to 'sing the Lord's song in a strange land' – and their experience
of his favour was sometimes transmitted to the homeland, where it

encouraged deeper piety and even revival. The chapels, of course, catered not only for Gaelic communities, firmly rooted in the Lowlands, but also for transient Highlanders, as they moved temporarily into the Lowlands, and then made their way homewards at the end of seasonal employment. Gleanings from 'the harvest of the Lord' sometimes accompanied their journeys, and seeds were sown in Highland soil. Gaelic chapels thus preserved a beneficially osmotic relationship with the Highland homeland, as this book demonstrates splendidly.

In 1995 Dr MacDonald gave us a fine study of Glasgow's Gaelic Churches. In this volume, he offers us an in-depth study – a social, spiritual and cultural biography – of one Gaelic chapel in Scotland which is, naturally, very close to his heart. It is the mother church of Bon Accord Free Church of Scotland in Aberdeen. By a wonderful providence, the records of the early years of Aberdeen's Gaelic chapel have been preserved virtually intact, and this happy circumstance has allowed Dr MacDonald to present a remarkably detailed story. He does so meticulously. The result is a book of very considerable importance to our understanding of Scotland's churches and especially its Gaelic chapels.

Several aspects of the life and work of the Aberdeen chapel are worthy of some emphasis in this introduction. First and foremost, the evidence so skilfully exploited by Dr MacDonald allows us to see virtually the whole life of the church, from its foundation, through many trials and tribulations, to its twentieth century metamorphosis. We meet a rich gallery of characters – ministers, elders and people – who fought the good fight of faith in various ways – and no one more so than the redoubtable John Ewen, one of the first managers of the chapel and a friend of the Gaels whose memory deserves commemoration. The book contains a wealth of miniature biographies of key figures, both in Aberdeen and in the wider Gaelic world.

No less significantly, this book allows us to see the ambivalent relationship which existed between Gaelic chapels and the parishes in which they were situated. It is evident that, in its early years, the Aberdeen chapel enjoyed a considerable degree of independence relative to its parish. This allowed it to appoint its own elders and call its own ministers without restriction. In effect, the chapel was a 'gathered congregation', conforming in some respects to the Baptist and Congregational chapels elsewhere in Scotland. Such independence was both a strength and a weakness: a strength because doctrinal standards could be safeguarded; a weakness since the chapel was perhaps more than usually vulnerable to the loss of its congregation as industries rose and fell. Eventually the position of the Aberdeen chapel was regularised within the parochial system, but, as in the case of most churches which functioned as Gaelic chapels, its awareness of being a 'special' charge transcended the many vicissitudes which came its way. Aberdeen's Gaelic chapel was itself something of a 'migrant', moving to several different locations (notably Gaelic Lane) as the city grew and developed, but part of its Gaelic character remained, and continues to the present.

The cultural profile of the Aberdeen chapel is of particular interest. The nature of the surviving evidence permits Dr MacDonald to look in some detail, not only at the chapel in relation to its urban environment, but also at the social status of those who were its leaders in the eldership. In the bygoing, he is able to challenge previous historian's views on the social mobility and aspirations of those who led their churches out of the establishment in 1843. Elders at the Gaelic chapel were rugged individualists who were chosen to lead the flock because of the quality of their spiritual experience, not the success of their social climbing. This is all too often a neglected perspective among those historians who tend to approach the Christian faith merely as a sociological phenomenon. Again, while this was Aberdeen's Gaelic chapel, it is clear that it provided spiritual nourishment for monoglot English speakers too. Such a congregation was not devoid of tensions between the two groups. This book shows us how such tensions were created and resolved.

Tension between ecclesiastical groups, who define their distinctive tenets theologically or culturally, is a theme of no small relevance to the present day. Indeed, this book offers a timely set of perspectives to those who grapple with such issues. In Aberdeen itself, the boom-time of the oil industry introduced specialist workers from different parts of the world, notably Americans from the southern United States. Some of the new arrivals established churches and chapels with a distinctive cultural ethos, based on their respective homelands, and employing much the same principles as inspired Aberdeen's Gaelic speakers to create their own Gaelic chapel back in 1785. In the course of time, questions arose within these modern chapels about the extent to which they should become part of their immediate cultural contexts. Should they insist on appointing a native Scotsman as minister, for example? How far should the theological perspectives of Scotland, rather than those of the United States, be allowed to determine the complexion of the church? Of course, this theme is not only Gaelic, Scottish or American. It is, in truth, global, and this book is potentially of interest wherever different ethnic groups have migrated and, in their own languages, have endeavoured to 'sing the Lord's song in a strange land'.

As Professor of Celtic at the University of Aberdeen, and as an evangelical Highlander with an insatiable interest in the different cultural expressions of 'the faith once for all delivered to the saints', I count it a particular privilege to write the Foreword to this illuminating book. It is a rich contribution to the planting of a field which, prior to Dr MacDonald's diligent labours, was largely untilled. His crop is now maturing. May the seed that comes from it lead to further seminal thinking and study in the years ahead.

Donald E Meek
King's College
OLD ABERDEEN 1999

*

INTRODUCTION

IN the summer of 1982, I returned home one day to find a cardboard carton sitting on the doorstep. It subsequently transpired that the minister of Bon Accord Free Church, who was about to leave Aberdeen for Killearnan, thought that the church records should be left in the safe-keeping of the Session Clerk rather than in an empty manse; and so he deposited a large box of assorted minute books to await my lunch-hour return. The box included old folios bound in sail-cloth. This was my first sighting of the records of the Aberdeen Gaelic Chapel. It seems that sometime after 1970 they had been deposited in the manse by my predecessor who had been appointed to the clerkship of the congregation (St Columba Free Church, Dee Street, as it then was) in 1929. How they came into his possession is unknown. Alex Gammie, writing as the Ecclesiastical Correspondent of the Aberdeen *Evening Express* in 1909, reported that the Gaelic Church records had been allocated to the United Free High Church. If so, they must have been transferred to the Free Church congregation at a later date, most probably in the 1930s. All of which is typical of the haphazard way in which irreplaceable church records are transferred from one pair of hands to another. The paucity of surviving records is a consequence of such treatment.

Happily the earliest records of the Highland Congregation remain to tell the story of impoverished Highlanders who, long before the Clearances, made their way to Aberdeen in search of remunerative employment. The commonest names in the 1795 congregational roll — Mackay, Mackenzie, Sutherland and Ross — suggest that the early migrants came from the eastern seaboard of Northern Scotland. In due time others came 'frae a' the airts' to establish a community chiefly distinguishable from the native Aberdonians by their predilection to 'gabbit in Gaelic'.

Monolingual Highlanders arriving in Aberdeen with no understanding of the English language suffered under a considerable social and economic handicap. It was a disability which many, through time, overcame. But however willing the Gaels were to resort to English for commerce or companionship, Gaelic remained the language of worship. So they bent their energies to secure a chapel in which they could join in the worship of God 'in the manner to which they had been accustomed from their infancy'. In 1795 they gathered in their newly-built chapel to join with their minister to (as he put it) give thanks to God who, 'Having in His providence gathered us from North, South, East and West and brought us among strangers and a language we did not understand, and though for a time He made us to hang our harps on the willow trees, yet at length, in His grace, He gave us His Word and ordinances in our native language'. Aberdeen could now add a Highland congregation to its Ecclesiastical Directory.

The history of the church is sometimes presented as a chronicle of its buildings or its ministerial succession or its place in the life of the community or the nation. These are of course, valid, although incomplete, portraits. The true history of the church is to be found in its people, especially its converts, their encounter with God and their interaction with one another in the life of the church. In the 19th century the church in the Highlands was not short of annalists to record the wonderful works of God, especially those works which were wrought through the agency of the Free Church of Scotland. But much of the reporting was hagiographic, written for the purpose of immortalising the godly lives and self-denying service of the leaders of the Disruption Church. In the nature of the case these accounts focussed on unique events and eminent ministers. Consequently they cannot be regarded as typical of the mainstream life of the church.

Moreover, the largely biographical, Highland Church histories of last century were, for the most part, constructed from folk-memories and are lacking in documentation. Although Highland people justly enjoyed a reputation for accurate recall, the suspicion remains that in some instances distance lent enchantment to the view. This element of uncertainty attaching to Highland Church histories which were based on an oral tradition, has the corresponding effect of investing minute books such as those of the Gaelic Chapel with added interest; for in these we have a candid, impartial record of the influence of events, both great and small, on the ongoing life of a Highland congregation.

There is another feature which distinguishes the present account from earlier histories of the Highland Church. These accounts were centred round national or provincial leaders. The story of the church on Gaelic Lane includes the contribution of some very ordinary people. It was true of that church, as of the church in Corinth, that 'not many mighty, not many noble' were to be found in its ranks. There were some who were influential in public life but the great majority were ordinary people, nondescript newcomers at the lower end of the social scale. But even in the lives of obscure and shadowy figures such as those that flit across the pages of the Gaelic Chapel records, there are incidents worth telling and lessons worth learning.

While the true history of the church must take to do with eternal things, the account which follows necessarily focuses on temporal things for it is based on records which have to do with the material and business concerns of the congregation rather than the spiritual and devotional experiences of its members. The reader should also bear in mind that what is written here is not a complete, or perfectly pro-portioned, account of the Highland church in Aberdeen. Inevitably it tends to highlight points of disagreement in the congregation because it was the function of the church's management to adjudicate on contentious issues and, having done so, to keep a record of their decisions. Consequently disputes attain an undue prominence in the story. On the other hand, even in days of bitter controversy, the church, although doubtless wounded by ill report, continued with its mission to bring men and women to an awareness of things unseen and eternal. Every year new names were added to the roll of communicants, testi-fying to the ongoing work of the Gospel in bringing people out of darkness into light; but the circumstances of that divine encounter are known only in the records of heaven itself. That aspect of the life of the congregation is certainly under-represented in the narrative.

In recounting the story of the Highland congregation from 1785 to 1900, I have set it in the context of contemporary church developments both in Aberdeen and in the Highlands in so far as these impinged on the life of the Gaelic Chapel. For the most part the narrative is treated chronologically, that form being more readily comprehensible to the average reader whose interest is in the people and events concerned with the Scottish church and especially the Highland church. Where possible, events recorded in the chapel records have been amplified from other sources such as Presbytery and Assembly Committee minutes or from the literature of the period, much of it obscure or not easily obtained. Some readers would no doubt have preferred a thematic to a chronological approach, but that would have eclipsed the persevering service rendered by some participants over an extended period, service that was in striking contrast to that of the majority of people who feature fleetingly in the minute books.

The church in the Highlands still has its representatives in Aberdeen. In claiming to be one of them, I concede that I write from the stand-point of the worshipping community. That should not be a disquali-fication. On the contrary, from that vantage ground, it should be possible, the better to take account of the spiritual dimension which ought not to be overlooked. In recent years the history of the church has become a topic of interest to social historians who set out to account for its development in terms of social changes and economic forces. Some historians have linked the development of evangelical Christianity in Scotland to the collapse of the old order. According to this theory, loyalties that were formerly given to the clan chief were transferred to prominent, charismatic preachers. (Incidentally, this view was shared by some Free Church ministers last century). Others have traced the rise of evangelicalism to economic hardship consequent to the Clearances, the dispossessed finding solace for their sufferings in the consolations of the Gospel. Others stress social upheaval rather than economic privations as the springboard for religious revival. While it is possible to demonstrate a correlation between social trends and religious enthusiasm, to claim that they are causally related involves major assumptions. Demographic and other factors do influence the development of a congregation, but in common with every other branch of the Christian church, the Highland church, like the church of the New Testament, owes its growth to the quickening power of the Spirit of God. That conviction underlies the writing of this account.

In pursuit of my researches into people and places referred to in this book, I have been greatly assisted by the helpfulness shown to me both by the staff of the Local Studies Section of Aberdeen Central Library and also the Special Collections Librarians of the University of Aberdeen. The access which I was given to newspaper archives in the Woodside Library, together with freedom from surveillance, a freedom such that it led to my being unintentionally shut in the basement when the library closed early one afternoon for its Christmas vacation, were equally appreciated. The staff of the Scottish Record Office, Edinburgh gave me much assistance, and I was made to feel especially welcome any time I sought help from New College Library, Edinburgh. When libraries failed, Winram's Antiquarian Bookshop, Aberdeen, more than once came up with material highly relevant to my task.

Many friends from Church and University contributed to my knowledge of events. Invidious though it is to single out any of these, I cannot forbear to acknowledge the stimulus I have received from Professor Donald Macleod of the Free Church College, Edinburgh. From the outset of this project his insights into all things Highland, theological and ecclesiastical, have helped to clarify my thoughts. From among a younger generation, John A Smith's ardent interest in Highland church life and his acquaintance with its literature has been to my certain benefit on several occasions.

Professor Donald E Meek of the Chair of Celtic in the University of Aberdeen has honoured me with his willingness to write a Foreword, so renewing the bond with the University which contributed so markedly to the successful establishment of the Gaelic Chapel two centuries ago. In addition to being a notable Gaelic scholar, his own allegiance to the church of his fathers has won for him a distinguished place as a historian of the Scottish Church.

I am especially grateful to the Governors of the McCaig Trust, the Hope Trust, the Drummond Trust and the Highland Fund Ltd, for their generous financial contribution to the cost of publication, support which I value not least for the recognition it conveys of my concern to write a serious account of a hidden byway of Scottish church history. Lesley Ann Taylor, publishing manager of Saint Andrew Press offered encouragement of the most practical kind and has given invaluable help and advice. As with an earlier book, Donald W Macleod, former Rector of Fortrose Academy, has by his computer skills and personal interest, assisted me to an extent known only to myself.

Amidst the inevitable fret and frustration from attempting what sometimes seemed beyond my reach, the comforts of home were unfailingly present. And so to May, and to all who encouraged me to complete this memoir of the Gaelic Chapel, 'perhaps a frail memorial, but sincere', I extend my warmest thanks.

Ian R MacDonald
ABERDEEN 1999

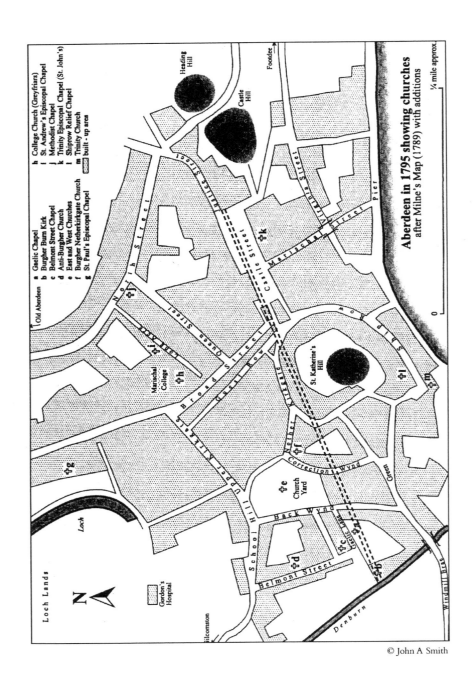

Aberdeen in 1795 showing churches
after Milne's Map (1789) with additions

Old Aberdeen
a Gaelic Chapel
b Burgher Burn Kirk
c Belmont Street Chapel
d Anti-Burgher Church
e East and West Churches
f Burgher Netherkirkgate Church
g St. Paul's Episcopal Chapel

h College Church (Greyfriars)
i   St. Andrew's Episcopal Chapel
j   Methodist Chapel
k Trinity Episcopal Chapel (St. John's)
l   Shiprow Relief Chapel
m Trinity Church
▨ built - up area

© John A Smith

MAP OF ABERDEEN IN 1795 SHOWING THE CHURCHES IN THE AREA.
[DOTTED LINE INDICATES UNION STREET AS IT APPEARS TODAY.]

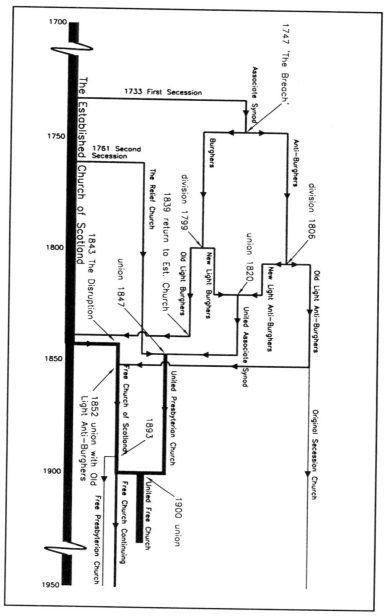

SOME OF THE DIVISIONS AND RE-UNIONS IN THE PRESBYTERIAN CHURCH
IN SCOTLAND BETWEEN 1733 AND 1900.

Chapter 1

*

THE FOUNDING FATHER

AS the year 1784 was drawing to a close, it was observed that the Rev. Ronald Bayne was among the Sunday morning worshippers in the Church of East St Nicholas in Aberdeen. The arrival of the tall distinguished looking Highlander was especially remarked on by some of his Gaelic-speaking compatriots from the Highlands. Almost five years had passed since Ronald Bayne had left Aberdeen following his enlistment for chaplaincy service with the 2nd battalion of the 42nd Regiment of Foot.[1] The regiment had been raised by Colonel Lord Macleod of Raasay for service in India, and very demanding service it proved to be. The hazards of the outward voyage, the rigours of the climate and the ferocity of the campaign waged against the forces of Tippoo Sahib, took a heavy toll of officers and men. From among the survivors, Ronald Bayne was invalided home.[2]

In his boyhood days, home for Ronald Bayne was the Highland burgh of Dingwall where he had been born *circa* 1755. As a family, the Baynes, lineal descendants of the Knights of Tulloch, hereditary keepers of Dingwall Castle, were said to be remarkable for their distinguished personal appearance and charm of manner.[3] Ronald was not lacking in these qualities. He was a natural leader, described by Donald Sage who knew him intimately, as a man of great mental acuteness. Like most of his compatriots who aspired to a university education, Ronald Bayne went to Aberdeen to study, but contrary to the usual practice of Highland students which was to matriculate at King's College, he enrolled at Marischal College. This quite separate university was the one generally favoured by the sons of Aberdeen citizens and, in later years, Bayne's intimacy with many of the prominent families in Aberdeen, was to benefit Highlanders residing in the city.

Although his ancestral home was in Dingwall, his ties with Aberdeen were of a kind that made him regard that city as his journey's end. For Aberdeen was the home of Miss Elizabeth Bentley, a daughter of a wealthy hosiery manufacturer who, in 1770, had moved from the Midlands of England to Aberdeen, at that time a flourishing centre for the manufacture of woollen goods. The Bentleys came of a highly distinguished Yorkshire family, one of whom was Richard Bentley, Master of Trinity College Cambridge, and, in his day, a very able apologist for the Christian faith. The friendship between Ronald Bayne and Elizabeth Bentley, which had begun during his student days in Aberdeen, survived the long years of his absence in India, and on 2nd February 1785[4] they were married and took up residence in Aberdeen.

Paid employment was not something that Ronald had need of. His wife, coming from a prosperous family, almost certainly enjoyed independent means, but, that apart, his own income from his army commission, gave him more than enough to support them both. Nor was he under any obligation to rejoin his regiment, even although he continued to hold his chaplain's commission. His name appears in the Army lists right up to 1796 when chaplains ceased to be listed. After 1800 he is still referred to in Presbytery minutes as Chaplain to His Majesty's 73rd Regiment. But he did not go overseas again and, as his regiment did not return to Britain until 1806, he saw no further military service.

Nominal army service of this kind was by no means exceptional at that time. Indeed the appointment of army chaplains was something of a financial racket. The choice of a regimental chaplain lay with the Colonel. He sold the commission and the appointee, as long as he retained the commission, was guaranteed 6s 8d per day or £120 per annum, a very substantial sum in the late 18th century. For a fraction of that sum the chaplain could engage a deputy to undertake the duties of the post and this was what commonly occurred.[5] But if, because he enjoyed a sinecure of this kind, it should be thought that Ronald Bayne was devoid of pastoral instincts, that would be wholly to misjudge his character, for at that time Aberdeen was receiving an influx of Gaelic-speaking Highlanders whose spiritual needs gave him great concern.

Highlanders in search of work

In earlier times Aberdonians were inclined to be suspicious of Gaelic speakers. Indeed since the Battle of Harlaw (1411), in which many of Aberdeen's most illustrious citizens died defending their city against the Lord of the Isles and his pillage-bent clansmen, Highlanders had been regarded as undesirables. But now economic forces were at work which encouraged the recruitment of Highlanders as a cheap source of labour for the city's developing industries, notably quarrying and weaving.[6] Consequently, long before the Clearances, there was a significant movement of Highland people into the city. Labourers for the stone quarries were the first to arrive, closely followed by their families and friends. The opportunities which the city offered for regular and remunerative employment, were irresistible, especially when set against the grinding poverty and ever-present threat of starvation that accompanied subsistence on an infertile terrain, and soon a Highland community, a community with a distinctive language, a distinctive background and, in some ways, a distinctive outlook, took shape within the city.

Despite the many advantages which Gaelic-speaking Highlanders enjoyed in Aberdeen, they were conscious of one major deprivation. There was no opportunity to join in the public worship of God in their own language. Even for those Gaels who had a working knowledge of English, Gaelic was felt to be indispensable for the purpose of worship. To them the language was not merely a vehicle of communication, it was a creative force giving reality to the religious life. There were others of course, who had no English and, in the absence of a Gaelic-speaking minister, their deprivation was irremediable.

As it happened, after 1776, an itinerant Gaelic-speaking preacher was stationed in Aberdeen from time to time. He was the Rev. Duncan McAllum, a native of Argyll who lived from 1756-1834. Under the Methodist system of circuit preachers McAllum was sent north, to places such as Speyside, Inverness and Cromarty but, in a departure from the normal practice, Wesley kept sending his 'North Star' (as he called McAllum) back to Aberdeen and he was resident there in 1776, 1778, 1783-84, 1789-90, 1798-99, and 1812-14.[7] As an English preacher he was popular with the Methodist society in Aberdeen, but he does not appear to have engaged in regular Gaelic preaching in the city itself.

In the Presbyterian churches, the only minister who might have laid claim to being a Gaelic speaker, was the Rev. George Mark, minister of Peterculter Parish Church from 1775-1811. Although a native of Banff, he had been presented in 1770 to the Parish of Kirkhill, Inverness-shire, but his induction there was opposed by the congregation on the grounds that he was not bilingual. A committee appointed to assess his competence in Gaelic concluded that 'for the short time he has applied to it, he seems to understand the principles thereof'; but their opinion that he would be 'fully capable to teach them to a Gaelic congregation if he continue the diligence he has hitherto done' did not carry conviction with the Assembly who set aside the appointment. In the circumstances, it is unlikely that he maintained his 'diligence', and it seems certain that a Gaelic preacher to minister to the needs of the immigrant community was not to be found in any of the local pulpits. And if any were, none did.

In this media-saturated age it is difficult to visualise a world in which people were wholly dependent on their ministers or their memories for the consolations of the Gospel. Yet that was the situation which confronted the Gaelic-speaking community. In those days no one could read Gaelic who had not first learned to read English. As late as 1772, it was only a minority of the Highland clergy who were truly literate in Gaelic.[8] It is not surprising, therefore, that the common people, unaided, could make nothing of the written word. Moreover the written word, as far as Gaelic was concerned, was incomplete. The New Testament had been published in Gaelic in 1767 but the entire Bible did not become available in a Scottish Gaelic version until 1801. For access to the Scriptures the people were dependent on a reader who could translate from the English Bible. Scripture reading did not always form a part even of public worship and family worship involving Scripture reading must have been a rarity. Under these circumstances, it is obvious that the Highlanders would have felt very acutely the lack of provision for their spiritual welfare.

As it happened, the Presbytery were not wholly indifferent to the Gaelic problem. In June 1785, presumably acting on Assembly instructions, they had appointed that a collection for defraying the cost of translating the Old Testament into Gaelic should be taken in all the churches of the Presbytery.[9] At their meeting in September, they again urged that a collection be made on Sunday 2nd October. Perhaps these intimations served to draw attention to the need for some local provision. In any case, the matter came to the notice of Ronald Bayne who 'moved with compassion for the souls of his countrymen according to the flesh, and zeal for the glory of God, readily and freely offered to preach to them in Gaelic if they could get a place to meet in for that purpose'.[10]

It is to be noted that the pledge that came from the compassionate heart of the Rev. Ronald Bayne was not given without regard to the practicability of the undertaking. He would preach to the Highlanders in Gaelic 'if they could get a place to meet in for that purpose'. In 1785 that was no easy matter. The range of halls, ecclesiastical, educational and recreational, available today, was undreamt of then. If accommodation was to be obtained it could only be from existing churches. These buildings, in most cases, had only a single auditorium and, if permission were to be granted, it would be necessary to congregate at some uncanonical hour. However, even that concession was seldom forthcoming. When, several years later, some citizens of Aberdeen were won to the cause of the Congregational Church then being promoted in Scotland by the Haldane brothers, they found themselves in a similar predicament. Recalling the problem one wrote, 'our next step was to look out for some place in which to observe the ordinances of Christ; but no one could be found, and an application for the use of any of the Churches in the city would have been vain, for ministers and Sessions of all sects are our greatest opponents in this affair'.[11] Another went so far as to refer to the clergy as 'our declared enemies'.[12] Dissent, whatever form it took, received no encouragement from the Established Church. The Congregationalists were thus laid under the necessity of building a place of worship from the outset. However the spiritual aspirations of the Highlanders fell into a different category from dissent and commanded greater sympathy.

The commencement of Gaelic services

Through the good offices of the Rev. Mr Abercrombie, minister of the second charge and doubtless well acquainted with Ronald Bayne, permission was granted for the Highlanders to meet in the choir of the Parish Church of East St Nicholas 'before the town's people assembled for public worship'. A second service was held 'in the interval of public worship in the forenoon.'[13] This arrangement was not without its difficulties for both groups of worshippers, but the Gaelic folk were thankful to have regular diets of worship at which the Rev. Ronald Bayne officiated. Even so it was at best a temporary arrangement and the congregation were anxious to attain to a more permanent status. Whether it was with a view to obtaining official recognition for their congregation that Ronald Bayne might thereby be persuaded to remain with them, or whether it was as a consequence of his urging them to find financial support for a Gaelic preacher in order that he might be released from his self-imposed commitment, it is impossible to say; but, whatever the reason, by February of 1786 a group of individuals representative of the congregation presented a petition to the Presbytery of Aberdeen requesting the 'Presbytery's aid in an application to the Committee for Managing the Royal Bounty, for a missionary to preach the Gospel and perform other acts of religious worship in the Gaelic language'.[14] The wording indicates that it was the services of an ordained minister that was envisaged.

The Royal Bounty was an annual subvention amounting to £1000 donated from 1725 onwards by George I, and thereafter his successors, for the purpose of supporting ministers and catechists in remote areas of the Highlands and Islands which were without teind stipends. Since it was largely with a view to evangelising the Gaelic areas of Scotland that the fund was established, it was not inappropriate for the Highlanders resident in Aberdeen to seek a share of it. The disbursement of the Royal Bounty Fund was entrusted to a committee of the General Assembly.

The Petition which the Highlanders presented to the Presbytery affirmed that there were in Aberdeen 800 persons incapable of deriving edification from public worship in the English language and a list of their names was appended. The Presbytery appointed a three-man committee comprising the ministers of Aberdeen and Old Machar and Mr Gregory of the chapel-of-ease (Gilcomston) to ascertain 'how far the facts asserted are founded in truth', and on this committee confirming the facts as stated, the Presbytery agreed in March to support the crave of the petition.[15] They appointed 'the minister of Aberdeen' to prepare the petition for transmission to the Assembly and there present it. This was a promising start for 'the minister of Aberdeen' was Dr Duncan Shaw who that year was elected Moderator of the General Assembly and who, therefore, presided at the meeting of the Royal Bounty Committee held on 31st May 1786 at which the petition 'to grant out of the Royal Bounty what may appear proper for employing one to preach to the Highlanders in and about this place' was presented.[16] The petition was remitted to a sub-committee which met in July but, before agreeing to any new appointments, they 'resolved to examine the state of the Fund and upon enquiry found that the former appointments exceed the sum annually to be divided considerably and therefore were of opinion that in this state of the Fund the Committee cannot appoint any new stations'.[17] Thus ended the first attempt to obtain official support for a Gaelic minister in Aberdeen.

In March of the following year (1787) the Presbytery renewed its application to the General Assembly on behalf of the Highlanders in and about Aberdeen, but again the state of the Fund was not such as would allow new appointments. Indeed the situation had deteriorated so that vacant stations had now to be left unfilled and all salaries were cut by ten per cent.[18] Still the deficit mounted and in 1788 the Committee found it 'unnecessary to enter on consideration of applications'.[19] Had the Committee been in a position to support a preacher in Aberdeen, the grant could have been anything from £10 to £30.

Ronald Bayne's Elgin ministry

By the time that the Highlanders learned, in the summer of 1788, that support from the Royal Bounty Committee in the foreseeable future was exceedingly improbable, they had already received even more disconcerting news. In February Ronald Bayne had been approached by the congregation of the Little Kirk in Elgin. The Little Kirk, so called to distinguish it from the Parish Church (the Muckle Kirk) functioned as a chapel-of-ease within the Established Church. It had a reputation for independency, probably a consequence of its right to elect its own minister and for that and other reasons it was generally viewed with suspicion and disfavour by the Presbytery of Elgin. The minister was dependent for his support on subscriptions from the people. He was authorised to marry and, within limits, baptise, but he lacked the right to administer the Lord's Supper, the members of his congregation being required to attend the Parish Church for communion.[20] It was far from being a plum charge but it had enjoyed an evangelical ministry from the Rev. Wm McBean who, at that time, was under call to Moy. In response to the approach made to him Ronald Bayne replied as follows.[21]

Aberdeen, 4th March, 1788

Sir,

I had the favour of your letter, and am certainly much obliged to you and the other good people that you say would be glad to have me for their minister in the event of Mr. McBean's leaving you. That I have a desire to be employed in the Redeemer's work, and that it would give me joy to be made instrumental in promoting his kingdom, I do acknowledge to the praise of the glory of his grace. But your Little Kirk is not a charge that I can see suited to my poor gifts and weak graces. It has peculiar difficulties. However, a bond servant has no right to dictate to his Master. I can, therefore, say neither yea nor nay to your proposal in this early stage of it. See you ask counsel of God. Pray Him to make the lot fall on the one that he would choose, and if it should fall upon me, oh! may the Lord make his way straight before my face, and hedge me in so as that I cannot elude it if I would. Your writing to me shall be a secret (so far as it depends upon me) as long as you please. Your letter found me easily. With compliments to Mrs Duncan,
    I am, Sir,

Your very humble servant,
R Bayne.

It may be that when Ronald Bayne took up residence in Aberdeen, he cherished hopes of obtaining a presentation to a local charge from which he could give some superintendence to the Gaelic-speaking community. As it happened, a vacancy arose in the Parish of Old Machar (St Machar's Cathedral) in September 1787, but it was Alex Henderson, one of his class-mates in Marischal College, who got that presentation, being ordained to the second charge of Old Machar in May 1788. With no immediate prospect of a presentation to a charge in the Aberdeen area, and the anticipated vacancy in Elgin having been confirmed, Ronald Bayne concluded that he was not meant to elude the offer made to him by the managers of the Little Kirk. When replying to their first approach, he acknowledged that the invitation was 'in the event of Mr. McBean's leaving you'. The uncertainty was not on the part of Mr McBean. He had been nominated as a candidate to fill a vacancy in the Parish of Moy and Dalarossie, some ten miles south of Inverness, and his willingness to go need not be doubted for a pastorate in a Parish was always more attractive than that of a chapel-of-ease such as the Little Kirk, if only because it conferred the right to full participation in the Church courts. The chapel ministers had a status little better than that of assistants in the parish and, having no seat in the Presbytery, could not be sent as commissioners to the General Assembly. The query as to whether Mr McBean would go to Moy arose from the fact that he had not received a presentation or a call in the usual way. In a complex situation he had been recommended by the Presbytery on 12th February as one of four possible appointees, but as there was some resistance on the part of the congregation, the Presbytery at their meeting on 1st April left open the question of making an appointment from the suggested list and it was not until 6th May that the matter was finally decided in favour of Wm MacBean.[22] In August 1788 he was inducted to Moy and Dalarossie and shortly after, Ronald Bayne commenced his ministry in Elgin.[23]

Ronald Bayne's comment that the charge in Elgin had 'peculiar difficulties' was a considerable understatement. There he had to endure all manner of opposition from the Moderate-dominated Presbytery of Elgin. Even so, he stayed at the Little Kirk for twelve years in the course of which he declined several calls to other places, among them a call in 1798 to the rapidly growing Aberdeen Gaelic Chapel. This call he declined on the grounds that 'his own new chapel was in building'. He stayed in Elgin until 1800 when he was, in effect, forced out by a decision of the General Assembly withdrawing recognition from the congregation and dissolving the charge. This was a direct consequence of the new building which his congregation had erected. In the course of his Elgin ministry, the Little Kirk had become crowded with worshippers, people flocking from far and wide to sit under Ronald Bayne's preaching.[24] This proved to be too much for the 'Moderate' Presbytery. As long as it remained a little Kirk they could put up with it; but a flourishing evangelical congregation in a new building threatened to undermine the influence of the Parish Church and such a situation could not be allowed to develop. The charge had to be suppressed. When the Assembly of 1800 upheld the judgement of the Presbytery that 'the chapel-of-ease in the town of Elgin is at present unnecessary and inexpedient', Ronald Bayne, forced to choose between continuing as a minister of the Church of Scotland or accompanying his congregation into secession, saw it as his duty not to become a Seceder minister[25] and instead accepted the offer of the chapel-of-ease (the East Church) in Inverness.

In 1808, the year in which he had conferred on him a Doctor of Divinity degree by King's College, Aberdeen, he was admitted to the Parish of Kiltarlity and Glen Convinth where he remained until his death in 1821. The clerical tradition in the Bayne family was continued by his son the Rev. Charles John Bayne (1797-1832), minister of Fodderty. A grandson, Dr Peter Bayne, was a writer of considerable distinction, biographies of Martin Luther and Hugh Miller being among his works, as well as a volume on the history and testimony of the Free Church of Scotland.

Ronald Bayne's personality

Ronald Bayne was a man of great energy and ability who possessed an 'exuberant imagination' which, no doubt, was the basis of his kirk-filling eloquence. In his day he was recognised as one of the most eminent ministers of the Highlands, a man for whom Dr John Macdonald of Ferintosh (1779-1849) 'cherished the warmest affection with profound respect'. According to a son of the Ferintosh manse, who, having lived in the Elgin area for several years had every opportunity to discover the opinions of those who had known him personally, Ronald Bayne's 'knowledge of the truth was large – his experience of grace was deep. He dealt with every man's heart – he cared for no man's face. His discourse was rich, his manner bold, his style original'.[26]

Of course, he was not without his faults. He possessed a quick temper and his tongue could be an unruly member,[27] but like many other hot-tempered men, he was generous and warm-hearted. Although he declined to leave the Established Church, he showed no antipathy to seceders. His home was open to receive as honoured guests brethren of other denominations.[28] He had a truly catholic spirit and for a quarter of a century he served on the editorial panel of the *Evangelical Magazine*, but no period of his ministry was more timely or needful than his selfless service in Aberdeen. An early chronicler of the Gaelic Chapel epitomised his contribution with becoming restraint. 'There is ground to hope,' wrote the anonymous annalist, 'that much good was done during that time both in edifying such as had formerly a relish for the Gospel and also in arousing the careless to a concern for their salvation.'

Notes to Chapter 1

1. *Army Lists*, 1780-1796.
2. J Macdonald: *Isobel Hood's memoirs and manuscript* (Aberdeen, 1843), p 86. See also D Sage: *Memorabilia Domestica* (Wick, 1889, reprinted 1975), p 223.
3. N Macrae: *The romance of a royal burgh: Dingwall's story of a thousand years* (Dingwall, 1923; reprinted 1974), p 113. See also *Disruption Worthies of the Highlands* (Edinburgh, 1877), p 38.
4. A Dingwall Fordyce: *Family record of the name of Dingwall Fordyce in Aberdeenshire* (Fergus, Ontario, Canada, 1885 and 1888), volume1, pp 14-17; vol. 2, appendix, pp xi-xii.
5. A C Dow: *Ministers to the Soldiers of Scotland* (Edinburgh, 1962), p 226.
6. W Kennedy: *Annals of Aberdeen* (London, 1818), vol. 2, p 213.
7. A F Walls: *Some Personalities of Aberdeen Methodism 1760-1970* (Aberdeen, 1973), p 5.
8. J MacInnes: *The Evangelical Movement in the Highlands of Scotland 1688 to 1800* (Aberdeen, 1951), p 64.
9. *Records of Aberdeen Presbytery*, vol. 8 , p 354 (29th June, 1785) (CH2-1-10).

9

10. MS *circa* 1795, *The origin of the Gaelic congregation in Aberdeen.*
11. J H Wilson: *The Bon-Accord repository* (Aberdeen, 1842), p 113.
12. J Bulloch: *Centenary memorials of the first congregational church in Aberdeen* (Aberdeen, 1898), p 13.
13. J Macdonald: op. cit., p 86.
14. *Records of Aberdeen Presbytery*, vol. 8, p 361 (8th February, 1786) (CH2-1-10).
15. Ibid., pp 361-362.
16. *Minutes of the Royal Bounty Committee* (31st May, 1786), p 62 (CH1-5-60). Dr Duncan Shaw was a son of Lachlan Shaw, the historian of Moray.
17. Ibid., p 70 (30th August, 1786).
18. Ibid., p 91f (29th August, 1787).
19. Ibid., p 118 (4th June, 1788).
20. J Macdonald: op. cit., p 83.
21. Ibid., p 87.
22. *Records of the Presbytery of Inverness* (6th May, 1788), p 175, vol. 1758-1821 (CH2-553-7).
23. The date of Ronald Bayne's induction to the Little Kirk, Elgin is erroneously given in *Fasti Ecclesiae Scoticanae* (vol. 6, pp 396 and 470) as 1798. The information regarding his chaplaincy service in India is also incorrect.
24. J Macdonald: op. cit., p 87.
25. Ibid., p 94.
26. J Macdonald: op. cit., p 10.
27. J Kennedy: *The Apostle of the North* (Inverness, 1886; new edition, 1932), p 216.
28. J Macdonald: op. cit., p. 96.

Chapter 2

*

Temporal Pillars

Colquhoun McGrigor

IN 1788, although bereft of their preacher, the fledgling Highland Congregation was not devoid of leadership. They had at least one man of exceptional ability in their ranks. This was Colquhoun McGrigor, a Gaelic speaker from Cromdale, Strathspey and a man who, in the few years in which he had been in Aberdeen, had become well established in the business community. Like many others, he went to Aberdeen in connection with the hosiery industry in which he rapidly prospered.

Born about 1740, he married a Miss Ann Grant of Lethendry, Strathspey and when their family of three boys, James, Robert and Charles, were still young, they moved to Aberdeen. James, born at Cromdale in 1770, was a brilliant child. Perhaps the achievement that gave him most satisfaction was being dux of Aberdeen Grammar School in 1784.[1] Graduating from Marischal College in 1788, he pursued an Army Medical career, eventually becoming Director General of the Army Medical Department. In 1831 he was created a baronet for his services to king and country, being credited with having ensured a British victory in the Peninsular War by his medical supervision of Wellington's troops. Three times in the course of a long and distinguished career he was elected Rector of Marischal College,[2] as was, more than a century later, his equally distinguished great-grandson, Admiral of the Fleet Sir Roderick McGrigor. An imposing obelisk to the memory of Sir James McGrigor Bart KCB still stands in the Duthie Park, Aberdeen having been moved there from the quadrangle of Marischal College where it was first erected shortly after his death in 1858.

Following the departure of Ronald Bayne for Elgin, Colquhoun McGrigor assumed the leadership of the congregation. He was the first of many office-bearers who down the years were to take an active interest in the welfare of Highland students.[3] His strategy for the congregation was to see it established as a distinctively Highland congregation catering for the needs of Highland people while, at the same time, integrated with and enjoying the support of, the whole community. The first step was to constitute themselves as a charitable body to be known as 'The Gaelic Society'. As such they could solicit financial support from local sources such as the firms that were major employers of Highland labour. Although the Society could count on the support of 'several respectable individuals from the Highlands who were resident in Aberdeen', the outworking of the McGrigor strategy called for the involvement of other prominent citizens in the community. Their identity is given in the following notice which appeared in the *Aberdeen Journal* of 12th August 1788:

GAELIC PREACHER

A subscription is now opened for the purpose of fitting up a Place of Worship, and paying a Gaelic Preacher, for the benefit of the numerous Highland Inhabitants of Aberdeen and its Vicinity.

It is sufficient to state to the benevolent Public, that there are upwards of 800 Highlanders residing here, the greatest part of whom understand English so imperfectly, as not to reap Instruction from the ordinances of Religion in the English Tongue.

Subscriptions and Donations for this pious purpose will be received by Mr. Charles Farquharson, Mr. Alex. Ross, Mr. Alex. Leslie, Mr. Colquhoun McGregor, Provost Cruden, Mr. Ewen, Mess. Angus and Son, and by the Publisher.

The sponsors of this appeal were all men of standing in the community, but of the names appended to the notice only that of Colquhoun McGrigor can be positively identified with the Gaelic congregation.

The others include two members of the Town Council – Charles Farquharson and Provost Wm Cruden, a cousin of the author of Cruden's Concordance.[4] Mr Alex Leslie was probably Mr Leslie of Berryden, a merchant [druggist?] in the town and a director of the Aberdeen Banking Company. He died in 1799 in his 77th year. Mr Alex. Ross may well have been the person of that name who was then treasurer of Aberdeen Infirmary. Both of these men were directors of the Poor's Hospital and obviously concerned with charitable enterprises.[5] Messrs Angus and Son, booksellers on Narrow Wynd, offered a convenient location at which donations could be deposited.[6] The publisher was James Chalmers (1742-1810) who since 1764 had been proprietor and editor of the *Aberdeen Journal*, a weekly newspaper launched by his father in 1748 to acquaint Aberdonians with 'domestic and London intelligence'. Renamed the *Press and Journal,* it still survives as Scotland's oldest newspaper. The remaining sponsor was Mr John Ewen, a civic celebrity and by far the most stalwart and enduring of the original backers. As principal manager of the Gaelic Chapel for more than thirty years he merits an extended reference.

John Ewen

By any standard, John Ewen was a remarkable man. He was born in Montrose in 1745, his father being a wandering tinker or, possibly, an itinerant trader. He himself began making his living as a travelling salesman or packman, selling trinkets and small items of hardware. In the course of time he opened his own shop specialising in jewellery and hardware and he has been variously described as merchant, jeweller and goldsmith. In the course of a long business life he amassed a substantial fortune, the testamentary disposition of which became the subject of lengthy litigation terminating in the House of Lords.[7] Although entirely self-educated, he was equally at home in the world of learning as in the world of business and fittingly took his place alongside, if not slightly above, the local literati of his day, with all of whom he was on the most companionable terms.[8] Music and art alike engaged his faculties and enjoyed his patronage. Perhaps as a consequence of some astute trading with the Low Countries, or possibly through his marriage, he acquired an astonishing collection of Old Masters including, seemingly, works by Caravaggio, Van Dyck, Rubens, Titian, Barroccio, Rembrandt, Breughel and Poussin.[9] The accreditation may have rested on no other authority than his own, perhaps over-optimistic, assessment.

The most beneficial service which he rendered to the city of his adoption was in the related fields of local government reform and the improvement of civic amenities. As regards the former, he achieved distinction as Secretary of the Convention for Burgh Reform for Scotland in which role he corresponded with Pitt, making, it is said, a deep impression on those politicians in favour of reform.[10] His achievement in the improvement of local amenities was a consequence of a Police Bill for the 'better paving, lighting, cleansing and otherwise improving the streets, lanes and other public passages of the city of Aberdeen' which, despite the early opposition of the magistrates, he succeeded in getting on the Statute Book in 1795.[11] One of the clauses of this Act provided for the systematic naming of streets and numbering of houses,[12] a provision which, if it had been implemented earlier, would have facilitated the identification of the many individuals referred to only by name in documents dating from the eighteenth century. The early records of the Gaelic Chapel give no addresses and few designations.

In pursuing, as he did, single-mindedly and disinterestedly, the reform of corrupt practices in local government, it would have been easy for John Ewen to have made enemies; yet all contemporary accounts describe him as a most courteous and attractive person whose company was much in demand. His emporium, conveniently situated at the Castlegate Narrow Wynd[13] (in 1818 the Athenaeum was erected on the site of the jeweller's shop), was in its day the gossiping-place of the town, largely, it seems, owing to 'the singular politeness and urbanity of its tenant'.[14] These qualities of urbanity and courtly refinement are beautifully displayed in the correspondence which John Ewen conducted as principal manager of the Gaelic Society.

What considerations influenced the Gaelic folk to invite John Ewen to be their principal manager it is impossible to discover; but the choice was a happy one and, in retrospect, it is clear that the advice they followed (whatever the source) was sound. The basis for John Ewen's benevolent interest in the welfare of the Gaelic congregation is similarly a matter for conjecture. His involvement with road improvements in Aberdeen could have brought him into contact with the Highlanders both as quarriers and, perhaps more significantly, as road overseers and surveyors, several of whom were to be found in the congregation at an early stage. Another business link that John Ewen had with the Highland community is that he acted as agent for many of the chapmen who traversed the Highlands and Islands as itinerant merchants.[15] But in all likelihood his willingness to be involved in the secular affairs of the Gaelic Society was simply a reflection of his public-spirited outlook. As the obituarist in the *Aberdeen Journal* remarked, 'His exertions in favour of charitable institutions and for every individual case of distress that came under his notice were zealous and unremitting'.[16] Liberal in politics, zealous in every good work and willing to be identified with any cause that could lay claim to be benevolent or philanthropic, he deserves a better epitaph than 'a busybody to the backbone' accorded to him by one writer.[17]

Although a man familiar with the spiritual as well as the temporal concerns of Christianity, John Ewen did not seem to have a firm ecclesiastical affiliation. At one period in his life he was attached to the Methodist Church, being a trustee of the Queen Street Chapel founded in 1764, and it has been suggested that he was indebted to his Methodist connections for the elevated rank which he came to enjoy in Aberdeen society.[18] Apparently Mr Hanby, the local Methodist preacher, was 'a person of very accomplished manners' on account of which he had access to the patrician families of Aberdeen. He introduced John Ewen to his friends, 'among whom was Mrs Middleton, a lady of some fortune, who, with her daughter was a member of the society'. This daughter married John Ewen.

She maintained her attachment to the Methodist Society, but 'Mr Ewen, for reasons best known to himself, afterward forsook the

Methodists, yet he was never ashamed of accompanying Mr Wesley on his visits in the city'. Some of the Wesleyan preachers had to endure both verbal and physical abuse when preaching on the Castlehill and Wesley himself 'experienced treatment little better than what had been bestowed on some of his assistants'.[19] And so it must have called for some courage on the part of John Ewen to take his stand with Wesley. Beyond that and the fact that he left legacies to the Poor's Fund of the Kirk Session of Laurencekirk (where his mother lived) and Old Machar, we know nothing of his personal church commitment.

An appeal for funds

The terms of the appeal printed in the *Journal* of 12th August 1788 indicate that the managers anticipated expenditure in two areas. One outlay was by way of stipend, from which it may be concluded that Ronald Bayne had left, or was on the point of leaving, Aberdeen. The other outlay was 'to fit up a place of worship'. From this it is evident that the Gaelic Society took the view that it was time to find alternative premises to those which they were using in the Choir of East St Nicholas. The major factor that led them to this decision was the desire for extended hours of worship. In St Nicholas, the available time for worship was limited because of the English services that had to be accommodated either before, or after, the Gaelic services. In winter the problem was further aggravated by the restricted hours of daylight, which meant that normally only one Gaelic service could be accommodated. Now with the intention of employing a full-time preacher, it was natural that the people would want to get the maximum benefit from his services. Alternative premises had, therefore, to be found or built. The response that the earlier appeal prompted, whether gratifying or otherwise is not known; but now the managers decided to renew the appeal in more explicit terms. Consequently, the *Journal* of 19th January 1789 carried the following notice which bears all the hallmarks of John Ewen's honey-tongued persuasiveness.

HIGHLAND CONGREGATION ABERDEEN

The quarrying of Granite in the vicinity of this city, for the purpose of paving the streets of London, it is well known, drew from the country some years since a number of day labourers, and the greatest part of these were Highlanders – building and improvements in agriculture have increased their number. Associating very closely together, and accustomed to speak the language of their forefathers, they are exceedingly at a loss for the Benefits of Public Worship. Unacquainted with the idiom, energy and peculiarities of the

English language, they are, in their present situation, precluded from the advantage of public instruction and social worship on the Sabbath. In a Christian country, and in a city famed for the liberality and generosity of its citizens, the situation of this little society of strangers need only be mentioned, that they may meet with that countenance and support which will enable them to worship God in the only language with which they are acquainted. Their number in Aberdeen, and its environs, is about six hundred. Every exertion on their part has hitherto been made to obtain this advantage, and the utmost ardour has been manifested by them to accomplish it. They have appointed managers to collect from among themselves, what their funds will allow, and they rest upon the generosity of the Public for such addition as will enable them to pay a moderate stipend to a Preacher who shall officiate in public worship, and instruct them in the principles and duties of our holy Religion, in the Gaelic tongue. Such a Preacher is already found, but a place of worship, and a fund for fitting it up, as well as what is necessary for the support of a Preacher is still wanting. The Magistrand Class in the King's College have the honour of furnishing the first fruits of this benevolent fund. They have just paid in Three Guineas to the Managers, by an unsolicited contribution among themselves: it is at once a proof of the good sense, generosity, and public spirit of these young gentlemen.

Contributions, to enable the Highland Congregation to fit up a place of public Worship, and to support a Preacher, will be received by Mr. Colquhoun McGregor, Mr. Ewen, or by the Publisher of this Paper, the Managers.

This appeal with its judiciously chosen references to the Highlanders' reserve, their cultural deprivation, their diminutive presence, their laudable yet unavailing exertions, coupled with their sensible submission to oversight by competent managers, all of which was set against the background of the city's richly deserved reputation for open-handedness, as now witnessed to by the selfless gesture from the students of King's College, was both skilfully presented and informative. The class list for the final year (Magistrand) class does not include the names of any obvious fund raisers for the Gaelic congregation and who took the initiative in this gesture of support remains unidentified.

James Stalker, resident preacher

The most intriguing comment in the published appeal is the remark that 'a preacher is already found'. The anonymous chronicler of the Gaelic congregation, after referring to the departure of Ronald Bayne in 1788 wrote, 'Encouraged by his counsel and exhortation ... they chose a Reader from among themselves and so continued to assemble in this manner for two years'. It is puzzling that the chronicler chose not to disclose the identity of the Reader. However, the preacher referred to in the *Journal* of 19th January 1789, can be identified from the *Aberdeen Almanack* for the year 1789, published on 20th December 1788.[20] This was the first year in which the *Almanack* carried an entry for the Highland Congregation, probably another helpful gesture on the part of the publisher of the *Almanack*, James Chalmers. The entry named the three managers, John Ewen, Colquhoun McGregor and James Chalmers, together with the Minister of the Highland Congregation – the Rev. Mr James Stalker. Given the publication date of the *Almanack*, the information reported there must have represented the situation prevailing in the latter part of 1788. The unanswered question is whether or not the advertised minister – James Stalker – and the 'Reader chosen from among themselves' are different persons or one preacher given two different descriptions. The congregation continued to be listed in the *Almanack* published in 1790 and in 1791, but both of these entries list only the managers, making no reference to a preacher. That would seem to imply that James Stalker's tenure of office may have been less than a year, or, if longer, it was judged inappropriate to identify him with the title of minister to the congregation. Perhaps the latter is the more likely of the alternatives.

James Stalker was born in the Parish of Edinkillie near Dunphail in Morayshire. He enrolled as a student at Marischal College in 1772, the class junior to that of Ronald Bayne. Among his classmates was Lachlan Mackenzie, the future minister of Lochcarron. For some reason he did not continue at Marischal but he graduated from King's College in 1777, having transferred there in 1774. It is probable that, like many others whose ultimate aim it was to enter the ministry, he acted as a schoolmaster or tutor before applying for licence. His application to be licensed came before the Presbytery of Chanonry in May 1782 when he is described as having been introduced to the Presbytery as a student in divinity in the town of Chanonry. The Presbytery, satisfied with the testimonials which he furnished, 'agreed to take some trials of him'.[21] The trials, extending over eighteen months and five meetings of Presbytery, were not inconsiderable for they involved the delivery of a homily, an exegesis, a lecture, an exercise and a popular sermon. Having completed that to the satisfaction of the Presbytery, he was licensed to preach on 6th January 1784.

His first engagement to give resident supply arose out of unhappy circumstances. In 1779 it was rumoured that the minister of the United Parishes of Moy and Dalarossie, the Rev. James MacKintosh, was the father of a child born to a woman who had been a servant in his manse. In March 1782 the Presbytery of Inverness deposed James MacKintosh from the ministry but because of various appeals and referrals to Synod and Assembly the case was not finally disposed of until 1787. Throughout this long drawn out process, the Presbytery had to make arrangements for the supply of religious ordinances to the parish, and in June 1784 they asked the Royal Bounty Committee to provide a salary for a preacher. This the committee agreed to do at the rate of £30 per annum.[22] Two years later they were to take a different view, giving it as their opinion that this provision was a misappropriation of the Royal Bounty (which it was) but they let it run its course nevertheless.[23] Funding having been provided, the Presbytery were authorised to employ 'a proper person to dispense the ordinances of religion in the Parishes of Moy and Dalarossie' and James Stalker was appointed from July 1784 to preach, catechise and visit the sick.

On 6th September of the following year, the case against James MacKintosh being no nearer a conclusion, the Presbytery received a letter from the Laird of MacKintosh on behalf of the heritors of Moy and Dalarossie requesting that James Stalker be ordained as this would increase his usefulness in the Parish. The Presbytery agreed 'to ordain Mr. Stalker forthwith and with that in view prescribed John 4:10 as a subject of a popular sermon and 23rd Psalm for a lecture'. Since these were the same passages prescribed by the Presbytery of Chanonry for James Stalker's licensing, it may be that the Presbytery of Inverness invited the probationer to suggest the subjects. Satisfied with his handling of the topics, the Presbytery ordained Mr Stalker later that month.[24]

In 1787 the General Assembly finally decided against the appeal from the Rev. James MacKintosh, ordered that he be deposed from the ministry and declared the Church of Moy to be vacant. The right to appoint a successor fell to the patron, the Laird of MacKintosh, but when he initiated proceedings the Presbytery claimed the right to fill the vacancy *tanquam jure devoluto,* the patron having failed to exercise his right within the statutory six months. The petition from the patron was in favour of James Stalker, but it would seem that the Moy parishioners had had enough of Mr Stalker for they counter-petitioned requesting the Presbytery to appoint either a Mr Wm Ross[25] or Mr Lachlan Mackenzie, missionary at Uist and the future minister of Lochcarron, or Mr Alex Macadam, minister of the recently opened Cromarty Gaelic Chapel.

The Presbytery deliberating on the two petitions 'thought the business of consenting to either of them a matter of great importance' and consented to neither. Instead they invited the heritors and people to express a preference for one of the following – Mr Wm MacBean of the Little Kirk, Elgin; Mr Fraser, missionary at Strathglass; Mr Dallas in Lewis; and Mr Simpson at Knockbain – with the ultimatum that if the people would not choose one of these, the Presbytery would choose for them. Further resistance from the heritors on the one hand, and the people on the other, was unavailing and the Presbytery appointed Wm

MacBean from Elgin. James Stalker lost that presentation because of dilatoriness on the part of the patron. By such means it happened that Wm MacBean went to Moy and Ronald Bayne went to Elgin. Did Ronald Bayne, being part of the train of events that shunted James Stalker out of Moy, feel some qualm of conscience pressing him to help James Stalker find some new sphere of service? And when the Aberdeen congregation, encouraged by Ronald Bayne, 'chose a Reader from among themselves', was James Stalker already in the congregation awaiting the appointment? Within months of his leaving Moy, he was advertised as minister to the Highland Congregation. But the following year his name had been dropped from the post of stated preacher. The next year the congregation 'after hearing of several candidates' called a minister. If James Stalker was among the candidates, he proved to be no more acceptable in Aberdeen than he had been in Moy. His career for the following 15 years is veiled in obscurity, but it seems that he was for some time an assistant chaplain at Fort George.[26] Perhaps Ronald Bayne's army contacts had something to do with that appointment.

In Moy, James Stalker had made a favourable impression on the Laird, and no doubt there must have been others in different places who thought highly of him. One such was William Lord Bellenden to whom James Stalker had proved to be 'singularly serviceable' in the role of assistant chaplain at Fort George. This Lord Bellenden was a near kinsman of the 3rd Duke of Roxburghe and, in March 1804, following the death of the 3rd Duke, he succeeded to the Dukedom. On learning of this elevation, the erstwhile chaplain conceived it as his duty to convey his respects in person. Arriving at the door of Fleurs Castle, he intimated his business, but the butler, observing that the caller had neither carriage nor full dress, told him that His Grace was at dinner and could not see him, being engaged with company. 'His Grace, however, thought otherwise, and learning who it was, came himself, hailed and received him at the door, ushered him into the dining room, and expressed to the company his obligations and his happiness at seeing his old and tried friend'.[27] He then kept the chaplain at Fleurs Castle until he could offer him a benefice. Lilliesleaf became vacant on 28th September 1804 and, one week later, James Stalker was presented to the charge. His benefactor died a mere six months after his nominee's admission to the charge.

Lilliesleaf offered a particularly good living in terms of stipend and glebe; so good, in fact, that it gave rise to some dissatisfaction among other incumbents in the Presbytery of Selkirk.[28] James Stalker remained in Lilliesleaf until he died, unmarried, on 23rd March 1816. Brief though his service was in Aberdeen he earned a place among those who served the Gaelic congregation there.

Notes to Chapter 2

1. J McGrigor: *Autobiography of Sir James McGrigor* (London, 1861), p 1.
2. P J Anderson (ed): *Records of Marischal College* (Aberdeen, 1898), vol. 2, pp 21-23.
3. E H B Rodger: *Aberdeen doctors at home and abroad* (Edinburgh, 1893), p 54.
4. A M Munro: *Memorials of the aldermen, provosts and lord provosts of Aberdeen 1272-1895* (Aberdeen, 1897), p 250.
5. *Aberdeen Almanack* (1787), p 180.
6. J Rettie: *Aberdeen fifty years ago* (Aberdeen, 1868), p 52.
7. W Bannerman: *The Aberdeen worthies* (Aberdeen, 1840), pp 107-115.
8. W Walker: *The bards of Bon-Accord* (Aberdeen, 1887), p 330.
9. W Thom: *The history of Aberdeen* (Aberdeen, 1811), vol. 2, p 206. This chapter on literature and the arts in Thom's history was contributed by a 'gentleman'. The authorship has been attributed to John Ewen. See George Walker: *Aberdeen Awa'* (Aberdeen, 1897), p 387.
10. W Kennedy: *Annals of Aberdeen* (Aberdeen, 1818), vol. 1, p 317.
11. A Keith: *A thousand years of Aberdeen* (Aberdeen, 1972), p 303.
12. G M Fraser: *Aberdeen street names* (Aberdeen, 1911), p 6.
13. J Rettie: op. cit., p 52.
14. J Robertson: *The book of Bon-Accord* (Aberdeen, 1839), p 10.
15. I am indebted to Mr Stuart Maxwell, Edinburgh for information on Ewen's business connections.
16. *Aberdeen Journal* (31st October, 1821).
17. G M Fraser: op. cit., p 6.
18. R Wilson: *An historical account and delineation of Aberdeen* (Aberdeen, 1822), p 143.
19. Ibid., pp 142-144.
20. *Aberdeen Journal* (15th December, 1788), p 4.
21. *Records of the Presbytery of Chanonry*, vol. 5, p 165 (8th May, 1782) (CH2-66-5).
22. *Minutes of the Royal Bounty Committee* (12th August, 1784), vol. 1776-1785 (CH1-5-59).
23. Ibid. (31st May, 1786), p 62, vol. 1785-1794 (CH1-5-60).
24. The *Fasti* has been mistakenly taken to imply that James Stalker was ordained by the Presbytery of Chanonry as assistant to the chaplain at Fort George (*eg* A C Dow: *Ministers to the soldiers of Scotland*, p 239).
25. Probably the Wm Ross who was at the time in Rothiemurchus. He was subsequently minister of Cromarty Gaelic Chapel and was said by Donald Sage to be 'very popular among the humbler classes'.
26. *Records of the Presbytery of Inverness*, vol. 1758-1821, p 173 (12th February, 1788) (CH2-553-7).
27. *Fasti Ecclesiae Scoticanae* (Edinburgh, first edition, 1867), vol. 1, p 555.
28. *Records of the Presbytery of Selkirk*, vol. 1792-1825, pp 146 ff (6th April, 1813) (CH2-327-8).

Chapter 3

*

FITTING UP ST MARY'S

THE Rev. Micah Balwhidder's estimate of parish life in Dalmailing in the year 1789, might aptly describe the mood of the Highland Congregation that same year. 'It was not remarkable for any extraordinary occurrence; but there was a hopefulness in the minds of men, and a planning of new undertakings, of which, whatever may be the upshot, the devising is ever rich in the cheerful anticipations of good.'[1]

St Mary's (Gaelic) Chapel

There was no major change in the affairs of the Highland Congregation until the end of 1789 but, in the course of the year, the managers had been contemplating new developments, especially as regards better accommodation. The solution they adopted was to petition the Town Council for permission to hold the Gaelic services in St Mary's Chapel, then, as now, the crypt or undercroft of East St Nicholas. This ancient part of the Kirk of St Nicholas dates from 1438 and is not only the finest piece of medieval architecture remaining in Aberdeen, but also, the only medieval building in the city constructed entirely of granite.[2] Down the centuries it has served a variety of purposes, both sacred and profane.[3] In the 18th century it had been used for a time as a plumber's shop, but presumably, it was not being used for any particular purpose when the Highland Congregation made their request to the Town Council, the owners of the building. The crave of the petition submitted on 17th November 1789 was as follows:

> *To the Honourable the Magistrates and Council, from the Highland Congregation in Aberdeen.*
>> *Unto the Hon. the Lord Provost, Magistrates, and remnant members of Council of the City of Aberdeen. The petition of the subscribing Highlanders, in their own name and in the name of many others impowering them,*
>> *Humbly Sheweth,*
>> *That there are of their number upwards of five hundred persons of both sexes, residing in this city and its environs, employed in honest labour, who, by their imperfect knowledge of the English language, are incapable of reaping the benefit they could wish, from public or private instructions in that language.*

That from a desire of having the ordinances of religion dispensed in the language which they can best understand, and from which they may reap most edification, they have executed a deed (which they have put into the hands of certain trustees) for the payment of ten pounds sterling quarterly to one who should undertake the office of a Preacher and Catechist among them. That they purpose to raise this salary from a voluntary subscription among themselves; a collection to be taken up at the door of their place of meeting, and a small rent to be imposed upon the seats in it. That their indigent circumstances will not admit their building a place of worship for themselves, and therefore they are obliged to apply to the generosity and benevolence of the council for their accommodation in this respect. That they acknowledge with the warmest gratitude, the goodness of the council, in vouchsafing them the liberty for so long a time of assembling for public worship and catechising in one of their churches. But as this privilege, tho' they should please to continue it with them, would allow them the opportunity of public worship only once every Lord's Day, especially in the Winter season, and must deprive them of every advantage they might hope for from the seat rents, they would humbly intreat, that the council would be graciously pleased to allow them the use of St Mary's Chapel under the East Church, for the purpose of public worship, and that for any time and under any restrictions, which to them shall seem meet. That in such event your petitioners will, at their own expence, put proper windows and seats in it, and take all possible care of it.

That the goodness of the council to them hitherto, and their readiness to encourage any reasonable scheme for promoting the success of religion, and the best interests of the poor inhabitants, in this city, have encouraged them at once to present this their humble petition to them, and to hope that they will be pleased to grant it.

May it therefore please the Honourable Council to take the above petition into their serious consideration, and if they see cause to grant the request of it, and your petitioners, etc.,

For, and behalf of	*Colquhoun McGregor,*
the Petitioners,	*James Chalmers,*
Aberdeen, 17 Novr. 1789.	*John Ewen, Trustees.*

Given the fact that the Provost and one of the Councillors had already identified themselves as being in sympathy with the aspirations of the Highland Congregation, it is not surprising that, following an on-site inspection of the premises, the Council reached the following decision:

10 December 1789. The Provost and four baillies, Dean of Guild and Treasurer. Provost John Abercrombie, Baillie Hadden, Alex Dingwall, Wm. Black, Alex Robertson, Charles Farquharson, Robert Garden, Deacon Imray, Deacon Leask.

The said day the Council having resumed the consideration of the Petition from a Committee of managers for the Highland congregation in this place desiring liberty for the performance of public worship in that apartment under the East Church called St Mary's Chapel and the Magistrates having reported that they had gone and visited that place and were of the opinion that the use of it might be granted to the Petitioners without doing any kind of prejudice either to the Church or to the public. They unanimously agreed to allow the petitioners the use of the said chapel for the purpose of performing public worship and catechising but during the Council's pleasure only and under the express condition not only that they shall be at all kind of expence in repairing and fitting up the same for the forsaid purpose but also that the preacher or catechist to be employed by the petitioners shall be first regularly licenced and authorised by the proper Judicature of the Established Church.

The conditions attached to the magistrates' consent presented no difficulty to the Gaelic managers. They had already indicated their willingness to meet the expense of fitting up a place of worship, putting in proper seats and windows. How much they did as regards inserting new windows is uncertain. Their funds amounted to no more than £26 and the 'fitting up' may not have extended beyond furnishing the chapel with seats and a reading desk. Five years later 'the darkness of the place' was to be adduced as one of the reasons for vacating it, but, however gloomy the interior, the important thing was that now they had a place to meet in which they could call their own.[4] St Mary's comforts were decidedly austere, but the Highlanders revelled in the freedom to worship at a time of their own choosing, free from external constraints of any kind.

An enlarged income was a further benefit which could be anticipated from their segregation. In the 18th century there was very little pressure on worshippers in the Established Church to contribute to the Church's revenue. The Burgh Churches in Aberdeen, as in other towns and cities in Scotland, were maintained by the municipal authorities and stipends paid out of the Common Good Fund.[5] Income such as there was came either from seat rents – an annual, or twice-yearly, payment made by those who wished to have the right to occupy a seat at all services – or from church door collections. The income from seat rents was used to defray sundry expenses while the church door collections were appropriated by the parish authorities to be used for poor relief. It was taken for granted that only the well-to-do would contribute to the church door collections.[6] Worshippers in the Parish Church, therefore, could, and did, attend services without making any monetary contribution and so there was no tradition of voluntary giving in the Established Church. On the other hand, in the Secession Church, buildings and pastors had to be supported out of the free-will offerings of the people. Seceders accepted that financial burden as the price that had to be paid for the privilege of choosing their own minister as against having one imposed on them by the patron, be it the Town Council or the heritors.

The Highland Congregation fell into a third category. Although within the fold of the Established Church, it had no access to Parish Funds for the support of its minister. Neither could it raise money from seat rents, for the seats in East St Nicholas did not belong to the Gaelic congregation. By the same token, they were debarred, in theory at least, from retaining any door collections taken at the Gaelic services, for the Parish had a claim on these for poor relief. In fact, the only income available to the Highland Congregation was that from private donations, by far the most erratic source in terms of a steady cash-flow. Clearly therefore, the position would be greatly improved by their occupying premises which were exclusive to their own use, for then they could exact seat rents and more easily retain church door collections. The managers made clear in their petition to the magistrates that such was their desire and intention. These income sources were, in fact, essential for the proper establishment of the congregation. In anticipation of the freedom to collect funds, the managers had sanctioned an arrangement by which a preacher was to be guaranteed an annual stipend of £40. Although considerably below a parish stipend, this figure was not unattractive, being more than most Royal Bounty preachers could expect at that time.

Kenneth Bayne's irregular appointment

In 1790 the congregation commenced the process of selecting a minister. The early chronicle recounts: 'after the hearing of several candidates, they gave a unanimous call to Mr. Kenneth Bayne, preacher of the Gospel in the Presbytery of Dingwall and the Synod of Ross, to be their pastor'. Who the other candidates were is not revealed, but the successful one was a younger brother of Ronald Bayne, a relationship which would have done nothing to hinder his candidature. Born in 1767, Kenneth Bayne matriculated at Marischal College in the class of 1782-1786. His scholastic attainments were said to be quite average. Donald Sage contrasting him with his brother Ronald, described him as 'his equal and contemporary in the Christian life but his inferior in natural abilities'. Although he attended Marischal College for four years he did not graduate. Non-graduation was not uncommon at that time because the additional fee payable on graduation could be a disincentive. On the other hand, a contemporary recalled that although he was a diligent and serious student at Aberdeen 'an enfeebled and relaxed state of nerves checked the ardour and activity of his literary pursuits'.[7] That, however, did not disqualify him from attending the four year divinity course which he had to complete before he could apply for licensing.

Dingwall being his home Presbytery, it would have been natural for him to have received licensing there, and it seems that he was also ordained by the Presbytery of Dingwall to the charge of the Aberdeen Highland Congregation, but as there is a gap in the records of that Presbytery between 1787 and 1793 that cannot be confirmed.[8] However, he was not ordained by the Presbytery of Aberdeen and, although ordination of licentiates by a Presbytery other than the Presbytery of the bounds may not have been exceptional at that time, it would seem that the Town Council's direction that the preacher be 'authorised by the proper Judicature of the Established Church' was not complied with. Irregular though the procedure may have been, Kenneth Bayne was the first minister to be ordained to the charge of the Gaelic congregation in Aberdeen.

First ordination of elders

Having their own minister and their own accommodation opened the way for further development in the congregation. As the chronicler put it: 'From this date they had all divine ordinances regularly administered to them, for the effecting of which Mr. Kenneth Bayne, with the approbation of the congregation, ordained elders to join with him in the government of the Church and exercise of discipline and watch over the manners of the people.' The elders were named as Angus Munro, Donald Chrystie, Donald Mackenzie and William Fraser. None of them subsequently achieved any prominence in the temporal management of the congregation.

Judged by the practice of the Church at that time, the ordination of elders in the Gaelic congregation was irregular. There was only one Parish – St Nicholas – in Aberdeen and although it was a collegiate charge having three ministers, it had only one Session the General Kirk Session from which elders were allocated to the various Established Churches in the town. In 1788 a claim by the Session of Aberdeen that they were entitled to have three representative elders (to offset their three ministers) attend the Presbytery, was rejected without a vote by the General Assembly.[9] The Presbytery acquiesced with the view that Aberdeen Kirk Session was entitled to only one representative elder in the Presbytery. Technically, although not yet officially, the Highland Congregation had the status of a chapel-of-ease and could not appoint elders or exercise discipline; but the Highlanders in their concern to have a Kirk Session, seemed to be oblivious to these niceties of church government. The ordination of elders, which would have been conducted in Gaelic, would not have come under the purview of the managers who were mainly concerned with the temporal affairs of the congregation.

SSPCK support for Gaelic Congregation

All things considered, by 1791 the Highland Congregation had reason to be satisfied with their progress. However, finance was a recurring problem and in an attempt to achieve greater security, it was agreed with the Presbytery that another appeal would be made to the Royal Bounty Committee.

The representative of Aberdeen Presbytery on the Royal Bounty Committee that year was Dr Alex Gerard who was instructed 'to use his endeavours to get some assistance out of their funds'.[10]

Dr Gerard (1728-1795) was Professor of Divinity at King's College and a very experienced and influential member of Assembly having been Moderator in 1764.[11] Although Dr Gerard informed the Presbytery that he had recommended the Highland Congregation to the Royal Bounty Committee, he was not listed in the sederunt as being present and his endeavours, such as they were, failed to produce any result.[12] The congregation might have been better served the following year when the Presbytery representative was the Rev. Hugh Hay, then newly appointed to the second charge of St Nicholas. Probably he would have been well disposed to the cause of the Highland Congregation for, in 1793, his sister was to become wife to Kenneth Bayne. Sadly, before the wedding took place, Hugh Hay had died at the early age of 29. But the application was not renewed in 1792 because a parallel application made in 1791 to the Society in Scotland for Propagating Christian Knowledge (SSPCK), was more sympathetically received.

In April 1792, the Presbytery received intimation from the SSPCK secretary that the Society had 'allowed £10 for the catechetical instruction of the Highlanders settled in Aberdeen in their own language';[13] whereupon, the Presbytery appointed 'Mr Kenneth Bayne, minister of the Gaelic Chapel in this place' to undertake the duty. Kenneth Bayne was not, of course, a member of the Presbytery but it is interesting that although the Presbytery had not ordained or inducted him, he is referred to as 'minister of the Gaelic Chapel in this place'. The term 'Gaelic Chapel' was now to displace the former 'Highland Congregation'.

At the same time that Kenneth Bayne was told of the willingness of the SSPCK to support his work among the Aberdeen Highlanders, events were occurring elsewhere which were to forestall its implementation. A new Gaelic chapel in Greenock was officially opened on 8th April 1792. Shortly thereafter, Kenneth Bayne was called to be its first minister and by the end of the summer, he had been inducted to his second and last charge. He remained there until he died, three months after his brother Ronald, in April 1821.

Kenneth Bayne's personality

Kenneth Bayne's ministry in Aberdeen did not extend beyond two years and in that time he did not make the impact that he was subsequently to make in Greenock. He lacked his brother's eloquence. One estimate states that 'his preaching was profoundly experimental, but his enunciation was slow and difficult'.[14] His close friend, Dr Love of Anderston Chapel, who preached his funeral oration, remarked that he was easily exhausted on account of his nervous debility, but this was not without benefit for 'without this restraint his delivery would probably have had rather an excess of animation and vehemence'. He was at his best when addressing those who were spiritually enlightened, when his exposition of the mysteries of salvation were, according to the same source, 'remarkably clear, copious, comprehensive, attractive and refreshing'. On the other hand, to those whom he regarded as deficient in their profession of faith, he was perhaps unduly sharp and severe. A particularly revealing comment on his ministry is that he had a 'great and salutary influence over people from the Highlands in the lower classes of society; and which extended itself to serious people in general and in some remarkable instances, to persons in the higher situations of society'.[15] That last remark may cast some light on Donald Sage's statement that 'natives of Greenock who did not understand Gaelic, went to reside in the Highlands for the express purpose of acquiring the language in order to profit by his preaching'.[16]

The wholesome influence which he had on the community in general, was reflected within the microcosm of his own home. His family, one son and seven daughters, was stricken by tragedy. Two of his daughters drowned at Bridge of Allan, the older trying to rescue the younger.[17] Of the remaining five, three went out as missionaries to India. The first to go was Margaret. She and her husband, Dr John Wilson FRS, left Scotland for Bombay under the auspices of the Scottish Missionary Society in 1828,[18] a year before Alexander Duff, the first missionary sponsored by the Church of Scotland, set out for India. Margaret Bayne was a gifted woman who, it seems, spent some time at the University of Aberdeen receiving an education much in advance of her day.[19] In 1835 she started a school for girls in Bombay and when she died the following year, her two sisters, Anna and Hay, went out to India at their own expense to carry on the work she had begun. Anna lived only four years before she too died in India, and seven years later Hay died at sea.[20] John, the only son, continuing the Bayne tradition, became a minister and played a prominent role in the Church in Canada.[21]

Notes to Chapter 3

1. J Galt: *Annals of the Parish* (Foulis edition, London, 1911), p 182.
2. F Wyness: *City by the grey North Sea* (Aberdeen, 1965), p 33.
3. J Cooper: *Cartularium ecclesiae Sancti Nicholai Aberdonensis* (Aberdeen, 1892), pp xlvii–xlviii.
4. R Wilson: *An historical account and delineation of Aberdeen* (Aberdeen, 1822), p 130. The account of the Gaelic congregation given by Wilson was largely copied from an entry in the Gaelic congregation managers' minute book which carries the title 'A short narrative of the rise, progress and present establishment of the Gaelic congregation in Aberdeen drawn up and read with approbation to several of the principal members of the congregation and at their desire recorded by Mr John Ewen originally chosen as one of their first managers by whom the narrative was written. Aberdeen 20th March 1818'.
5. A J H Gibson: *Stipend in the Church of Scotland* (Edinburgh, 1961), pp 25–26.
6. A L Drummond and J Bulloch: *The Church in Victorian Scotland 1843-1874* (Edinburgh, 1975), p 38.
7. P McBride (ed.): *Sermons and letters of Dr John Love of Anderston Chapel* (Glasgow, 1838), p 29. A sermon preached in the Gaelic Chapel, Greenock at the funeral of the Rev. Kenneth Bayne, 1821.
8. The information relative to Kenneth Bayne given under the entry for the Aberdeen Gaelic Chapel in *Fasti Ecclesiae Scoticanae* (first edition, 1871, vol. 3, p 481; third edition, 1926, vol. 6, p 6), is erroneous at several places. He was not appointed to the Gaelic Chapel in 1781 (he was then aged 14), nor was he ordained by the Presbytery of Nairn. He commenced his ministry in Aberdeen in 1790 and was most probably ordained by the Presbytery of Dingwall that year.
9. *Records of the Presbytery of Aberdeen*, vol. 8, p 404 (30th July, 1788) (CH2-1-10).
10. Ibid., vol. 8, p 434 (11th May, 1791) (CH2-1-10).
11. G D Henderson: *The burning bush. Studies in Scottish church history* (Edinburgh, 1957). Chapter XI, 'A typical moderate', pp 163–179, gives a highly interesting account of the career of Dr Gerard.
12. *Minutes of the Royal Bounty Committee* (1st June, 1791), vol. 1785–1794, p 261 (CH1-5-60).
13. *Records of the Presbytery of Aberdeen*, vol. 8, p 453 (12th April, 1792) (CH2-1-10).
14. D MacGregor in *Disruption Worthies of the Highlands* (Edinburgh, 1877), p 42.
15. P McBride: op. cit., p 30.
16. D Sage: *Memorabilia Domestica* (Wick, 1889, reprinted 1975), p 224.
17. C Roger: *A week at Bridge of Allan* (Edinburgh, 1851), pp 20–22.
18. For an account of Margaret Bayne, see J Wilson: *A memoir of Mrs Margaret Wilson* (Edinburgh, 2nd edition, 1838).
19. E G K Hewat: *Vision and achievement 1796-1956* (Edinburgh, 1960), p 46.
20. For a short account of the splendid service given to the church in India by the three Bayne sisters, see D P Thomson: *Women of the Scottish Church* (Perth, 1975), pp 181–191.
21. W Gregg: *A short history of the Presbyterian Church in the Dominion of Canada* (Toronto, 1892), p 109.

Chapter 4

*

ABERDEEN'S CHURCHES IN 1790

IN the closing quarter of the 18th century, Aberdeen's ecclesiastical landscape underwent some major changes.[1] The changing scene was a consequence of an expanding population and an increasing tendency to divisiveness within the Established Church. The medieval burgh of Aberdeen was a highly compact community centering round the Kirkgate, the Gallowgate, the Castlegate, the Shiprow and the Green. The parish churches (West St Nicholas, East St Nicholas and the College or Greyfriars Church) were situated in this precinct and, a little further to the east, was St Clement's Footdee. The city still had village-like qualities in the compactness of its corporate life.

About 1760 buildings began to be erected on the lands of Gilcomston, the high ground lying to the north-west of the Denburn, and soon there was a considerable community of artisans living in the area comprising Jack's Brae, Leadside and Loanhead.[2] This territory fell within the bounds of the Parish of Old Machar (or St Machar's Cathedral) and for the convenience of the one thousand strong community, a chapel-of-ease was built in 1771 by voluntary subscription. Approval by the Church for the erection of a chapel-of-ease, or extension charge, was by no means a common occurrence. One of the great weaknesses of the Established Church was its inability to adapt the parish system to cope with the needs of the expanding cities. One church in each parish was all that the ecclesiastical infrastructure allowed for.[3] Additional churches, intended to cater for the expanding industrial population, had to be funded by voluntary subscriptions without any assistance from ecclesiastical sources. Even when this level of support could be achieved, there was often a marked reluctance on the part of the ecclesiastical authorities to sanction such a development.

The reasons for this obstructive attitude were basically two-fold – first, a suspicion that not infrequently dissatisfaction with the services of the parish minister was a factor in the proposed extension, and second, a concern that a flourishing chapel-of-ease would divert resources (the church door collections), hitherto allocated to the poor, to the support of alternative ministries.[4] The Church as a whole was divided on this, as on most other issues, and by 1798 the General Assembly ruled that chapels-of-ease were not to be sanctioned without Assembly approval. Previously, some chapels had been sanctioned at Presbytery level but, as early as 1779, the Assembly was involved in granting permission for a chapel in Dunfermline, approval there being conditional on the allocation of church door collections to the Parish Poor's Fund. It was restrictive legislation of this kind that induced many church extensionists to sever their links with the Established Church. They saw no reason why, having paid for their buildings and their ministers, they should then put themselves under the yoke of the Establishment. Independence was an easier and a cheaper option.

Secession Churches in Aberdeen

The trend to independency and divisiveness was a product of the movement towards toleration which had been gaining in momentum since the beginning of the century and which culminated in the abolition of the Penal Statutes in 1792. The fragmentation of the Church had begun in 1733 with the formation of the Associate Presbytery by the Erskines and their supporters. In 1747 a dichotomy within this first secession Church gave rise to the Burghers and the Anti-burghers. Later still, in 1761, Thomas Gillespie and his followers left the Established Church to form the Relief Church. Aberdeen was not immune to the attractions of separatism and, by 1780, each of these three strands of secessionism – Burgher, Anti-burgher and Relief – was represented in the town.

The first of these secession congregations was formed by a group which hived off from East St Nicholas in 1756 and adhered to the principles of the Associate (Burgher) Synod.[5] Its first meeting place was near the quay at the corner of Virginia Street and Weigh-house Square, but in 1772 a new church, still within the city limits, was opened in the Netherkirkgate. Another hive-off from East St Nicholas gave rise to a congregation which adhered to the second strand of secessionism – the General Associate (Anti-burgher) Synod.[6] When, in 1779, this group came to erect a place of worship, they had to be content with a site outwith the old city and so they feued part of the Caberstone Croft – pastureland at the north end of what is now Belmont Street, a street then just beginning to be developed from the Schoolhill end.

By this time (1780) the city was irrevocably committed to a westwards expansion. Beginning at Back Wynd, which for two hundred years had served as the city's western perimeter road, the building line moved downward into the valley of the Denburn and from there northwards to the suburb of Gilcomston. In this process, Belmont Street continued to be developed in a southerly direction and, in 1780, the third strand of secessionism, the Relief Church, obtained a feu on the east side of Belmont Street opposite Patagonian Court. This congregation was formed in 1778 following dissension within Gilcomston

Chapel-of-Ease over the choice of a minister.[7] The disappointed section of the congregation hived off and, attaching themselves to the Relief Presbytery, built a chapel capable of accommodating one thousand people. However by 1791 they disjoined themselves from the Relief Church and, being re-admitted to the Established Church, became Belmont Chapel-of-Ease.

The next decade saw the construction of another two churches. Trinity Chapel was erected on the Shiprow in 1794 and it was followed in 1795 by the New Light Burger church which was built at the south end of Belmont Street at a point where the descent to the Denburn was so steep that no stairs were required for access to the gallery.[8] From the foregoing it is evident that, in the decade which saw the formation of the Highland Congregation, the establishment of new congregations and the erection of new churches was something of a growth industry in Aberdeen, and a fashionable area for development was the eastern slope of the Denburn valley.[9] To complete the ecclesiastical directory relative to the period at which the Highland Congregation was worshipping in St Mary's Chapel, it should be said that there were 15 sizeable congregations in Aberdeen at that time. Of these, eight belonged to the Established Church, *viz* West St Nicholas, East St Nicholas, the College or Greyfriars Church (the fabric of which was demolished in 1903 to make way for the extension of Marischal College), St Clement's Footdee, Gilcomston Chapel-of-Ease, Belmont Chapel-of-Ease, Trinity Chapel-of-Ease and St Mary's Gaelic Chapel. In addition to the three Burgher and Anti-burgher congregations already mentioned, there was also a Relief congregation which, in 1780, had split off from the Belmont Relief before that congregation returned to the Established Church. This group built their chapel in the Shiprow to the east of Market Street, and eventually, as the sole representative of the Relief Church in Aberdeen, built St Paul's on Rosemount Viaduct.[10]

There were three Episcopal churches, one of which, St Andrews, belonged to the Scottish Episcopal Church. Although in 1784 the scene of the consecration of the first Episcopal Bishop of America, it was little more than the upper floor of a dwelling-house; but a proper chapel was built on the same site in Longacre in 1795. It too was eventually demolished in the interests of extending Marischal College. The English Episcopal churches were Trinity and St Paul's both long since demolished. These 15 congregations, together with small individual congregations of Methodists, Quakers, Roman Catholics, Bereans and Glasites, constituted the Christian Church in Aberdeen in the year 1792 when the Rev. John Mackenzie came to the place vacated by Kenneth Bayne.

Notes to Chapter 4

1. I R MacDonald: 'Aberdeen's Churches in the Late Eighteenth Century' in *Northern Scotland,* vol. 19 (1999), pp 75-83.
2. W Robbie: *Aberdeen: its traditions and history* (Aberdeen, 1893), p 287.
3. J Cunningham: *The church history of Scotland* (Edinburgh, 2nd edition, 1882), vol. 2, p 401.
4. Ibid., p 418.
5. A Gammie: *The churches of Aberdeen* (Aberdeen, 1909), pp 149 ff.
6. Ibid., pp 88 ff.
7. Ibid., pp 69 ff.
8. R Small: *History of the Congregations of the United Presbyterian Church 1733-1900* (Edinburgh, 1904), vol. 1, p 12.
9. I R MacDonald: op. cit., pp 75 ff.
10. A Gammie: op. cit., pp 202 ff.

Chapter 5

*

GAELIC LANE

JOHN Mackenzie was a native of Ross-shire and, having been a student at Marischal College from 1783-1787, he would have attended the Gaelic services held by Ronald Bayne and so would have been known to the congregation. On 7th August 1792, four weeks before Kenneth Bayne was inducted in Greenock, John Mackenzie applied to the Presbytery of Chanonry for licensing. Perhaps there had been some communication between himself and the congregation regarding his decision to apply for licensing, for some two months later, as reported in the anonymous manuscript *The Origin of the Gaelic Congregation in Aberdeen*: 'Upon the 8th day of October 1792, they gave a unanimous call to Mr. John Mackenzie Preacher of the Gospel in the Presbytery of Chanonry and Synod of Ross to be their Pastor with which call he closed and being ordained to the charge came to Aberdeen in December 1792.' This is the first entry in *The Origin* which is specific as regards days and months; and this feature, together with the fact that from this point 'they' in the narrative is replaced by 'we', suggests that it was John Mackenzie who wrote it.

On 27th November 1792 John Mackenzie compeared with the Presbytery of Chanonry, when, according to its minutes, he 'delivered a discourse on Romans 8 v. 32 which was approved and having a prospect of being chosen to supply the vacancy in the Gaelic Chapel at Aberdeen requested of the Presbytery to be ordained'. This the Presbytery agreed to on the grounds of his 'not having come under the usual engagements to submit to the judicature of this church'.[1] This may be taken to imply that the Aberdeen Gaelic Congregation was not considered to be subject to the jurisdiction of the Presbytery of Aberdeen and is a clear indication of the extent to which an attitude of independency prevailed in this outpost of Highland evangelicalism. But if true *de facto*, it was not true *de jure*. Several years later, in a review of the ecclesiastical status of the congregation, the Presbytery acknowledged that 'there had been irregularities in the manner of introducing and settling a minister there, owing probably to its coming gradually forward from small beginnings'.[2]

The fact of the matter was that in selecting a minister, the congregation disregarded the Presbytery. They looked to Ronald Bayne for advice and then made their own arrangements with Highland presbyteries for the ordination of their ministers, all of which was contrary to the approved procedure of the Church. Of course the fact that chapel ministers had no seat in the Presbytery tended to confirm their isolation and the consequent independence of their congregations. Only the need to obtain a Presbyterial certificate of diligence before he could claim the annual SSPCK grant of £10, brought the Gaelic Chapel minister into contact with the Presbytery; and as regards the procedural irregularities in the admission of John Mackenzie to the chapel, it seems that the Presbytery, in neglecting their supervisory role, were as much to blame as the congregation. On 6th February 1793, John Mackenzie compeared with the Presbytery of Aberdeen, produced his call to the Gaelic congregation and informed the Presbytery that he had been ordained to the chapel, whereupon the Presbytery agreed to receive him.[3] Any further formalities were dispensed with.

The congregation continued to act as if they were independent of the Presbytery when the minister 'in concurrence of the elders then in office and approbation of the congregation, appointed five persons more for that office *viz.*, Alexander Murray, James Davidson, Simon Fraser, William Macleod and Alex Fraser'. Of these, only the first mentioned attained any prominence in the subsequent history of the congregation.

Following the induction of John Mackenzie the congregation continued to grow, or, as he himself put it, 'the Lord made the cause upon the whole to prosper'. The result was that the congregation outgrew the available space in St Mary's Chapel and the decision was taken to build a chapel of their own. The leadership for this project was provided by the managers more than the minister; but together, pastor and people had seen sufficient evidence of flourishing ecclesiastical building projects to encourage them in their own plans. In 1793 two new congregations had been formed in the city and, in no time, both had chapels under construction. One was Trinity Chapel-of-Ease which had its origin like so many others in disaffection over the filling of a vacancy – this time in East St Nicholas.[4] The dissentients erected yet another commodious chapel at the lower end of the Shiprow and it was opened in April 1794. Still nearer, both in respect of time and place, was the 'Burn' Kirk which resulted from a split in the Burgher congregation located in the Netherkirkgate. Following the death of their minister in 1793, the Burgher congregation split over the choice of a new minister.[5] As usual the losing minority hived off and the year 1795 found them building their own place of worship close by the Denburn (hence the name Burn Kirk) at the position now occupied by the eastern pier of Union Bridge.

Feu purchase for Chapel

Emboldened by the enthusiasm and achievements of others, the High-landers now joined the ranks of the church builders. The first step was to obtain a feu and to this end they negotiated with Andrew Simpson, merchant in Aberdeen and proprietor of the ground now delimited by Back Wynd, Union Street, Belmont Street and Gaelic Lane, but which, in 1795, had only Back Wynd as an easily recognisable reference point. Consequently the feu was described as 'part of that Tail or Croft of Land lying in the Green of Aberdeen on the West side of the West way there-of which leads from St Nicholas Kirk to the place of the Carmelite or White Friars'. As has already been mentioned, Belmont Street was being developed from the Schoolhill end, ie downhill towards the Green.[6] There was, of course, no Union Street then and when, several years later, that thorough-fare was built on a series of arches that carried it from the Castlegate and across the Denburn, Belmont Street, instead of continuing on its downhill course, had to be graded uphill to intersect with the elevated Union Street. Hence the low point of Belmont Street to this day is at its junction with Gaelic Lane. Needless to say, Gaelic Lane took its name from the chapel which, when completed, fronted on to it.

At that time, the area from the Green northwards to Back Wynd and St Nicholas Kirk, must have been steeply sloping garden, or pasture, ground. Some impression of the steepness of the ascent can be had from a consideration of the difference in level between the Green (at the bottom of the steps ascending to Union Street) and Back Wynd. The Green itself was the termination of the main approach road from the south which came into the city via the Hardgate and Whinmill Brae. The selected site therefore, was, at the time, an open and promi-nent one, although, subsequently, the construction of Union Street turned it into a back lane. This, however, was a lesser inconvenience than the effect which Union Street had on the Burn Kirk which opened its doors for worship two weeks prior to the Gaelic Chapel. The Burn Kirk happened to be directly in line with the proposed route for Union Street and it had to be demolished to allow the foundation stone of Union Bridge to be laid in 1801. The New Light Burghers, to give the Burn Kirk adherents their proper description, were then rehoused in a building which until recent times still stood in St Nicholas Lane. But so obscure was its location that it was said of it that 'its approach was scarcely to be discovered by the most determined explorer'.[7]

The Gaelic feu as marked off by 'Peter Ross, mason in Aberdeen and George Duncan, wright there', had a 60 foot frontage and extended backwards (towards Union Street) to a depth of 54 feet. The transfer took effect from Martinmas 1795 and the disposition was in favour of Colquhoun McGregor, merchant; Patrick Robertson, shoemaker; Simon Fraser, Pensioner; Alex Murray, woolcomber; Angus Mackay, woolcomber; Ebenezer Murray, merchant; Angus Sutherland, slater; and John Mackay, shoemaker. A memo dated April 1834, states that the chapel was founded on 10th March 1795. Building was completed in less than six months at a cost of £850.[8]

It might be said of the Highlanders, as it was said of the seceders, that they bade defiance to aesthetics, but Wilson generously describes their chapel as 'handsome',[9] while Kennedy, more cautiously, credits them with having built a 'very neat chapel'. The building itself was rectangular with the long axis running east-west; four windows were inserted along the south side, three of which are still visible. The feu superior undertook to refrain from any action which might 'obstruct the light of the said church or prove obnoxious to the hearers'. The entrance door was on the north side and the pulpit was against the east wall.

Public appeal for building fund

While the building was under construction the managers decided on a further appeal in the columns of the *Aberdeen Journal*. On 23rd June 1795 the following appeared:

THE GAELIC CONGREGATION
TO THE PUBLIC

The Gaelic congregation in Aberdeen acknowledge with gratitude, the kindness of Providence, in having favoured their association as a religious Society; and in the indulgence and protection afforded them hitherto, under the guidance of a Pastor and Managers. They find their numbers increasing, and the attendance on public worship subjected to many inconveniences, from the smallness and darkness of the place, in which they at present meet.

To obtain the necessary accommodation for public Worship, they have rented a piece of ground in the neighbourhood of Belmont Street, on which a chapel is at present building, and will be finished in the course of the season. — Their funds, however, are very far short of the undertaking — but they desire to acknowledge, in this public manner, the benevolence of many well disposed Individuals, while at the same time, they presume to solicit the Contributions of such as may be inclined to think favourably of an Establishment calculated to promote the Interests of Religion and Virtue in a particular manner, among the lower Ranks of the community, who depend entirely upon their own personal industry for the support of themselves and families.

Contributions will be gratefully received by the Managers — and by any of the Elders or other members of the congregation who have subscription papers.

John Ewen, James Chalmers, Colq. M'Gregor, Pat. Robertson
MANAGERS

It is to be noted that the three original managers had now been joined by Patrick Robertson, variously described as a shoemaker or leather merchant. Like Colquhoun McGregor, he was an adherent in the congregation.

List of subscribers

Included among the records of the Gaelic congregation is a list of all those who contributed five shillings (25 'new' pence) or more to the financial appeals made between 1788 and 1795. There are separate lists for (i) the Town Inhabitants – some 60 persons plus three corporate donations contributing in all £46 17s 3d; (ii) the Women of the Congregation – 24 donations amounting to £19 16s 2d including £4 1s of sundry amounts; and (iii) Members of the Congregation – some 75 persons contributing £70 5s 1d inclusive of £6 14s 10d of sundry donations. Altogether £137 was raised. The largest donations were from the Rev. Kenneth Bayne and the Rev. John Mackenzie who each contributed five guineas. The managers each gave one guinea, except Patrick Robertson who gave two. Several of the town's inhabitants also contributed a guinea – among them: Andrew Simpson, the feudal superior, and the feu surveyors George Duncan, wright, and Peter Ross, mason, the latter giving £1 11s 6d. Civic dignitaries such as Baillie Alex Hadden, whose sons, student contemporaries of Ronald Bayne, became distinguished provosts of the city, are also to be found on the list. John Ewen would appear to have persuaded some of his friends both in the University (*eg* Professor James Beattie) and in the Aberdeen Volunteers (*eg* Alex Brebner of Learney) to make a contribution. Other university teachers who contributed were Professors Copland, Hamilton and Macleod. The names of ministers such as the Rev. George Gordon of East St Nicholas and the Rev. Wm Blake of the English Episcopal Church (Trinity), are also included, as are supporters of other Christian charities such as George Symmers of Cults, a committee member of the Aberdeen Auxiliary of the Bible Society and a merchant in Broad Street. Most of the contributors were merchants in the city, among them Alex Scott of Broad Street, John Robertson, glazier and George Gordon, smith. The shopkeepers whose premises were close to John Ewen's shop in the Narrow Wynd also contributed, for example James Smith, grocer, R & J Catto and Wm Paterson, bookseller. Many of these traders are listed in a contemporary account.[10]

The opening of the Gaelic Chapel

The end of the summer saw the building completed and it was officially opened by the Rev. John Mackenzie on Monday 30th August 1795. It was to serve the Highlanders for 87 years during which time the Gaelic worshippers could be seen slowly wending their way up the Green, or, after the construction of Union Street, making their way along the Denburn, up through Patagonian Court and into Gaelic Lane where they stood and 'gabbit in Gaelic' before disappearing through the narrow doorway of the chapel. The sculptured granite lintel of the doorway is still to be seen in Gaelic Lane. Although the frontage on the north side has been altered and the roof raised to give an additional storey, the original walls on the remaining sides still stand; and three of the original windows can be seen on the south side. Of the other churches in existence in Aberdeen at that time, all with the exception of West St Nicholas and St Mary's Chapel, have disappeared or have been rebuilt so that the original fabric is no longer recognisable. The Gaelic Chapel was an unpretentious, severely functional, building, but it served its day and generation. Many there were for whom it was the gate of heaven, the place where they first found peace with God through faith in Jesus Christ.

The congregation was not a large one by Aberdeen standards. The number of hearers attached to the Gaelic Chapel in 1795 was 330, of whom 119 resided in the Gallowgate Quarter including the Tannarie Street and the Printfield, 73 resided in the Castlegate, 63 in Gilcomston, and the remaining 75, which included those living on the other side of the Dee, were listed as being in the Green Quarter. The roll of hearers at that date is included in the records of the congregation.

The ranks of the permanent hearers were swollen from time to time by those temporarily resident in the city. Especially prominent in this category were students and soldiers. Highland regiments were regularly stationed in Aberdeen, especially after the opening of the new Castlehill barracks, the building of which began in 1794. Indeed, the first regiment to be quartered there was the 2nd battalion of the Breadalbane Fencibles and the extent of their appreciation of the Gaelic services is evidenced by the fact that they contributed the largest corporate donation to the appeal fund. The sum of £3 13s 9d from soldiers, whose weekly income after deductions was only 1s 6d, was quite substantial.[11] The celebrated Gaelic bard, Duncan Ban MacIntyre, was at that time a sergeant in the Breadalbane Fencibles and his influence could only have been beneficial.

Another ardent Celt and gifted Gaelic poet and scholar who made his appearance in Aberdeen at this time was Ewen Maclachlan. First bursar in the bursary competition for King's College, he came to

Aberdeen in 1796 and, as rector of Old Aberdeen Grammar School and then librarian of King's College, he was to remain there until his tragically early death in 1822. Latterly his attachment was probably more to the Parish Church of Old Machar, where he lived and where he held the salaried post of Session Clerk, than to the Gaelic Chapel. But like many other occasional hearers he would be found there when eminent Highland preachers occupied the pulpit. These occasions were not infrequent, for the managers were determined to ensure that the Aberdeen Gaelic Chapel would command its share of notable preachers.

Notes to Chapter 5

1. *Records of the Presbytery of Chanonry*, vol. 5, p 234 (27th November, 1792) (CH2-66-5).
2. *Records of the Presbytery of Aberdeen*, vol. 10, p 288 (28th July, 1819) (CH2-1-12).
3. Ibid., vol 8, p 465 (6th February, 1793) (CH2-1-10).
4. A Gammie: op. cit., pp 73 ff.
5. Ibid., pp 197 ff.
6. G M Fraser: *Historical Aberdeen* (Aberdeen, 1905), p 121.
7. R Angus: *Sermons by the late Rev. Henry Angus with a memoir of his life* (Aberdeen, 1861), p xl.
8. W Kennedy: *Annals of Aberdeen* (Aberdeen, 1818), vol. 2, p 188.
9. R Wilson: *An historical account and delineation of Aberdeen* (Aberdeen, 1822), p 131. Wilson, of course, was quoting from John Ewen's narrative in which the chapel is described as 'very handsome'.
10. R S Walker (ed.): *James Beattie's day-book 1773-1798* (Aberdeen, 1948).
11. The Marchioness of Tullibardine: *A military history of Perthshire* (Perth, 1908), p 156, footnote.

Chapter 6

*

Brief Pastorates

THE management of the Gaelic Chapel was well aware of the need for a proper constitution to regulate the congregation's business. Aberdeen's recently formed congregations, most of which had had their origin in disputes of one kind or another, were an ever present reminder of that need. Consequently, 'considering that in all societies whether civil or religious, it is necessary to lay down rules for the government and management of the same', the head managers and subscribers of the Gaelic congregation met on 1st July 1796 'to establish fundamental rules for the management of the spiritual and temporal concerns of the congregation'. A draft constitution which had been previously prepared for signature was submitted, discussed and several adjustments made to it, the insertions being clearly discernible on the original document, all of it written in English. Finally, the rules 'being read in the Gaelic language by the Rev. John Mackenzie, the meeting unanimously agreed to the contents thereof in full'. If Gaelic was the language for worship, English was the language for business. In none of the records of the Gaelic congregation is a single word of Gaelic to be found.

The Chapel's constitution and management

The constitution as approved consisted of six articles and it was signed by five of the elders, Simon Fraser, Angus Munro, Alex Fraser, Donald Christie and Alex Murray, the last two of whom were unable to write their names. Three of the managers, James Chalmers, Patrick Robertson and John Ewen, also signed the constitution; but the fourth, Colquhoun McGrigor, apparently was not present and indeed his name does not appear again in the congregational records. It is, of course, highly probable that he attended subsequent meetings of the management committee, but, as it was not the practice to list the sederunt in the minutes, it is not possible to say when the prime mover in the formation of the Highland Congregation, made his last appearance.

Latterly life had not been easy for Colquhoun McGrigor. His first wife, the mother of his three sons, died on 22nd December 1792 only months before James, her eldest son, took ship to London to commence his brilliant career. On 24th December 1795 Colquhoun remarried, but this second wife, Grizel Finlayson, daughter of John Finlayson, supervisor of excise in Aberdeen and widow of Peter Gordon of Bellatrich Glenmuick, died only a year later on 1st January 1797. That month he retired from his business leaving it in the hands of his second son, Robert. Then, on 20th October 1798 in his 59th year, he himself died, at Banchory House, the home of Andrew Thomson, son-in-law of Professor Hamilton, one of the subscribers to the Gaelic Chapel Appeal Fund. Colquhoun McGrigor was buried in St Nicholas Churchyard, Aberdeen, in the shadow of the Gaelic Chapel, there to be joined by his son Robert, merchant in the Gallowgate, who died the following year aged 27 years.[1]

The constitution as approved laid down that all major policy decisions, including such matters as the choice of a minister, were to be determined by 'a majority of voices of the elders, heads of families and unmarried men who have been regular hearers and have had seats in the chapel for twelve months and understand the Gaelic language'. It may be significant that the language requirement was one of the insertions made to the original draft constitution from the floor of the meeting. It did not appear in the draft submitted by the managers. In the 18th century 'heads of families' did not require further definition and the women of the congregation had no say (at least not constitutionally) in the choice of their minister. It may be that they had no voice in any of the management decisions. The franchise for the election of the management committee extended to 'contributors to the amount of five shillings and upwards' and since this does not specify the gender of the contributors it could be taken to include women along with men. But, neither is the gender of the committee personnel specified and the committee was strictly men only.

The constitution required that a committee of management, consisting of eight persons plus a clerk and a treasurer, be elected annually in May. The committee was to elect its own preses (chairman). In addition to the elected members (the under managers), the committee included the four head managers, one of whom had the status of principal manager. The meeting of 1st July 1796 elected to the committee Angus Mackay (treasurer), Simon Fraser (clerk), John Mackay, Murdoch Mackenzie, Duncan Mackenzie, Angus Sutherland, Donald Macdonald, Alex Sutherland, John Miller and Ebenezer Murray, five of these being among the original feu assignees. The committee, at their first meeting, appointed Simon Fraser, the only elder amongst them, as their preses. The clerk was voted a salary of two guineas. The treasurer was required to produce sureties but was given no salary, presumably the use of the funds (or the interest thereon) being considered adequate recompense.

Beadle, treasurer, clerk, precentor – duties and rewards

The committee soon got down to business and at their meeting on 5th August 1796 ordered the treasurer to 'settle all accounts and debates with Peter Ross relating to the pavement', adding ominously that 'in case their proposals be objected by him, to refer the matter to the Head Managers'. The need for a church officer was then considered whereupon they 'appointed Angus Mackay to regulate the clock and have charge of the sacramental furniture, of all utensils, to draw and set the communion tables, to see the chapel always clean, and, on completing his charge, the committee unanimously agreed to pay him ten shillings yearly'. As an afterthought they added that he was 'bound in his charge to see the chapel properly lighted in time of lecture and windows drawn for air when necessary; also to observe that the walk within the parapet dyke be kept in clean and decent order'.

Despite the fact that frequently the same name appertained to different people, as in the case of the treasurer and the church officer, the clerks down the years made no attempt to distinguish people according to their address or occupation and thus there is often some uncertainty as to who is being referred to. After a year, Simon Fraser, whose minutes are of excellent quality, resigned the clerkship. In fact there is a gap of six months between April and October 1797 for which there are no minutes and the statutory annual general meeting seems not to have been convened until November that year. Fraser was not among those reappointed to the committee in November of 1797 and at this point his name disappears from the records. But having been one of the original feuars of the congregation, its first clerk and preses and an elder, he certainly made a significant contribution to its early life.

Simon Fraser was succeeded in the clerkship by John Hendry who occupied a prominent role in the affairs of the congregation for the next ten years before he also disappeared from view. The now accepted practice of inserting in the Session or committee minutes a tribute to a retiring or deceased member was certainly not followed in the 18th or early 19th century. For instance, Aberdeen Presbytery in 1787 recorded without comment the death of its clerk, the mention of his decease being simply to explain the appointment of another.[2] At that time it was not the practice even to express regret, let alone engross a tribute, and in this respect the records of the Gaelic Chapel follow the accepted practice of the day. The minute recording John Hendry's appointment as clerk does not suggest that his election was contested, but for the appointment of a clerk in 1818 a short leet of three was drawn up and the candidates were asked to submit a specimen of their writing. When John Hendry was appointed Clerk in October 1797 with a salary of £2 2s, he already enjoyed another salaried post – that of precentor – to which he had been appointed from among three candidates a year earlier at a salary of £1 6s, a figure obviously arrived at on the basis of sixpence per week. In October 1798 he demanded that his precentor's salary be increased to £2, but the committee claimed that such an increase could only be authorised by a general meeting of the congregation. The next annual general meeting, by a majority vote, conceded the increase which brought John Hendry's emoluments up to £4 2s or more than 10 per cent of the minister's stipend.

Glasgow's interest in John Mackenzie

If the committee felt unable to concede on their own authority an increased disbursement to John Hendry, they felt no such inhibition with regard to some other charitable gifts. In April 1797 they met 'to take under their consideration the necessity of giving a small donation in cash to the Rev. John Mackenzie in order to defray in part the present expense in his family'. It was agreed by a majority that he be given a donation of 25 shillings from the funds. What the particular circumstance was, is not specified. It may have had to do with the birth of his son Kenneth. More unaccountably, in October 1797 the committee agreed 'with one voice' to give a present to Mrs Ronald Bayne to the value of £10. By December the gift, which cost £9 10s, had been chosen and they ordered the treasurer 'to deliver the same to John Winks the Elgin carrier'. A letter was sent to Ronald Bayne advising him of the gift in transit and the committee, wisely, 'thought it proper to have a copy of the letter in their books to make people sensible for what it was given'.

To round off their charity, the committee agreed to give £2 5s to the poor's house, but the under-managers were not, generally speaking, overly sympathetic to the plight of the poor. A recommendation from the Kirk Session that the poor should be allocated seats in the chapel gratis, was received with a distinct lack of enthusiasm, the committee insisting that there should be no 'public intimation from the pulpit for that purpose knowing the consequence of doing so will be to create a general animosity in the whole congregation even in the Session itself ... and to increase the poor among us and burden the cause'.

The letter to Ronald Bayne, written by the treasurer Angus MacKay and dated 6th December 1797, explained that the gift to Mrs Bayne was in recognition of his being 'the instrument in the hand of the Lord, of planting and forming into a congregation; and for your constant disinterested labour of love ever since in occasional watering and seasonable refreshing ....' But almost ten years had passed since Ronald Bayne had left Aberdeen and it may be wondered if the gift was not given more with an eye to the future than to the past. Some six months earlier, on Sunday 30th July, the Rev. James Kidd, Professor of Oriental Languages at Marischal College, was prevailed upon 'with but a few minutes notice' to take an evening service in the Gaelic Chapel. Recording the incident in his diary, he wrote, 'I took occasion to address them on their situation as Christians likely to lose their present pastor'.[3] He was referring to a widely supported move to call John Mackenzie to Ingram Street Gaelic Chapel, Glasgow, a campaign that was thwarted by the Glasgow Chapel managers in favour of their own nominee, so prompting events which were to lead to the formation of Duke Street Gaelic Chapel to which Mackenzie was eventually called.[4]

If, as seems probable, the gift to Mrs Bayne was linked to the possibility of a vacancy occurring in Aberdeen, the Aberdeen folk did seem genuinely concerned to retain their minister if they could. In November 1797 the committee informed the managers that they wished to augment their minister's salary. The managers responded favourably to the proposal and 'empowered the committee to do the same when they thought proper'. At that time the minister received £40, of which £10 came from the SSPCK. He was responsible for his own accommodation, but in January 1798 the committee agreed to give the minister £10 to pay his house rent. This appears to have been the only augmentation given.

At the General Assembly in May 1798 the New Gaelic Chapel in Duke Street, Glasgow was granted a constitution which stipulated that the ministerial stipend would be not less than £70. Within six weeks of permission being granted to call a minister, the Duke Street Chapel had sent a call to John Mackenzie. On 9th July John Mackenzie called a meeting of his Session and committee to inform them that he intended to close with the call and would be leaving some time in September.

This decision was one that 'the congregation yielded to with great reluctance', but they were not slow in coming to a decision about filling the vacancy. By 1st August it had been unanimously agreed to send a call to Ronald Bayne. Characteristically Ronald Bayne appeared in person on 10th September to meet with the committee and then 'gave them his final denial that he could not answer their call, that his own new chapel was in building'. It must have been galling for the Aberdeen Highlanders to learn that the chapel building enterprises of 1798 now took precedence over their earlier achievement. John Mackenzie was inducted to Duke Street Gaelic Chapel on 3rd October. His parting gesture of kindly concern for his first pastorate was to gift to them his Gaelic Bible to be read to the congregation. In a sense, it was a holding operation for he was, in due course, to return to Aberdeen.

The pastorate of William Forbes 1798–1800

At the meeting held on 10th September 1798, at which Ronald Bayne intimated his intention of staying in Elgin, the Session and committee agreed 'to send for Mr William Forbes to have him for a Sabbath or two as he was the only young man that was known to be free'. This William Forbes was born in Avoch in 1767.[5] His father was a man of substance, factor to Sir Roderick Mackenzie of Rosehaugh, as well as farming on his own account. His mother was said to be a deeply pious woman and an adherent of the Seceders. Educated at Fortrose Academy, he went to King's College, Aberdeen in 1782 and so was a contemporary of Kenneth Bayne and John Mackenzie. Licensed by the Presbytery of Nairn in August 1791, his first assistantship was with the Rev. Hugh Calder at Croy and from there he went as assistant in Strachur in the Presbytery of Dunoon. For some time he tutored for the Roses of Kilravock Castle and he was probably there, and therefore free, when approached by the Aberdeen Gaelic Chapel. As a candidate in Aberdeen his ministry was well received and on 12th October he was given a unanimous call. The call, which was sanctioned by the Rev. Dr James Shirrefs of West St Nicholas and the Rev. Dr William Brown, Principal of Marischal College, came before a hastily convened meeting of the Presbytery of Nairn which agreed on 30th October to take William Forbes on trials for ordination. At a subsequent meeting of Presbytery held at Kilravock Castle on 5th November he was ordained. By 18th November 1798 he had commenced his ministry in Aberdeen.[6]

The vacancy had been brief and would have seemed so to the congregation as the supply preacher was the Rev. Professor James Kidd of Marischal College, the redoubtable Irishman who, as minister of Gilcomston Chapel-of-Ease from 1801–1834, exercised the most remarkable ministry that Aberdeen has ever known, the impact of which continued to be felt for at least a generation after his death. James Kidd came to Aberdeen in January 1794 as Professor of Hebrew in Marischal College and the Gaelic folk were quick to recognise in him a kindred spirit. He was a highly talented man and a most enthralling and effective preacher. He frequently preached in the Gaelic Chapel and his popularity won him invitations to other similar pulpits. As early as March 1796 (only a month after being licensed) he was assisting Kenneth Bayne at the Greenock Gaelic Chapel communion.[7] He seems to have enjoyed a special rapport with the Aberdeen Gaelic Chapel and the entries in his diary have fewer laments about 'deadness' and 'want of assistance' in respect of his preaching there. Although he would have been familiar with Irish Gaelic, he preached only in English. In his diary entry for 25th June 1797, he lamented that he was unable to preach to a Gaelic-speaking regiment in camp outside Aberdeen, but instead he offered to take John Mackenzie's services that the latter might preach in Gaelic to the Highland soldiers.[8] His English preaching was much appreciated by the Gaelic congregation, and the fact that he accepted no more than £2 for preaching through the vacancy raised him still higher in their esteem.

In April 1800 William Forbes received a presentation to the congregation of Tarbat (Portmahomack) in the Presbytery of Tain, where he remained until his death in 1838 aged 71 years. His ministry in Aberdeen lasted only 18 months but, according to Donald Sage, 'if brief in point of time, it was eternal in regard to its real effects'. A bachelor in his Aberdeen days, in 1813 he married a sister of Donald Sage and Sage was well acquainted with the eccentricities of his brother-in-law. According to Dr Kennedy of Dingwall, his was a stern regime which had the effect of imposing 'an order and propriety in the demeanour of his congregation in the house of God such as could not elsewhere be found'.[9] He had a vigorous intellect and was scrupulous in his pulpit preparation: 'his manuscripts were often quite as ready for the press as for the pulpit, though they never found their way to either.' If the sermons were polished, the same could not be said for the preacher: 'there was a rough crust on the outside of him, but there was much sterling love beneath it, though too deep for all to find it.' Happily some did, among them Jean Sage his wife, and 'through the mists which so often overspread them, she was capable of discerning and fully appreciating, the excellencies of his Christian character'.[10] They had two sons, the elder of whom aspired to the ministry, but both died while studying at King's College. Before he left Aberdeen in April 1800, Mr Forbes made the seemingly traditional gesture of presenting a gift to his congregation; in this instance, a donation of two guineas.

The pastorate of James Macphail 1800–1802

Confronted again with the problem of filling a vacancy in the pastoral office, the managers took soundings as to who might be available and in July the committee authorised the expenditure of £2 by Patrick Robertson 'to pay horse hire to the North Country on business belonging to the congregation'. His mission was successful. A meeting of the congregation held in August for the purpose of ascertaining reaction to Mr James Macphail, preacher of the Gospel from the Parish of Croy, who had been preaching in the chapel for the previous two Sabbaths, agreed to give him a call, only three members dissenting. The call was signed on 18th August and John Ewen was requested to send it with an accompanying letter setting out the duties and the emoluments and urging the nominee to come with all convenient speed.

'The duty,' wrote John Ewen, 'which I hope you will have much satisfaction in discharging, is to preach in Gaelic twice and lecture once in the evening, every Sabbath day. The annual stipend which these good people mean to give is £70 and I find that they also intend to afford you the House lately occupied by Mr. Forbes your predecessor, rent-free. Wishing you and them much happiness together.' Here John Ewen rested his case.

The call, which was subscribed by three of the city ministers, came before the Presbytery of Nairn on 25th September, along with a request from James Macphail for ordination as this would 'contribute to his usefulness in the charge'. The Presbytery 'after some consideration agreed to the propriety of the measure and resolved to take Mr Macphail upon trials for ordination as being well acquainted with him from his long residence within the bounds of the Presbytery and his having often preached in their pulpits and in their hearing'. Accordingly, as with Wm Forbes, the trials imposed by the Presbytery of Nairn were somewhat perfunctory and James Macphail was ordained five days later whereupon he proceeded to Aberdeen. Like his predecessor when in Aberdeen, James Macphail was unmarried and remained so thereafter.

The vacancy presented the managers with no major difficulties. Once again the Rev. James Kidd gave regular supply and there would have been no complaints about that. At their October meeting the managers commissioned Angus Mackay (the treasurer) and Patrick Robertson 'to speak with the Rev. Mr Kidd and pay him for his good service in supplying our vacant Sabbaths during the summer half year'. The negotiators reported to the February meeting that they paid the Rev. Mr Kidd £10 which, for six months service in an office carrying an annual stipend of £70, seemed well below the rate for the job.

As sometimes happens, the difficulties emerged not in the vacancy but in the settlement. James Macphail, the new minister, was the second son of Hector Macphail, minister of Resolis, whom, according to Donald Sage, he very much resembled in the simplicity of his Christian character. However, the father had suffered from severe depression[11] and, it would appear, the son resembled him in that respect also. Shortly after his induction to Aberdeen, he gave up the evening English lecture and instead preached in English at the afternoon service while continuing with Gaelic at the morning service. However, his English preaching commanded support neither from the Gaelic folk nor from 'the town's inhabitants', with the result that the managers were alarmed to find that 'the collections were getting lighter every Sabbath'. In these circumstances it was agreed at a general meeting of the congregation held in March 1801, 'to have Gaelic forenoon and afternoon till such time as their minister would be able to lecture as formerly as he was but tender in health at present and not able for that heavy work'. But James Macphail never resumed the evening lecture.

In August the committee met 'to consult with one another about their situation in regard of a minister as their present one got a call to another charge'. Macphail made clear his intention of accepting this call and although he did not leave Aberdeen until March, as early as December the congregation were 'getting a hearing' of prospective candidates. The charge that James Macphail accepted and into which he was admitted on 13th May 1802, was that of Daviot and Dunlichity in the Presbytery of Inverness. There he remained until his death in 1839 aged 74 years. He is perhaps best remembered on account of the fact that he was one of four members of the Presbytery of Inverness rebuked at the bar of the General Assembly in 1824 for their part in a public protest which they mounted against the induction of the minister presented to the Parish of Kiltarlity following the death of Ronald Bayne. The minister in question was the Rev. Colin Fraser. He was objected to by some of the parishioners, ostensibly on the grounds that the patron, Thomas Fraser of Lovat, was a Roman Catholic and they did not think that a Roman Catholic was capable of making a right judgment in the settlement. The parishioners took their case to the Court of Session which ultimately found in favour of the patron, a finding accepted by the Synod but not by the Presbytery, so that, at the admission, only two of the six ministers of Presbytery present, gave the new minister the right hand of fellowship. The remaining four, of which Macphail was one, staged a protest for which conduct they were subsequently rebuked by the Assembly.[12]

Discord in the lectern

Dissatisfaction with a minister's performance, especially as regards the effectiveness of his pulpit work, often creates an atmosphere in which other grievances are brought into the open. Evidence of this can be seen during James Macphail's pastorate. Two months after Macphail's induction, Patrick Robertson convened a meeting of the management committee to inform them 'that he was daily getting complaints about the way of singing in this chapel'. He further reported that it was 'owing to the precentor' that the discord had arisen, which remark John Hendry the clerk (and precentor) dutifully recorded in the minutes.

The solution which the committee proposed was that the precentor would resign his office, although still be paid for it, and Ebenezer Murray would be invited to assume the function of leader of the praise. The precentor, however, having the previous year worsted the committee in securing congregational support for an increase in his salary, was in no mood for laying down his tuning-fork and he insisted that the matter be referred to a general meeting of the congregation. When this meeting was held a week later, a compromise was reached by which the precentor was to continue in his office with 'occasional assistance' from Thomas Sutherland, Ebenezer Murray and Murdoch Mackenzie at the evening service. John Hendry continued to hold the salaried post of precentor until 1806 when he seemingly resigned all his offices. The appointment of his successor was not minuted, but may be inferred from the minute of 30th December 1806 which records that the committee 'took up consideration of a demand made by David Ross for paying certain people for teaching him to sing vocal musick but as he had not yet given satisfaction as a precentor they refused it'.

Sanctions and economies

The decreased income which first became apparent in 1801 gave the managers considerable concern. The decrease was attributable to fewer services, lower attendances and a reluctance on the part of seat-holders to renew their subscriptions. It was urged that a strong line should be taken with defaulters and the committee agreed that none was 'to receive any benefits in this chapel except the hearing of the Word only, none to receive the privilege of the communion nor a line to the infirmary or to the workhouse except their seats be paid'.

The indebtedness of the trustees amounted to £424 and the March meeting of the managers 'agreed to give the rights of the chapel to any gentleman of property as heritable security that would advance them the demands on the house at present'. Interest at 5 per cent was being paid on money loaned to the congregation. In the course of a discussion on ways of containing expenditure, it was suggested at the annual meeting held in May 1801 that no office-bearer in the congregation should receive any wages except the minister. Since the only salaried posts were those of the church officer (10 shillings), clerk (£2 2s) and precentor (£2), the latter two posts being held by John Hendry, the suggestion was obviously aimed at the clerk. Others suggested compromise – payment for every second year only – and the debate became confused. John Hendry's minute of the outcome of the discussion is typical of his style. 'Some was for one way, others for another way. Then they agreed to put the same to a vote and the stating of the vote was for payment and for nothing. The most number was for payment. The man that was in the office then agreed for this year only to do it for £3 2s. in place of £4 2s. considering the goodwill towards him'. Three years were to pass before his voluntary cut was restored.

Perhaps the most significant decision taken at this meeting was the appointment of a new treasurer. Angus Mackay, woolcomber, had held the office for five years and no reason is given for his resignation or replacement. He was succeeded by John Macdonald, tailor in Queen

Street, who had been elected to the committee three years earlier and who was to continue as treasurer until 1815. At the same meeting, six of the ten under-managers appointed the previous year were now replaced, among them four of the five members who had served continuously since the first election in 1796. Of the original appointees, only Duncan Mackenzie, shoemaker, continued in office. Whether this represents dissatisfaction with the committee on the part of the electorate, or a reluctance on the part of committee members to continue in a time consuming job, or simply the natural turnover rate to be expected in committee appointments, it is impossible to say. But the head-managers, John Ewen, James Chalmers and Patrick Robertson were more durable.

Notes to Chapter 6

1. A S Maxwell: *Monumental inscriptions St Nicholas Aberdeen* (Aberdeen, 1972), section D, p 6, entry 27.
2. *Records of the Presbytery of Aberdeen,* vol. 8, p 391 (9th October, 1787) (CH2-1-10).
3. J Stark: *Dr Kidd of Aberdeen* (Aberdeen, third edition, 1898), p 70.
4. I R MacDonald: *Glasgow's Gaelic Churches* (Edinburgh, 1995), p 11.
5. J Noble: *Religious life in Ross* (Inverness, 1909), p 209. For some account of the life of Wm Forbes, see pp 209-217.
6. *Records of the Presbytery of Nairn,* vol. 1773-1820, p 140 (5th November, 1798) (CH2-554-1). Sage in *Memorabilia Domestica* incorrectly states that Wm Forbes succeeded James Macphail in Aberdeen Gaelic Chapel.
7. J Stark: op. cit., p 55.
8. Ibid., pp 69-70.
9. J Kennedy: *The days of the fathers in Ross-shire* (Edinburgh, 1861; new edition, Inverness, 1927), pp 75-77.
10. D Sage: *Memorabilia Domestica* (Wick, 1889; 2nd edition 1899, reprinted 1975), p 224.
11. D Sage: op. cit., p 265.
12. *Fasti Ecclesiae Scoticanae* (1926), vol. 6, p 471.

Chapter 7

*

HIGHLAND TRANSPORT

THE year 1801, when the Highland Congregation, only ten months after a settlement, were again faced with the prospect of a vacancy, was a year which in many ways emphasised the hardship that was a feature of life in Northern Scotland at the turn of the century. For that year, like the previous one, was a year of dearth and crop failure. Although less serious than the catastrophic famines of some earlier years, such as 1782 when widespread starvation added significantly to the national mortality,[1] it was, nevertheless, bad enough to have a noticeable effect on the community generally. A run of poor harvests inevitably had an adverse effect on living conditions, pushing up the price not just of grain and other foods, but also of manufactured goods. The end of the 18th century coincided with a time of serious price escalation[2] and this may have been a contributory factor in bringing about the lighter collections uplifted in the Gaelic Chapel.

With rising prices, the prospect of resuming the search for a pastor to come to a charge which could offer neither glebe nor stipend indexed to the price of grain, was a daunting one. Had the managers been able to anticipate that it would take all of three years, they might well have despaired of holding the congregation together. The vacancy, when it took effect in early 1802, was made more difficult by the fact that the congregation's favourite supply preacher, Professor James Kidd, was no longer available, having been inducted as minister of Gilcomston Chapel-of-Ease in June 1801. From a management point of view, the inability to provide the congregation with the supply preacher they would like is bad enough, but to have that same man preaching further up the road is little short of disastrous. Hence there was a need to get a satisfactory settlement as soon as possible and, in the meantime, to ensure that Gaelic-speaking supply preachers be obtained. Only on that basis could they hope to arrest drifting of the lightly attached hearers to Gilcomston.

Supply problems

Basically, the supply problem was the problem of bringing Highland preachers to Aberdeen at a time when the city was effectively an enclave accessible mainly by ship, a means of transport which was at best unpredictable, often hazardous, and always infrequent. It is difficult today to get a proper conception of the remoteness of Aberdeen from the other centres of population in Scotland at the end of the 18th century. Its remoteness and inaccessibility by road from Glasgow and St Andrews in the 15th century was one of the arguments used by Bishop Elphinstone in his campaign to establish a university in Aberdeen[3], and the situation as regards travelling south did not alter significantly until the last decade of the 18th century. Although it was intended in 1785 to continue to Aberdeen the newly established mail coach service between London and Edinburgh, the state of the roads between Perth and Aberdeen made this impossible. It was not until 1st August 1798 that a mail coach service was established between Edinburgh, Perth and Aberdeen.[4] The coach 'denominated, perhaps facetiously, the Fly' required about 32 hours for the journey and the fare was £2 2s.[5]

If wheeled transport southwards was slow and expensive, north-wards it was non-existent. The problem here was the lack of proper roads and bridges, especially over the Spey at Fochabers and the Findhorn at Forres, and these obstacles were not overcome until the Highland Commission for Roads and Bridges was established in 1803 with Thomas Telford as engineer-in-charge. Even then, despite the fact that the Fochabers bridge was completed in 1805, it was 1811 before a regular daily stage-coach service operated between Aberdeen and Inverness. North of Inverness, the introduction of public vehicular transport was delayed even longer. The rivers Beauly and Conon had both to be bridged and it was 1819 before the first stage-coach ran from Inverness to Thurso,[6] although a service as far as Tain had been established at an earlier date. From all of this it is evident that the problem of getting supply from the Highland presbyteries to Aberdeen in the opening years of the 19th century was a formidable one. Horse-back was the standard means of travel for those who could afford it. The alternative was to walk. Both means required a robust constitution.

Walking and riding

One of the best contemporary accounts of travel between Aberdeen and the North in the years 1800-1820, is to be found in Donald Sage's *Memorabilia Domestica*. Its relevance to the conditions applicable to the supply of the Gaelic Chapel is not in question, at least for the later period, since the journeys described in Sage's account were undertaken at the behest of the Gaelic Chapel.

His first journey to Aberdeen was made in 1804 when, aged 15, he enrolled as a student at Marischal College. Accompanied by a family servant referred to as Muckle Donald, he left his father's manse in Kildonan, Sutherland, and walked 35 miles to Dornoch where they made an overnight stop. The next day, crossing the Dornoch Firth and the Cromarty Firth by ferry, they reached Balblair in the Black Isle. Another ferry brought them to Ardersier from where they tramped to Aberdeen. But the long walk was too much for the teenager and, two miles west of Inverurie, he collapsed from exhaustion. Muckle Donald carried him into a nearby farmhouse where he was revived with a drink of warm milk and pepper. Then the occupant of the farmhouse, seeing that the lad was incapable of walking any further, put him on his horse and conveyed him to an Inverurie inn. Finding himself the recipient of such large-hearted humanity, the stricken student's heart overflowed with gratitude. 'I offered him a dram and he took it, I offered him money and a feed for his horse but he refused it. He bade me adieu, mounted his horse, disappeared in the dark, and I never again met him.'[7] The next day Donald Sage completed the walk to Aberdeen and Muckle Donald set off on the 160 mile return journey. It was not just the distance to be traversed, but the difficulty of the route, especially the softness of the terrain, that made the journey so formidable. At the end of the session, Sage returned from Aberdeen to Helmsdale on a salmon-fishing smack. Such was the storm that they encountered that, leaving Aberdeen on a Friday, it was the Tuesday before Helmsdale was reached.

In 1805 Donald Sage again walked from Kildonan to Aberdeen accompanied by Muckle Donald, but, as luck would have it, 'at Fochabers we fell in with a returning hired horse belonging to a man of the name of Campbell, an innkeeper and horse-hirer in Aberdeen. This lucky cast made our journey comparatively easy. Muckle Donald and I rode alternately, the horse carrying our baggage also'.[8] Curiously enough, some years later, the premises adjoining the Gaelic Chapel were occupied by livery stables belonging to a man Campbell which in time became Campbells Motor Hirers. On the return journey at the end of his second session, Sage set out at 6 am accompanied by a number of other students, among them Ronald Bayne's eldest son, James, and another 'very young man little more than 12 years of age'. Their first stretch was from Aberdeen to Keith, 'a most overwhelming journey for one day being little less than 50 miles'. Again he comments on the difficulty of the terrain '… a wretched floundering track. On this road, in the olden times, horses have sunk to the very girths in mud.'

In June 1819, when Sage went to Aberdeen to preach as a candidate for the Gaelic Chapel, travel had undergone a quantum change. He took the mail coach from Inverness to Aberdeen and, on the return journey, he claims to have travelled on the inaugural run of the coaching service operating between Inverness and Thurso. Similarly when he arrived in Aberdeen to commence his ministry in the Gaelic Chapel, it was from the 'Duke of Gordon' stage-coach that he alighted into the welcoming arms of some of the leading men of the chapel.[9] On that journey, he doubtless reflected that he was living in a different world from that in which, some 15 years earlier, he had made his first acquaintance with Aberdeen.

Notes to Chapter 7

1. H Hamilton: *An economic history of Scotland in the eighteenth century* (Oxford, 1963), p 8.
2. Ibid., p 378.
3. W Robbie: *Aberdeen: its traditions and history* (Aberdeen, 1928), p 91.
4. A R B Haldane: *Three centuries of Scottish posts* (Edinburgh, 1971), p 58.
5. Aberdeen Almanack (1798), p 185; Wm Kennedy: *Annals of Aberdeen,* vol. 2, p 277.
6. J Barron: *The Northern Highlands in the Nineteenth Century* (Inverness, 1903), vol. 1 p 166.
7. D Sage: *Memorabilia Domestica* (Wick, 1889; second edition, 1899, reprinted 1975), pp 138-139.
8. Ibid., pp 145-146.
9. Ibid., p 223.

Chapter 8

*

JOCKEYING FOR POSITION

IN August 1801 the managers of the Gaelic Chapel met to consider a suitable successor to James Macphail whose short-lived pastorate was to end the following March. Obviously travel difficulties, if nothing else, made it impracticable to have a succession of preachers from which the people could subsequently make a choice. Instead the managers of a chapel-of-ease would invite a preacher known to be looking for a charge to come in effect as sole nominee, and take the services in their chapel over a period of two or three weeks, after which the people were given the opportunity to vote for or against the candidate.

John Kennedy's ambitions

The first preacher on whom the people were asked to pass judgment was John Kennedy. This John Kennedy (father of the renowned Rev. Dr John Kennedy of Dingwall) was a native of Kishorn, near Lochcarron; and as he had been a student at King's College, Aberdeen from 1788-1792 he was not a stranger to the congregation.[1] Following his trial services in Aberdeen in December 1801, the congregation elected him with but one dissenting vote. As usual, John Ewen dispatched the call, enclosing with it a letter virtually identical to that which, a year previously, he had written to James Macphail, but with one additional insertion. After writing 'the annual stipend which these good people mean to give', he now added parenthetically 'and I can assure you it is as much as they can well afford'.

The £70 stipend and the relative independence of the chapel pulpit would not have been unattractive to one in John Kennedy's situation. Since 1798 he had been assistant to the parish minister of Lochbroom, Alex Stronach, who that year had been suspended from his duties for flagrant drunkenness. Later Alex Stronach was to allege that it was John Kennedy, at the time schoolmaster in Lochcarron, who had fomented the public outcry which forced a reluctant Presbytery to proceed against him.[2] Whether or not there was any truth in this allegation, following Alex Stronach's suspension Kennedy was appointed assistant at Lochbroom in which capacity he received £45 of the £85 stipend.[3] In addition to the improved emoluments attaching to the Gaelic Chapel, there was a further reason for optimism in the Aberdeen camp.

It was known that Stronach had intended petitioning the 1801 General Assembly to lift his suspension, but on the advice of his friends he deferred his petition until 1802 when it was considered that his chances would be better. With Stronach's suspension lifted, Kennedy would then be 'available', assuming no other offers came his way. In these days gossip concerning ministerial moods and movements seemed to travel no less rapidly than it does nowadays and, in the absence of rumours of rival approaches, hopes were high in Aberdeen that John Kennedy would accept their call. Alas these hopes were to be disappointed.

In March Kennedy replied to the call sent at the end of December. He said that he 'could not give them a determinate answer until the first of June'. The date was significant. By then the Assembly would have come to a decision regarding Alex Stronach. But that was not the only decision that John Kennedy was waiting for. After preaching in Aberdeen, he had been alerted to the possibility of an appointment to the Eriboll mission in the Parish of Durness in north-west Sutherland. He had earlier expressed an interest in that station. In 1799, when a previous vacancy had occurred there, his younger brother Neil had written to the Directors of the SSPCK, who funded the mission, 'applying for the Mission of Eriboll to his brother'.[4] As it happened, the directors of the SSPCK had, on that occasion, already offered Eriboll to Neil McBride, but now that McBride was moving to Arran the secretary of the SSPCK wrote to John Kennedy enquiring if he was still interested, and pointing out that the directors met after the Assembly to authorise appointments, in effect to confirm invitations already made by the Secretary.[5]

Although the Aberdeen congregation were unaware of this offer, they sensed that, having delayed acceptance of their call, John Kennedy's decision was not likely to be in their favour. Noting that 'their present pastor would be away next week to his other charge', they decided at their meeting in March, that to wait 'would be much against our cause', especially as Kennedy had given them no indication of the likelihood of his coming. Their intuition was correct. The Assembly lifted the suspension on Alex Stronach thereby making his assistant redundant, and the directors of the SSPCK at their meeting of 1st July 1802 approved the offer made by their secretary and accordingly appointed John Kennedy 'to be missionary minister of Eriboll, his salary to commence from the time of entering upon the duties of his office'.[6] The SSPCK left it to the Presbytery of Tongue to attest the date of his 'entering the duties of his office'. John Kennedy himself was present at the meeting of Presbytery held on 3rd November at which this matter was considered, and as he then reported that he had already made occasional visits to Eriboll the Presbytery sportingly agreed that 'he was appointed by the SSPCK to be missionary at Eriboll from 1st

May last, and as he has officiated in the bounds of the mission several times since, he is certificated as being in the bounds'.[7]

In later years another attempt was to be made to get John Kennedy to Aberdeen, but meantime the congregation agreed to write to Ronald Bayne explaining their predicament and inviting his opinion as to their best course of action. The advice they got (on 8th April) was to try the Rev. Wm MacKintosh, at that time minister in Bruan and Berriedale, Caithness, which station, like Eriboll, was an SSPCK mission. MacKintosh, future father-in-law to Donald Sage, had been in Bruan since 1795 and according to his grandson was 'much esteemed as an eloquent preacher'.[8] A letter was sent forthwith, but the response, if any, was not recorded.

Aberdeen overture to John Mackenzie

Six months passed and in October the Committee met and, having despaired of attracting Wm. MacKintosh, agreed to write to James McLauchlan, minister of the Edinburgh Gaelic Chapel, that he might arrange for a certain Mr Macfarlane to come and preach for three or four Sabbaths as a candidate. Macfarlane duly appeared, but after hearing him for only two Sabbaths the congregation agreed to 'wait for a few weeks until such time as they could get a hearing of Mr. Mackenzie from Glasgow'. Mr Macfarlane must have been an exceptionally dreary preacher, for it seems he failed to attain to the ranks of the ordained ministry. References to a Mr Patrick Macfarlane who translated the Catechism into Gaelic, but was having difficulty in finding a publisher for it, are to be found in the SSPCK minutes. Perhaps this was the unprepossessing preacher.

Whether or not the congregation got a hearing of John Mackenzie who had earlier gone to Glasgow from Aberdeen, is not recorded; but, by January 1803, they unanimously resolved that he 'be earnestly solicited to again become their pastor'. The call was signed and John Ewen was requested to write a letter that would 'express their utmost anxiety' that John Mackenzie would return to Aberdeen. The principal manager rose to the occasion as only he could.

Aberdeen 21 Jany. 1803
To the Revd Mr. John Mackenzie, Glasgow.

Sir,

I address you at the earnest request of the Gaelic Congregation in this City, and could my address correspond to their anxious desire to obtain your consent to become again their Pastor, their object in this application, would be, for them, happily obtained.

They justly estimate your worth and the importance of your services, at no ordinary rate – and were their wealth equal to their inclination, and liberality, you would not be without your reward. Their only regret is that their abilities does not at present admit of what is adequate to your merit, or their own wishes, but what they can afford they offer with great cordiality, and if Providence shall enable them to do more, it will not be wanting on their part. They bid me assure you, in the meantime, One Hundred and Twenty pounds per annum, and I think I may safely add my own assurance, that every consideration of duty and attachment will concur in prompting them to add to this sum, as soon as they are able.

When I consider from what small beginnings they have arrived, by the blessing of Heaven, at their present comparatively, prosperous condition that they have obtained it by means of their sobriety, industry, piety, and uniform good conduct, I cannot doubt, under your superintendence, of their farther prosperity. And that you may disinterestedly be disposed to comply with their request, looking for better, and more ample, reward, from that source from whence every good flows – I inclose an unanimous Call from the Congregation, and I can assure you, that never was a Call given with greater cordiality.

I am, very respectfully, and truly Revd Sir,

Your humble servant,
(signed) John Ewen.

If the managers thought that the promise of a stipend above that obtaining in Glasgow would achieve their object, they were soon to discover otherwise. Gratified though he doubtless was at being the subject of such laudatory opinion, John Mackenzie remained unpersuaded by John Ewen's earnest pleading. The increased stipend was not promised regardless of the wherewithal to meet it. The congregation's finances appear to have improved during the vacancy and when it was reported to the annual general meeting in May 1803 that the treasurer had a credit balance of £68, he was ordered 'to give what money he had in charge of Mr. Alex Webster, lawyer, to get bank interest for the same, till he would have use for the same'.

Meantime the congregation continued to pay interest at 5 per cent on their various loans.

Wm MacKintosh of Berriedale makes his demands

By August 1803, all their efforts to obtain a minister having been thwarted, the congregation again reverted to Ronald Bayne's suggestion. They agreed to call the Rev. Wm MacKintosh of Berriedale, but, in the light of past experience, it was resolved to delay 'extending the call till they should be certified of his willingness to accept the charge and resolved to wait one month from this date [29th August] to receive his definitive answer; and further resolved that in case of his acceptance and as he cannot leave his present charge vacant till Whitsunday next [May 15th] he be requested to provide a proper pastor to supply said charge till that time, or send one to Aberdeen till that period that the congregation may no longer be wanting of the Gospel ordinances regularly dispensed among them; and in regard to the preaching in English as well as Gaelic, they agreed to leave the regulation of that to the discretion of the said Mr. MacKintosh to act therein as he shall see it most for the edification of the people'.

The tenor of the minute suggests a measure of exasperation with ministers unable, or unwilling, to give a prompt decision. Predictably MacKintosh failed to reply within the stated period. It was not until 29th November that the congregation heard his answer to their proposition. His reply took the form of an enumeration of counter demands as follows. First, he wanted the names of six men as managers, presumably who would stand surety for his stipend. Second, he announced that he would lecture (*ie* take an English service) only for four or five months in the year. Third, he wanted 'a house with the convenience of four rooms'. He concluded by saying that if they did not write to him in the course of four weeks, 'he looked on them as provided already'.

The peremptory tone of his letter added to the feelings of annoyance already created by the lateness of the reply. And yet to terminate negotiations was not in the interests of the congregation. The managers had no alternative but to act as reasonably as was possible in the circumstances. And so Patrick Robertson, the preses, was ordered to write to the minister of Berriedale by the first post and to inform him first of all that they had read his letter; second, that they were to pay his house rent; third, that his managers would be Patrick Robertson, John Ross, Wm Macdonald, Wm Graham, Angus Sutherland and Robert Gordon; and fourth, that 'if he did not lecture both the seasons, they looked on themselves as unable to agree with his propositions'. The minute of the next meeting of the committee, dated 10th January 1804, simply reads, 'The Rev. Mr. Wm. MacKintosh's final answer came to the Gaelic congregation in Aberdeen, that he was to stay with his own congregation in Berriedale, Caithness'.

The absence of any other comment, the failure to take matters further or discuss any other business, conveys better than words the sense of weariness and dejection now felt by the committee. They met again on 1st February and took the only course of action conceivable to them. They wrote to Ronald Bayne 'requesting him to come in April to dispense the Sacrament of the Lord's Supper among them and at the same time requesting him if he knew of any young man that would come with him at that time and would preach to them as a candidate'.

Neil Kennedy's vacillations

Ronald Bayne could always be relied on to offer a solution. He now suggested Neil Kennedy, the younger brother of John Kennedy, whose preference for Eriboll had so disappointed the Aberdeen congregation. Since 1801 Neil Kennedy had been missioner in Strathconon.[9] In the company of Ronald Bayne, Kennedy attended the Aberdeen communion, and following his visit the managers, on behalf of the congregation, expressed an interest in his coming to Aberdeen as pastor. When the annual meeting of the congregation was held in the following month, letters were read both from Ronald Bayne and Neil Kennedy. The *précis* of Kennedy's letter is tantalisingly condensed. It reports Kennedy as saying that 'he had an offer from the Parish of Assynt in the shire of Sutherland but that they might depend upon it that he would inform them as soon as it would be in his power concerning the same'. The meeting agreed to wait his answer.

Subsequent developments indicate that the offer of the Parish of Assynt had to do with the appointment of an assistant to the parish minister, the Rev. Wm Mackenzie who, in the words of Dr John Kennedy, 'was almost all a minister ought not to be'.[10] Elaborating further on his unflattering description of 'Parson William' (as the minister of Assynt was affectionately termed by his parishioners), Dr John Kennedy wrote, 'Always accustomed to regard his pastoral work as an unpleasant condition of his drawing his stipend, he reduced it to the smallest possible dimensions, and would not infrequently be absent without reason and without leave for many weeks from his charge'. The minister of Assynt was already over 70 years of age and, with an addiction to drink exacerbating the incapacity occasioned by natural indolence and bodily infirmity, it is not to be wondered at that he was thought to have need of the services of an assistant. But, no further developments having taken place in that direction, the Aberdeen congregation, by the end of the month of July, sent a call to Neil Kennedy.

In September it was announced that he had written accepting the call and intended taking up his duties in November. But the sense of relief which the managers experienced on the receipt of this news was shortlived. On 29th October 1804 a general meeting of the congregation was called 'to hear a letter that came from the Rev. Mr. Neil Kennedy informing them that he got a call from the Parish of Assynt to be a helper and successor of their present pastor but at the same time wishes to come to Aberdeen for the space of six months'. The congregation were devastated by this news but, taking the view that half-a-loaf was better that no bread, they agreed, putting it on record that as he had closed with their call sent to him in August, they considered that they 'had first right to him'. In the event he came in November as promised and remained for four years.

Three years were to pass before 'Parson William' got his assistant. Curiously the appointee was not Neil Kennedy, but his brother John. Although it was known in September 1806 that Eriboll was likely to lose its minister,[11] it was the following July before John Kennedy actually moved to Assynt.[12] Dr John Kennedy, in his memoir of his father, says with regard to the Assynt offer, 'He had been enabled to decide unhesitatingly, and at once, that it was his duty to accept the offered appointment. What his reasons for this decision were, and how the Lord had revealed His mind to him, there are now no means of ascertaining'.[13]

When Kennedy of Dingwall wrote these words more than 50 years after the event, it was at a time when evangelical ministers were more inclined than their fathers had been to clothe with a pious altruism decisions which earlier generations would have recognised as being determined by more practical considerations. Among these, one of the most decisive factors as regards a minister's willingness to accept the offer of a charge was whether that charge carried parish status. Seldom could the mission stations or the chapels-of-ease compete against the drawing power of the parish churches; not because the parish stipend was invariably higher, but because the parish appointment always carried the right to a seat in Presbytery and Synod. To teach but not to rule, which was the unenviable lot of the non-parish ministers, was regarded as an emasculation of ministerial authority. If, as Neil Kennedy's letter said, the Assynt appointment was as 'helper and successor', there is little doubt that John Kennedy, or anyone else in his position, would have seen it as his duty to accept it. And accept it he did. But 'amidst his happiness and success in Assynt, he had to bear what in some respects was the greatest trial of his life'.[14] At that point Aberdeen thought it saw its opportunity to enlist John Kennedy to its cause – but that is to run ahead of events. For the present they were content to have Neil Kennedy.

Notes to Chapter 8

1. For some account of the life of John Kennedy, see J Kennedy: *The days of the fathers in Ross-shire* (Inverness, 1927, new and enlarged edition), pp 149-239.
2. *Assembly Papers* (1802), Petition dated 22nd May, 1802 (CH1-2-137).
3. *Records of the Presbytery of Lochcarron*, vol 3, p 73 (29th August, 1798) (CH2-567-3).
4. *SSPCK Records: Minutes of committee meetings*, vol. 12, p 14 (September 1799) (GD95-2-12).
5. Ibid., p 219 (July, 1802).

6. Ibid., p 219 (1st July, 1802) (GD95-2-12).
7. *Records of the Presbytery of Tongue,* vol. 2, p 202 (3rd November, 1802) (CH2-508-2).
8. D Sage: *Memorabila domestica* (Wick 1889; 2nd edition, 1899; reprinted 1975), p 290, footnote.
9. *Records of the Presbytery of Lochcarron,* vol. 3, p 83 (23rd December, 1800) (CH2-567-3).
10. J Kennedy: op. cit., p 178.
11. *SSPCK Records: Minutes of committee meetings,* vol 13, p 85 (December, 1806).
12. Ibid., p 136 (July, 1807).
13. J Kennedy: op. cit., p 176.
14. Ibid., p 180.

Chapter 9

*

His Brother's Keeper

IN terms of ministerial effectiveness, Neil Kennedy seems always to
have been overshadowed by his brother; but that may have been the
estimate of a later generation whose view had been coloured by Dr
Kennedy's adulation of his revered parent. Neil Kennedy is described in
Scott's *Fasti* as 'one of the best known ministers in the North, a man of
great pulpit power and apostolical zeal',[1] a verdict that scarcely equates
with Dr Kennedy's own description of his uncle's preaching – 'his
manner quiet, and his style unadorned and simple, there were few who
felt attractiveness in his preaching but such as relished the savour of its
spirituality'.[2] A description of Neil Kennedy's pulpit characteristics,
probably the work of Dr Gustavus Aird but oddly reminiscent of Dr
John Love's description of Kenneth Bayne's pulpit gifts, gives a slightly
different presentation to that of Dr Kennedy.[3] All, however, agree that
he was a man of saintly character and one much given to prayer.

Benevolent demands

On arriving in Aberdeen, Neil Kennedy's first request was for a Session
house to be built onto the chapel and the managers agreed to its being
erected without delay 'as it was the pastor's desire to have the privilege
of the same between sermons'. To that end they negotiated building
permission with Mr Lamont, the adjoining proprietor and the Session
house was completed without its having occurred to the committee
that the congregation had a right to be consulted in the matter, a
procedure that gave rise to some criticism at the next congregational
meeting in May 1805. That year the treasurer was having difficulty in
getting in seat rents and it was agreed to have an across-the-board
reduction in charges. This may be taken as indicating that the availability of the accommodation exceeded the demand. The minister's
stipend had been fixed at £120, but the committee had made no
allowance for accommodation.

In January 1806, probably in anticipation of his marriage later that
year, Neil Kennedy wrote requesting that his house rent be paid.
Perhaps the managers felt that a housing subsidy which the minister
already enjoyed from the Laird of Dundonnell (see below) relieved
them of any responsibility in the matter. The minute recording the

committee's decision to refuse this request made it sound wholly reasonable. 'They took under their consideration their charge and discharge, and seeing the former less than the latter, show themselves unable to answer the same as they were not bound to do it by promise.' Obviously the contract offered to Neil Kennedy did not include the concessions extracted by MacKintosh of Berriedale. The committee appointed three of their number to convey their decision to the minister and 'inform him of the state of their funds'. Perhaps with a view to making an unpleasant duty less disagreeable, they consented to give him a gratuity of £5. The mollifying effect of this benefaction on the minister's self-esteem would have been considerably diminished had he been told that the same meeting of the committee 'agreed to give Mrs Kidd a present of a dozen of silver spoons with a dividing spoon as the Rev. Mr. Kidd had been of great service formerly and at present'.

There were other occasions on which the committee made additional gestures of support. In September, 'having taken into consideration the extra burden he had sustained through not having any assistant at the communion', they agreed that he should receive an extra £5. In effect they were sharing with the minister the sum which would have been expended on a visiting communion preacher. For example, the following April Ronald Bayne was assisting at the communion and he received £10 to meet his expenses in coming from Inverness. This would seem to have been quite generous as the coach fare to Aberdeen was £2 inside or £1 2s outside.[4] Perhaps Ronald Bayne was given special consideration. In June 1807 the committee had on its agenda another request from the minister for a rent allowance and, on this occasion, 'the propriety of complying with Mr. Kennedy's request being explained to them, they unanimously agreed to grant him the sum of £15 15s. per annum for house rent in testimony of their esteem for him − the said sum to be given annually as long as the Society can afford it'.

Managerial changes

The wording of the minute suggests that some fresh voices were in evidence in the committee and indeed there had been changes. In 1806 John Hendry resigned the clerkship after ten years service and his name faded from the records. He was succeeded by Duncan McGregor whose beautiful calligraphy was to inscribe the minutes for the next ten years. He lived in George Street, at that time a new housing development, and on occasion the committee convened in his home. A notable addition to the committee was James Bentley, brother-in-law of Ronald Bayne and Professor of Oriental Languages in King's College − the equivalent post to that occupied by James Kidd in Marischal College. Professor Bentley was probably an external manager. He was appointed chairman of the committee but appears not to have signed the minutes as such. Patrick Robertson, who had acted as chairman for almost ten years, died between September 1806 and June 1807. Perhaps the new voices on the committee were also responsible for the decision to insure the chapel for the sum of £500. Having agreed to meet the minister's rent, the committee resolved that a retiring collection for this purpose should be taken twice a year in June and December. The sums raised by this means have not been recorded, but retiring collections were not uncommon. The *Aberdeen Journal* of 27th April 1808 reported, 'We hear the sum collected at the Gaelic Chapel last Sunday evening for the Foreign Mission Society amounted to £15 1s. 8d.'. Clearly the Highlanders could be generous in supporting a deserving cause.

Shortly after the commencement of Neil Kennedy's ministry, the third ordination of elders in the congregation took place. 'Some of the former elders being dead and some others of them by age and infirmities rendered unable to attend their office', there was a need to strengthen the Session and to that end Ebenezer Murray, Duncan McGregor and Alex Macdonald were ordained. All of them subsequently took a prominent part in the congregation's affairs.

The Highland minister's fool

During his stay in Aberdeen Neil Kennedy acted as tutor and guardian to a difficult teenager, Kenneth Mackenzie, second son of George Mackenzie, Laird of Dundonnell. 'Mr Neil' had been tutor to the family in Dundonnell from 1798-1801 when his brother John succeeded him. Kenneth, born in 1790, was described as 'a person of very defective natural capacity'. In 1804 his father, concerned for his mental and social development, arranged for him to be boarded with Neil Kennedy in Aberdeen. There he became known as 'the Highland minister's fool'. The Grammar School, after a probationary period, declined to cope with him, whereupon Kennedy sent him to the Old Aberdeen School of Ewen Maclachlan 'who, however, gave up on him as desperate'. That assessment was no doubt shared by Neil Kennedy. On one occasion Kennedy had to gatecrash a party at a public house at the Bridge of Don to extricate his charge from some undesirable company.

These and other events were recalled in 1830 in the course of a celebrated legal case concerning the succession to the Dundonnell Estate at which it was averred that Kenneth Mackenzie had been duped into signing a will which he was incapable of comprehending and which transferred the estate to his wife's relatives. Neil Kennedy was the first witness called by the pursuer, Thomas, the younger brother of Kenneth. At the trial Henry Cockburn, for the defendants, pointed out that Neil Kennedy's evidence, to the effect that he had found Kenneth to be virtually ineducable, was somewhat at variance with letters he had sent to the teenager's father in 1807-1808; but as the trial judge said by way of excusing the discrepancy, 'When a tutor comes to write to a father about the education of his son, it is natural for him to put a gloss upon his progress'.[5]

His willingness to provide 'care in the community' accommodation for the disadvantaged son of Dundonnell did not prevent Neil Kennedy from taking a wife who loyally shared the burden with him. Anne Downie, who married Kennedy in July 1806, was the eleventh of 16 children born to John Downie, minister of Urray, whose wife, Charlotte, was a descendant of the Baynes of Tulloch and therefore related to Ronald Bayne. It would seem that this attachment was the means of disjoining Neil Kennedy from Aberdeen for, according to the minutes, by the summer of 1808 the committee were again taking steps to fill an anticipated vacancy. In October of that year, Neil Kennedy left to become 'assistant-minister to the Parish of Urray', *ie* assistant to his father-in-law then aged 81 and probably in indifferent health, although three years were to pass before he died. In the case of an ailing minister who was unwilling to resign from his charge as long as he had hopes of eventual recovery, funds for the temporary support of an assistant were sometimes made available from sources such as the SSPCK. But it appears that no such recognition attached to the Urray assistantship. It was simply a private arrangement between John Downie and his son-in-law, the latter being given what the minister deemed appropriate from his own income. No doubt it was a modest sum.

Even before he left Aberdeen, Neil Kennedy was short of money and in August 1808 the congregational managers gave him a loan of £40 repayable with interest at 5 per cent. His first repayment amounting to £10 was not sent until April 1810 when, in an accompanying letter, he explained that 'owing to certain embarrassments that came in his way lately he could not send them the remainder at that time'. He went on to express the hope that 'they would put him to no uneasiness about it until it be in his power to remit the balance'. In July 1811 he was requesting another twelve months in which to pay, but the committee were prepared to allow only six months.

Fraternal competition

In October 1811 the minister of Urray died. If Neil Kennedy had entertained hopes of being appointed successor to his father-in-law, they were to be disappointed. A successor was nominated to the vacant charge in January 1812 and the following month the SSPCK, noting that 'Mr Neil Kennedy, some time ago Society catechist in Aberdeen, was at present out of employment', decided to offer him the mission at

Strathfillan in Perthshire.[6] He replied acknowledging his gratitude for the offer, but avoided giving a decision, his letter indicating 'that he is at present so situated that he cannot come to an immediate determination on the subject'.[7] The reason, apparently, was that some weeks previously an approach had been made to the Presbytery of Chanonry by some elders and heritors of the Parish of Killearnan asking for permission to 'employ the Rev. Neil Kennedy, late minister of the Gaelic Chapel at Aberdeen and assistant for some time to the late worthy minister of Urray'.

Killearnan had been vacant for more than five years as a result of a dispute over the ownership of the patronage and the request was that Neil Kennedy be allowed to supply the pulpit until it could be filled by a proper presentation.[8] The Presbytery, insisting that the supply preacher be given at least one guinea a week 'for his trouble', agreed to Neil Kennedy's appointment, subject to approval being given by another of the heritors in the parish. In due course that approval was given, but it was still awaited when the Strathfillan offer came from the SSPCK. In May 1812 Neil Kennedy wrote officially declining Strathfillan, whereupon the SSPCK offered him Ullapool.[9] This he might have welcomed, for by May John Kennedy had managed to displace his brother as supply preacher of Killearnan.[10] But before Neil received notice to quit, Mrs Hay Mackenzie of Cromartie, who, as patron of Urray, had declined to offer him that living, presented him with the Parish of Logie Easter in the Presbytery of Tain, which he was pleased to accept. There he was to remain until his death in 1836 at the comparatively early age of 58. He had four daughters and five sons, two of whom entered the ministry. A grandson attained distinction as Lord Kennedy, chairman of the Scottish Land Court.

Notes to Chapter 9

1. *Fasti Ecclesiae Scoticanae* (1928), vol 7, p 63.
2. J Kennedy: op. cit., p 224.
3. J Noble: *Religious life in Ross* (Inverness, 1909), p 156.
4. T A Anderson: *Inverness before railways* (Inverness, 1885), p 31. The coach services did not, of course, operate daily until 1811, but in 1806 the alternative equestrian travel would have been no more costly.
5. Dundonnell Cause. *Report of the Trial by Jury, Thomas Mackenzie, Esq., against Robert Roy, Esq. WS,* reported by Simon MacGregor (11th May, 1830) (Edinburgh).
6. *SSPCK Records: Minutes of committee meetings,* vol 13, p. 375 (February, 1812) (GD95-2-13).
7. Ibid., p 386 (April, 1812).
8. *Records of the Presbytery of Chanonry,* vol. 6, p 148 (17th December, 1811) (CH2-66-6).
9. *SSPCK Records: Minutes of committee meetings,* vol 13, p 392 (May 1812) (GD95-2-13).
10. Records of the Presbytery of Chanonry. vol 6, p 154. 17 June 1812 (CH2-66-6).

Chapter 10

*

STRIVING FOR THE MASTERY

IN the summer of 1808 the Gaelic Chapel managers began to look for a replacement for the Rev. Neil Kennedy. They wrote to the Rev. John Munro, since 1806 a Royal Bounty preacher in the Achreny mission, Caithness, inviting him to come forward as a candidate. Like so many others he was known to the Aberdeen congregation as a former student at King's College, but with this difference – it was as a tradesman that he had first come to Aberdeen. Having had only an elementary education, he served his apprenticeship as a carpenter in his native Parish of Kiltearn in Ross-shire and then went to Aberdeen to work at his trade.[1] In his spare time he took to studying and eventually abandoned carpentry to train for the ministry. His wife was a sister of Wm Forbes, minister of the Aberdeen Gaelic Chapel from 1798-1800, and she may also have been known to the congregation. Whatever memories he had of Aberdeen, the invitation to present himself as a candidate for the Gaelic Chapel did not appeal to him and he declined the offer. Subsequently he accepted a call to the Edinburgh Gaelic Chapel and, from 1821 until his death in 1847, he was minister in the Parish of Halkirk, Caithness, where he was much esteemed, probably more on account of his personal qualities than his literary gifts.

David Carment

The managers learned of John Munro's refusal on 19th September at a time when the Rev. David Carment, assistant to the Rev. Hugh Calder, Croy, was officiating at the autumn communion. There can be little doubt that Carment's attitude to a call from Aberdeen would have been sounded, for he was the type that would have been very acceptable to the congregation. Probably it was for that reason that he had been invited to take the communion services at that time. Although born and reared in Keiss, Caithness, he was of lowland parentage and was far from being an archetypical Highland preacher. His preaching was practical, with a directness and terseness to which Highlanders, at least at that time, were not much accustomed. Yet he was highly popular with every kind of audience.[2] Donald Sage, in a picturesque if slightly belittling reference, explained why.

He was a sound, scriptural preacher and a ready speaker. But he unhappily disturbed the gravity of his hearers by indulging no ordinary powers of humour and drollery in his public orations. His sermons and speeches teemed with anecdotes and quaint and ludicrous expressions, and whether he mounted the pulpit or stood on the platform, this was exactly what his audience expected. A broad grin settled down on the face of every one of them, plainly intimating that they had made up their minds, so long as Carment was speaking, to have some fun.[3]

Sage's strictures may not have been altogether devoid of professional envy. If, on occasion, the congregation felt 'disturbed' on account of Carment's diversions, their protestations would not have been intended too seriously. Neither the Highlanders nor the Aberdonians were averse to instruction being lightened with a little buffoonery from David Carment. He would certainly have been a welcome candidate for their chapel, but at the time he was content with Croy. In 1810 he went to Duke Street Chapel in Glasgow where he remained until presented to the Parish of Rosskeen in 1822. As a parish minister he enjoyed going to the General Assembly and made some very effective appearances there, his speeches, like his Synod addresses, being delivered with hard knocks against all who did not fall in with his views. Towards the end of his ministry, a revival occurred in his parish and in 1840 he admitted more communicants than during the whole of the preceding 18 years of his ministry.

Donald MacGillivray

The next person to receive an invitation from the managers was a Mr Donald MacGillivray who was residing in Edinburgh. Brought up in the Episcopal Church in Strathnairn, he became a zealous Presbyterian while a student at King's College, Aberdeen (1799-1803).[4] He readily agreed to preach in Aberdeen and by the middle of October he was officiating in the chapel. Given £9 for his expenses, he returned to Edinburgh while the managers convened a meeting of the congregation at which his name was proposed. Alas 'but few of the congregation appearing on his side, it was judged expedient by the managers to adjourn the meeting until the people made up their minds in bringing forward another candidate'. Rejected by Aberdeen, Donald MacGillivray took a post as a teacher in Ferintosh and subsequently held mission charges at Fort William, Berriedale, Strathfillan and Lochgoilhead before being presented to the Parish of Kilmallie in 1831. His ministry there was brief, for he died in 1835, but it has been said that it marked the beginning of a widespread revival in Lochaber.[5]

It was in an atmosphere of some excitement that the next meeting

69

of the committee was held on 1st November 1808. The excitement was occasioned by the fact that the managers had received 'some information concerning the Rev. John Kennedy of Assynt which was thought to be favourable to them in their present situation'. The prospect of securing the services of this preacher was clearly an exhilarating one and they responded quickly. It was agreed to call a congregational meeting with the minimum of notice while Professor Bentley would write immediately to John Kennedy advising him 'that he might expect a call to follow with the least possible delay'.

A tint of Normanism

John Kennedy had been in Assynt for little more than a year when news reached Aberdeen that he might be persuaded to leave it. According to his son and biographer, it was during his stay in Assynt that he experienced the sorest trial of his life.[6] This was a consequence of the actions of Norman Macleod (1780-1866), a native of Assynt and a very talented personality who seemingly won the hearts of the people.[7] This was a new experience for John Kennedy who, if his son is to be believed, had been almost idolised by the parishioners of his previous charge at Eriboll. When he left there, 'strong men were bathed in tears, women in groups were wailing as he passed, and all watched to get the last look of him as he went out of sight'.[8] In contrast to such adulatory treatment, he had not been long in Assynt when a group, including some who claimed to have benefited from his preaching, left the stated services of the Established Church in favour of separatist meetings led by Norman Macleod. So captivating was Norman that his rival services eventually attracted the support of all but two of the communicants of the district. His separatist movement had been launched as a protest against what he claimed to be the moral laxity of the Established Church, a laxity with which, in the view of Norman Macleod, John Kennedy acquiesced for reasons of self-interest.[9] Specifically, he pointed out that 'Parson William' of Assynt was a known inebriate and yet John Kennedy did not protest against the loose discipline and other abuses that prevailed at that time. Taking this high ground obviously had a strong appeal for the pious people and Kennedy found himself placed in a very uncomfortable position, being upstaged by a rival spiritual leader claiming to have superior godliness and a greater loyalty to the truth.

The decisive battles in this ecclesiastical warfare occurred prior to 1812, the year in which Kennedy left Assynt, but the question of interest in relation to the Aberdeen vacancy is whether contumacious behaviour from Norman Macleod was evident in the year 1808 to the extent that it could be the source of the information thought to be favourable to the aspirations of the Aberdeen congregation. The evidence would suggest that this was a possibility. Dr Kennedy says of Norman that, following his conversion, his spiritual development was at an unseemly rate of growth: 'He all at once started in the course of profession at a stature and with a courage that seemed never to have known a childhood at all. He began at once to prepare for the ministry'. It was in 1808 that he commenced his academic studies with a view to the ministry and so his precociousness must have registered in the mind of John Kennedy by then at least. Indeed in the light of subsequent developments, it seems likely that he had already begun to preach without due authority, the ultimate act of insubordination.

There was, however, another matter giving concern as regards John Kennedy's position in Assynt which might have filtered through to Aberdeen. In April 1809, 'Parson William' wrote to the SSPCK for financial help for Kennedy on the grounds that there had been 'a failure in the payment of subscriptions to his assistant Mr. Kennedy'.[10] He attributed this failure to 'the great hardships experienced in that country in consequence of the late scarcity and the high price of provisions'. It may safely be assumed that 'Parson William' would not have written at the first hint of a shortfall and that the situation reported in April 1809 had made itself felt the previous autumn. Perhaps it merely reflected a bad harvest. But it could also be the reflection of the withdrawal of the support of the community. To this appeal, the directors of the SSPCK, while regretting the reported distress, replied that it was not in their power to apply any part of the Society's fund to the support of his assistant. The fact remains that whatever the precise nature of the information reaching Aberdeen, John Kennedy had problems in Assynt which raised the hopes of the congregation. Once again, however, they were to be disappointed in their attempt to secure his engagement. In January 1809, he wrote to say that he did not see his way to close with their call. Perhaps the fact that Norman Macleod of Assynt was now a student in the Aberdeen congregation, influenced his decision. Whatever the reasons, he stuck to his post in Assynt. But even with Norman in Aberdeen for much of the year, his task continued to be a difficult one.

The Killearnan careerist

Two years later, in April 1811, the SSPCK, looking for someone to take Alex Flyter's place in Berriedale, decided to approach John Kennedy who, 'there was reason to expect, would accept of the appointment if it was now offered to him'.[11] In fact, he did accept it, in letters dated 5th and 15th July, but, as happened with his previous appointments, he then prevaricated and by 22nd April 1812, Robert Gunn, the minister of Latheron, the parish that included Berriedale, was writing to the Society to say that he understood that 'the Rev. John Kennedy whom the Society had nominated to the mission at Berriedale had been appointed to officiate in the vacant Parish of Killearnan till the process respecting the right of patronage shall be determined by the House of Peers'.[12] The minister of Latheron was obviously close to reliable sources of information. A month later, on 19th May, John Kennedy himself wrote to the Presbytery of Chanonry to say that he had been appointed by 'the Right Honourable the Lord Chief Barons and Remanent Barons of His Majesty's Exchequer in Scotland as interim minister of the Parish of Killearnan with the concurrence of Mr and Mrs Hay Mackenzie of Cromartie'.[13] He reported to the Presbytery his intention of accepting the appointment, although, because of engagements which he had 'in the West Country', he anticipated that it would be some weeks before he moved to Killearnan. Meantime he assured them that his brother Neil would continue to officiate at Killearnan until his arrival. The Presbytery, on receipt of this unexpected information which, as the minute cryptically put it, 'they had every reason to believe authentic', could do no other than request him to 'enter upon and fulfil the functions of the same charge with his earliest convenience until the patronage be decided'.

As already remarked, the right of patronage of Killearnan Parish was the subject of competing claims by the Crown and the Mackenzies of Cromartie. On the parish having fallen vacant some five years previously, the Crown had nominated the Rev. William Macrae of Barvas, while the Mackenzies, who appeared to have the better claim, nominated the Rev. Thomas Ross who had succeeded the inebriate Alex Stronach in Lochbroom. The Presbytery of Chanonry were willing to induct Ross, but remitted the question to the Church Procurator.[14] Although the Mackenzies issued a second presentation to Thomas Ross, the Procurator advised the Presbytery to defer his induction until the Crown made its position clear regarding a possible appeal. The Presbytery, 'out of proper caution and impartiality towards either of the presentees', agreed to this, obviously taking the view that for Dr Ross to be in the parish gave him some advantage.[15] Subsequent events were to bear out the correctness of that view.

If John Kennedy seemed especially interested in Killearnan, it was not because he was without supporters elsewhere. When Kennedy left Assynt, 'Parson William' asked the SSPCK for another assistant.[16] They declined the request, and he then agreed to the appointment (by the patron) of 'an assistant and successor'. Duncan MacGillivray, at that time missioner at Achness, was appointed. The people of Assynt were not consulted in the matter; if they had been, their preference would have been for John Kennedy. In fact, so aggrieved were the parishioners, that a body of Assynt Highlanders forcibly interrupted the induction proceedings by staging a pro-Kennedy riot, in consequence of which the induction was delayed and some of the rioters imprisoned.[17]

Again, Aberdeen was not the only city whose Highland population would have welcomed him. In October 1813 he was given a call by Edinburgh Gaelic Chapel.[18] Characteristically he delayed his decision. Nine months later John Macdonald, Ferintosh, the previous minister of the charge, wrote to the SSPCK, who paid the chapel stipend, to say that Kennedy had 'not been able to determine as to his acceptance of the Edinburgh Gaelic Chapel' and that they should invite him for a further two or three Sabbaths supply.[19] This the directors declined to do. Finally, on 12th July 1814, Kennedy wrote to say that he 'did not wish to keep the congregation any longer in suspense'.[20] He declined the offer.

That same month the House of Lords judgment in the matter of the disputed patronage was officially announced.[21] As expected it was in favour of the Mackenzies of Cromartie. That John Kennedy was advantageously placed to obtain the presentation was now evident and the fact that he was married to a kinswomen of the Mackenzies would not have hindered his suit.[22] On 17th August 1814 Dr Thomas Ross of Lochbroom wrote to the Presbytery of Chanonry withdrawing from the presentation given to him in 1808 by the Hon. Mrs Mackenzie.[23] By November John Kennedy had his position as minister of the Parish of Killearnan officially confirmed.[24] Dr Kennedy, in his memoir of his father, remarks without any explanation, 'In coming to Killearnan at first, he looked forward to the prospect of being minister of Lochbroom, the scene of his first stated labours as a preacher'.[25] Perhaps the thought was that Dr Ross, appointed to Lochbroom in 1807 and given the presentation to Killearnan in 1808, would ultimately succeed in his claim to Killearnan and, in turn, would be succeeded in Lochbroom by John Kennedy. In the event Kennedy's achievement in obtaining the temporary incumbency of Killearnan reversed the anticipated succession, and Dr Thomas Ross remained in Lochbroom until his death in 1843.

The Assynt Separatist

Back in Aberdeen, the managers, following John Kennedy's rejection of their call, showed their freedom from partisanship by their willingness to employ (or, more correctly, continue to employ) that ecclesiastical Ishmael, Norman Macleod of Assynt, as their regular supply through the winter of 1808–1809. The fact that he was engaged to do this would suggest that he had gained some previous experience by preaching in Assynt. It was of course a grave irregularity that one who was not even a licentiate of the church should undertake to preach in any of the church's pulpits. For this infringement Dr Thomas Ross refused baptism to Norman's child when the father was schoolmaster in Lochbroom,[26] a decision which launched Norman on his remarkable odyssey to St Ann's, Nova Scotia, and ultimately, to Waipu, New Zealand.[27] But, to the Highlanders in Aberdeen, these matters were of little consequence compared to the elevation of spirit that they experienced from listening to the Assynt separatist, who sounded to them as a watchman of Israel as he rebuked the sins of the church and the self-interest of its ministers. For all of which, 'and his labours among them in the course of the winter season', he received the sum of £5 from the chapel managers.

Notes to Chapter 10

1. For a brief account of the life of the Rev. John Munro, Halkirk, see Rev. Alex Auld: *Ministers and men in the far North* (Wick, 1869; reprinted Glasgow, 1956), pp 56-70.
2. For a brief account of the life of the Rev. David Carment, Rosskeen, see Rev. J. A. Wylie (ed.): *Disruption Worthies: A Memorial of 1843* (Edinburgh, 1881), vol. II, pp 147-151.
3. D Sage: *Memorabilia Domestica* (Wick, 1889; 2nd edition 1899, reprinted 1975), p 283.
4. For some details of the life of the Rev Donald MacGillivray, Kilmallie, see Principal John Macleod: *By-paths of Highland church history* (Edinburgh, 1965), pp 10-14.
5. G N M Collins: *John Macleod DD* (Edinburgh, 1951), p 9.
6. J Kennedy: *The days of the fathers in Ross-shire* (Edinburgh, 1861; Inverness, 1927, new and enlarged edition), p 180.
7. For a brief account of the life of Norman Macleod, the Assynt Separatist, see John Macleod: op. cit., pp 136-147; and Donald Munro (comp.): *Records of Grace in Sutherland* (Edinburgh, 1953), pp 186-188.
8. J Kennedy: op. cit., p 177.
9. The substance of Norman Macleod of Assynt's criticism of the Rev. John Kennedy and the Established Church can be found in a letter from Norman Macleod addressed to the Rev. Dr John Kennedy of Dingwall and reprinted in a chapter aptly entitled 'A Separatist Blast' in Macleod: *By-paths of Highland church history* (Edinburgh, 1965).
10. *SSPCK Records: Minutes of committee meetings*, vol. 12, p 243 (May, 1809) (GD95-2-12).
11. Ibid., p 333 (April, 1811).
12. Ibid., p 399 (June, 1812).
13. *Records of the Presbytery of Chanonry*, vol. 6, p 154 (17th June, 1812) (CH2-66-6).
14. Ibid., vol. 6, p 80 (21st June, 1808).
15. Ibid., vol. 6, p 85 (11th July, 1808).
16. *SSPCK Records: Minutes of committee meetings*, vol. 12, p 401 (June, 1812) (GD95-2-12).
17. D Sage: op. cit., p 193.
18. *SSPCK Records: Minutes of committee meetings*, vol 14, p 1 (October 1813) (GD95-2-14).
19. Ibid., p 35 (July, 1814).
20. Ibid., p 41 (August, 1814).

21. J Barron: *The Northern Highlands in the nineteenth century* (Inverness, 1903), vol. 1, p 76.
22. *Fasti Ecclesiae Scoticanae* (1928), vol. 7, p 158.
23. *Records of the Presbytery of Chanonry,* vol. 6, p 177 (20th September, 1814) (CH2-66-6).
24. Ibid., vol. 6, p 180 (1st November, 1814).
25. J Kennedy: op. cit., p 185.
26. J Macleod: *By-paths of Highland church history* (Edinburgh, 1965), p 138.
27. G Macdonald: *The Highlanders of Waipu* (Dunedin, 1928).

Chapter 11

*

A CAPITAL OFFENCE

ON January 16th 1809, three days after it was intimated that John Kennedy had refused the call to Aberdeen, the congregation, acting on the managers' recommendation, agreed to call their former pastor, the Rev. John Mackenzie of Duke Street Gaelic Chapel, Glasgow. According to Donald Sage, Mackenzie 'not feeling himself suited as pastor of the Duke St. Chapel, readily returned to his former charge'.[1] Sage, however, was sometimes given to discerning difficulties regarding which the parties concerned were quite insensible. Mackenzie had been ten years in Glasgow and six years earlier had declined a pressing invitation to return to Aberdeen. Clearly he did not leave Glasgow at the first opportunity, but his sons were now approaching the age for university entrance and perhaps that influenced him in accepting the call. Whatever the reason he demitted his charge in Glasgow, where he was succeeded by David Carment, Croy, whose pulpit display of drollery and humour incurred Sage's censure.

John Mackenzie returns to Aberdeen

It was June before John Mackenzie began his second pastorate in Aberdeen, but as early as February 1809 the managers not only agreed to meet his removal expenses but in addition they sent him a £50 loan 'to relieve him of any embarrassment on his removal from Glasgow', assuring him at the same time that more would be advanced if necessary. Apparently more was necessary and by the time he came to Aberdeen he had received an interest-free loan of £80 – the equivalent of two thirds of his annual stipend.

His ministry opened in circumstances of undisclosed personal or domestic difficulty which evoked the practical sympathy of the managers. In May 1810 they gave him a donation of £8 'to make his situation as comfortable as lies in their power'. In October they decided to intimate 'that a special collection be uplifted for behoof of their present pastor' pending which they agreed to a loan of £20 'to relieve him out of some embarrassment that he was under'. The following August, 'having taken into consideration the present situation of their pastor and the breach made lately in his family', they gave him a donation of another £20, 'the said sum to be raised by subscription among the congregation and such other well-wishers as incline to contribute to the same'. Almost certainly his wife died at that time.

In these difficult months the stipulation that the SSPCK annual catechist grant of £10 had to be applied for through the Presbytery was forgotten, and two years payment lost as the Society would not pay arrears. Again the managers felt bound to make good the deficiency, which they did by deducting £20 from the minister's indebtedness which at the time was £100. Then they advanced another £10, making his debt £90, and this at a time when Neil Kennedy was seeking to defer repayment of his £40 loan. The Presbytery, receiving in March 1810 their first intimation of John Mackenzie's induction the previous year, pointedly noted that he had been received by the ministers of Aberdeen without a call having been sustained by the Presbytery, but the presumptuous action of the ministers responsible was excused on the grounds of 'there being an actual vacancy and the Presbytery having a long adjournment'.[2]

The managers' sympathetic treatment of the minister's personal circumstances was not a reflection of buoyant revenue in the congregational fund. On the contrary, the debt on the chapel stood at £493, essential repairs and improvements to the fabric were long overdue, and economies were being imposed such as a reduction in the number of candles lit at the time of evening lecture, these items being, it seems, very costly at that time. Improvements which it was agreed should be embarked on included white-washing the interior of the chapel, this to be undertaken by one of the congregation, *viz* 'John Graham, plaisterer' who was instructed to 'furnish materials and do the work at the ordinary rate that such work is done at, likewise to provide scaffolding to suit himself to be paid for distinct from the white-washing'. Angus Sutherland, prominent in the management committee since 1796, was instructed to examine and repair the roof. Mr (the designation suggesting that he was an outside tradesman) Booth, painter, was engaged to paint the chapel windows. New guttering was ordered, as was a new gate and a new outer door. Alex Pirie, who at the time was engaged in laying the kerbstone in Gaelic Lane, was given the job of laying the pavement in front of the chapel, while 'John Macdonald, contractor, one of the committee, was appointed to see the said pavement properly laid and report the same to the committee before the charges thereof be paid'.

Fund-raising by Dr Kidd

These improvements all cost money, and although the minutes contain no mention of special fund-raising efforts, fund-raising services were held periodically. The biographer of Dr Kidd, basing his remarks on the testimony of Dr Aird of Creich, tells of an occasion when Dr Kidd was asked to take a Sunday afternoon fund-raising service in the Gaelic Chapel. Since the immediate need was occasioned by improvements to the chapel's exterior, the occasion could have been during John Mackenzie's ministry. Quite apart from his popularity with the Gaelic worshippers, Dr Kidd was the obvious choice for such a service, for 'he begged with an importunity and success which no other man in Aberdeen could rival'.[3] Being of a practical outlook, he took for his subject the contributions given for erecting the Tabernacle and, suiting action to words, he called on the beadle to bring the collection plate, into which he then proceeded to toss a crown piece. Then identifying certain individuals in the congregation by name, he suggested what they might fitly contribute – a muff, a silk mantle, a gold watch, *etc.* Finally, turning to one of the most prominent men, an elder and one of the original trustees, he urged, 'And you, Ebenezer Murray, you have I know not how many houses, and none to leave them to but a wife as old as yourself; put one of them in the plate'.

The extent to which Ebenezer Murray had the grace of giving is not recorded, but he had, at least, the grace of going on, even in the face of such bracing and gratuitous advice. To the end of his days he remained active in the congregation. He was a general merchant whose business was located at the foot of Broad Street, but he must also have enjoyed the reputation of being something of a man of property. Before John Mackenzie flitted from Glasgow, the committee agreed 'to take a dwelling house for him and it was left to Ebenezer Murray to settle with Christie, the shoemaker who owned the house'.

Fama clamosa

Each year saw some changes in the management personnel. James Chalmers, editor and proprietor of the *Aberdeen Journal*, died in June 1810 leaving only John Ewen of the original external managers. Chalmers' place was taken by Arthur Thomson, Agent of the Aberdeen Bank and a crony of John Ewen in the Aberdeen Musical Society.[4] Prominent though these men were in the life of the community, there would have been some, perhaps many, in the congregation quite unaware of the transition from one to the other. But that same month in which Chalmers died there was another change of which none was ignorant, for it was the talk of the town. A meeting of the elders and committee was convened on 26th June 1810 to deal with a *fama clamosa* that had unexpectedly arisen. The minute recorded it with unusual fulness:

The meeting being constituted, they took into consideration the murmurs and prejudices raised in the minds of the congregation against Angus Mackay their present beadle on account of him digging a grave for the body of the man lately executed here, himself acknowledging the same. It was unanimously agreed upon that he should be superceded from his office for a time for the satisfaction of the people.

The event referred to was the execution on 15th June of Andrew Fraser or Hosack (Fraser being an assumed name) who had been apprehended the previous August for house-breaking and theft while employed at Rubislaw quarry.[5] One night he broke into a nearby cottage and took articles of clothing. A watchdog aroused the neighbours and the housebreaker was apprehended after a chase. A search of his home revealed other stolen items and Hosack stood trial in April 1810. Found guilty, he was sentenced to death, and an appeal to the Crown for clemency was unavailing.

The barbarous penalty, so monstrously disproportionate to the crime, was not so regarded in these days. Eight years later an orphan boy aged 17, a first offender, was hanged for sheep–stealing, even though public sympathy in the case was openly on the lad's side.[6] Public sympathy was not, however, similarly extended to Andrew Hosack, perhaps because it was also rumoured that he was guilty of the murder, in 1797, of an octogenarian, George Milne, and his only daughter, both of whom were axed to death before their cottage, near Keith, was set fire to. Hosack strenuously denied any involvement in that crime and there seems to have been no good evidence for charging him with it. But the rumour ensured that the execution was carried through in an atmosphere of public hostility to the accused. Why public hostility should have been directed at the man who undertook to dig the criminal's grave is by no means clear, but the circumstances surrounding the disposal of the body were unusual enough to be newsworthy at the time. The *Black Kalendar of Aberdeen* (1840) gives the following account.[7]

Hosack, a stout-built man fifty-six years of age at the time of his death, died penitently. On the occasion of his execution, a scene of a curious description took place. It had been arranged to carry his body to the Gallowhill, and there bury it, or rather lay it barely below the ground. It was necessary to get a cart for the carrying away of the body, and various attempts were made to seize the carts of the coalmen and others on the quay for this purpose. These attempts, on the part of the civil power, were, however, successfully resisted by the carters, with the assistance of some sailors; and no one appeared willing to lend his cart or horse for such a purpose. In this difficulty, it was recollected that the hangman, John Milne, kept a cart, and while he was engaged in his official duties in Castle Street, his cart and horse were seized, and brought up the town, in spite of some resistance on the part of his daughter, who, it was said, was also roughly handled by the people. The news reached the executioner before he had left the scaffold, from which he made a speech to the spectators, and appealed to their sympathy against the indignities which had been offered to himself and his daughter. He asked the public whether he had not done his duty honourably, and was answered by cheers from the rabble. He then formally resigned his situation in presence of the people, and for this magnanimity he was again greeted with applause. He was, however, that same night, prevailed upon to continue in office. Hosack's body having been laid down on the Gallowhill, was carried off during the night by the surgeons.

It may be doubted that Angus Mackay's involvement was wholly altruistic. Perhaps he was in the employ of the surgeons. But whatever the reason for his co-operation, it earned the censure of the community with the result that it was needful 'for the satisfaction of the people' that now he should be superseded in the office which he had honourably discharged since the chapel had opened its doors some 15 years earlier. The following month the committee met to appoint a successor when, 'agreeable to the desire of the Rev. Mr. Mackenzie their present pastor, they appointed Alex Murray, elder, to officiate as officer or beadle in the room of Angus Mackay lately dismissed'. This Alex Murray was one of the original feu assignees when he was designated a woolcomber. He had been ordained to the eldership during John Mackenzie's first pastorate.

Irregular ordination

During the remaining three years of John Mackenzie's ministry, the work of the congregation continued along familiar lines. Four additional elders – Alex Ross, Gilchrist Sutherland, John Macleod and Patrick Mackenzie – were ordained to office. This ordination, carried out as were the preceding ones without the sanction of the Presbytery and contrary to the law of the Church, was the last of its kind. Not until the Gaelic Chapel was given independence by being made a *quoad sacra* parish in 1834 were further elders ordained. In all, since the foundation of the chapel, 16 elders had been ordained, five of them in John Mackenzie's first pastorate and four in his second. When Donald Sage drew up the congregational roll in 1820, only six of the 16 elders ordained, remained in office, *viz* Angus Munro from the first ordination carried out by Kenneth Bayne, Alex Murray from John Mackenzie's first pastorate, Ebenezer Murray and Alex Macdonald from Neil Kennedy's appointments and Gilchrist Sutherland and John Macleod from the last ordination.

In July 1813, four years after his induction, John Mackenzie intimated his intention to accept a call which he had received from another newly established Gaelic congregation in Glasgow, that of Kirkfield or Gorbals. It was 1814 before he commenced his ministry there and in Kirkfield he remained until his death on 30th November 1823. He had two sons: one, Alan John, of whom it is recorded that he was a student of philosophy; the other, Kenneth, was a student at Marischal College from 1812-1813 when he transferred to the University of Glasgow. On the death of his father, this son was called to be his successor in Kirk-field Chapel.[8] His second and last charge was that of Bo'ness where, at the Disruption, he adhered to the Church of Scotland and died in 1867.[9]

Notes to Chapter 11

1. D Sage: *Memorabilia Domestica* (Wick, 2nd edition, 1899; reprinted 1975), p 224.
2. *Records of Aberdeen Presbytery*, vol 9, p 358 (28th March, 1810) (CH2-1-11).
3. J Stark: *Dr Kidd of Aberdeen* (Aberdeen, 3rd edition, 1898), p 246.
4. G Walker: *Aberdeen awa'* (Aberdeen, 1897), p 218.
5. *Aberdeen Journal* (18th June, 1810), p 4.
6. L Mackinnon: *Recollections of an old lawyer* (Aberdeen, 1935), pp 21-22.
7. *The Black Kalendar of Aberdeen* (Aberdeen, 4th edition, 1878), p 167.
8. I R MacDonald: *Glasgow's Gaelic Churches* (Edinburgh 1995), pp 16-17.
9. *Fasti Ecclesiae Scoticanae* (1915), vol. 1, p 197.

Chapter 12

*

RUNNERS AND PURSUERS

USUALLY a chapel minister, having accepted a call to another charge, gave timeous notice of his intention to leave. Sometimes he even saw it as his duty to ensure that his congregation would be provided with a suitable successor.[1] In Aberdeen the Gaelic Chapel Session were able to undertake this duty themselves and on 6th September 1813 the managers agreed that 'the elders should be empowered to enquire after and bring forward from time to time such ministers of the Gospel as candidates or otherwise as they think may be for the benefit and satisfaction of the society'. The Session delegated this duty to three of their number – Ebenezer Murray, the general merchant with an interest in property; Alex Murray, the elder who had replaced Angus Mackay as church officer; and Alex Macdonald, a merchant in East North Street who had been ordained to office by Neil Kennedy and who, with the passing of the years, came to be one of the most assertive office-bearers in the congregation. At the end of November these men reported to the committee that they had corresponded with Mr Angus Macbean at Croy and Mr Robertson at Fort William.

Angus Macbean and Wm Robertson

Angus Macbean had graduated from King's College in 1809 before taking a post as schoolmaster at Dores.[2] When approached by the Aberdeen Gaelic Chapel, he had just been appointed as assistant to the Rev. Hugh Calder, minister of Croy. In effect he was preacher to the Parish of Croy, as Hugh Calder suffered from some nervous disorder that prevented him from addressing any public audience with the result that, over a period of forty years he had to employ a succession of assistant preachers, among whom were David Carment and Angus Macbean.[3] Angus Macbean declined the approach from Aberdeen and remained as assistant in Croy until 1821 when he succeeded Kenneth Bayne as minister of Greenock Gaelic Chapel.

Wm Robertson of Fort William was a son of a greatly esteemed Gaelic preacher, the Rev. John Robertson, minister successively in Achreny, Rothesay and Kingussie. Wm Robertson had been ordained to the mission church in Fort William only a few months before he was invited to become a candidate for the Aberdeen Gaelic Chapel. Like

Angus Macbean he declined the offer from Aberdeen, choosing instead to remain at Fort William until 1816 when he went to Laggan and eventually in 1818 to Kinloss.[4]

Duncan Grant

Although the elders' report was a negative one, the committee never-theless approved of their endeavours and agreed that they 'should still continue to correspond with such ministers as they get notice of until the present vacancy in their chapel be supplied'. The task was soon completed. In the middle of December a young man, 24 years of age, came to preach. He was Duncan Grant, a native of Strathdearn in Inverness-shire, who had graduated from King's College in 1808 thereafter becoming a teacher in the public academy at Fortrose. Licensed to preach at the comparatively early age of 23, he had obvious gifts for the work of the ministry. After listening to him over two Sundays, the managers found themselves 'so far satisfied with the said Mr. D Grant's abilities and character as to agree to call a general meet-ing to get the sense of the people concerning giving a call to the said Mr. D Grant'. Another Sabbath's preaching did nothing to impair the favourable opinion already created. The 'sense of the people' was affir-mative, unanimously and enthusiastically so. The meeting held on 10th January 1814 agreed that the stipend should be increased to £150 and, if necessary, seat rents would be raised to meet the higher outlay.

Since the meeting was an important one, John Ewen was present and was invited to preside; the Committee chairman, Ebenezer Murray, giving place to him. John Ewen likewise assumed responsibility for the minute which he inscribed in characteristic vein, the preamble virtually rehearsing the early history of the congregation:

> *The meeting having previously deliberated on the subject and chosen Mr. Ebenezer Murray as their preses, it was their unanimous desire that Mr. John Ewen, merchant, a gentleman who had been a manager since the first estab-lishment of the congregation as a collective body for religious worship in St Mary's Chapel under the East Church granted them by the honourable the magistrates and council of Aberdeen, for that important purpose should be called in and preside on the occasion.*

The call having been drawn up and signed, it was dispatched along with the customary letter of courteous entreaty from the principal manager. It brought a ready response. Duncan Grant was not one given to temporising.

In 1812, when Grant was parochial schoolmaster of Kirkmichael and Cullicudden, and not much over the minimum age of 21, he had applied for licensing from the Presbytery of Chanonry.[5] Now he requested ordination in order to qualify for his appointment to Aberdeen. His petition was supported by a letter from Dr James Ross, minister of the third charge of Aberdeen, informing the Presbytery that 'it would be agreeable to the Rev. doctors, his colleagues the other parochial ministers of Aberdeen that this Presbytery would proceed to the ordination of Mr Grant before he left their bounds'.[6] It will be recalled that when John Mackenzie was ordained to the Aberdeen Gaelic Chapel by the Presbytery of Chanonry in 1792, there were no obstacles put in his way, the Presbytery taking the view that he did not 'come under the usual engagements to submit to the judicature of this church'. Now, however, a member of Presbytery voiced a note of caution and suggested that the request made by Dr Ross had to be supported either by 'the Presbytery of Aberdeen as a body, or at least from the parochial ministers of Aberdeen conjunctly, as a proper ground for this Presbytery's procedure to ordain a minister for that corner of the church'.[7]

Duncan Grant undertook to obtain such support which he did in the form of a letter dated 5th April from three ministers of Aberdeen who urged that 'the state of the Gaelic congregation so long without a minister will we hope be sustained as an apology for making this request'. The Presbytery of Chanonry, having considered this letter, 'sustained it as a good and valid ground for them to proceed upon', whereupon they ordained Duncan Grant 'to the office of the Holy Ministry with a special view to the charge of the Gaelic Chapel and congregation at Aberdeen, his call by whom he has laid before this Presbytery bearing *ipsa facie* that said call has been sustained and approved by the whole ministers of that extensive Parish of Aberdeen or St Nicholas'.[8] By the middle of April 1814, Duncan Grant, at 24 years of age one of the youngest ministers in the Church, entered on the duties and the problems of his first pastorate.

In the opening months of his ministry the entries in the minute book record the familiar and predictable items of congregational business. It was agreed that the minister's travelling expenses from Fortrose should be met and that a letter of thanks should be sent to Professor Kidd 'for his great attention to the interests of the Gaelic congregation and more especially during the late vacancy'. Note was taken of the fact that their previous minister was in debt to the managers to the extent of £90 of which £40 was still to be outstanding two years later. The first reference to communion expenses in the course of Duncan Grant's ministry occurs in April 1816 when the assisting minister was Angus MacKintosh of Tain, a greatly venerated Highland divine and, like Duncan Grant, a native of Strathdearn.[9] Two years later, in April 1818, the name of the most famous of all the Highland preachers – the Rev. John Macdonald of Urquhart or Ferintosh, generally referred to as the Apostle of the North – appears for the first time. This, however, was not the first occasion on which John Macdonald assisted at the April administration of the sacrament in Aberdeen. He had been there the previous year and it was as a consequence of that visit that his peripatetic preaching became the subject of a complaint to the General Assembly. The incident highlights the continuing struggle between the Moderates and the Evangelicals in the National Church.

Muzzling the Apostle of the North

John Macdonald, although himself a parish minister, spent the greater part of the year doing the work of an itinerant evangelist. His services were in constant demand, his eloquence being almost mesmeric in its effects. But his very popularity no doubt gave rise to some resentment on the part of his brother ministers, especially those who were of a less evangelical persuasion. Such was the situation in the Presbytery of Strathbogie, the ministers of which were mainly of the Moderate persuasion.[10] The occasion of the complaint to the General Assembly, as reported by the Rev. George Munro, parish minister of Huntly, was as follows.[11] A member of the parish church in Huntly received a letter from the Rev. John Philip of Aberdeen,[12] informing him that the following day Duncan Grant of the Gaelic Chapel and John Macdonald of Ferintosh would be passing through Huntly and the latter requested the Rev. George Munro's permission to allow him preach in the parish church. When the request was conveyed to the parish minister, he refused permission on the grounds that 'it was not customary in this place for ministers of the Established Church to preach on weekdays'. He offered his pulpit for the Sunday which, of course, given the pressure of preaching engagements in Macdonald's diary (he preached more than 300 times every year[13]) was out of the question. But, on being pressed as to whether Macdonald could preach elsewhere in the parish, Munro said he could preach where he pleased. A service was then arranged in the Seceder church which was packed for the occasion.

At the same time the minister of Keith, the Rev. John Maclean, reported that two persons acting on behalf of the auxiliary Bible Society of Keith, had requested the use of the parish church for Macdonald to preach for the benefit of the Bible Society. After some consideration the minister 'did not think it right to comply'. The minister of the adjoining Parish of Cairnie, the Rev. John Findlater, was then approached by one of his elders who asked that Macdonald might be given permission to preach in the Cairnie Church. Findlater refused, but when asked if the Highland minister could have permission to preach elsewhere in the parish, he replied that 'he did not care though he would preach on the top of the Beinn hill [the highest point in the parish] if he chose'. Macdonald then preached on this hill near its boundary with the Parish of Keith. Almost a year after this took place, the matter was raised at a meeting of the Presbytery of Strathbogie as something which had 'given great offence to every sincere well-wisher of the peace and order of this church'. It was agreed to refer the case to the General Assembly and, as required by the law of the Church, notice of this was sent to the Dingwall Presbytery and its itinerant preacher.

Replying to the charge, John Macdonald pointed out (i) that the requests made for liberty to preach had come wholly from the people within the parish; (ii) that the permission of the parish minister had in each case been sought and granted for liberty to preach within the bounds of the parish; and (iii) that he invariably made it clear in reply to any invitation to preach that without the positive permission of the parish minister he would refuse all such requests. He went on to say that had he been informed that the ministers of Huntly and Cairnie objected to his preaching on these occasions, no solicitation of other persons, however well-meant, would have induced him to do so. He ended up by saying, 'I am now sincerely sorry that in so doing I should have offended the brethren or any others; and assure you and the Presbytery of Strathbogie that I shall be careful to give no such offence in time to come; and should similar services be hereafter proposed to me, without the absolute request or permission of the parish minister under his own hand, shall utterly decline them'. One would have thought that such an ample acknowledgment of the prerogatives of the parochial clergy would have satisfied the most clamorous litigant, but the Presbytery having considered 'the nature and tendency of the offence in question refused to sustain the letter as a sufficient apology'. Disclaiming any prejudice against the individual, they judged it important to obtain the sense of the Assembly on the practice in general.

The reign of the Moderates in the General Assembly is usually reckoned to have ended in 1805, but even in 1818 they could still exert a decisive influence on Assembly findings, especially towards the close of the Assembly when the attendance was thinner. On the last day of the Assembly the reference from the Presbytery of Strathbogie was sustained and, although John Macdonald was not explicitly mentioned, he was clearly in view when the Assembly ruled that 'the conduct of any minister who exercised his pastoral functions in a vagrant manner, preaching during his journeys from place to place in other Parishes than his own without the special invitation of the minister of the parish, is disorderly and calculated to injure the interests of sound religion'. It probably had little effect on the peripatetic ministry of the Apostle of the North. There were not enough days in the week for him to fit in all the invitations that came his way. But it did deprive the Parishes of

Strathbogie of a hearing of the Rev. John Macdonald as he made his way to the April communion in the Aberdeen Gaelic Chapel which he continued to do for the next ten years[14] at least, and probably much longer.

Dr Kennedy, in his biography of the Apostle of the North, makes no reference to Macdonald's self-defence when arraigned by the Presbytery of Strathbogie. Instead he conveys the impression that nothing would seal his lips. 'With his zeal for the salvation of sinners, his constant readiness to preach, and the manifold proofs he had received that the blessing of the Lord was descending on his labours we cannot wonder though Mr. Macdonald could not always keep silence while passing through Strathbogie.'[15] Writing in 1866, or indeed any time after 1843, that sentiment would have seemed appropriate enough, but it did not reflect John Macdonald's attitude in 1818 for he deferred to the Assembly's finding even when he did not agree with it.

Being a member of the 1818 Assembly he was able to record his dissent from the Act on vagrant preaching. Among the reasons given for dissent he said the Act could be 'followed with such consequences as the Reverend Mover could not have intended – obstructing or discouraging the ministers of this Church or exposing them to unnecessary and unbecoming challenges for joining with Christians of other denominations in promoting the use of the sacred Scriptures and the interests of religion and civilisation throughout the Globe'. In listing the names of those who adhered to the dissent, Dr Kennedy follows a contemporary press report[16] in which the names of the dissentients are not in accordance with the signatures on the original document. Some names are given which do not appear on the manuscript and others are omitted. John Kennedy, Killearnan and Dr Thomas Ross of Lochbroom are among the names omitted. Dr Ross was the only signatory to append his parish to his name. Perhaps he did this to distinguish himself from his namesake Dr Thomas Ross of Kilmonivaig, but as it was said of the latter that 'never did clergyman unite so much zeal for religion with such unbounded charity towards those who differed from him',[17] it might be thought to have been an unnecessary precaution.

Dr Mearns looks to his laurels

Whether or not Dr Duncan Mearns was the Reverend Mover of the Strathbogie reference, he was given the credit for it by Dr Andrew Thomson,[18] the formidable standard-bearer of the Evangelical Party in the Assembly – 'in himself a host', to quote Sage's graphic expression.[19] Thomson's view was that Mearns, who had recently been elected to the chair of Divinity in King's College, and who was the acknowledged leader of the Moderate Party in the Synod of Aberdeen, was anxious to make a name for himself in a similar capacity in the Assembly, and, casting around for an issue to take to the Assembly, found the peripatetic preaching of the Apostle of the North in Moderate territory, a suitable subject on which to exercise his legislative skills. Certainly the fact that the matter lay dormant almost for twelve months before the Presbytery of Strathbogie took it up, suggests that their action was very much an afterthought to the alleged offence.

Whatever impoverishment may have been suffered by the parishioners of Strathbogie as a result of Duncan Mearns' ambitions on the floor of the Assembly, the Gaelic congregation in Aberdeen was left untouched in its enjoyment of visiting preachers. But Duncan Mearns' aspirations in the academic field did have the effect of depriving the Highlanders of the services of another evangelical stalwart in the person of Dr John Love of Anderston Chapel in Glasgow. The chair of Divinity in King's College, for which these men were rival candidates in 1816, was vested in a committee of electors comprising representatives from King's College and from the Synod of Aberdeen. The Synod, being in the control of the Moderate Party, would obviously have favoured the appointment of Dr Mearns; but it was not directly involved in the election. Indeed, judging from the Synod minutes, its discussion of the vacant post was confined to the emoluments which it considered to have been 'so diminished as to hold out no sufficient inducement to any person of respectability to come forward as a candidate'.[20] Inducement or no, the post attracted the interest of Dr Mearns, Dr Love and Dr Alexander Black, all of them candidates with impeccable academic credentials. For this university chair the appointments procedure was unique in that it involved a competitive examination in the course of which the candidates were invited to criticise a sermon chosen from one of several volumes brought in from the library and opened at random.[21] However searching the interrogation, Dr Mearns, perhaps not surprisingly, was elected. Donald Sage, who regarded Love as much superior to Mearns in ability, nevertheless conceded that the latter was by no means unworthy of the post. While Dr Love's attachment to High Calvinism would have given him close links with the Highland Church, Dr Mearns' appointment was not without benefit to the evangelical cause. 'Rabbi' Duncan was to say of him, 'I was much indebted to Dr Mearns. I was an atheist when I entered his class. It was under him that I gave up atheism'.[22]

The absconding treasurer

While the Assembly of 1818 was deliberating on the Strathbogie repercussions of the visit of Macdonald of Ferintosh to Aberdeen, the managers of the Gaelic Chapel were themselves embroiled with local difficulties revealing all too clearly that the Church had not succeeded in her task of bringing men to perfection. Some changes in personnel had taken place in the recent past. In May 1816 Alex Murray informed the managers 'that he was to resign his office as beadle for the future', but at the following meeting he was re-elected without explanation. However, shortly afterwards, Robert Hamilton is referred to as church officer. In 1817 the clerk, Duncan McGregor, died and John Macdonald, road surveyor, took over the clerkship temporarily. In June 1818 Robert Hamilton was appointed clerk on condition that he relinquish his post as beadle. Both Robert Hamilton as clerk, and Donald Bain, his replacement as beadle, were each to give twenty years of service in their respective offices. John Macdonald, tailor in Queen Street, who had served as treasurer since 1801, was succeeded in May 1815 by George Sutherland, an appointment which, in the event, turned out to be ill-judged. Contrary to the usual practice, the names of his sureties, if such he had, for the office, are not minuted.

At a meeting held on 29th May 1818 there was some hint of dissatisfaction with the system prevailing in respect of borrowing money. Alex Macdonald, merchant in East North Street, the new president appointed at the annual general meeting held earlier that month, and the leader of a strongly conservative group within the congregation, when asked if he would follow the customary practice of signing Bills on behalf of the congregation, replied that he would not, and should there be anyone 'who was not satisfied with the signature of the treasurer, he [the treasurer] would pay them off with banknotes'. It was agreed at that meeting that 'enquiry should be made into the mode of borrowing money on other chapels-of-ease through the town and that such information as could be gathered would be brought up to the next meeting'. The information, if obtained, was not minuted at their June meeting, but a new form of Bill was agreed.

The managers held their July meeting on Friday the 3rd when little business was discussed. Unusually, they met again three days later when the chair was taken by one of the outside managers, Alex Webster, a prominent lawyer who had taken the place of Arthur Thomson, agent of the Aberdeen Bank. The business was 'to elect a treasurer instead of their late treasurer [George Sutherland] who had disappeared at their last meeting'. After discussion they elected Robert Sutherland, plasterer, as treasurer. Two other points are minuted: that the loss to the chapel consequent to the treasurer's departure, was £82 11s 2d; and that they had before them 'a letter from their late treasurer which Mr. Webster ordered to be transcribed into their minute book verbatim'.

The letter, which is itself dated 3rd July, is a mixture of apology, explanation, an appeal for understanding and a plea for time in which to make restitution. It begins, 'To the committee of the Gaelic Chapel I must confess with deep regret that I became under the disagreeable necessity of disappearing at your last meeting, a degrade to my character as a professing Christian including deep loss to the Gaelic Society'. The content of the letter is very confused, but he was at pains to explain that having got himself involved in debt (the failure of a business enterprise is implied), he made use of the Society's funds in order to meet his creditors thereby 'adding misery to sorrow'. One creditor to whom he owed £63 was leaving for America and insisted on having his money. To meet this demand, the treasurer borrowed £40 in the name of the congregation from a Wm Mackay. He borrowed £20 from a Mr Annand to pay the minister's salary. Having explained the current position for the benefit of his successor, he assured the committee that he 'never spent any of your money in unbecoming manner' adding that his 'hopes being blasted at the meantime although not altogether perished as yet, I trust if I be spared in health that I shall be enabled to redeem the Society the present sustained loss with interest'.

The committee met again the following week to consider if it would be proper to take legal proceedings to recover their money, when they were advised 'it would be vain to lay out good money upon bad'. However, Robert Hamilton the clerk and Robert Sutherland the new treasurer were asked to 'go and take a view of such furniture as might be in George Sutherland's house and that they should give information to Mr. Webster respecting the same'. The findings of this commission are not reported. Perhaps the plight of George Sutherland's destitute family aroused some feelings of compassion in the church's emissaries.

The other matter that came under review was the status of the loan of £40 advanced by Wm Mackay. Since the Bill had been drawn contrary to their rules and without the knowledge of the managers, the committee were inclined to the view that they would not be obliged in law to meet it. John Macdonald, road surveyor, was asked to obtain counsel from 'three men of business' and he subsequently reported the unanimous view of three lawyers that the Society were not obliged to pay the Bill. Fortified by this legal opinion, Macdonald delivered the Bill to its hapless proprietor 'leaving him to do as he thought good; only requesting him at the same time not to be too rash in his proceedings concerning his Bill'. Later, after further reflection, 'the managers out of sympathy with the young man Wm. Mackay, and likewise for the honour of the congregation, agreed to call a meeting of the subscribers in order to ascertain their opinion concerning the Bill'. The subscribers unhesitatingly agreed to the payment of the Bill 'as a debt of honour'.

Three years later, on 15th March 1821, a meeting was held of which the minute reads:

A meeting of the managers of the Gaelic Chapel called by private intimation,

Mr. Alex Webster advocate, being in the chair when George Sutherland, their late treasurer, appeared before them and acknowledged his sorrow for the debt which he had unfortunately contracted and come under to the congregation amounting to £82 11s. 2d; after deducting the £10 which he had remitted before, since he left Aberdeen, and agreed to give his voucher for the amount due at present (the payments when made to be credited thereon till the debt be extinguished), the meeting approved of the foregoing proposal, and empowered the present treasurer to receive George Sutherland's Bill for the amount due by him on the conditions before specified or expressed.

In 1836 a George Sutherland of Carmelite Lane was admitted to the communicant membership of the congregation. It cannot be claimed with any certainty the entry relates to the erstwhile treasurer, but perhaps it did; and in any case the episode is illustrative of a congregation taking to heart the Pauline injunction 'be kind one to another, tender-hearted, forgiving one another even as God, for Christ's sake, has forgiven you'.

Notes to Chapter 12

1. D Sage: *Memorabilia Domestica* (Wick, 2nd edition, 1899; reprinted 1975), p 281.
2. *Fasti Ecclesiae Scoticanae* (1920), vol. 3, p 200.
3. J Macleod: *By-paths of Highland church history* (Edinburgh, 1965), p 90.
4. R Cowan: *Our church fathers* (Elgin, 1899) gives some account of the ministry of Wm Robertson.
5. *Records of Presbytery of Chanonry*, vol. 6, p 152 (31st March, 1812) (CH2-2-66-6).
6. Ibid., p 167 (29th March, 1814).
7. Ibid., p 168 (29th March, 1814).
8. Ibid., p 170 (12th April, 1814).
9. J Noble: *Religious life in Ross* (Inverness, 1909) gives some account of the ministry of Angus MacKintosh, pp 228-236.
10. J Burleigh: *A church history of Scotland* (London, 1960), p 344.
11. *Assembly Papers* (1818). Petition from the Presbytery of Strathbogie (CH1-2-143).
12. Minister of George Street Congregational Church, Aberdeen. John Philip had a particular concern for evangelical outreach 'in the extensive and destitute country which lies between Aberdeen and Inverness'. See Andrew Ross: *John Philip (1775-1851)* (Aberdeen, 1986), p 75.
13. J Kennedy: *The apostle of the North* (Edinburgh, 1866; new ed., Inverness, 1932), p 148.
14. J Stark: *Dr Kidd of Aberdeen* (Aberdeen, 3rd edition, 1898), p 199.
15. J Kennedy: op. cit., p 74.
16. J Kennedy: op. cit., p 75 gives the reference as The Christian Instructor (1819). It is also to be found in the *Aberdeen Journal* (10th June, 1818), p 4.
17. J Barron: *The Northern Highlands in the nineteenth century* (Inverness, 1903), vol. 1, p 214.
18. J Kennedy: op. cit., p 77.
19. D Sage: op. cit., p 279.
20. *Register of the Synod of Aberdeen*, vol. 8, p 545 (10th October, 1815) (CH2-840-5).
21. G D Henderson: 'The Divinity Chair of King's College' in *Aberdeen University Review*, vol. 25, pp 120-131 (1928).
22. D Brown: *Life of John Duncan LL.D.* (Edinburgh, 1872), p 49.

Chapter 13

*

The Strife of Tongues

THE harmony within the congregation, and especially in its committee, in respect of their defaulting treasurer, was not reflected in every area of its life and witness. Several matters of contention are reported in the minutes, disputes concerning the rights of seat-holders being especially notable, but with such absence of detail that it is usually impossible to determine the rights or wrongs of any particular case. Whereas the number affected by these wrangles was small, there was one controversial issue regarding which few, if any, were unaffected. That had to do with the language of worship. In the life of every Gaelic Chapel a time came when the introduction of an English service became a necessity if priority was to be given to the mission of the Church rather than the maintenance of the tradition. When, as in the cities, the language of the community was no longer Gaelic, the children inevitably grew up in ignorance of it. If families were to be retained within the fellowship, sooner or later English had to be introduced and, when the attempt was made, it was sure to be resisted by those who considered a sermon in a language other than Gaelic to be not worth 'a hearing'. Every Gaelic congregation on the mainland was confronted by this problem and in Aberdeen it was a matter of contention almost from the day that they opened their chapel.

English preaching

The issue was first officially discussed at a general meeting of the congregation held on 21st October 1796 when the Rev. John Mackenzie 'made the following proposals to the meeting, to wit, that he was willing to preach two Gaelic sermons every Sabbath day and an English lecture in the evening at the hour of six during the summer or winter – or to continue in his usual course of preaching. Immediately the meeting was desired to divide themselves in two parties, this being the method proposed in place of votes. A majority of nineteen was found on the Gaelic side which embraced the proposal of two Gaelic sermons and the English lecture'. What that minute fails to make clear is whether the minister's 'usual course of preaching' included an English sermon in which case there would have been as much English as Gaelic in 1796. But, whatever his practice had been, English was now to be given a secondary place. At the annual general meeting in 1797, 'both charge and discharge was read by which they understood that the house could not be supported without an English discourse wance a day'. The meeting paid tribute to John Mackenzie's willingness to carry the burden of three services each Sunday.

It was a burden that the Rev. James Macphail, who came to the chapel in September 1800, was unable, or unwilling, to carry. He dropped the evening English lecture and changed the afternoon Gaelic service to an English service. By March, a general meeting was called 'to consult about the form of worship as they had at present Gaelic in the forenoon and English in the afternoon which made their own people backward to the cause and very few of the town's inhabitants giving attendance, by which we was getting fewer in number and our collections getting lighter every Sabbath'. The meeting agreed that it would be preferable in the circumstances to have two Gaelic services and no English.

When Neil Kennedy took over the pastorate, the evening English lecture was resumed and the practice continued under Duncan Grant's ministry. But Grant was, in some respects, different from his predecessors. For one thing, he got more involved in the life of the Christian community in Aberdeen. He associated with the Bible Society collaborating with John Philip, minister of the George Street Congregational Church, who, in addition to being intellectually gifted, was greatly interested in foreign missions and left Aberdeen in 1818 to give 30 years of service to the South African stations of the London Missionary Society.[1] Grant also had contacts with the Methodist Church[2] and, within two years of his coming to Aberdeen, he gave the annual sermon for the benefit of the Society for the Relief of Aged and Indigent Women.[3] One consequence of his outgoing attitude was that the town's inhabitants were attracted to his preaching. In fact, at the time of evening lecture, which was in English, the chapel was crowded with Aberdeen people. Impressed by the interest shown in his English preaching, and perhaps seeing a comparatively poor attendance at the afternoon Gaelic service, Duncan Grant came round to the view that the afternoon diet of worship, which for the greater part of the year was a much more convenient time for worship, should be in English. Although it has been said that in arriving at this decision he was responding to the urging of the Aberdonians,[4] he also saw it as catering more effectively for the spiritual welfare of the families in the congregation.

The year 1817 was the year in which Duncan McGregor, clerk since 1806, died. At the annual general meeting, held on 30th April that year, he had been reappointed clerk and it would seem his health was not then in question. But that was the last minute inscribed by him. Perhaps his ill-health had something to do with the fact that the next meeting to be minuted was held six months later on 2nd October. Obviously another pen wrote this minute, and the next; and although John Macdonald, surveyor, acted as clerk *pro tem* until the next general meeting, it is possible that the minutes of October 1817 were drafted by Duncan Grant. The thrust of the meeting cannot be better conveyed than by quoting the minute of the managers' meeting and of the resultant congregational meeting.

> *Gaelic Chapel,*
> *Aberdeen October 27th 1817.*

> *At a meeting of the Session and committee of managers of this chapel called by public intimation from the pulpit and regularly constituted, the Rev. Duncan Grant mentioned that this meeting had been called at the request of the Session in order to deliberate on the manner in which the public administrations of the Lord's Day should be conducted in future. It was mentioned that many of the congregation had for several years expressed the strongest desire to have an English sermon preached here either on the forenoon or afternoon of every Sabbath day and that it was necessary to determine at this time whether this wish should be gratified or not. After the subject had been considered maturely, and discussed at considerable length, it appeared that all the members of Session present, with the exception of two, and all the members of committee, were of opinion that the spiritual and temporal interests of the congregation rendered it necessary to have English preached regularly every Lord's Day at either of the stated diets. Mr Grant was requested to mention this as the opinion of the Session and committee to the General Meeting that is to be held here tomorrow evening. This meeting are also of opinion that the English service should be in the afternoon of the Lord's Day. The meeting wish it to be understood that in the event of an English sermon being preached in the Gaelic chapel, the present occupiers of seats shall have a preference at the time of letting the seats and that the rules already formed for determining all matters of importance be strictly adhered to by all concerned.*

The minute was signed by John Macdonald, as was the one after that, which reads as follows:

> *Gaelic Chapel,*
> *Aberdeen 29th October 1817.*

> *A meeting of the Session, committee of management, Heads of Families and young men who have seats in the Chapel having been called by public intimation from the pulpit on Sabbath last, was held here this night. Mr. Grant after having regularly constituted the meeting informed those present*

that the object of the meeting was to decide whether public worship was to be conducted in future as formerly exclusively in the Gaelic language or partly in Gaelic and partly in English. After the subject had been discussed at some length and the advantages and disadvantages resulting from a change of this nature considered, it appeared to be expedient to determine the matter by the opinions and votes of the meeting. Those who wished to have English preached regularly once every Lord's Day were requested to stand up whilst those who wished to have no change were instructed to sit in their seats. When these instructions were followed, it was found that a very great majority voted for having the English language introduced. The persons who were for the continuance of the present system, did not form one third of the meeting. It was consequently decided that after the seats are let in November next, a sermon should be regularly preached in English in the afternoon of each Lord's Day in the chapel. It is to be understood, however, that the Rules in regard to the election of Ministers and the management of the chapel shall be strictly followed and that those who understand Gaelic shall have the preference at the letting of the seats.

Before John Macdonald signed this minute he added a postscript which reads:

The English to be continued as long as it shall be found beneficial for the Cause only, by order of the committee.

John Macdonald.

Duncan Grant had reason to be satisfied with the level of support he found for introducing English to the stated diets of worship. It had, he reckoned, the support of two-thirds of those who attended the meeting. The management committee were unanimously in favour of change and, in the Session, consisting of at least eight elders, it would seem that no more than two were opposed to change. He was probably satisfied with subsequent developments. Six months was a short time in which to look for an appreciable improvement but, at the general meeting next April, it was reported that the overall debt on the chapel was now at £281, down from a figure of £409 at the commencement of his ministry, and about £40 down on the figure twelve months ago; and that despite the fact that the treasurer had been incurring additional debt on his own behalf. Obviously there had been a considerable surplus of income over expenditure during the year.

In April 1818 the managers met in the week previous to the annual general meeting. There was only one item of business and it was duly minuted by John Macdonald:

Held a meeting of the committee of managers for the purpose of ascertaining whether they were of the same mind as they were regarding the continuation of the present system of worshipping when all agreed unanimously to continue the same at present. By order of the committee.

Gaelic rearguard

The annual meeting in 1818 fell on the first day of May. Traditionally the minister did not attend. Probably then, as now, annual meetings held little appeal for the ordinary worshipper. Only the activists would be present. This year, however, there seemed to be a better than usual attendance. After the accounts were presented and approved, the meeting proceeded to elect the managers, when it became evident that change was in the air. Of the twelve then in office, only five were re-elected. Angus Sutherland, slater, who had acted as preses for the past ten years and had been prominent since 1796, was now displaced as preses (although remaining a member of committee) by Alex Macdonald, merchant in East North Street. Although an elder since 1805, when he was ordained by Neil Kennedy along with Duncan McGregor, now deceased, and Ebenezer Murray, Alex Macdonald had not been a member of the management committee for the past seven years, and he had served only briefly before then. Now, as chairman of the meeting, he, according to the minute, 'proceeded to observe that he understood by the unusual fulness of the meeting, that there were some grievances which the meeting wished to be removed, which, as he, Mr Macdonald, understood, were occasioned by the late change from Gaelic to English in the afternoon of every Sabbath day'.

This introduction was probably intended as an invitation, or pre-arranged signal, to the discontented to express their mind, for the minute continues ... 'to which it was answered that it was by no means to hear the accounts read that they came up but to ascertain whether they were to have their old, valuable and much esteemed privilege, a Gaelic sermon preached at both the diets every Lord's Day as it was previous to the last six months'. After some debate, 'it was proposed that those who were for having Gaelic at both diets should retire out of the house, while those who were for having Gaelic and English should remain in their seats; and it was found by this division that only a few remained for the English'.

The English lobby now tried to sist proceedings, for 'it was proposed by a quorum of the managers' that a special meeting be called for the purpose of deciding the issue, a meeting at which 'the Rev. Duncan Grant would be requested to come up on their head as preses'. No formal decision was minuted regarding this proposal. Perhaps it was not opposed. At any rate, on 5th May, a meeting of the congregation consisting of the Heads of Families, subscribers and young men was held. The minister was present and, the meeting being constituted by prayer, the rules of the house were read. Then battle commenced. Who was to chair the meeting? The minister who had constituted it with prayer? Or Alex Macdonald, the preses appointed by the annual general meeting? Alex Macdonald made his position clear. 'He would not speak one word until the meeting should impower him for the same and shew their desire by giving their votes for whom they choised to act as preses for the night. Accordingly Mr. Alex Macdonald was chosen by a majority of the meeting to act as preses.' The chairman then spoke of the 'disagreeable effects' of the introduction of an English sermon, and, after some discussion, it was decided to take a vote by dividing the house. The chairman, disregarding any symbolic regional connection, commanded that 'those who were for having Gaelic altogether would go into the East end of the house, and those who were for having Gaelic and English would go into the West end of the house; then it was found that a great majority were for the Gaelic alone'.

English routed

Duncan Grant was not one to concede defeat if any prospect of victory, however faint, remained. Another general meeting took place on 13th May 'called by public intimation by the Rev. Duncan Grant their pastor who considered their last meeting illegal'. After constituting the meeting, 'Mr Grant proceeded to urge the necessity of having an English sermon once every Lord's Day and that he judged it needful both for the spiritual and temporal prosperity of the congregation'. The minute suggests that only the minister spoke on that side, whereas a number of the members spoke on the Gaelic side; after which 'our worthy friend and principal manager, Mr. John Ewen, delivered a very agreeable discourse on the points in dispute in which he signified his wish that the English should be continued if it was agreeable to the whole, let it be at whatever diet they saw meet, but urged nothing so much as peace and unanimity in all things'. He ended his peroration 'by declaring that he wished heartily the welfare of the congregation in all its affairs'.

The man who had guided the congregation's affairs since its formation 30 years previously had, in this situation at least, the instincts of a peacemaker. The meeting temporarily suspended hostilities to accord their principal manager a vote of thanks 'for his kind attention to the welfare of the congregation upon the present and former occasions'. That done, 'the Rev. Duncan Grant continued his arguments in favour of the English side but finding that he could not prevail, he proceeded to take the votes by calling a scroll prepared for the purpose beginning at No. 1'. The scroll carried the names of those who, according to the constitution, were entitled to vote in the election of a minister, *ie* elders, heads of families and unmarried men who were regular hearers and had had seats in the chapel for twelve months and understood the Gaelic language. When the votes were counted, it was found 'that a considerable majority voted for the Gaelic'. It is disappointing that, if a count was taken, the numbers were not recorded. In a separate statement on the controversy recorded in the Session book,[5] and possibly written by Duncan Grant, it is reported that 'it was resolved by a small majority of the voters that the Gaelic language should be again resumed in the afternoon. With this resolution Mr. Grant complied tho' he was disposed to think that the temporal and spiritual interests of the congregation would be promoted by having the service conducted once every Lord's Day in the English language'. Given the fact that non-Gaelic speakers were excluded from voting, it is evident that the congregation was fairly evenly divided in the matter.

The way of the aggressor

Grant's intentions certainly were good and had regard to the long-term welfare of the congregation. He was a far-sighted man and it must have been galling for him to see the light of the Gospel being arrested by the lengthening shadows of a Celtic twilight. Perhaps his impatience hindered the achievement of his objective and, on occasion, he may have lacked discretion. His youthfulness left him quite unabashed when confronted by those with more experience than himself. How others reacted to this self-confidence is apparent from an incident concerning Dr Kidd.[6] The two of them, while on a social visit to some mutual acquaintance, happened to get involved in a discussion of Jonathan Edwards' views on Divine sovereignty. They could not agree on a quotation from Edwards' work and, both men being remarkable for tenacious memories, neither would yield. When the company dispersed, Grant went home to bed while Kidd went home to research the works of Edwards. When he had found the disputed passage, phrased as he had recollected it, he strode along to Grant's house shouting, 'Is the Pope in?' The door being opened, Kidd placed the volume in his adversary's hands and, having extracted an admission of defeat, left him with the parting shot: 'Never again contradict a man so strenuously who is older than yourself.'

It is Kidd we have to thank for a glimpse of Alex Macdonald's temperament. On the occasion of a Sabbath communion evening, Kidd had gone along to the Gaelic Chapel. Although a large crowd had gathered waiting admission, the officials of the chapel were in no hurry to open the doors. Such a thoughtless and unwelcoming attitude incensed the Irishman who gave vent to his feelings in a manner that constituted a breach of the peace. The indignation of the chapel elders at this behaviour prompted them to send a deputation to Dr Kidd to express their displeasure. Reconciliation was soon achieved, but, as Dr Kidd later told Donald Sage,[7] their stern, pertinacious faces had made him uneasy for a moment. 'Of two of them,' he said, 'I had an instinctive terror. I was afraid of Alexander Murray's prayers, and equally so of Alexander Macdonald's fists.' This is an illuminating comment on Murray the elder who became church officer following the grave-digging stramash; and on Macdonald the elder who was voted preses at the height of the language controversy. Sage goes on to explain the reference to Alexander Macdonald's bellicosity:

> *The allusion evidently was to a pugilistic encounter of Macdonald's with a drunken nephew. 'Poor Saunders,' he used to say, 'was sorely tried; it was really too much for flesh and blood. There was a pitched battle between Saunder's Highland blood and Saunder's godliness, and the Highland blood won the day.'*

With Alexander 'Saunders' Macdonald as chairman of the management committee, Duncan Grant continued, as best he could in the circumstances, to minister to the spiritual needs of the congregation and the community. At the end of May 1818 the minute reports that 'a great number of the seats are still unlet'. The prospect of two Gaelic services doubtless discouraged those whose preference or requirement was for English and the Gaelic folk knew that there would be room enough for them without having to pay for a seat. At the end of November that year, the managers agreed to purchase black cloth with which to drape the pulpit as a mark of respect on the death of Queen Charlotte.

Duncan Grant's gifts

In May 1819 they had before them a letter from Mr Burnett, advocate, on behalf of the County Gentlemen of Aberdeenshire who were desirous of building in the vicinity of the Gaelic Chapel and wished to know if the managers were willing to sell their building. The meeting agreed to sell for £1100 while retaining all the materials of the chapel. Since the chapel had only cost £850, that seemed to be a fairly demanding price and negotiations went no further. It was later that month, on 31st May 1819, that Duncan Grant intimated his resignation to the managers, three weeks after he had received a presentation from the Earl of Moray to the Church and Parish of Alves. At the same time he told the committee 'that he was to leave the 10 patent lamps that he had planted in the chapel'. Obviously, to make the conditions at the evening English sermon more congenial, he had at his own expense furnished the chapel with oil lamps. Perhaps this was an expense which the managers had declined to incur, and in the aftermath of the embezzlement of their funds, resources would have been fully stretched. On the other hand, lighting supplied by people bringing their own candles often gave rise to unpleasant consequences.[8] In his concern for the spiritual welfare of his flock, Grant did not overlook their material comforts.

Donald Sage, in a typically acerbic comment on his predecessor in Aberdeen, remarked that Duncan Grant and his flock had quarrelled and the minister left in a huff, his parting sermon being 'one of the most perfect scolds I ever heard'.[9] He went on to suggest that Grant's irascibility was attributable in part to a stomach complaint; but Sage himself was not without symptoms of hyperacidity, and if Duncan Grant was as ill-disposed to his people when he left, as his successor implies, he had an unusual way of demonstrating it. The early tradition in the congregation seemed to be that the departing minister presented the congregation with a gift. Ronald Bayne, Kenneth Bayne, John Mackenzie and William Forbes were all credited with such a gesture. James Macphail, Neil Kennedy, and John Mackenzie in his second pastorate, were not so credited. Perhaps the latter two took their departure with so much borrowed money that they felt it was inappropriate to leave a gift. Now, Duncan Grant not only promised the committee that he would leave the chapel lamps, which would have been useful anywhere, but also undertook to give the congregation two silver communion cups. It was a benefaction that, to this day, was to perpetuate his memory in the congregation.

Duncan Grant went to Alves as successor to his uncle, the Rev. Wm Macbean, whose departure to Moy from the Little Kirk in Elgin in 1788 had had the effect of detaching Ronald Bayne from the superintendence of the Gaelic congregation in Aberdeen. Wm Macbean had been four years in Moy when, in 1792, he obtained the presentation to the Parish of Alves. From this vantage point in the courts of the Church, he secured his place in the Church's annals by being the opening speaker in the historic debate of 1796 which urged on the General Assembly the need to support Foreign Missions. Wm Macbean had himself a link with the promoters of the Aberdeen Gaelic Chapel in that his second wife, whom he married in 1810, was a daughter of the Aberdeen merchant Alex Leslie whose name was one of those attached to the first appeal for funds to support a Gaelic preacher in Aberdeen. Macbean died in 1818 and his nominated successor, one Walter Stuart, a probationer, also died — a week before his intended ordination fixed for 6th May 1819.

At the request of the parishioners, Duncan Grant was given the presentation by the Earl of Moray on 12th May 1819. He remained in Alves until 1827 when the same patron presented him with the Church and Parish of Forres. Remaining a bachelor throughout his life, he nevertheless had a wide circle of friends secured by his eminent abilities, genial manners and affectionate disposition.[10] It has been said of him that at the height of his power, he was a singularly devoted and active minister.[11] That could equally be true of his Aberdeen ministry. His strength lay in his pulpit work. Consequently he enjoyed great popularity as a preacher which was not without its difficulties for him. One stormy winter's day he was driving from Alves to preach in Burghead where he intended to repeat a sermon which he had already given that day in Alves. However, on the way he caught up with an elder who, having had the benefit of the earlier diet, was obviously making his way to Burghead for another one. Somewhat irritated by the circumstance which he felt now required him to take a different theme, Grant said to the parishioner, 'John, I should have thought one sermon would serve you on a cold day like this'; to which he got the reply, ''Deed Mr. Grant, I need as good a diet of meat on a cold day as on a warm one'.[12]

Duncan Grant's gifts extended to giving special addresses to children, which apparently he did in Aberdeen under Dr Kidd's tutelage, and to writing poetry. The death of his mother prompted the following lines, illustrative of his talent in that direction:

> *To train our minds, in early youth,*
> *To heavenly wisdom, virtue, truth,*
> *Was still your chief pursuit;*
> *And then to teach our feet to climb*
> *The hill, where learning's fane sublime*
> *Presents the richest spoils of time*
> *And knowledge yields her fruit.*

Needless to say, he took a prominent part in the Disruption controversy and became minister of Forres Free Church in 1843. He died there on 17th March 1866, his funeral being attended by an immense gathering of people. The following Sunday the preacher at the memorial service was Dr Kennedy of Dingwall. His sermon, reported *in extenso* in the local paper,[13] well illustrates Dr Kennedy's gifts as a preacher and was a fitting valediction to the life of one who was probably the most impressive preacher on the register of the pastors of the Highland Congregation in Aberdeen.

Hugh Miller, the future editor of *The Witness*, sat under Duncan Grant's preaching while on a visit to Forres in 1833. Returning to Cromarty he wrote to his hostess, 'I trust you have tendered my best thanks to Mr. Grant for his elegant and truly excellent discourse. He carried me with him from beginning to end. I felt all he wished me to feel, and saw all he intended I should see'.[14] A finer tribute could not be paid to the pulpit from the pew.

Notes to Chapter 13

1. J Bulloch: *Centenary memorials of the first Congregational church in Aberdeen* (Aberdeen, 1898), pp 53-63. See also Andrew Ross: *John Philip (1775-1851)* (Aberdeen, 1986).
2. D Brown: *Memoir of the life of Dr John Duncan* (London, 1872), p 94.
3. This sermon entitled 'The claims of the afflicted on the compassion of friends' was preached in the West Church of Aberdeen and published in 1816. Grant's text is from Job 19:21: 'Have pity upon me, O ye my friends; for the hand of God hath touched me.' It can be consulted in the Thomson collection in King's College Library, Aberdeen (T169). Other sermons by Duncan Grant are also to be found in this collection.
4. D Sage: *Memorabilia Domestica* (Wick, 1889; 2nd edition 1899; reprinted 1975), p 221, footnote. This footnote, added by Donald Sage's son, states that a dispute on the language question was appealed to the Presbytery who ruled in favour of Gaelic. There is, however, no mention in the Presbytery records of any discussion of a dispute over Gaelic or any other matter in the congregation.
5. This minute book is, in fact, a continuation of the pages of *The origin of the Gaelic congregation in Aberdeen,* and gives information on ministerial changes, ordination of elders and admission of communicants.
6. J Stark: *Dr Kidd of Aberdeen* (Aberdeen, 3rd edition, 1898), pp 265-266.
7. D Sage: op. cit. p 232.
8. R M Smith: *The history of Greenock* (Greenock, 1921), p 276.
9. D Sage: op. cit., pp 220-221.
10. Obituary notice in *The Free Church of Scotland Monthly Record* (May 1866, p 18).
11. *Fasti Ecclesiae Scoticanae* (1926), vol. 6, p 423.
12. This incident is recounted in R Cowan (ed.): *Our church fathers* (Elgin, 1899), chapter 9 being an account of D Grant (pp 73-81, W Winter).
13. *Forres, Elgin and Nairn Gazette* (28th March, 1866).
14. P Bayne: *Life and letters of Hugh Miller* (London, 1871), vol. 1, p 343.

Chapter 14

*

MEMORABILIA ABERDONENSIS

WHEN Duncan Grant, on the last day of May 1819, intimated his resignation to the managers of the Gaelic Chapel, they already had a clear plan of campaign before them. 'They agreed to send a letter to the Rev. Donald Sage, Preacher of the Gospel, Kildonan, to come and preach in the chapel as a candidate for three several Sabbaths and they appointed Mr. Grant to write to Mr. Sage the next day to that effect.' The description of Donald Sage as Preacher of the Gospel, Kildonan, reveals that the committee were well-informed as to his situation. The designation referred to his location, not his office. His father, the Rev. Alex Sage, was parish minister of Kildonan. Donald, born in 1789 and a graduate of Marischal College, had been appointed Royal Bounty preacher at Achness and Ach-na-h'uaighe in May 1815 and remained as such until May 1819 when the Royal Bounty committee extinguished the charge consequent to the Strathnaver Clearances of April and May that year.[1] In anticipation of this development, he had vacated his Achness manse in the previous November and had gone to his father's manse at Kildonan. His suitability for the Gaelic Chapel had been urged by Robert Sutherland, a plasterer from Loth in Sutherland, one of the new faces elected to the committee in 1818 and the one who had taken over the treasurership when George Sutherland absconded in July of that year. According to Donald Sage, Robert Sutherland, on a visit north to be married to a daughter of the Kildonan SSPCK schoolmaster, had been 'expressly deputed by the congregation at Aberdeen to make enquiries after me in the prospect of a vacancy occurring, by the appointment of their minister, Mr. Duncan Grant, to the Parish of Alves'.

The invitation to preach as a candidate in Aberdeen was received by Sage at a time made inconvenient by his sister's wedding and his stepmother's terminal illness. Nevertheless he set off. Arriving in Aberdeen on Saturday 26th June 1819, he was met at the coaching inn on Union Street by Robert Sutherland and some other committee members. The following day Duncan Grant preached his farewell sermon in the morning. Sage took the afternoon and evening services, his sermons being listened to, according to his own account, by 'most attentive audiences. During the course of the week my election and call as minister were harmoniously entered into by the congregation'. However, the committee minutes reveal that he preached, as was intended, for three Sundays before the, undoubtedly harmonious, election took place on Tuesday 13th July. By this time he was already on his way back to Inverness if, as he claimed, he travelled on the inaugural stagecoach run to Thurso. By the end of July he was back in Aberdeen and on 1st August he performed his first official duties as minister.

To begin with he stayed in lodgings in Virginia Street before moving, in November, to his own house at Braehead of Gilcomston. A description of some of his experiences while in Aberdeen, is given in *Memorabilia Domestica,* an autobiographical account of his life and times which he commenced to write in 1840. This work was not published until 1889, 20 years after his death, and, it has been suggested, that the reason for the delay was that some of the remarks which he made about his contemporaries were too pungent to print when the near relatives of those pilloried were still alive. Sadly the published account is an abbreviated version, his son, who edited it, having conceived it necessary 'to eliminate repetitious and irrelevant matter and, here and there, to condense the narrative'. In fulfilment of this filial act of wanton redaction, thumbnail sketches of prominent people in the Aberdeen Gaelic Chapel were consigned to the flames. In a volume entitled *Disruption Worthies of the Highlands,* published in 1877, or twelve years before *Memorabilia Domestica,* Dr John Kennedy of Dingwall wrote the article on Donald Sage. In this article he makes frequent reference to Sage's *Memorabilia* and quotes several paragraphs from it. Clearly he had the manuscript before him; and none of it would he have found more fascinating than the account of the Aberdeen congregation, which Kennedy himself knew well from his student days. Of this period, Kennedy writes:[2]

> *In 1819 he went to Aberdeen, and was minister of the Gaelic chapel there for two years and nine months. In his* Memorabilia *he gives the history of that congregation, from its first formation by Dr Bayne to the date of his own settlement; a description of the most remarkable of his hearers; an account of his mode of conducting his work; and his estimate of each of the ministers and leading men in the granite city during the time of his residence there. Most graphic are his descriptions of the religion, morals, language, and habits of the Aberdonians; and the portraits he draws are, at any rate, not deficient in strength. His* Memorabilia *of Aberdeen would form a very interesting volume.*

Excerpts of all that is referred to in that paragraph, can be found in the published volume with the exception of 'a description of the most remarkable of his hearers'. Sage's portrait gallery of any, even the least remarkable, of his hearers in Aberdeen, would have made an invaluable contribution to the history of the Aberdeen Gaelic Chapel.

A constitution for the Chapel

His ministry commenced in August 1819, but Sage was not formally inducted into his charge until 1st February, 1821. The reason for the long delay was that the status of the chapel had come under the review of the Presbytery. Perhaps the Assembly of 1818 had drawn attention to the fact that there existed in Aberdeen a chapel that was not officially recognised by the Church. At any rate, at the meeting of Presbytery on 22nd June 1819, at which Duncan Grant tendered his resignation, the Presbytery, 'entertaining doubts respecting the footing upon which the Gaelic Chapel stands', appointed a committee to investigate.[3] John Ewen, Alex Macdonald and Gilchrist Sutherland appeared before this committee as the congregation's representatives. Following a historical review which revealed that the congregation had 'grown up from small beginnings without any formal sanction by the church', the Presbytery agreed that it was entitled to 'the countenance and protection of the church and should receive a regular constitution'.[4] Meanwhile, Donald Sage was sanctioned to officiate in the chapel until the following Assembly.

The constitution that was drawn up by the Presbytery was broadly acceptable to the committee. Representations were made to the effect that the managers 'judged it inconvenient to have more stated collections than what they already have' – a reference to collections for charitable purposes appointed by the General Kirk Session or other courts – and at the same time they wanted more flexibility as regards the payment of communion expenses, obviously regarding the normal £10 per annum as insufficient in the context of a Highland congregation. On the whole the constitution left them little different in respect of the liberties they had previously enjoyed. They were inhibited of course from appointing any new elders and the election of managers was to take place quinquennially instead of annually. The position of Gaelic was safeguarded as determined by the majority vote in 1818.

The constitution was approved by the General Assembly of 1820. Donald Sage was not qualified to be a member of Assembly, but it would seem from the comprehensive account which he gave of the proceedings of that Assembly, that he had judged it expedient to attend.[5] The Gaelic Chapel having become a fully sanctioned chapel-of-ease, the Presbytery, with what it claimed to be all convenient speed, arranged for the induction of Donald Sage to take place on 1st February 1821, when the Rev. Robert Doig of the second charge of St Nicholas preached 'an excellent and appropriate discourse' from Malachi 2: 7 ('a priest … is the messenger of the Lord').

In the interim the work of the pastorate had of course been carried on under the superintendence of Donald Sage, and the committee found themselves dealing with the usual transactions. Sage commenced his ministry by asking for his salary quarterly in advance and, to meet this demand, a further loan was obtained from John Macdonald, tailor in Queen Street. At the same meeting the committee agreed that the chapel lamps would be lit during the winter evenings and Donald Bain, the church officer, was told to apply to Mr Rettie for oil. Donald Sage invited his first cousin, the Rev. Donald Fraser, minister of Kirkhill, to assist at the September communion both in 1819 and 1820. This preacher had a richly deserved reputation for being a gifted divine who was exceptionally fastidious about his personal appearance.[6] He was one of four ministers (James MacPhail a former minister of the Gaelic Chapel, was another) of the Presbytery of Inverness rebuked at the bar of the Assembly in 1824 for refusing to attend the Kiltarlity induction. In 1836 he was to achieve the further and more unfortunate distinction of being one of the first road casualties in the Highlands. He was killed in an accident involving his gig.

Communion vessels for the Chapel

The first opportunity to use the communion cups presented to the congregation by Duncan Grant occurred in September 1819. At their meeting on 26th June, the committee had asked John Macdonald, their preses (Alex Macdonald having held the office for only one year), to write a letter of thanks to Mr Grant for the communion cups which he had presented to the congregation as 'a token of his affectionate regard for them'. The cups are the work of an Aberdeen silversmith, Wm Jamieson whose name is retained in the firm of Jamieson & Carry, Union Street, Aberdeen. The vessels are beaker-shaped, a form traditional to the north-east of Scotland,[7] and have engraved on them the inscription:

To
The Gaelic Chapel
From
THE REV. DUNCAN GRANT
1819

The experience of using these silver beaker-shaped cups alongside pewter goblet-shaped vessels must have persuaded the committee that they should obtain another two matching cups. This purchase was agreed to at a meeting on 4th February 1820. Unaccountably the work was given to a London firm of silversmiths. Their reproductions are so perfectly matched that one of Wm Jamieson's vessels must have been loaned as a pattern. Apart from the inscriptions, the vessels, in all other respects including weight (410 grams), are identical; but Duncan Grant's vessels, being the work of an Aberdeen silversmith, are rarer and more valuable. On the London vessels the inscription reads:

Gaelic Chapel
ABERDEEN
1820

In the manuscript entitled *The origin of the Gaelic congregation in Aberdeen,* the entry dealing with Duncan Grant's ministry concludes: 'Mr Grant presented the congregation when leaving them with a set of ten patent lamps value £10 10s. and with two silver communion cups value £14'. This entry may, or may not, have been written by Duncan Grant; but whoever wrote it, did not, in the opinion of another (and the handwriting points to that other as being Donald Sage), tell the whole story. For following on from 'cups value £14' there is a later insertion adding 'which was in fact paid by the money collected at the church doors during the evening lectures'. Someone did not want posterity to give more credit to Duncan Grant than was his due.

Other pastures beckon

When Donald Sage came to Aberdeen as Gaelic Chapel minister he was back in familiar surroundings. Having been a student at Marischal College from 1804-1810, he knew the city, and also the congregation, one in which he had enjoyed the hospitality of the minister, the Rev. Neil Kennedy, and probably that of other homes as well.[8] But he was never very settled as minister in Aberdeen. Had he not been unemployed, it is unlikely that he would have come at all. But having come to Aberdeen, he did not have long to wait before he received other approaches. These, however, lacked that most desirable feature, parish status, which earlier interest suggested might come his way sooner rather than later. In 1816, when the minister of Golspie died, the parishioners got up a petition in his favour, but it met with a flat refusal at the hands of the patron, Lady Stafford.[9] Again when Dornoch, that same year, became vacant on the death of John Bethune, the parishioners petitioned in favour of Donald Sage, but Lady Stafford, taking the attitude that 'he had so many patrons among the people as not to stand in need of any provision which she had in her power to extend to him', appointed his cousin Angus Kennedy instead.[10]

In 1821 Sage received a call to the Gaelic Chapel in Rothesay which he says was so advantageous that the wonder was that he could have declined it.[11] That charge certainly had a succession of notable preachers, among them Robertson of Kingussie, Flyter of Alness,

Stewart of Cromarty, and McBride of Rothesay. Perhaps at the time he had in view Kiltarlity, where Ronald Bayne had just died in January of that year; or Greenock Gaelic Chapel where Kenneth Bayne died in April. He did in fact go to preach in Greenock as a candidate, although afterwards he protested that it was because he did not 'precisely understand the general regulations by which chapels-of-ease were guided particularly during vacancies'.[12] It seems, however, that he withdrew his name from consideration only when he sensed that things were not going his way. Later in his reminiscences he conceded that, having preached as a candidate for Kenneth Bayne's pulpit, he was followed by Angus Macbean, Hugh Calder's assistant at Croy. 'In the choice of a minister which followed, Mr. Macbean was chosen. But there was a minority for myself so dissatisfied with the choice of the majority that they resolved to withdraw.' On his recommendation this minority eventually called his friend Nathaniel Morren as their minister.[13]

In the summer of 1821, Sage was walking up the Gallowgate in Aberdeen when he met a member of his congregation who informed him that he had recently been home visiting his relations in the Black Isle where he had learned that the parishioners of Resolis were desirous of having him as their minister. Sage knew that Resolis was a parish in which the patron deferred to the wishes of the people, and, as he left the Gallowgate, he was gripped with a sudden sense of destiny. 'The intelligence, however undecisive, took a stronger hold of my mind than I had anticipated. Could it be true?'[14] He very much hoped that it could be and his suspense was short-lived. By 14th August, two years after his ministry commenced in Aberdeen, he had signed his acceptance of the presentation to Resolis. It was not an issue on which he had to wrestle for divine guidance; sufficient light was to be found in the facts of the situation. Altogether it was an eventful time for him as his marriage to Harriet Robertson of Pitstrunie and of Tanfield House, Woodside took place in Aberdeen on 21st July 1821. Although he had closed with the call to Resolis in August 1821, it was not until May 1822 that he was inducted there and through the winter he continued to officiate from time to time in the Gaelic Chapel.

The life of the congregation continued along the usual lines. Macdonald of Ferintosh officiated at the April communion in 1822 as he had done every year since 1817. To the September communion in 1821, instead of his cousin from Kirkhill, whom he had invited to the previous autumn celebrations, Donald Sage now asked the minister of the Edinburgh Gaelic Chapel, John Munro, who in 1808 had declined to be a candidate for the Aberdeen congregation, and who in fact was the alternative candidate for the Resolis vacancy when the parishioners elected Sage. It is likely of course that the arrangement for John Munro to officiate at the Aberdeen sacrament, had been made long before the

Resolis election. He was an old and valued friend, one who, having witnessed an early and disastrously inept preaching performance by Sage, had comforted him in his distress and had encouraged him not to abandon his aspirations to be a preacher of the Gospel.[15]

John Ewen's passing

A notable, if sorrowful, event that occurred on 21st October 1821 was the passing, at the age of 75, of the worthy principal manager, John Ewen. It is to be hoped that more notice was taken of his decease than appears in the minutes, for nowhere is his death remarked on in the congregation's records. Yet over a period of 35 years, he attended every significant meeting of the congregation, corresponded with all its ministers, and represented it at any meeting of church or municipal authorities when the need arose. Only three years earlier he had given a lecture on the history of the congregation and, at the request of the committee, engrossed its substance in the minute book. In retrospect it is almost as if his passing was the harbinger of departing glory. The tide which, since the formation of the congregation, had been flowing strongly in its favour, had now reached its flood and was about to ebb. Highlights there would be still, when Macdonald of Ferintosh and similarly gifted preachers came on special occasions. But they would be as rays of the setting sun, piercing the lengthening shadows. The day of small things was fast approaching.

The Sage of Gaelic Lane

For pulpit eloquence and preaching elegance, Donald Sage could not compete with Duncan Grant. But he exercised a thoroughly satisfactory ministry; and if he had less appeal for the Aberdonians than Grant had, he may well have had more appeal for the Highlanders. Congregations were large and probably reached their peak in his time. In December 1819 the managers had to seek advice 'whether it would be convenient to have boards in the passes [aisles] on purpose to be used when the house would be crowded'. Unquestionably Donald Sage had mental endowments of a high order. According to his obituarist his gifts were assiduously cultivated by habits of energetic research.[16] The same source credits him with polishing his sermons with careful emendation and as 'having a taste for accomplished composition', a feature which of course is evident from his *Memorabilia*. But he was also a spiritually-minded man, perhaps more so after he left Aberdeen and had passed through the furnace of affliction in the early death in childbirth of his beloved Harriet. Sage's talent for conveying an unforgettable picture, and the feelings of those caught up in it, is displayed most vividly and movingly in his descriptions of scenes such as his mother's death, the parting of his congregation following the clearances in Strathnaver, and the inconsolable grief which he experienced following Harriet's death.

As a minister he had another valuable asset in that he was a most efficient administrator. In his *Memorabilia* he refers to the chaotic condition in which he found the records of the Parish of Resolis and how he set about rectifying the situation. In this respect also, he had served his apprenticeship in Aberdeen. He left behind him the first and only complete baptismal roll of any pastorate in the Gaelic Chapel. In the two years and eight months of his ministry, he baptised 78 children – 42 boys, 34 girls and two unspecified – for all of whom he left details of parentage. He was even more thorough with the communion roll. When the chapel was erected in 1795, John Mackenzie drew up a list of hearers consisting of 330 persons. No other record was extant when Sage commenced his pastorate. On 20th September 1820 the Session 'took into their consideration a proposal for enrolling the names of all those who have been admitted as communicants in this chapel. They unanimously approved of it and appointed that all the communicants of this congregation should meet in the chapel and give in their names, place of abode, and the minister's name by whom, and the Parishes where, they were admitted'. Sage himself, in his neat and highly legible handwriting, drew up the roll which he found to consist of 204 communicants. Having done the same exercise in Resolis, he found 'the roll of communicants for 1823 amounted to only forty-seven; it received no further additions until the year 1826 when eight more were associated'.

The last of the fathers

One is left with the feeling that in the Gaelic Chapel in Aberdeen, Donald Sage had a far more influential ministry to a mixed congregation of artisans, merchants and students. He himself remarked that the peculiarity of Ross-shire was that 'while in other parts of the country true religion was to be found among the middle classes, in Ross-shire it was almost entirely confined to the peasantry'.[17] Sage's gifts, on the other hand, seemed more suited to an educated congregation which the Gaelic Chapel was showing signs of becoming. And he did not leave Aberdeen because he had fallen out with his congregation. 'I had abundant proof of their attachment to me, especially from such of them who truly feared God. There were but few of these comparatively; in going to Ross-shire, certainly, true Christian intercourse would be very much increased'. Was that then the reason for his going to Ross-shire? If so, it scarcely called for a very exalted sense of duty. Financially he would have been better off in Resolis, but perhaps not decisively so;

and instead of finding the managers willing to put the congregation into debt so that he could be paid quarterly in advance, he found that 'I did not receive a farthing of my stipend without a grudge or even without the curse of my heritors along with it. The delays they ever made in paying at the term ... and the disputes into which they led me to enforce payment were calculated to deprive me of procuring the most ordinary necessaries of life'.[18] Yet even had he anticipated that he would encounter such difficulties at the hands of the heritors, it would not have deterred him from accepting the presentation. Ministerial prospects, to use his own phrase, were always to be assessed in terms of the parish ministry. To have the status of a parish minister was an emblem of ecclesiastical authority, and to have that emblem in the Black Isle, was to have it where it mattered most. In the days of the fathers, the Black Isle was 'the Garden of the Lord'. Ferintosh had its Macdonald, Cromarty had its Stewart, Killearnan had its Kennedy, and Resolis was to have its Sage. There he went in 1822; there he ministered in word and ordinance for 47 years; and there, in 1869 in his 80th year, he died, the last of the Fathers in Ross-shire.

Notes to Chapter 14

1. D Sage, *Memorabilia Domestica* (Wick, 1889; 2nd edition, 1899, reprinted 1975), p 218.
2. J Graham (ed.): *Disruption worthies of the Highlands* (Edinburgh, 1877), p 48.
3. *Records of the Presbytery of Aberdeen,* vol. 10, p. 285 (22nd June, 1819) (CH2-1-12).
4. Ibid., vol. 10, pp 287-290 (28th July, 1819).
5. D Sage: op. cit., pp 239-253.
6. J Kennedy: *The apostle of the North* (Edinburgh, 1866; new edition, Inverness, 1932), pp 224-225.
7. T Burns: *Old Scottish communion plate* (Edinburgh, 1892).
8. D Sage: op. cit., p 172.
9. Ibid., p 206.
10. Ibid., p 213
11. Ibid., p 254.
12. Ibid., p 255.
13. Ibid., p 270.
14. Ibid., p 257.
15. Ibid., p 191.
16. *The Free Church of Scotland Monthly Record* (June, 1869), pp 137-138.
17. D Sage: op. cit., p 262.
18. Ibid., p 326.

Chapter 15

*

Misfits and Misdeeds

DONALD Sage's resignation was accepted by Aberdeen Presbytery on 5th December 1821 but, as his departure was to be deferred until April, the Presbytery agreed that he should continue to officiate as long as convenient. It was also noted by the Presbytery that Mr Duncan MacCaig, Lismore, would be giving supply.[1] The new constitution required the managers to present a list of three candidates to the Presbytery, and the lawyer, Mr Alex Webster, who represented the managers at the Presbytery, reported to the committee on 11th December that their list had to be submitted by 20th December. The managers could not have anticipated this need for, on 11th December, 'judging that they had not information enough they agreed to postpone the giving in of their list till the 19th curt'. On the appointed day they submitted 'without a dissenting voice' the names of Duncan MacCaig, Lismore; Angus Macmillan, Strathfillan; and Robert Clark, Tongue. It may be assumed that the order was deliberate.

Duncan MacCaig cedes Uig to Alex Macleod

The circumstance that Donald Sage's continuance *pro tem* was bracketed with Duncan MacCaig's officiating in the vacancy, together with the obvious unpreparedness of the managers to offer additional suggestions, points to Duncan MacCaig as being the anticipated appointment. But events turned out otherwise and Robert Clark was inducted. The minutes cast no light on the reason for his selection. Following the minute of 19th December, at which a list of candidates was agreed, there is no further reference to the vacancy, not even to Robert Clark's election, presumably because the appointment was now more firmly in the hands of the Presbytery. Consequently it is impossible to say whether it was the congregation or, as seems more likely, Duncan MacCaig who withdrew interest.

After a promising start to his career, the subsequent history of the licenciate from Lismore was sadly inglorious. He served briefly as missionary at Fort William until he was nominated by the SSPCK to the Edinburgh Gaelic Chapel which was vacant at the same time as the Aberdeen Chapel. He commenced his ministry in Edinburgh in April 1823 and only two months later he was offered the Parish of Uig in

Lewis.[2] With a sublime disregard for convention and an indifference to ministerial prospects that bordered on the eccentric, he declined the presentation. His decision had momentous consequences for the history of the Church in Lewis, for the presentation was then offered to Alexander Macleod, the first evangelical minister to be appointed to the Long Island. It is interesting that this Alex Macleod, born in Stoer in 1786, was one of those who had been influenced by Norman Macleod of Assynt during the time that John Kennedy was minister there. When Alex Macleod applied to the Presbytery of Tongue for licensing in 1818, he had explicitly to disavow any 'tint of Normanism'.[3] After brief pastorates in Dundee Gaelic Chapel and Cromarty Gaelic Chapel, he was given the presentation to Uig and shortly after he went there a remarkable revival began under his preaching, eventually spreading from Uig to the rest of the island. The islanders, previously distinguished for their godlessness, now became noted for their piety.[4]

Hugh Miller's strictures on Duncan MacCaig

Whatever attraction Edinburgh had for Duncan MacCaig, he remained there until 1831 when, following a trial in the High Court, he was convicted of theft and sentenced to transportation to Van Diemen's Land for 14 years. Inevitably his conviction led to his being deposed from the ministry 'for stealing books and contumacy'. In Van Diemen's Land, from which he never returned, he became a teacher, but the last report of him portrayed him 'as in a state of complete destitution'.[5] The same source suggests that insanity was the cause of his offences, but there is other evidence indicative of a fundamental lack of integrity. For example, Hugh Miller recounts the case of his own cousin, George Munro, who, whatever other attainments he may have lacked, had a very good grasp of Gaelic. In 1829, anxious to improve his situation in life, he applied for an appointment with the Edinburgh Gaelic School Society which supported teachers in needy Highland areas. He was called to Edinburgh for interview and language test, but George Munro's dress was not conducive to his success for 'instead of bringing with him his ordinary Sabbath-day suit of dark brown and blue, he had provided himself with a suit of tartan and appeared before the committee apparently as well suited to enact the part of colour-serjeant to the Forty-Second, as to teach children their letters'.[6]

The Secretary of the Society, the Rev. Walter Tait, a devout but naïve Evangelical who, as minister of Trinity College Church in Edinburgh, was himself deposed in 1834 for a reference to the doctrines of the Irvingite sect, concluded from the interview that a man 'encased in tartan' was deficient both in taste and grace. But since it could scarcely be alleged with any show of decency that George Munro was inadmissible on the basis of his partiality for tartan, it became necessary to fail him on the paucity of his Gaelic. Duncan MacCaig was the Society's chief examiner and, in the words of Hugh Miller, 'not being a remarkably scrupulous man, he seems to have stretched a point or two, in compliance with the pious wishes and occult judgment of the Society's Secretary'. From this it would appear that his conduct was not always consistent with his profession.

The Eriboll training ground

It was Robert Clark, the last named on the list submitted to the Presbytery, who became successor to Donald Sage in Aberdeen. Like the latter he was a native of Sutherland, but, although five years older, he was later in going to University. He graduated from King's College in 1814 and, in keeping with the usual practice of those aspiring to the ministry, he became a schoolmaster and taught in Eddrachillis and Tongue. Although described in the minutes as Robert Clark, Tongue, it was as a missionary in Eriboll that he came as a candidate to the Aberdeen Gaelic Chapel.

John Kennedy had chosen Eriboll in preference to Aberdeen in 1802, but in later years the mission had fallen on hard times. When Kennedy left Eriboll in 1807 to be assistant to 'Parson William' in Assynt, three letters were addressed to the SSPCK concerning a successor.[7] One was from 'Mr Tait, doer for Lord Reay', informing the committee that 'the gentlemen and inhabitants are determined to add something handsome to the living of the person to be appointed, if he is one to their mind'. He omitted to say who such an one might be. The second letter was from John Kennedy himself, recommending Mr Wm Findlater as his successor. The third was from the Rev. Wm Mackenzie, minister of the Parish of Tongue, asking that his son, the Rev. Hugh Mackay Mackenzie, who some months earlier had been appointed his assistant and successor in the Parish of Tongue, might be given the appointment at least for such time as 'he, Mr. Wm. Mackenzie, does not stand in need of his son's assistance'. The advantage from the Mackenzies' standpoint was that whereas the Tongue parish stipend was being shared by father and son, if the son were given Eriboll this would increase their joint income, perhaps substantially, if 'something handsome' were to be added to the living. The father, who was then aged 70 and lived on to the age of 96, had been in ill-health when his son was appointed as his assistant; but as the son's health was if anything worse than the father's, the father found himself getting little benefit from having an assistant.[8] However this arrangement, advantageous as it was for its proposer, did not find favour with the SSPCK and Wm Findlater was appointed.

Although the Society directors took the precaution of making 'enquiry at Lord Reay's doer and others interested in the mission' whether Mr. Findlater would be acceptable,[9] there is no evidence that the promised 'handsome' support ever materialised. Wm Findlater remained in Eriboll until 1812 when he was presented with Durness, the parish in which the Eriboll mission was located. After 1812 it seems that no further appointment was made to Eriboll until 1816 when the Presbytery petitioned the SSPCK to re-establish the mission.[10] This they did, appointing as missionary the Rev. Hugh Mackenzie. This arrangement has the appearance of being another self-help scheme devised in the Tongue manse, for the appointee was not only a nephew of the minister of Tongue but also a son-in-law, having married his first cousin Helen, a daughter of the Tongue manse. Appointed to Eriboll in November 1816, Hugh Mackenzie a year later was given the Parish of Assynt, his admission there being free from the rioting that accompanied the induction of his predecessor, Duncan MacGillivray. While he was minister in Assynt, Hugh Mackenzie succeeded both in qualifying as a doctor of medicine in King's College, Aberdeen and in obtaining his membership of the Royal College of Surgeons in Edinburgh. His last charge was the historic Parish of Killin in Perthshire where, sadly, he died prematurely, aged 47, another victim of a gig accident en route from Taymouth Castle to his manse at Killin.[11]

The fact that Dr Hugh Mackenzie, during his brief tenure of Eriboll, was able to reside with his in-laws in the Tongue manse was a considerable convenience to the SSPCK, for the Eriboll missionary accommodation had become ruinous. When the charge again became vacant the minister of Tongue wrote to the SSPCK recommending the Tongue schoolmaster, Robert Clark, for the appointment. The Society were agreeable to the suggestion, but as the minister of Durness, in whose parish the mission was located, pointed out that the accommodation was in need of repair, his appointment was deferred for a time.[12] Eventually ordained to the charge in November 1819, Robert Clark was, nevertheless, refused admission to the mission house by the Tacksman of Eriboll. Following further representations, the Tacksman, in July 1820, promised access in May 1821.[13] Being a victim of such circumstances may give significance to the designation accorded to Robert Clark by the Presbytery of Aberdeen as 'itinerant minister of the mission of Eriboll'.

Robert Clark in Aberdeen and Glasgow

Clark was inducted to the Gaelic Chapel on 20th June 1822 with Dr Mearns preaching 'an appropriate and excellent discourse' from Proverbs 23: 18 – 'Surely there is an end; and thine expectation shall not be cut off.'[14] Unlike most of his predecessors, Robert Clark made no demands on his managers and no areas of disagreement appear in the minutes. Perhaps there was not time for disputes to surface. His pastorate, which lasted a mere nine months, was the shortest of any in the annals of the Gaelic Chapel. But in the course of it there were the hoped-for additions to the communion roll suggesting that in the course of this ministry, as in others, there were those who had been born again to a living hope and a steadfast walk.

In April 1823, Clark left Aberdeen to go to Duke Street Gaelic Chapel, Glasgow, made vacant by the translation of the Rev. David Carment to the Parish of Rosskeen. He remained there for eleven years. By 1831, if not sooner, his congregation was longing for a new voice. In the words of a contemporary, Robert Clark was 'in feeble health' and his pulpit ministrations were not 'quite suited to the strong appetite of his thoughtful Highlanders'.[15] Some of his elders suggested that an assistant be employed to give Sunday afternoon lectures, the expense being met by the congregation. As often happens when such a suggestion is made, they already had a man in view. In this case the nominee was John 'Rabbi' Duncan who, shortly before, had been a candidate for Anderston Chapel, made vacant by the death of Dr John Love. To the disappointment of his sponsors in Anderston Chapel, 'Rabbi' Duncan had been passed over in favour of a fellow Aberdonian, Charles Brown, but this new attempt to bring him to Glasgow was more successful, the minister of Duke Street Chapel offering no objection to the proposed assistantship. Whether the recruitment made much difference to the cause there is unclear. One of 'Rabbi' Duncan's biographers says that he was not popular in Duke Street.[16]

Robert Clark returns to Sutherland

In 1834 Robert Clark returned to his native Sutherland as minister of the *quoad sacra* Parish of Kinlochbervie. Although it was said of him that before the Disruption he professed great zeal for the non-intrusion cause, he chose to remain in the Established Church in 1843. In that part of Scotland his would have been a very unpopular decision. As it happened, in the Presbytery of Tongue, all the ministers of the *quoad civilia* Parishes (Durness, Eddrachillis, Farr, and Tongue) left the Established Church, while the ministers of the lower status *quoad sacra* charges of Kinlochbervie and Strathy remained in. Consequently Robert Clark was censured by the Evangelical Party as one who turned back in the day of battle.[17]

Perhaps he was a lonely man. He remained unmarried and, given the extent of inter-marriage between manse families in Northern Scotland, he may have felt a degree of isolation. In any case he was a man of independent mind, able to think for himself and not given to slavish adherence to the tradition. He could also express himself effectively – at least with his pen. In a letter to the Edinburgh Gaelic Schools Society he refers to the benefits which had accrued from the availability of the printed Gaelic Bible and from the recently acquired ability of the people to read it. His comments throw light on an earlier practice when the Scripture-reader had only the English text from which he gave a free rendering in Gaelic. Clark also brings out the tendency of the religious Highlander to hallow practices which, useful and necessary in their day, ultimately ossify and so frustrate proper understanding and growth. Referring to the English-to-Gaelic Scripture-reading of earlier days he wrote,

> *In their Sabbath meetings there was only an attempt to translate; and great was the injustice which the good Word suffered from such attempts; for, though the Translators were willing to do it justice, they wanted the ability. No doubt the Society in Scotland for propagating Christian Knowledge gave many copies of their excellent Translation of the Bible as far as it had then proceeded; but so wedded are men to long contracted habits that people in general preferred to hear the Scriptures mangled by a babbler of a Translator than hear the pure Translation read. I do not go by report. Many were the instances I saw of this; and although the ridiculous practice has given way it is not wholly rooted out in some parts within my acquaintance.*[18]

These places would have been in his native Sutherland and his comments are in keeping with remarks made by Hugh Miller in his autobiographical work *My Schools and Schoolmasters*. Born in Cromarty in 1802, Hugh Miller spoke no Gaelic,[19] but he gives a fine description of family worship being conducted in Gaelic in the home of his Sutherlandshire relatives. His uncle who led the worship (or in the time-honoured phrase 'took the Book') read the English Bible, but because some of those present understood only Gaelic he translated into Gaelic and did it with great fluency. Hugh Miller then makes the point that the family preferred a translation into Gaelic to a straight reading from the recently published Gaelic Bible because the latter was written in Argyllshire Gaelic, which differed sufficiently from Sutherland-shire Gaelic, to make the North Country people prefer a translation by a native speaker.[20] Perhaps in Robert Clark's strictures against this practice there was a trace of impatience born of intellectual superiority.

Notes to Chapter 15

1. *Records of the Presbytery of Aberdeen,* vol. 10, p 368 (5th December, 1821) (CH2-1-12).
2. *Fasti Ecclesiae Scoticanae* (Edinburgh, first edition, 1871), vol 1, p 78.
3. *Records of the Presbytery of Tongue,* vol. 2, p 277 (19th October, 1818) (CH2-508-2).
4. J Graham (ed.): *Disruption worthies of the Highlands* (Edinburgh, 1877; enlarged edition, 1886). For an account of the ministry of the Rev. Alexander Macleod, see pp 221-232.
5. J Kay: *A series of original portraits with biographical sketches* (Edinburgh, 1877), vol. 1, p 154, footnote.
6. H Miller: *My schools and schoolmasters* (Edinburgh, 1854, reprinted 1886), pp 114-115.
7. *SSPCK Records: Minutes of committee meetings,* vol. 13, p 36 (2nd July, 1807) (GD95-2-13).
8. D Sage: *Memorabilia Domestica* (Wick, 1889, 2nd edition, 1899, reprinted 1975), p 205.
9. *SSPCK Records,* op. cit., p 144 (3rd September, 1807).
10. *Records of the Presbytery of Tongue,* op. cit., p 268 (28th November, 1816).
11. *Fasti Ecclesiae Scoticanae* (1923), vol. 4, p 185.
12. *Records of the Presbytery of Tongue,* op. cit., p 282 (24th November, 1819).
13. Ibid., p 294 (20th July, 1820).
14. *Records of the Presbytery of Aberdeen,* op. cit., p 399 (20th June, 1822).
15. D Brown: *Life of John Duncan* (Edinburgh, 1872), p 251.
16. W Knight: *Colloquia peripatetica* (Edinburgh, 5th edition, 1879). Biographical sketch of Dr J Duncan, p lvii.
17. J Graham: op. cit., p 93.
18. *The eleventh annual report of the Society for the support of Gaelic schools,* appendix no. 1, letter 2.
19. P Bayne: *Life and letters of Hugh Miller* (London, 1871), vol 1, p 8. (The Gaelic chapel that was built in Cromarty in 1783 was for the benefit of incomers.)
20. H Miller: op. cit., p 98. See also H Miller: *Leading Articles* (Edinburgh, 1890), pp 408-409.

Chapter 16

*

A SUNSET GLOW

ONLY four weeks elapsed between the intimation of Robert Clark's resignation and his induction in Duke Street Gaelic Chapel, Glasgow. The clerk recorded on 7th April that in intimating his resignation, the minister gave them 'full authority to be on the outlook for themselves for candidates without any lose of time or opportunity'. Later that month there was 'held a meeting of the committee of managers called by public intimation', at which point the minute ends. Perhaps the clerk had not been present, but Mr Alex Webster laid before the Presbytery on 17th April an application from the Gaelic Chapel for permission to invite Mr Archibald Cook, missionary at Berriedale, as a candidate.[1] Three weeks later Mr Webster informed the Presbytery that Mr Cook had declined coming forward as a candidate, but that, at a further meeting of the managers on 25th April (again unminuted), their list of candidates had been completed with the addition of the Rev. Hugh Mackenzie, Ardeonaig and Mr Donald Gordon, Farr.[2] The Presbytery gave permission for these candidates to preach 'after producing to the ministers of Aberdeen satisfactory certificates'.

Archibald Cook

The fact that the managers put Archibald Cook, missionary at Berriedale, first on their list, suggests that they, or their advisers, had an eye for discerning quality in the bud. The previous year he had completed his arts and divinity training at the University of Glasgow and he would not have been known personally to the Aberdeen congregation. However, he was a protégé of Dr John Love of Anderston Chapel[3] and the congregation's links with Glasgow ministers may have led to Archibald Cook being recommended to them. In Berriedale he had taken the place of Ronald Bayne's son Charles who, curiously, failed to be nominated at any time as a candidate for Aberdeen – perhaps indicative of the fact that a generation had passed away since the formation of the Aberdeen Gaelic Chapel. When he was approached by Aberdeen, Archibald Cook had only been a few months in Berriedale and he was content to stay. In fact he remained in Caithness until 1837 when he went to Inverness as first minister of the North Church, then newly

119

constituted as an extension charge consequent to a split occurring in the East Church over the election of a successor to his brother Finlay Cook.

Donald Sage was well acquainted with the Cook brothers, his sister being Finlay Cook's wife. In his description of Archibald, Sage lets rip with his most withering invective:[4]

> *His literary attainments are not high; his Gaelic is bad, his English worse. He rigidly adheres to the dialect of his native district the Isle of Arran, one of the worst dialects in Scotland. His attempts to preach in the English language, both in regard to pronunciation and grammatical construction, are provocative of the ridicule of thoughtless men in the audience. He had of course attended school ....*

Perhaps that last phrase was the most cutting of all. In Sage's view 'no man was ever afflicted with a larger measure of human frailities and failings'. Yet despite all that, Donald Sage had to concede that in respect of disinterested zeal, indifference to worldly concerns and devotion to the eternal interests of the kingdom of heaven, it was questionable if anyone ever more closely approximated to the divinely-trained disciples of Galilee than Archibald Cook. From the testimony of others, it is evident that there was a quality in his preaching and in his personal dealing with people, which made him an exceptionally effective evangelist. Principal John Macleod summed him up as 'a religious genius ... with the defects of his qualities'.[5]

Donald Gordon

Archibald Cook having declined their invitation, the congregation invited Hugh Mackenzie, the second on their list, to preach. On June 9th 1823, a general meeting was held to ascertain 'whether the meeting was to rest satisfied with the candidate already called and heard, or whether the managers was to call the next candidate on their list'. In the event the Rev. Hugh Mackenzie from the Ardeonaig Mission, having 'preached for two Sabbath days in Gaelic and English much to their satisfaction, the meeting, being unanimous without a dissenting voice', agreed to ask the Presbytery for permission to sign a call. Almost 34 years had passed since the first call to the Gaelic Chapel was sent to Kenneth Bayne. Another 34 years would pass before another opportunity would come to them to chose a minister. Had that been known to them, they might have exercised their option to hear the third candidate – Mr Donald Gordon, Farr. He had been appointed schoolmaster in Farr in 1817, but by 1823 he had moved to the adjoining Parish of Eddrachillis where he had been ordained assistant to the minister, the

Rev. John Mackenzie, one of the ministers whom Norman Macleod of Assynt categorized as 'most notorious inebriates'.[6] He was to remain an assistant in Eddrachillis until 1829 when he was presented with the Parish of Stoer in the Presbytery of Dornoch; after seven years in Stoer he was given the Parish of Edderton.[7] He joined the Free Church in 1843 and died in 1847 at the comparatively early age of 51. In the hagiographical literature of Ross-shire he is not credited as having achieved any distinction in the annals of the Church, but it may be supposed that he was capable of worthy, if not always exciting, preaching.

Robert Findlater's revival aftermath

That Hugh Mackenzie was listed above Donald Gordon may have been deliberate or fortuitous. Both had been educated at King's College: the latter graduating in 1819, the former in 1811. Mackenzie was from Kiltarlity while Donald Gordon was born in Strathaven (Lanarkshire). It is conceivable that one feature in Hugh Mackenzie's favour was that he was minister in a pulpit from which, in the recent past, the Gospel had been preached as 'with the Holy Ghost sent down from heaven'. To be the successor, as Hugh Mackenzie was, of one associated with a revival, was to be identified, at one remove, with the wonderful works of God. Such was Hugh Mackenzie's situation in Ardeonaig.

The Chapels of Ardeonaig and Lawers were preaching stations which formed the Lochtayside Mission, established by the SSPCK in 1791 with funds provided by Lady Glenorchy.[8] The district comprised parts of the Parishes of Kenmore, Killin and Weem, then in the Presbytery of Dunkeld. In 1810 Robert Findlater (a brother of Wm Findlater of Eriboll and Durness) was appointed missionary at Lochtayside and, from the time of his settlement there, his impact on the community was such that many were added to the Church. However in 1816, when John Macdonald of Ferintosh, the Apostle of the North, came to the autumn Communion, 'the work assumed abnormal proportions'.[9] Services were held in the open air at Lawers and a great crowd, estimated at 5000 persons, gathered to hear this remarkable evangelist. In the view of his biographer this was the occasion when Macdonald of Ferintosh preached his most memorable sermon.[10] Taking as his text 'Thy Maker is thine husband' (Isaiah 54: 5), the discourse took two hours and twenty minutes to deliver. Robert Findlater, describing the occasion to his brother William, wrote, 'I could compare it to nothing but the days of the Apostles after the day of Pentecost'.[11]

It sometimes happened on these occasions that the people were brought to such a pitch of excitement that they were verging on the point of collapse. An eyewitness of a similar occasion, when John Macdonald was preaching in Invermoriston, wrote, 'The impression of that day was extraordinary. The place was like a battlefield strewn with the dead and dying. Not a few survived to testify that the Lord was present of a truth that day'.[12] The spiritual quickening of which this was but one evidence continued to be experienced in Breadalbane generally from 1815-1820. It was, however, identified more with the SSPCK ministers than with the parish ministers, and those most closely involved were Robert Findlater, Lochtayside, and in Strathfillan Donald MacGillivray, the candidate that the Aberdeen Gaelic Chapel had heard and rejected in 1808.

As a consequence of the prominence given to his ministry by this revival, Robert Findlater was called from Lochtayside to the East Church in Inverness in 1821 and there he laboured 'a singularly devoted minister and preacher' until he died in the cholera outbreak of 1832 at the age of 47.[13] While he was in Inverness, vacancies occurred in the Perthshire Parishes of Killin, Comrie and Moulin, but although the parishioners almost unanimously petitioned to have Robert Findlater appointed, he was not favoured by the patrons.[14] When he received the call to Inverness, he found it hard to part company from the people who had meant so much to him in Ardeonaig and Lawers. But among the reasons which led him to accept the call he included his confident hope 'that under the patronage of the Society they would ere long be provided with a suitable minister. It relieved his mind to think that they were left in good hands'.[15] Whether the 'good hands' referred to the Most High, the SSPCK or the Rev. Hugh Mackenzie, he left to the judgment of the reader to discern.

On 20th June 1822, Hugh Mackenzie was inducted to the charge of Lochtayside. The emoluments were a stipend of £40, communion elements and a small grass glebe and manse at Ardeonaig.[16] The duties were to preach alternately at Lawers and at Ardeonaig for which it was necessary to cross the loch by boat. Hugh Mackenzie remained at Lochtayside for only one year. Although the religious history of the area, especially that of Lawers and Glenlyon, has been well documented, the literature is devoid of any comment on the fact of, let alone the quality of, Hugh Mackenzie's pastorate. In the volume that deals minutely with the ecclesiastical succession in the Parishes and missions of Breadalbane, even his name is incorrectly given as Alexander Mackenzie.[17] His presence was soon forgotten. He was succeeded briefly by Colin Hunter, who wrote a history of the SSPCK, and in 1827 by a nephew of Lachlan Mackenzie of Lochcarron, Donald Mackenzie, who inherited some of the eccentricities of his uncle and who ministered at Ardeonaig for 46 years until his death in 1873.[18]

Hugh Mackenzie comes to stay

The Presbytery of Aberdeen met with the Gaelic Chapel congregation on 26th June 1823 for the formal election of Hugh Mackenzie. When they met again on 7th August the clerk minuted that as they had no information on when Hugh Mackenzie was to come to Aberdeen, they could not fix the date of his induction, but they authorised him to preside at the Autumn communion if he was in Aberdeen.[19] Perhaps because of the uncertainty of developments, Donald Sage was present to assist at the September communion. In accordance with the usual practice, some of the managers were appointed as delegates 'to settle with the Rev. Mr. Donald Sage for his travelling expenses', whereupon Mr Sage 'directed that his travelling expenses would be appropriated to the purpose of furnishing the Chapel with a central lamp as a present from himself'. If his predecessor Duncan Grant's ten patent lamps cost one guinea each, Donald Sage's expenses would purchase a beacon, the luminosity of which would put all ten patent lamps in the shade. Sage's stratagem to outshine his rival, even in the matter of a parting gift, was brilliant. It was also the last recorded act of ministerial munificence to the Gaelic Chapel.

On 31st October 1823, the Presbytery met in the East Church at ten o'clock forenoon and adjourned to the Gaelic Chapel-of-Ease at one o'clock when 'an excellent and appropriate discourse' was preached on the occasion by Dr George Glennie from 1 Timothy 4:16 ('Take heed unto thyself and unto the doctrine'). Or so the occasion was recorded in the Kirk Session minutes. The text which the Presbytery Clerk minuted as being the subject of the sermon was 2 Timothy 2: 15 ('Study to shew thyself approved unto God, a workman that needeth not to be ashamed').[20] But an appropriate and, doubtlessly excellent, discourse could equally well be preached from either; and possibly the hermeneutic of the Professor of Moral Philosophy in Marischal College was sufficiently adroit to make the same sermon fit either text. After the sermon, Dr Glennie gave 'an affecting and suitable address', first to the minister and afterwards to the people. Hugh Mackenzie was now minister of the Gaelic Chapel and he was to remain so for 36 years, successfully resisting all efforts by the people, or many of them, to eject him.

Pew rights and wrongs

A new minister in the congregation did not affect the regular business of the managers, especially as the minister was not present, nor expected to be present, at the managers' meetings. Since the new constitution came into force in 1822, annual elections to the committee were a thing of the past. Some changes had been made prior to 1822. Duncan Mackenzie, shoemaker, Skene Square, the only manager to have given continuous service since the committee was formed in 1796, was not re-appointed in 1819 and his death is referred to in late 1823 with reference to the repayment of £40 which he had loaned to the managers. Robert Sutherland, plasterer, who was appointed treasurer in 1818, gave way in 1821 to Alex (Saunders) Macdonald, merchant of East North Street; but he continued on the committee. Another senior manager, Angus Sutherland, slater, was appointed to the committee for the last time in 1820.

The annual general meeting held in April 1824 was fairly peaceable, the congregation, on the whole, being satisfied with the diligence of the managers. The statement of account was read 'after which the books were offered to the meeting for their inspection, but being satisfied with the statement given, they refused the books but observed that the precentor had by far too little salary and urged that he should have two or three pounds more in the year'. Neither the name nor salary of the precentor is mentioned, but it may have been Murdoch Mackenzie. In October 1812 the committee, 'having taken into consideration that Murdoch Mackenzie, their present precentor, having made a present to the funds of the Society of the salary due to him for that office since his commencement thereto [agreed] that in case he should, in the course of providence, ever be reduced so as to be unable to pay for a seat in the chapel, he shall be accommodated with one or two seats as he has occasion for, from the interest of his said salary returned'. He had donated £8 to the Society. Between 1812 and 1824 there is no reference to a precentor and Murdoch Mackenzie may still have been in the post. The matter having been raised and 'debated at full length by the managers, it was agreed that the precentor should have £4 a year'. The clerk, Robert Hamilton, took advantage of the occasion to ask if 'the meeting would consider whether they would see meet to add anything to his salary'. The managers agreed to raise his salary from three guineas to £4.

Another reminder of the fact that a generation had passed away since 1795 is given in 1824 when the managers met 'for the purpose of enquiring into the extent of the right of subscribers as to their seats'. Two cases came up for consideration. William Fraser had lost his right by reason of long absence. 'Having left no relations in this place who could claim his right', it was judged that the seat became the property of the managers. More poignant was the case of Alex Mackenzie, possibly a son of Duncan Mackenzie, shoemaker. He had 'lost his father's right as he does not understand the Gaelic language'. He was not the only one, for the minute went on to note that 'widow Macdonald is in the same case'. Without Gaelic these worshippers had no say in the matter. No discussion took place as to a need for reviewing the basis of constituent membership. The meeting ended with Alex Macdonald indicating that 'he is no longer to claim right to his mother-in-law's seat; but resigns it in favour of the managers'. Another problem that came before the managers from time to time was the request for a whole family to be accommodated in one pew. In the early days of the congregation, seat rights were purchased for adults only. With the passing of the years, different family groups would have rights in the same pew. Consequently accommodating all of one family together was difficult, if not impossible, unless others had abandoned their rights. For services which were not well attended, a family could, perhaps, take liberties without fear of being ousted from the pew. The problem became most acute when communion preachers came to the chapel, when regular worshippers had to make way for occasional worshippers retaining ancient rights.

The renowned Highland preachers continued to appear on the communion circuit. Macdonald, Ferintosh, was regularly at the April communion, but the practice of mentioning the name of the assisting minister in the minutes, was no longer maintained. An exception occurred in the Autumn of 1826, when it was minuted that the Rev. John Kennedy, Killearnan, assisted.

Notes to Chapter 16

1. *Records of the Presbytery of Aberdeen,* vol. 10, p 445 (17th April, 1823) (CH2-1-12).
2. Ibid., p 450 (7th May, 1823).
3. A MacPherson: *Sidelights on two notable ministries* (Inverness, 1970), p 28. Some account of the life of the Rev. Archibald Cook is given in this Memoir by Professor J R Mackay (1907).
4. D Sage: *Memorabilia Domestica* (Wick, 1889; 2nd edition, 1899, reprinted 1975), p 298.
5. J Macleod: *By-paths of Highland church history* (Edinburgh, 1965), p 105.
6. Ibid., p 150.
7. *Fasti Ecclesiae Scoticanae* (1928), vol. 7, p 54.
8. D Duff: *The new statistical account of Scotland* (Edinburgh, 1845), vol. 10, p 480.
9. A Macrae: *Revivals in the Highlands and islands in the 19th century* (Stirling, 1905), p 136.
10. J Kennedy: *The apostle of the North* (Edinburgh, 1866; new edition, Inverness, 1932), p 66.
11. W Findlater: *Memoir of the Rev. Robert Findlater* (Glasgow 1840), p 182.
12. A Macrae: op. cit., p 97.
13. *Fasti Ecclesiae Scoticanae* (1926), vol. 6, p 468.
14. W Findlater: op. cit., p 294.
15. Ibid., p 283.
16. Ibid., pp 126 and 283.
17. W A Gillies: *In famed Breadalbane* (Perth, 1938), p 299.
18. D MacGregor: *Campbell of Kiltearn* (Edinburgh, 1874), p 120.
19. *Records of the Presbytery of Aberdeen*, op. cit., p 467 (7th August, 1823) (CH2-1-12).
20. Ibid., p 473 (31st October, 1823).

Chapter 17

*

A FALSE DAWN

BY September 1826 the Rev. Hugh Mackenzie had been three years in the pastorate. The merits that the congregation had once discerned in his sermons were now less obvious. People were beginning to weary of his preaching; attendances were beginning to flag. Perhaps it was John Kennedy who suggested a remedy, for it was at the meeting of the chapel managers convened for the purpose of settling his travelling expenses that 'it was proposed and agreed that a lecturer be employed this winter, if it were agreeable to Mr. Mackenzie, and if that such an one could be found whose parts and piety would be judged, or expected, to benefit the spiritual and temporal interests of the congregation, and one who could preach in Gaelic, at a time if necessity required his doing so'. The first hint by way of encouraging a minister to move on is to suggest that he would be the better of an assistant to share the preaching. In this case it was fairly pointedly stated that both the spiritual and temporal interests of the congregation were in need of attention. Interestingly, in this job description Gaelic appears to have been given a secondary role. Although the minute was couched in general terms, it appears certain that the committee had a specific individual in mind, namely, Robert Finlayson. Finlayson's name does not occur in any of the congregation's records, but other sources confirm that 'such an one' did minister in the congregation to its temporal and spiritual enrichment.

Robert Finlayson and Woodside Chapel

Robert Finlayson was born in 1793 in Latheron, Caithness, where his father was schoolmaster. He was a student at King's College from 1816–1821. After teaching in Lybster and Dunbeath, he was licensed by the Presbytery of Caithness in May 1826 and shortly afterwards he came to Aberdeen, although under what auspices is unclear. According to the *Fasti* (1870), he held an appointment as missionary in the East Parish of Aberdeen before becoming an assistant in the Gaelic Chapel.[1] A biographical sketch written about 1875 dated his ministry in Aberdeen as commencing in July 1826, 'partly as assistant in the Gaelic church and partly as missionary in connection with Dr Foote's congregation'. The reference to Dr Foote's congregation is most probably an extrapolation from the *Fasti*, not an independent corroboration of it, and, in the absence of other evidence there must be a question mark over the accuracy of the *Fasti* on this point. There is no reference in the Kirk Session records of East St Nicholas (Dr Foote's congregation), nor in the Presbytery records, to such an appointment. Neither, of course, is he named in any records in connection with the Gaelic Chapel. The accuracy of the *Fasti* identification of Robert Finlayson with the East Parish may, however, be questioned on the basis of another remark, namely that he preached regularly at Woodside.[2]

Woodside was in the Parish of Old Machar, not St Nicholas, and it is unlikely that a missionary attached to East St Nicholas would be involved in Woodside. It is easier to see a connection between Dr Kidd's church, which was in the Parish of Old Machar, and Woodside. There was no place of worship in Woodside belonging to the Established Church until a chapel-of-ease was opened there in 1830, but the first steps towards the formation of that congregation took place in 1826, the time that Robert Finlayson is said to have come to Aberdeen.[3] Sir John Anderson (1814-1886), in a manuscript which he prefaced to a collection of Assembly Papers concerning the Woodside Chapel, wrote of the origin of the congregation, 'That movement may be said to have commenced during the exceptional summer of 1826. The fatigue of walking to and from Gilcomston during the hot weather told severely on the aged and the writer of this preface can well remember the nature of the communings of the good folk on the long weary way'.[4]

It is of interest that the attachment of the people of Woodside here spoken of was not to the Parish Church of Old Machar (St Machar's), but to the chapel-of-ease at Gilcomston (now the Denburn Church) where Dr Kidd was minister. With an expanding population in Woodside and its elderly worshippers exhausted by the long walk to Gilcomston, it is not surprising that steps should have been taken to hold services in the village itself. Dr Kidd, who was well acquainted with Robert Finlayson's gifts (Finlayson had been a regular worshipper in Kidd's congregation during his student days), would have perceived the probationer's usefulness in a missionary role and supported his engagement at Woodside. Having been alerted to the plan to employ Finlayson at Woodside, the Gaelic congregation then aspired to enlist his services for their own benefit. Hence the September decision of the managers that 'a lecturer be employed this winter if that such an one could be found whose parts and piety would be judged to benefit the congregation'. The outcome was an amicable arrangement to share Robert Finlayson between Woodside and the Gaelic Chapel. Every Sunday evening he preached in the Gaelic Church and once a fortnight he preached at Woodside. At both places he had crowded congregations.[5]

Neil McKechnie

From another point of view it probably suited the managers of the Gaelic Chapel that Robert Finlayson should be preaching in Woodside, for his presence there would strengthen the presbyterian attachment of the Highland mill-workers at a time when their adherence to their own tradition was under strain from an independent chapel which had been opened for worship some years earlier. This chapel, the first place of worship in Woodside (or the Printfield as it was sometimes termed), was built by subscription in 1819 and was known as Cotton Chapel,[6] the terms 'Cotton' and 'Printfield' being derived from the textile factories in the area. Although it commenced as an independent mission, it soon came under the superintendence of the Congregational Church and was supported by the Rev. Dr John Philip of George Street.

In 1822 the Rev. Neil McKechnie, a native of Kilcolmonell, took the mission pastorate on condition that he would be released for eight weeks every summer to undertake evangelistic missions in the Gaelic-speaking parts of the Highlands, an indication of his interest in evangelising Highland people.[7] For some months prior to his induction, in March 1822, to Cotton Chapel, he had been giving supply there. It may therefore not be without significance that at a meeting of the managers of the Gaelic Chapel held on 8th April 1822, it was recorded that 'the following four members resigned their office as managers of the Gaelic Chapel, *viz*., Thomas Sutherland, John Clark, Joseph Mackay and Robert Sutherland. The reason of the above resignations is that a few members residing at the Printfield might be admitted into the management of the affairs of the chapel'. This would seem to indicate that at the time that Neil McKechnie settled in Woodside, the managers felt that steps had to be taken to encourage loyalty among the Gaelic Chapel worshippers residing in that area. At the annual general meeting which was held the following month, Angus Mackay and Peter Mackenzie were 'duly elected for the Printfield quarter', while, at the same time, of the four who had resigned, all except John Clark were re-appointed. With an Argyllshire Gaelic-speaking Congregationalist like Neil McKechnie busy in Woodside, every effort had to be made to retain the support of the Highlanders and the presence of Robert Finlayson would have provided a much needed counter-attraction in favour of the Established Church and the Gaelic Chapel.

Whatever uncertainties exist as to the ambit of his duties in Aberdeen, there can be no doubt as to the effectiveness of his ministry. He drew the crowds both by the attractiveness of his personality and the winsomeness of his preaching. His fondness for allegorical preaching won him the sobriquet 'The Highland John Bunyan'. Obviously his sermons had a strongly imaginative element and this feature had tremendous appeal for the people. An early biographer, describing the impact that his preaching made on the Gaelic congregation, said, 'After a few Sabbaths the congregation increased in number to such an extent that many had to return home from church before the sermon began'.[8] He stayed in Aberdeen until 1829 when he was ordained to the congregation of Knock in Lewis, and two years later he was presented with the Lewis Parish of Lochs. His last charge was in Helmsdale. He died in 1867 leaving behind him the most fragrant memories in every charge in which he had officiated.

Woodside factions and Andrew Gray

After the departure of Robert Finlayson, the Gaelic Chapel continued to take an interest in developments at Woodside. The building of a church commenced in 1829, but when it was opened for worship in May 1830 there were serious differences of opinion within the congregation, and especially among the office-bearers. Subsequent events, both in the calling[9] and later in the service of a minister in Woodside Chapel, reflected the rivalry for civic honours and commercial success that existed between two of Aberdeen's most prominent families, the Haddens and the Browns. The competing interests centred round James Hadden of Persley, a partner in the firm of Leys, Masson & Co. who owned the Grandholm Mill; and Alex Brown, a partner in the Woodside Works of Gordon, Barron & Co. Both of these firms were engaged in the manufacture of textiles and they were already in dispute over the extraction of water from the Don[10] when the managing partners found themselves taking opposite sides in the choice of a minister for the new chapel.

In a three-cornered contest, Alex Brown's candidate, Mr Andrew Gray, a probationer but even then a most formidable Evangelical, had a majority of 21 votes over the Rev. Alex Leitch of Gartmore, who enjoyed the support of James Hadden. The remaining candidate, Matthew Millar, a probationer from Edinburgh, received but one vote. The result of the election was disputed by the Leitch minority who claimed that 28 of Andrew Gray's votes were inadmissible.[11] Woodside Chapel, being a new congregation, had no communicants' roll and its constitution prescribed that the first election of a minister should be by a majority of subscribers to the amount of one guinea who were members of the Established Church and resident in the Parish of Old Machar. It further stipulated that 'after the managers shall have fixed on the three candidates, the subscribers' list shall be closed until after the election'. The reason for this restriction was to prevent the manufacture of votes in the heat of a contested election or what nowadays is known as entryism.

The dispute over Andrew Gray's election arose because the names of 28 new subscribers were intimated at the same meeting as that at which the list of candidates was chosen, but, it was asserted, were not collated on to the roll of subscribers until a later stage in the meeting. The new names, all submitted by Alex Brown, had been collected by his brother, Wm Brown, who, from the vantage point of the family business (Brown, Booksellers and Publishers, Broad Street), was able to solicit donations for the new Woodside Chapel in much the same way as John Ewen had acted for the Gaelic Chapel. Incidentally, the owner of the business, Provost Alex. Brown, married to a daughter of James Chalmers of the *Aberdeen Journal*, was a son of the esteemed Rev. Wm Brown of Craigdam and the family was steeped in the evangelical tradition, two of the Provost's sons becoming in turn Moderator of the Free Church General Assembly.[12]

The validity of Wm Brown's subscription list was not queried at the meeting at which it was submitted, but subsequently it was objected to on several counts. In addition to the objection already mentioned, it was argued that no fewer than ten of the names were entered in Wm Brown's handwriting and, at the time the lists were closed, four of the ten had failed to make good the subscription which had been paid on their behalf by Wm Brown. For these reasons the appellants urged that the votes were inadmissible. The Presbytery and Assembly thought otherwise, and pointed out that even if the ten entries in Wm Brown's hand were disallowed (an action which the Courts viewed as both unwarranted and unjust), it would still not affect the final issue since Andrew Gray had a majority of 21. The objection to the 28 votes (an objection based on the order of the agenda of the nomination meeting), was rejected as incompetent. The support of the minister of the Gaelic Chapel had been enlisted on behalf of Andrew Gray, the Rev. Hugh Mackenzie being one of the forgetful four who paid their subscriptions after the lists were closed. Following the Assembly decision, Andrew Gray was duly inducted and he gave five years of vigorous service to the congregation while, at the same time, running a highly effective campaign for the admission of chapel ministers to the Church Courts, a crusade which led to the passing of the Chapels Act of 1834.

The Woodside Chapel was opened in May 1830, but because of the disputed election it was September 1831 before Andrew Gray was inducted. At the time the chapel was opened, the Presbytery agreed to a suggestion from the managers that, pending a settlement, the regular supply preacher should be a local probationer named John Duncan, later to be known as 'Rabbi' Duncan, Professor of Hebrew in New College, Edinburgh. 'Rabbi' John Duncan was known to the Browns and, perhaps, Alex Brown's influence can again be seen in the appointment. He did not stay for more than a few months in Woodside for, later that year, he took up an appointment in Persie Chapel, Blairgowrie. When Anderston Chapel, Glasgow, became vacant on the death of Dr John Love, the three candidates were 'Rabbi' Duncan and two of Provost Brown's sons, David and Charles, the last mentioned being the successful candidate. Some of Duncan's Glasgow admirers then succeeded in having him appointed as assistant to Robert Clark in Duke Street Gaelic Chapel. Gaelic was one of the few languages with which 'Rabbi' Duncan had no acquaintance, but he was held in considerable esteem by the Highlanders. While he was assisting at Woodside Chapel, he was engaged to give a weekly course of lectures in the Aberdeen Gaelic Chapel.[13] The subject of the lectures was the Westminster Confession of Faith, but he got no further than the chapter on the Fall of Man before he went to Persie. The wonder was that a mind to whom a single word would suggest a train of thought sufficient to furnish an entire lecture had got as far as chapter six of the Confession. 'Rabbi' Duncan's lectures called for special aptitudes on the part of the hearer, but he had his followers and very devoted followers they were. Among those who attended his Gaelic Chapel lectures was Gavin Parker,[14] the minister of Union Terrace (Bon Accord) Church.

Notes to Chapter 17

1. *Fasti Ecclesiae Scoticanae* (Edinburgh, first edition, 1870), vol. 3, part 1, p 145.
2. J Graham: *Disruption worthies of the Highlands* (Edinburgh, 1877), p 147. Biographical sketch of Robert Finlayson by Rev. Colin Sinclair.
3. J MacPherson: *Cunntas Aithghearr mu Bheatha 'n Urramaich Raibeart Fiunlason* (Lochalsh, 1870). I am indebted to the Rev. Dr Roderick Macleod of Cumlodden for this reference.
4. J Anderson: *A fragment of history* (1885). Preface to Assembly Papers on Woodside Chapel-of-Ease (1831). MS in Aberdeen Central Library.
5. D MacGregor: *The Shepherd of Israel* (London, 1869), p 245.
6. P Morgan: *Annals of Woodside and Newhills* (Aberdeen, 1909), p 80.
7. R Duthie: *Records of the first church in Woodside (Independent or Congregational) 1818-1945* (Banff, 1946), pp 10-11. For biographical details re. McKechnie, see W D McNaughton: *The Scottish Congregational Ministry 1794-1993* (Glasgow, 1993), p 93.
8. J MacPherson: op. cit. I am indebted to the Rev. Dr Roderick Macleod for the translation.
9. P Morgan: op. cit., p 83.
10. Ibid., pp 58-63.
11. *Assembly Papers* (1831): 'Cause of the Chapel-of-Ease Woodside. Case for Alex Brown and others, managers, and Robert Alexander and other subscribers, appellants', p 19.
12. A M Munro: *Memorials of the aldermen, provosts and lord provosts of Aberdeen 1272-1895* (Aberdeen, 1897), pp 26-27.
13. W Knight: *Colloquia peripatetica* (Edinburgh, 5th edition, 1879). Biographical sketch of Dr J Duncan, p lv.
14. D Brown, *Life of John Duncan* (Edinburgh, 1872), p 210.

Chapter 18

*

ST NICHOLAS DISJOINED

MAJOR changes took place in the territorial organisation of the Established Church in Aberdeen in 1828, and again in 1834. Reorganisation of parochial boundaries was long overdue. From the time of the Reformation there had been but one parish, the Parish of St Nicholas, in Aberdeen. It comprised a triangular area to the east of the Denburn with the River Dee as the base of the triangle and the Gallowgate as its northern extremity.[1] On all landward sides the Parish of St Nicholas was surrounded by the Parish of Old Machar. Under both Presbytery and Episcopacy, St Nicholas was a collegiate charge with at least three ministers attached to it. In November 1595 the Town Council, 'seeing the daily increase of people of this burgh', resolved that the town should be divided into four congregations.[2] The first step in that direction was taken in June 1596 when the Council decided that the choir of St Nicholas Church should be isolated from the nave. To that end they ordained that 'the hail carvit tymmer wark betuixt the pilleris in the queir be removit that ane stane wall may be biggit betuixt the said queir and the bodie of the kirk, that the said queir may be maid ane preiching kirk'.[3] When the Master of the Kirk-wark refused to implement this instruction, he was replaced by a more compliant mason and the Church of St Nicholas was thereafter divided into the Old Church and the New Church.[4]

Binary division

The proposal to make four congregations was taken no further at that time, but in September 1596 the citizens agreed to a division of the populace into two halves comprising, on the one hand, the Even and the Futtie Quarters inclusive of 'the four round tabillis' (thought to be four building blocks separating the Broadgate from the Guest Row), and, on the other hand, the Green and the Crooked Quarters.[5] Lots were drawn to determine which church and which minister should be assigned to each half of the town, with the result that the New (East) Church and Mr Peter Blackburn, minister of the first charge, fell to the 'Evin and Futtie Quarteris and four round tabillis', while the Old (West) Church with the bishop (David Cunningham, minister of the second charge) fell by lot to the 'Grene and Crukit Quarteris'.[6] This allotment involved switching the ministers of the first and second charges. Thereafter the West Kirk became associated with the first charge and the East Kirk with the second charge.

With two ministers the division of the parish into two pastoral districts, each comprising two Quarters, was simply done. But there were three charges and therefore three ministers, and in September 1596 the Council minuted their intention of having the Greyfriars or College Church repaired, after which the town would be divided into three parts and Parishes.[7] It is not clear when the division into thirds took place. Certainly Greyfriars Church had been repaired and brought back into use before the memorable General Assembly of 1640 was held there. But, irrespective of when the restoration and consequent division took place, it did not involve the minister attached to the benefice of Greyfriars. This benefice was the prerogative of the Professor of Divinity at Marischal College. He was required only to preach once each Lord's Day and he was specifically relieved of any further pastoral duties. Thus it was that only three ministers, the holders of the three charges of St Nicholas, had responsibility for the four Quarters.

Ternary division

When the division was made, the minister of the third charge was given the pastoral superintendence of the Even Quarter and half of the Futtie Quarter. The minister of the second charge, who had previously been responsible for the Even and Futtie Quarters, was given the Green Quarter along with the segment of the Futtie Quarter which had not been allocated to the third charge.[8] This effectively left the minister of the first charge with responsibility only for the Crooked Quarter. The ministers of the second and third charges were associated with the East Church. Later the minister of the first charge received, as a colleague in the West Church, the holder of the Greyfriars living after that building had yet again fallen into disuse because of its state of disrepair.[9] Thus both East and West St Nicholas came to have two ministers associated with each Church, but the pastoral duties, such as visitation, catechising and the administration of the sacraments, devolved on only three of the ministers, the holder of the Greyfriars living being exempt from pastoral responsibilities.

In 1759, the Council once again repaired Greyfriars Church and brought it back into service. Since the official duties of the minister of Greyfriars required him to preach only once a Sunday, and that in the West Kirk of St Nicholas, the Council agreed to meet the cost of paying a probationer to preach twice a Sunday in the Greyfriars Church. He was not, however, required to undertake any other pastoral duties, these having been allocated among the ministers of St Nicholas.

Quaternary division

In 1777 when the Greyfriars preacher left for another charge, the ministers of St Nicholas approached the Town Council with a view to having a fourth minister appointed to share in the pastoral work of the Parish of St Nicholas.[10] Their main concern was to have the parish sub-divided among four ministers instead of three. The council were not unsympathetic to the request, but deferred approval pending the report of a committee which was charged with making 'proper enquiry on the present state of the treasury funds'.[11] On this committee reporting that 'the Funds were considerably more than exhausted by the payment of the ministers' stipends already established',[12] the Council agreed to continue with the status quo and another probationer was appointed whose function was 'only to be preacher in the College Church by supplying both diets of sermon each Lord's Day with £40 salary'.[13] When in 1787 the next vacancy arose for a probationer to function in Greyfriars, the ministers of St Nicholas requested that the appointment would be such as to require the performance of all pastoral duties, this to include his having a section of the Town allocated for his superintendence 'but without being put upon the Establishment, only that he should be ordained by the Presbytery and settled as a preacher in the College Kirk as a kind of chapel-of-ease'.[14] In the event, the Council appointed a preacher, James Shand, on the same terms as his predecessors.[15]

In 1791 James Shand requested to be ordained. This the Presbytery then granted on the grounds that 'his charge although not a parochial charge is a permanent one'. The Town Council raised his stipend from £40 to £60 on the understanding that he undertook the entire range of ministerial duties and, thereafter, the Parochial clergy of St Nicholas took nothing more to do with ministry in Greyfriars Church.[16] Clearly the ordination of the preacher in Greyfriars was more of a benefit to the ministers of St Nicholas, whose workload was thereby reduced, than it was to the congregation; but it left unresolved the problem of a proper division of the city into pastoral districts, a problem that became more acute with the passing of the years inasmuch as the steadily expanding population was not evenly distributed within the three charges of St Nicholas. It bore most heavily on the Even Quarter for which Dr Duncan Shaw, minister of the third charge, had pastoral responsibility. When his senior colleague in the East Church died in July 1790, Duncan Shaw took advantage of the interregnum to suggest that a more equitable division might be made between the parochial responsibilities attaching to the second and third charges, he himself suggesting what a more appropriate division would be.[17] His suggestions were accepted by the Council with the result that most of the Futtie segment in Dr Shaw's 'Even' Quarter was transferred to his deceased colleague's pastoral district, *ie* the 'Green' Quarter which already embraced half of Futtie. But this was merely tinkering with the parochial problem. A solution was still a long way off and 30 years passed before any significant development took place.

Quinary division

It was in 1821 that the Town Council approached the Presbytery with the suggestion that the Parish of St Nicholas be divided into five *quoad sacra* Parishes, each having a separate Church and Session of its own. The proposed Churches were to be East and West St Nicholas, Greyfriars and St Clement's Footdee, for all of which the Town Council held the patronage. The fifth was envisaged as 'a new and additional parish church built and put upon the Establishment provided the necessary funds can be raised for that purpose'.[18] The Council were willing, if necessary, to go even further and tentatively suggested it might be possible to make six Parishes by raising one of the chapels-of-ease to parish status. The Presbytery responded by expressing their 'decided approbation of the measures proposed'. However, nearly four years passed before the matter again came before the Presbytery. On this occasion the proposal from the Town Council was to make five Parishes, the four above-mentioned together with Belmont Street Chapel-of-Ease.[19] In the intervening years the plan to erect a new building had been shelved and the Council had also to change its mind regarding the chapel to be accorded parish status. In 1823 this dignity had been offered to Trinity Chapel. The offer was one that the minister – the Rev. John Murray – and many of the congregation were disposed to accept. But a majority led by an elder – Wm Gray, father of Andrew Gray, the prospective minister of Woodside Chapel – opposed the move and the offer was then made to Belmont Street Chapel.[20]

The 1825 proposals were duly endorsed by the Presbytery, but the approval was less wholehearted, the Court concluding that 'the plan of disjunction was upon the whole, a proper one'. At the same time the Presbytery also gave its support to a petition from the ministers and Session of St Nicholas urging the need for the erection of a sixth parish church. This had the effect of arresting further progress. The following year the Town Council endeavoured to break the stalemate by taking advantage of the vacancy created in Greyfriars Church by the translation of its minister, Andrew Tawse. Stressing the impracticability of building a new church owing to the 'want of means', the Council urged that a division into five Parishes be proceeded with – in effect their original proposal of 1821 but incorporating an existing chapel instead of building a new church. This proposal was unacceptable to the

Presbytery because it was the Council's intention to fill the vacancy in Greyfriars with one of the three ministers of St Nicholas, a move which the Presbytery claimed 'diminished the number of officiating ordained clergymen in the place'.[21]

At the heart of the problem was the sinecure enjoyed by Dr Wm L Brown who, as Professor of Divinity in Marischal College, received the stipend attaching to Greyfriars Church but in return for which he did nothing other than take an occasional service in West St Nicholas. The Presbytery, in an overall review of the benefice of Greyfriars, had earlier conceded that 'it does not appear that the nominal minister of Greyfriars has ever performed any duty in the church to which he is presented'.[22] Even so they seemed unwilling to sanction any alteration in the status quo. It seems that no minister of the Church of Scotland ever held so many offices at one time as did Dr Brown. In addition to the Chair of Divinity and the benefice of Greyfriars, he held the Principalship of Marischal College, a royal chaplaincy, the deanery of the Chapel Royal and another lectureship. According to the acerbic James Bruce, he made atonement for his failings as a pluralist by doing all he could to prevent others from following his example.[23] Certainly he was most reluctant to part with the Greyfriars stipend. Consequently the division of the Parish of St Nicholas was delayed until 1828 when, in his 73rd year, Dr Brown agreed to relinquish his connection with Greyfriars Church. This opened the way for agreement to be reached between the Town Council and the Presbytery, the former now agreeing to the erection of a new church and the latter agreeing to the uncollegiating of St Nicholas Parish.

The disjunction of St Nicholas Parish

In March 1828 the Court of Teinds, on the application of the Town Council, pronounced a decree disjoining the Parish of St Nicholas and erecting it into six separate Parishes. The first three Parishes were to carry a stipend of £300. These were the East Parish with the Rev. James Foote as minister; the West Parish with Dr Glennie as minister; and the North Parish, its church yet to be built, with the Rev. John Murray as minister. This was the John Murray who, as minister of Trinity Chapel had been willing in 1823 to accept parish status for his congregation. The following year he was appointed by the Town Council to the second charge of St Nicholas and, on the disjunction of St Nicholas, he could have become minister of the East Parish but he elected to undertake the work of the new extension charge to be known as the North Parish. Belmont Street Chapel was designated the fourth, or South, Parish Church and the fifth and sixth Parishes were Greyfriars and St Clement's respectively. Each of these churches carried a stipend of

£250. Thus Aberdeen, last of all the major towns of Scotland, had its collegiate church disjoined.

Notes to Chapter 18

1. J Sinclair: *The statistical account of Scotland* (Edinburgh, 1797), vol. 19, p 148. See also J Milne: *Aberdeen: topographical, antiquarian and historical papers on the city of Aberdeen* (Aberdeen, 1911), p 69.
2. C Innes (ed.): *Extracts from the council register of the Burgh of Aberdeen 1570-1625* (Aberdeen, 1848), vol. 2, p 117 (17th November, 1595).
3. Ibid., p 135 (23rd June, 1596).
4. Ibid., p 136 (7th July, 1596).
5. The probable boundaries of the Four Quarters into which the burgh was divided are given in J A Ross: *Record of municipal affairs in Aberdeen* (Aberdeen, 1889), p 115. W Robbie in his book *Aberdeen: its traditions and history* (Aberdeen, 1893), p 83, wrongly transposes the Even and the Crooked Quarter.
6. C Innes: op. cit., pp 145-146 (14th September, 1596).
7. Ibid., p 145 (14th September, 1596).
8. *Aberdeen Town Council Register*, vol. 64, p 134 (20th June, 1778).
9. *Fasti Ecclesiae Scoticanae* (Edinburgh, first edition, 1871), vol. 3, p 473.
10. *Aberdeen Town Council Register*, vol. 64, p 107 (22nd September, 1777).
11. Ibid., p 110 (30th September, 1777).
12. Ibid., p 127 (22nd April, 1778).
13. Ibid., p 136 (2nd June, 1778).
14. *Aberdeen Town Council Register*, vol. 65, p 172 (26th February, 1787).
15. Ibid., p 176 (31st March, 1787).
16. *Records of the Presbytery of Aberdeen,* vol. 10, p 251 (25th March, 1818) (CH2-1-12).
17. *Aberdeen Town Council Register,* vol. 66, p 96 (20th August, 1790).
18. *Records of the Presbytery of Aberdeen,* vol. 10, p 366 (5th December, 1821) (CH2-1-12).
19. Ibid., p 535 (4th May, 1825).
20. R S Candlish: *Sermons and memoir of the Rev. Andrew Gray* (Edinburgh, 1862), p xi.
21. *Records of the Presbytery of Aberdeen*, vol. 11, p 22 (7th June, 1826) (CH2-1-13).
22. Ibid., vol. 10, p 252 (25th March, 1818) (CH2-1-12).
23. J Bruce: *Lives of eminent men of Aberdeen* (Aberdeen, 1841), p 398.

Chapter 19

*

SATELLITE TO THE SOUTH

THE disjunction of St Nicholas was not without effect on the Gaelic Chapel. Previously, like all other chapels in the town connected with the Establishment, it had fallen under the jurisdiction of the General Kirk Session. Now, under the newly drawn parish boundaries, it found itself attached to the South Parish, formerly Belmont Street Chapel situated on the other side of Gaelic Lane at its junction with Belmont Street. Trinity Chapel on the Shiprow was similarly attached to the South Parish. In 1829 the Presbytery remitted to the Kirk Session of the South Parish a request from the Gaelic Chapel for the ordination of additional elders,[1] and shortly thereafter the South Kirk Session appointed a committee 'to consider what addition it may be expedient to make to the Session'.[2] More than three years passed before the additions were made, and during that time the South Parish discovered that there were restrictions on its liberty of action that it had not anticipated.

Interference from St Machar

Basically the problem was that the South Parish, in nominating prospective elders for its Kirk Session (which included representative elders from Trinity Chapel and the Gaelic Chapel), selected some men who resided not in the former Parish of St Nicholas, but in the new town springing up across the Denburn within the boundaries of the Parish of Old Machar. This proposal was hotly contested by the Kirk Session of St Machar's who claimed that the South Parish was poaching on Old Machar territory. A long delay ensued while the matter was debated by the Presbytery. Eventually, in order to resolve the difficulty, some of the nominated elders transferred their residence from the Parish of Old Machar to that of the former St Nicholas.[3]

The Gaelic Chapel nominees were not seriously inconvenienced by the Old Machar interdict, but other difficulties arose to frustrate the intentions of the Gaelic Chapel minister. In November 1831 three men were nominated as elders for the Gaelic Chapel.[4] One was Hector Mackay, a ropemaker who resided on Nelson Street. This man, aged about 25, seems to have possessed exceptional gifts for spiritual leadership and he took a prominent part in the life of the Gaelic Chapel before eventually transferring his membership to Bon Accord Parish Church, an unhappy episode which falls to be considered at a later stage. In the published history of that church it is said that in 1829 Hector Mackay, when aged only 22 years, was ordained an elder in the Gaelic congregation.[5] Since the constitution of the Gaelic Chapel inhibited it from ordaining elders other than through the Parish Church, it would appear that this statement must be incorrect. It is true that as a consequence of the request for additional elders made by the Gaelic Chapel in 1829, Hector Mackay's name is the first nomination listed in the South Parish minutes, but his ordination as an elder was not proceeded with, probably because the Presbytery objected. On the other hand he could have declined the office, but if so his refusal was not minuted as was the case with the next name to appear − that of Alex Mackenzie, a skinner or currier residing at the Denburn near the Skene Street Bridge, an address that did fall within Old Machar territory.[6] The third person nominated was Donald Munro, a weaver whose address in 1831 is given as John Street. Possibly he was a son of Angus Munro, one of the first elders appointed in 1792. Angus Munro's address as recorded by Donald Sage in 1822 was John Street.

Gaelic elders in the General Kirk Session

Proceedings towards ordination were now delayed partly because of the attitude adopted by St Machar's Kirk Session and partly because of the death of the senior minister of the South Parish, John Bryce, and the death of his young colleague and successor, Wm Leith. When in February 1833 the business was again resumed, the South Parish minister was the Rev. Alex Dyce Davidson and the Kirk Session had before it a report from Presbytery recommending four members of the Gaelic Chapel for ordination.[7] These were the above-mentioned Alex Mackenzie, skinner, and Donald Munro, weaver (his address now being given as Union Street), together with Wm Gordon, bookseller of Summer Street, and Angus Mackay, tailor, of Gardener's Lane. The minister subsequently reported that Alex Mackenzie had declined the office and that Donald Munro was unsuitable in that, being a Chelsea Pensioner, he was liable to be called away from Aberdeen. When this circumstance was reported to the Rev. Hugh Mackenzie, minister of the Gaelic Chapel, he nominated Hugh Fraser, tailor at Broadford, for ordination.[8] Before the ordination took place, the South Parish minister discovered that another of the prospective elders, Angus Mackay, tailor of Gardener's Lane, was a Chelsea Pensioner and so he too was debarred from holding office, a decision which prompted a letter of protest from the Gaelic Chapel minister.[9] Effectively, therefore, only two new Gaelic elders were appointed − Wm Gordon, bookseller, and Hugh Fraser, tailor. Together they brought the Gaelic Church representation on the South Parish Session to four; Alex Macdonald, merchant of East North Street, and the plasterer, Robert Sutherland, who in 1819 had sponsored Donald Sage's candidature to the Gaelic Chapel, both being already members of that Session. In all the South Parish in 1833 had 30 elders, by far the largest section among the 96 elders that constituted the General Church Session.[10]

Alex Macdonald and Robert Sutherland were the first Gaelic elders to be ordained to the General Church Session of St Nicholas. In 1825, when the roll of St Nicholas Session comprised 57 ruling elders, it was agreed 'in view of the deficiency in the number of ruling elders in the city',[11] to enlarge the Session. The ministers were requested to make recommendations and 39 men were nominated of which twelve declined the office.[12] Among those proposed, Robert Sutherland, Longacre, Wm Murray, Gaelic Lane and Alex Macdonald, merchant, North Street, were described as 'sitters in the Gaelic Chapel'. Wm Murray, a communicant since September 1824, was not among those ordained, he apparently having 'removed to Caithness since the lists were given in'.[13] It is noteworthy that in nominating men to the General Kirk Session, the ministers of Aberdeen took no account of those who had been made elders in the Gaelic Chapel prior to its official recognition by the General Assembly. Of the three men nominated, Alex Macdonald was the only one who had officiated previously as an elder. Other senior elders such as Ebenezer Murray were passed over. In addition, at the ordination ceremony, no distinction was made between Alex Macdonald and Robert Sutherland, the former, despite his previous ordination, being, as was the latter, ordained rather than admitted to the General Kirk Session.

The South Parish and its satellite chapels were not alone in encountering difficulties with the minister and Kirk Session of Old Machar. The chapels-of-ease attached to Old Machar – Gilcomston, Union Terrace or Bon Accord, and Woodside – were all subjected to interference from their ecclesiastical superior. For example, Dr Kidd, minister of Gilcomston Chapel, was arraigned before the Presbytery for having arranged 'the appointment of a sermon on a weekday without any authority from this [St Machar] Kirk Session'. The visiting preacher on that occasion was Dr Macdonald, Ferintosh. In addition, Dr Kidd was charged with holding 'Divine Service by candlelight in the chapel-of-ease for a considerable part of the year notwithstanding an existing prohibition of the Presbytery on this point'.[14] Similarly the Rev. Andrew Gray, minister of Woodside Chapel, found that the elders chosen by the Old Machar Kirk Session for service in his congregation were all men who had strenuously opposed his induction to the Woodside Chapel, a proceeding which 'he had some difficulty in bringing himself to regard in any other light than that of an insult'.[15] Given such cynical disregard for brotherly co-operation in the service of the Church, it is not surprising that Andrew Gray should have been the spearhead of the movement to achieve the right of self-government for non-parish churches, a movement which culminated in the Chapels Act of 1834.

Discontented managers

A harmonious relationship between a minister and his office-bearers is not, however, guaranteed even when the minister has a decisive voice in selecting the men. The minister of the Gaelic Chapel had himself nominated Hugh Fraser, tailor at Broadford, for the eldership. Since, at the time, Hugh Mackenzie was also residing at Broadford, it would seem that he had every opportunity of becoming well acquainted with this parishioner. But Hugh Fraser had scarcely been admitted to office when he assumed the leadership of a ginger group whose object it was to shake up the dry bones in the Gaelic Chapel.

The year 1831 had been a difficult one for the Rev. Hugh Mackenzie. Two of his children died within weeks of one another. Furthermore it was reported at the annual general meeting of the chapel that 'funds were greatly on the decline'. The decrease was partly due to the unwillingness of hearers to pay seat rents, perhaps an indication of the fact that there was no longer pressure for accommodation. In view of the resistance to seat rents, the managers resolved that 'none will be allowed to possess seats in this chapel without paying for the same' and the minister was to be asked to intimate accordingly. 'Should he feel a delicacy in reading the same, one of their own number would go to the precentor's desk accompanied by one or two of his brother managers and execute the same after the pronouncing of the blessing.' The managers also decided that they themselves would need to 'take charge of the passes for some Sabbaths as their passkeepers are getting aged and frail and unfit for service, almost the whole of them'. New men would need to be recruited for this duty and it was agreed that intimation should be made for suitably qualified applicants, 'i.e., smart men of honest character and who understand figures a little and who, of course, understand the Gaelic language'. Six months later another meeting of the managers was called for the purpose 'of considering some measure or other for augmenting the necessary funds for defraying the regular and accidental expenses of the Chapel'.

The quinquennial election of managers took place in 1831 and the new blood introduced that year included Hector Mackay, ropemaker, and Wm Gordon, bookseller. The other men who had been nominated for the eldership were already serving as managers. The first indication of an attempt to enforce the decision taken in 1831 to the effect that 'none will receive any of the privileges connected with the chapel unless they have a seat and are otherwise found to support the funds of the chapel', appears in a minute of August 1832 when 'it was proposed and agreed that a list of communicants will be required against next communion stating where each sits, i.e., the number of pew they sit in; as it is intended that they will be served with tokens of admission agreeable to this list'. Clearly it was the intention to restrict communion to those who were paid-up members.

Occasionally the managers met monthly, but the usual pattern was that meetings were held quarterly. A sense of impending crisis may, therefore, be discerned in the fact that the managers held no fewer than four meetings in the month of February 1833. The regular quarterly meeting was held on the first of the month but the managers met again on the 15th 'by private intimation, agreed to at last meeting'. Hugh Fraser, tailor, was elected preses. The minute then reads as follows:

From the knowledge that Ebenezer Murray has of the low state of the funds of the Gaelic Chapel by the advice of Mr. Webster, advocate, he submitted to a meeting of the managers the following propositions, viz.:

1 *that the seat rents be raised from sixpence [2.5 pence] to one shilling [5 pence] per annum.*

2 *that all the subscribers be requested to give up their rights for the benefit of the General Fund.*

3 *to call a general meeting of the congregation and to show them the propriety of being more punctual in their attendance and more liberal with their collections.*

4 *to ascertain the propriety of calling an evening lecturer and how he is to be supported.*

5 *that a deputation be appointed to call on the Rev. Mr. Mackenzie to solicit his approbation and assistance in carrying the above propositions into affect.*

All these propositions were unanimously agreed to with the exception of Donald Munro who would not agree to call a lecturer.

Five days later, on 20th February, the managers met with the subscribers, the meeting having been called by public intimation from the precentor's desk. Hugh Fraser was re-elected to the chair. The minute somewhat obscurely states 'the subscribers agreed to raise their seats as proposed'. The only other decision taken was that Peter Duguid, Esq., Banker, be solicited to join Mr Webster, advocate, as a 'gentleman manager'. On 26th February the managers met with the heads of families, this meeting, like the previous one, having been called 'by intimation from the latren last Sabbath'. It was attended not just by Alex Webster, who was elected preses, and Peter Duguid, Esq., of Bourtie, but also by the Rev. Alex Dyce Davidson, minister of the South Parish Church. He and the preses both addressed the meeting and recommended the adoption of the first three propositions drawn up at the meeting of 15th February. These propositions having been read over 'two different times were unanimously approved by those assembled'. As regards the fourth proposition, Mr Webster informed the meeting that an evening lecturer could not be appointed 'without the previous consent and approbation of Mr. Mackenzie and therefore that the managers behove to arrange with him as to this matter before any steps could be taken thereanent. Alex Macdonald, the treasurer, and also Ebenezer Murray addressed the meeting and after a suitable exhortation by Mr Davidson on the propriety and necessity of following up the measures which had been recommended and agreed to for benefiting the funds, the meeting was closed with prayer'.

Resolutions urging greater faithfulness from the faithful are, as a rule, readily approved by ecclesiastical assemblies be they large or small, but the end result is seldom recognisably different from the starting point. Such now proved to be the case in the chapel on Gaelic Lane. No significant improvement fell to be recorded in subsequent months. In December the treasurer had to report that the amount collected at the seat-letting 'was found to be very deficient'. Everyone knew that the only effective counter-measure to dwindling numbers was for a Robert Finlayson, or some new voice, to appear in the pulpit. That was the reasoning that lay behind the proposition that an evening lecturer be appointed. However, the remedy could not be applied without the consent of the minister. Plead as they might with all the energy they could command, successive deputations found the Rev. Hugh Mackenzie implacably opposed to the suggestion. His was an understandably human reaction. No less human was the frustration provoked by his refusal to yield.

Notes to Chapter 19

1. *Records of the Presbytery of Aberdeen*, vol. 11, p 293 (2nd December, 1829) (CH2-1-13).
2. *Minutes of the South St Nicholas Kirk Session*, vol. 1 (1828-1849), p 79 (10th December 1829) (CH2-2-1).
3. Ibid., p 127 (5th January, 1832).
4. Ibid., p 124 (3rd November, 1831).
5. W Robbie: *Bon Accord Free Church, Aberdeen: a retrospect* (Aberdeen, 1887), p 88.
6. *Minutes of the South St Nicholas Kirk Session*, vol. 1 (1828-1849), p 132 (5th January, 1832).
7. Ibid., p 159 (14th February, 1833).

8. Ibid., p 160 (21st February, 1833).

9. Ibid., p 163 (7th March, 1833).

10. *Aberdeen Almanack* (Aberdeen 1834), p 237.

11. *Minutes of St Nicholas Kirk Session* (1822-1827), p 347 (17th October, 1825) (CH2-448-48).

12. Ibid., p 511 (14th May, 1827).

13. Ibid., p 523 (28th June, 1827).

14. *Records of the Presbytery of Aberdeen*, vol. 10, pp 257-258 (6th May, 1818) (CH2-1-12).

15. Ibid., vol. 11, p 511 (2nd May, 1832) (CH2-1-13).

Chapter 20

*

Spring Garden Blooms

BY 1834 fifty years had passed since the monolingual Gaels pleaded for the inauguration of Gaelic services in Aberdeen. In that time the Highland community had become bilingual and in these altered circumstances it became increasingly difficult for the minister of the Gaelic Chapel to retain the support of his fellow-countrymen. Preaching continued to have its attractions for the Highlanders, but for many of them heart-warming, soul-stirring sermons in English were to be preferred to pedestrian preaching in Gaelic. And Hugh Mackenzie's preaching was undeniably pedestrian. Even his obituarist conceded that he was 'not gifted with great eloquence'.[1] If his sermons possessed other merits, they were not discernible by ordinary mortals who preferred the diet on offer in other pulpits. Aberdeen was not short of attractive preachers. The beloved Dr Kidd was still active in Gilcomston Chapel, providing for his hearers spiritual nourishment in addition to soul-rousing exhilaration and entertainment. In Woodside Chapel Andrew Gray was getting into his stride and his preaching was such that he regularly drew hearers from Aberdeen.[2] Alex Dyce Davidson was settling into the South Church on Belmont Street. He was a fine evangelical preacher considered by many to be the ablest minister in Aberdeen. But possibly the pulpit which beckoned most alluringly to the theological sophisticates in the Gaelic Chapel was that of Union Terrace Chapel, in 1834 renamed Bon Accord Church.

Gavin Parker and Union Terrace Chapel

This congregation was of recent origin, having been formed in 1828. Its genesis can be traced back to a contested election for the pulpit of Trinity Chapel made vacant in 1824 when the magistrates promoted Trinity's popular minister, the Rev. John Murray, to the second charge of St Nicholas. Three men were nominated for the vacant charge – the Rev. David Simpson of Burghead who won the election; the Rev. Wm Leith who was subsequently called to Belmont Street Chapel (later the South Parish) and whose untimely death in 1832, aged only thirty years, delayed the appointment of elders in the Gaelic Chapel; and the Rev. Gavin Parker, then an assistant minister in Dundee. The whole community took a lively interest in this election and feeling ran high.[3]

Excitement of this kind is not to be wondered at when it is remembered that the appointment of chapel ministers was virtually the only occasion when elections took place in the community. The occasion was, therefore, more akin to the situation created by a general election nowadays. Before the passing of the Reform Bill in 1832 it was reckoned that in Scotland's population of two and a quarter millions, only 3000 persons possessed a vote.[4] Even under the 1832 Reform Act, only one person out of every 24 in the population had the vote. Similarly, local council elections were largely family affairs. Not surprisingly, therefore, the outcome of the election was awaited with intense interest.

The contest was effectively between David Simpson and Gavin Parker. It was won by Simpson, but the supporters of Gavin Parker never really acquiesced in the outcome and they resolved to go their separate way. Ultimately in 1828 the dissentients, whose leaders included the father of the Rev. Andrew Gray, persuaded the Presbytery to grant them (with Assembly approval) a constitution, or in other words, a licence, to function as a chapel-of-ease in the Parish of Old Machar.[5] At the same time they were able to purchase a redundant Baptist chapel on Union Terrace, and so to Union Terrace Chapel (not to be confused with Union Chapel built in 1822 on the Shiprow) a call was addressed to Gavin Parker and he commenced his ministry there in October 1828. Gavin Parker was an ardent follower of Dr John Love of Anderston Chapel and was accurately described as 'a high Calvinist who taught particular redemption as an essential doctrine of Christianity'.[6] He was instrumental in assisting 'Rabbi' John Duncan through his time of spiritual darkness and distress,[7] and it is not difficult to imagine the attraction that he would have held for Calvinistic Highlanders. Under his ministry the congregation grew[8] and in the process embraced a number of Highlanders whose subsequent contact with the Gaelic Chapel was largely confined to the annual visit of Dr Macdonald of Ferintosh to the Gaelic communion.[9] Since Union Terrace Chapel was in a different parish from that of the Gaelic Chapel, the communion services of the two congregations were held on different dates. 'Rabbi' Duncan was a regular visiting preacher in Gavin Parker's pulpit.[10]

Aberdeen ministers and the Chapels Act

In the light of these developments it can be seen that the church-going Gaelic community was no longer isolated from the general evangelical community and the drawing power of other evangelical pulpits placed a strain on the traditional loyalties of the Gaelic Highlanders. Rather than emphasise their own distinctiveness, the managers of the Gaelic Chapel attempted to adjust to the situation by asserting their equality with the Established chapels, a policy most obviously evidenced in their insistence on being accorded full parish status following the passage of the 1834 Chapels Act. This Act was one of two legislative decisions of the General Assembly of that year which set in motion events which culminated in the Disruption of the Church in 1843. These enactments were the Veto Act, which took account of the views of the congregation in the appointment of a parish minister; and the Chapels Acts which, among other things, gave chapel ministers parity with parish ministers in respect of membership of the church courts. Both these Acts gave rise to bitter controversy and voluminous litigation. In the historical development of the Disruption controversy the Veto Act occupied more of the legal limelight, but the Chapels Act was the more important and the more interesting innovation.[11] A quite disproportionate contribution to the ratification of that Act was made by the evangelical ministers of Aberdeen.

The first attempt to interest the General Assembly in the Chapel Question, as the agitation to achieve parity of rank for chapel ministers was termed, was made in 1825 by David Carment,[12] minister of the Parish of Rosskeen, who that year attended his first General Assembly as a commissioner. The overture which he introduced on that occasion made no progress in the Assembly, but the agitation continued in some presbyteries, notably in the Presbytery of Aberdeen where it was vigorously supported by Carment's friend Andrew Gray, at that time a divinity student in Marischal College (1824-1828). In 1828, and again in 1829, petitions relative to the Chapel Question drawn up by Andrew Gray on behalf of Aberdeen Chapel members, were submitted to the Assembly, but to no avail.[13]

In 1833 a meeting in Aberdeen of the Friends of Chapels-of-Ease, appointed a committee to campaign for recognition for chapel ministers. This committee, carrying the euphemistic title of 'The Committee for Promoting the Efficiency of Chapels-of-Ease', consisted of the chapel ministers themselves, *ie* Dr Kidd of Gilcomston, Andrew Gray of Woodside, David Simpson of Trinity, John Allan of Union, Gavin Parker of Union Terrace and Hugh Mackenzie of the Gaelic Chapel, together with four of the Parish ministers, *viz* James Foote, John Murray and Alex Davidson of the East, North and South Parishes respectively, and Abercrombie Gordon of Greyfriars. The committee also included Robert Smith who held the first charge of Old Machar, Principal Dewar of Marischal College, James Bentley, professor of Hebrew at King's College and Robert J Brown who was professor of Greek at Marischal College and a son of the pluralist Principal of Marischal, Dr W L Brown.[14] That same year the Presbytery of Aberdeen agreed to transmit to the General Assembly a petition on behalf of the chapel ministers.[15] The petition, to the effect that chapel-of-ease ministers be accorded the privileges of the regular clergy of the Established Church, was moved by Professor R J Brown of Aberdeen, but it was narrowly defeated by a motion in favour of appointing a committee to consider how best to implement the prayer of the petition,[16] in effect a delaying device.

The following year, 1834, the petitioners were back at the Assembly, and although as chapel ministers they were debarred from speaking as members of Assembly, they made clever use of a procedural device to allow two of their number address the house from the bar of the Assembly.[17] The men selected to present the case were Andrew Gray, minister of Woodside Chapel, Aberdeen, and the minister of Anderston Chapel, Glasgow, the Rev. Charles J Brown, an Aberdonian whose father, Provost Alex Brown, and brother had canvassed so effectively for Andrew Gray's election to Woodside Chapel. These men presented their case with consummate ability. As Principal Watt put it, 'Very few of their brethren in any position in the Church could have opened up the whole question in all its legal and historical bearings so cogently and brilliantly'.[18] The discussion having progressed from the bar to the body of the house, it then fell to Professor Brown of Marischal to move that the petition be granted, a motion which was carried by a large majority.[19] A committee was formed to complete the enactment and a later diet of the Assembly decreed that Kirk Sessions should be formed in, and parochial districts be assigned to, the chapels of the Establishment, their ministers to be members of the Church Courts equally with parish ministers.[20] The view then taken by the General Assembly, that it alone had powers to determine whom it might admit to, or exclude from, the membership of its own courts, was in due course to be successfully challenged in the Civil Courts. Nevertheless, the 1834 decision was, at the time, accepted so unquestioningly by all parties that only two years later a chapel minister was elected Moderator of the General Assembly. It was the final triumph of Andrew Gray's indefatigable campaign to get the Church to assert unequivocally, the Presbyterian doctrine of the parity of all ministers.

Spring Garden Parish Church

Following the passing of the Chapels Act, the Presbytery of Aberdeen appointed a committee to revise parish boundaries and to make recommendations concerning the new *quoad sacra* Parishes. The first report made to Presbytery by this committee took no account of the Gaelic Chapel which chapel it regarded as something of a special case as indeed it was. Strictly speaking, the Gaelic Chapels in lowland areas were not chapels-of-ease, that is to say they were not erected to relieve the pressure on accommodation in the parish church, or to convenience the population in an expanding community remote from the parish church. Their function was to cater for an immigrant group within the community. A Gaelic chapel was, in fact, a 'gathered' church. The committee appointed by the 1833 General Assembly to report on the implementation of legislation anent the elevation of chapels to parish status, recognised the anomalous position of the nine Gaelic Chapels in lowland districts. In their report, drawn up by the Rev. Wm Cunningham of the College Church, Edinburgh, later Principal Cunningham of New College, the committee took the view that it would be best to omit the Gaelic Chapels from any scheme of district allocation for pastoral superintendence.[21] But the Aberdeen Presbytery, doubtless at the behest of the Rev. Hugh Mackenzie, directed the Presbytery committee to include the Gaelic Chapel among the churches to be assigned parochial responsibilities. Consequently the committee, with considerable misgivings as to the fitness of the exercise, suggested the area bounded by Gerard Street on the north, George Street on the west, John Street and Innes Street on the south, and the Gallowgate on the east, a district comprising in all a population of 1287 souls. Hugh Mackenzie dissented from this report, as he did also in respect of the district assigned to Bon Accord Church, a district comprising 4409 persons, his dissent in the latter case being on the grounds that assigning so populous a district was contrary to the requirement of the Declaratory Act which specified that manageable districts be assigned to chapel ministers.[22]

A motion that the Gaelic Chapel be given neither Kirk Session nor parochial district, but that the matter, in consequence of the great difficulties connected with it, be referred to the following General Assembly for advice, was defeated and Spring Garden Parish Church, alias the Gaelic Chapel, came into being. The Rev. W R Pirie, already actively cultivating his reputation of being 'in ecclesiastical matters a man of war from his youth',[23] registered his dissent. The elders allocated to the Gaelic Chapel were the three already connected with it – Alex Macdonald, merchant, Wm Gordon, bookseller, and Hugh Fraser, tailor, the fourth, Robert Sutherland, having by now left Aberdeen. By 1836 another name had been added, that of Daniel Dewar, Principal of Marischal College.

Principal Daniel Dewar

Principal Dewar's attachment to the congregation was more honorary than functional, yet the people regarded him as one of themselves for he could address them in impeccable Gaelic. In September 1836, at yet another crisis meeting of the congregation, Alex Webster, advocate, proposed from the chair that Principal Dewar, who was present, be appointed an additional lay manager. By the end of the meeting a vote of thanks was accorded to the Principal 'for his unwearied exertions in promoting the spiritual and temporal welfare of this congregation', and, in a sense, he was no stranger to them. A native of Glen Dochart, Daniel Dewar had been appointed by the Town Council as preacher in the College Church (Greyfriars) in 1814 only a year after his ordination as missionary in Strontian. He was an exceptionally gifted man and while in Greyfriars he was nominated to the chair of Moral Philosophy at King's College, which post he held conjunctly with his preaching station. In 1817 the Presbytery received complaints that he was neglecting his preaching function in the College Church and, on being asked for an explanation, he offered the excuse: 'Being informed that it is usual with the professors in King's College to accompany the students to Church, I, in compliance with this custom, have generally gone with my class to the Old Town Church on the Sabbath forenoon while a licentiate officiated in the College Church.' The custom, however, was not intended to exempt the holder of a ministerial charge from the obligations of his preaching office and the Presbytery enjoined Dr Dewar 'to discharge his ministerial duties in the College Church personally and regularly in time to come as devolved upon him by the Presbytery and as discharged by his immediate predecessor'.[24]

Two years later Professor Dewar received a call to the Tron Church, Glasgow, in succession to the renowned Dr Thomas Chalmers who had moved to nearby St John's Church. In the Tron, Daniel Dewar exercised a very influential evangelical ministry until 1830 when, on the death of Dr W L Brown, he was appointed by the Crown to the vacant Principalship of Marischal College. It was said that he owed this appointment to a marriage connection with Lord Aberdeen's family.[25] The Senatus of Marischal College petitioned the Crown in favour of Professor George Glennie, Dewar's immediate predecessor in the College Church, and they unanimously expressed their disapproval of Dr Dewar's elevation.[26] However, his return to Aberdeen was warmly welcomed by the Evangelical Party and, no doubt, by the congregation of the Gaelic Chapel. Sadly, a character defect destroyed his later usefulness for, having taken a leading part in all the contendings and conflicts that preceded the Disruption, he, like the children of Ephraim, 'being armed and carrying bows, turned back in the day of battle'. He remained in the Establishment fearful lest by joining the Disruption Church he would forfeit his Principalship, in the event a needless fear. Donald Sage, who knew him intimately, gives a graphic, touching account of his rise from the humblest of circumstances to a place of power and eminence only to sink into dishonour and obloquy. He pinpoints his weakness with devastating terseness. 'He sat in a vehicle drawn by two horses, Ambition being the name of the one and Avarice that of the other'.[27]

Principal Dewar's fall from grace was, however, some years distant and Spring Garden Parish Church in 1836 welcomed whatever patronage he was disposed to give. Certainly the congregation needed all the support it could get for, not surprisingly, the parochial district assigned to it contributed no additional strength. A census taken in 1835 revealed that only 30 persons from a parish comprising 1486 souls had any connection with the Parish Church and that connection was attributable to its being a Gaelic church and not the parish church.[28] In the peculiar circumstances of the Gaelic congregation, the apportionment of any district could be no more than a concession to, or an indulgence of, its new parochial status. The enclave now designated the Spring Garden Parish was, in fact, a segment of the Greyfriars Parish which bounded it on both its east and north sides. Spring Garden was, of course, within the enclave, a street running parallel with Gerard Street but free from the overtones of Moderatism attaching to the street named after the Rev. Dr Alex Gerard. The Rev. Abercrombie Gordon, minister of Greyfriars Church, was already deeply committed to church extension work in this area and, in 1833, he had initiated the construction of a new building at Mounthooly which in 1835 was officially recognised by the Presbytery as John Knox Parish Church. This new church was practically on the doorstep of the Spring Garden Parish and its establishment must have extinguished any faint hopes which the Gaelic minister and Session may have had regarding their possible usefulness to non-Gaelic worshippers in that area. They continued to retain the name until the Disruption provided an excuse for a change of designation, but their commitment to an English language ministry must have been at best half-hearted. In 1839 a new issue of communion tokens was minted. While on one face was inscribed 'Spring Garden (Gaelic) Parish Church Aberdeen 1839', the wording of the Scripture text stamped on the reverse side was uncompromisingly Gaelic.

Notes to Chapter 20

1. *Aberdeen Free Press and Buchan News* (11th February, 1859), p 5.
2. R S Candlish: *Sermons and memoir of the Rev. Andrew Gray* (Edinburgh, 1862), p xxviii.
3. W Robbie: *Bon Accord Free Church, Aberdeen. A retrospect* (Aberdeen, 1887), p 2.
4. G T Warner and C H K Marten: *The groundwork of British history* (London, 1932; revised edition reprinted 1936), p 480.
5. *Records of the Presbytery of Aberdeen*, vol. 11, p 95 (20th June, 1827) (CH2-1-13).
6. *Fasti Ecclesiae Scoticanae* (Edinburgh, first edition, 1871), vol. 3, p 490.
7. D Brown: *Life of John Duncan* (Edinburgh, 1872), p 203.
8. *Selected portions from the diary and manuscripts of the Rev. Gavin Parker* (Aberdeen, 1848), p 26.

9. W Robbie: op. cit., p 16.

10. Ibid., p 18.

11. F Lyall: *Of presbyters and kings. Church and state in the law of Scotland* (Aberdeen, 1980), p 29.

12. A Gray (ed.): *The progress of the chapel question from its first discussion in 1825 to its settlement in 1834 by the elevation of the ministers of chapels to the rank of the parochial clergy* (Aberdeen, 1836), annotation by A Gray accompanying a letter reproduced from *Edinburgh Christian Instructor* (1825). This interesting volume containing all the proceedings on the chapel question from 1825-1836 was gifted to Christ College Library, Aberdeen by the Rev. A Gray; see R S Candlish, op. cit., p xxxiv, footnote.

13. Ibid., Petitions to the General Assemblies of 1828 and 1829.

14. Ibid., Minute of a meeting of the Friends of Chapels-of-Ease held 2nd May 1833.

15. *Records of the Presbytery of Aberdeen*, vol. 12, p 22 (27th March, 1833) (CH2-1-14).

16. R Buchanan: *The ten years' conflict* (Glasgow, new edition 1852), vol. 1, pp 235-236.

17. Ibid., pp 270-276.

18. H Watt: *Thomas Chalmers and the Disruption* (Edinburgh, 1943), p 138.

19. R Buchanan: op. cit., p 296.

20. *Declaratory enactment of the General Assembly regarding the status of Chapels of Ease* (31st May, 1834).

21. *Report of the Committee of the General Assembly on Chapels of Ease* (1834), p 6.

22. *Records of the Presbytery of Aberdeen,* vol. 12, pp 161-163 (7th October, 1834) (CH2-1-14).

23. P J Anderson (ed.): *Aurora Borealis Academica* (Aberdeen, 1899), p 173.

24. *Records of the Presbytery of Aberdeen*, vol. 10, p 245 (24th December, 1817) (CH2-1-12).

25. J Martin: *Eminent divines in Aberdeen and the North* (Aberdeen, 1888), p 224.

26. P J Anderson (ed.): *Records of Marischal College and University* (Aberdeen, 1898), vol. 2, p 30.

27. D Sage: *Memorabilia Domestica* (Wick, 1889; 2nd edition, 1899; reprinted 1975), p 228.

28. Parliamentary Papers. *Fifth Report of the Commissioners of Religious Instruction, Scotland* (1839), appendix, p 378.

Chapter 21

*

GLOOMY MEMORIES

THE quinquennial election of managers fell due at the annual general meeting held in April 1836. Four men were dropped – Robert Sutherland, plasterer, who had left the city; Donald Munro, the weaver who was opposed to the proposal to appoint an evening lecturer; John Stewart, also a weaver; and Hugh Fraser, formerly tailor of Broadford but now clothier of 227 George Street. Both the last mentioned were to be re-appointed in 1841, but Donald Munro, weaver and Chelsea Pensioner, finally faded from the records. Appointed in place of these men were Angus Mackay, tailor and Chelsea Pensioner, and Wm Murray, tailor, both of whom had given service earlier; and two newcomers to management, Robert Mackay, weaver, and James Dingwall, merchant at Woodside, later described as vintner at Woodside. Of these four, all but Wm Murray died before the end of their quinquennium. The treasurer, Alex Macdonald, reported that the congregational debt in 1836 stood at £380, an increase of more than £21 over the year. Following this depressing report it was agreed, on the proposal of Mr Webster, advocate, that a committee of enquiry be appointed 'to consider the present state of the funds of the church, and to report what may appear to them most likely to promote the benefit thereof and prevent an increase of the debt'. This committee comprised, Mr Duguid of Bourtie, banker; John Macdonald, road surveyor of Gerard Street, first appointed a manager in 1806; Ebenezer Murray, merchant of Broad Street, now residing at 27 Gordon Street; John Stewart, teacher on the Shiprow and possibly the same person previously designated a weaver; Hugh Fraser, clothier of 227 George Street; Wm Cormack, merchant of 33 Shiprow, who had joined the communicant membership earlier in the month; John MacKay, distiller; Alex Fraser, road contractor of Skene Street; John Macleod, road contractor; and Mr Alex Webster, advocate and convener.

This committee subsequently drew up a report which took account of both income and expenditure. Savings on expenditure were to be achieved by a reduction of £1 on the precentor's salary and a similar amount on the Clerk's salary. It was also proposed that 'the allowance formerly given to the church officer of £3 yearly be discontinued as he is now paid £5 per annum from the funds of the General Session'. It was the opinion of several members of the committee that money could also be saved by making use of local preachers for the Communion. Mr Webster was asked to 'communicate with Mr. Mackenzie anent this matter and ascertain his sentiments previous to a meeting of the congregation'.

Seat rents

On the income side the proposals had a familiar sound. Seat rents were to be increased, the minimum half-yearly payment being increased from one shilling (5 pence) to one shilling and sixpence (7.5 pence) which, taking into account the earlier increase, was a trebling of the cost over a three year period. At the top end of the seat rent scale (which comprised seven steps in all) the price was raised from three shillings (15 pence) to three shillings and sixpence (17.5 pence) or seven shillings per annum. The committee also went on to recommend that 'proper seat books should be prepared and delivered to the pew openers having the names of those who pay for seats correctly inserted so as no hearers may be accommodated who do not pay for the same with the exception of strangers or occasional hearers'. The final recommendation was that 'quarterly collections should be made for the benefit of the church and that the Very Reverend Principal Dewar should be requested to offi- ciate on these occasions'. When the report was brought before a general meeting of the congregation held on 9th September 1836, 'Dr Dewar addressed the meeting and pressed on them the propriety of uniting in supporting this place of worship. Messrs Ebenezer Murray and Alex Macdonald addressed the meeting to the same effect. The question being put from the chair whether or not the meeting approved of the report, it was unanimously agreed to, with the exception of four or five members'.

The increase in seat rents was reflected in the revenue from that source rising from £36 for the half year to June 1836 to £45 for the half year to December 1836. Whether or not the resignation of the clerk, Robert Hamilton, at the next general meeting held in May 1837 was a consequence of the reduction in his salary is uncertain. He had served as clerk for almost twenty years, but for much of 1834 he had been absent from ill-health. He was succeeded as clerk by Wm Murray, tailor.

Special lectures displaced

The most significant and contentious proposal was the appointment of special lectures. Implementation of this plan required the Rev. Hugh Mackenzie's agreement and it seems not to have been given. In February 1837 the managers requested Mr Mackenzie to invite Principal

Dewar, the Rev. Alex Dyce Davidson, now minister of the West Church, and his successor in the South Church, the Rev. Wm K Tweedie, to preach in the Gaelic Chapel the following month. However Hugh Mackenzie remained adamantly opposed to the idea and the exasperated managers decided that they had no alternative but to hold the special services in buildings over which Hugh Mackenzie had no jurisdiction. When the annual general meeting was held on 5th May 1837, Ebenezer Murray intimated that special services were to be held for the benefit of the funds of the Gaelic congregation. The first of these was to be held in the West Church on the evening of Sunday 28th May when the Rev. Alex Dyce Davidson would preach. On Wednesday 24th May the following notice appeared in the *Aberdeen Journal*:

GAELIC CHURCH

The Rev. Mr Davidson will preach a sermon in the West Church on the evening of Sabbath the 28th inst; and the Rev. Mr Tweedie in the South Church on a future evening, of which due notice will be given, when collections will be made in aid of the Funds of the Gaelic Church. The congregation assembling there was first brought together by the labours of the late Rev. Dr Ronald Bain. It is a fact worthy of being recorded that this excellent minister preached gratuitously for many years to the Gaelic population of Aberdeen. A large portion of the original members of the congregation have been removed by death and those who still survive are aged and few in number. Their offspring being brought up in this place are more conversant in the English than in the Gaelic – the language of their parents. Hence they worship not in the Gaelic Church but in other churches of the city. Owing to those causes the Funds are in a low state; and the managers feel themselves called upon to appeal to the Friends of the Church of Scotland for assistance to enable them to continue the ministration of the Word of Life to their fellow-christians and fellow creatures in their native tongue the only medium of communicating instruction to them on the subject of religion. English is preached on the Lord's Day afternoon for the benefit of those who do not understand Gaelic.

It was that same year that the minister reported to the Parliamentary Commissioners that in his congregation 'there are a few who do not understand any English and several hundreds who, although they understand it sufficiently to conduct the ordinary business of life, yet are incapable of understanding an English discourse'.[1] From the terms of the notice in the *Aberdeen Journal* it is clear that the primary mission of the Gaelic Church was to Gaelic speakers. Spring Garden Parish Church was an irrelevance as far as the Aberdeen citizenry were concerned – far more so than was the case twenty years earlier when the Rev. Duncan Grant had occupied the pulpit.

On Wednesday 5th July 1837 the *Aberdeen Journal* carried another notice:

GAELIC CHURCH

As already announced in a former advertisement the Rev. Mr. Tweedie will preach a sermon in the South Church on Sabbath 9 July at 6 o'clock evening when a collection will be made on behalf of the Funds of the Gaelic Church. The friends of the Church are earnestly invited to attend.

As minister of the South Church the Rev. Wm King Tweedie, although a native of Ayr, was most kindly disposed to the Highlanders. Before he came to the South Parish Church in 1836 he already had connections with the antecedents of the Gaelic congregation; for among his friends he numbered John Wilson of Bombay (married to a daughter of Kenneth Bayne) and especially John Macdonald, missionary son of Dr Macdonald, Ferintosh, who prior to his departure for Calcutta had been a minister in London as was W K Tweedie himself.[2] Tweedie was subsequently to write a biography of his missionary friend following John Macdonald's early death in 1847.[3]

Demise of the fathers

No indication is given in the Gaelic Church minutes of the extent to which the funds benefited from these services. At the meeting of the managers held on 6th June it was reported that Mr Duguid of Bourtie, agent of the Bank of Scotland, was indisposed. Perhaps after four years service he had had enough of the intractable problems of the Gaelic congregation. But the Gaelic Chapel never seemed to have difficulty in recruiting 'gentlemen managers'. It had Ebenezer Murray to thank for that. Although he was not one of the ten elected members of the committee, Ebenezer Murray attended the June meeting to report that in consequence of the indisposition of Mr Duguid he had approached Mr David Chalmers of Westburn, son and successor to James Chalmers, proprietor of the *Aberdeen Journal* and a former manager of the Gaelic Chapel, with a view to obtaining his consent to act as a manager in place of Mr Duguid. David Chalmers sent his letter of acceptance in the hand of his proposer who was warmly thanked by the committee for his good offices in this matter. It was Ebenezer Murray's last recorded appearance at the committee and as his last entry in the Aberdeen Directory appears in 1838 it may be presumed that he died in the latter half of 1837. His passing severed one of the few remaining links with the community that worshipped under Ronald Bayne. Ebenezer Murray had been appointed to the first committee of managers in 1796 and had served continuously until 1821. Thereafter although not an elected member, he had remained active and prominent in all the congregation's affairs. Ordained to the eldership in 1806 he was obviously a man of some substance and standing in the community and his genial presence in the congregation would have been sorely missed.

Another memorable event in the life of the congregation that year took place in September when it was agreed to install gas lighting in the chapel. The decision was a popular one with the congregation because the appeal for donations for this purpose raised more than the cost of the installation which amounted to £18 4s 6d. The total income for the year ending April 1838 was £232 and for the following year £243. Even so, in April 1839 the treasurer complained that he had not funds to answer all demands and he requested an increase in his borrowing powers which request was granted. At the annual general meeting in May 1839, at which the Rev. Hugh Mackenzie was present, it was agreed that servicing the debt of near £400 was the main source of the financial problem and that a new fund to liquidate the debt should be started. Income for this fund was to be looked for from quarterly special events, ie guest preachers. However, despite a series of deputations, the problem of ministerial consent remained unresolved and the financial situation continued to deteriorate.

In May 1840 the treasurer Alex Macdonald tendered his resignation on the grounds of 'advancing years and infirmities'. For more than thirty years he had devoted his energies to the service of the congregation according to his lights. Had he not so strenuously opposed the concessions which Duncan Grant had been anxious to make to English language hearers, the Highland Congregation might have been in better shape than proved to be the case in 1840. Even so, the congregation, such as it was, had reason to be grateful to Alex Macdonald who had been their treasurer for twenty years. Now he was accorded the distinction of being the first office-bearer in the congregation to have a tribute to his service engrossed in the minutes. When the quinquennial election came round the following year, he was the only one re-elected unanimously, ie without votes being counted. But the meeting at which he tendered his resignation was the last which he attended. He died on 23rd April 1842. He had the further distinction of being the first to leave a legacy to the congregation: £20 to the general fund and £20 to the bedridden poor, which legacies were not payable during the lifetime of his widow.

Alex Macdonald's place as treasurer was taken by Alex Mackenzie, skinner or currier of Denburn Terrace. He had been a member of the committee of management continuously since 1819, but in 1824 he had lost his father's rights as an original subscriber because he did not understand the Gaelic language. As treasurer he took office at a difficult time. The debt stood at £370 and he was immediately confronted with a demand for repayment of a loan of £100 which stood in the name of James Dingwall, vintner of Woodside, who had been elected a manager in 1836. James Dingwall had died earlier in the year and the demand by his widow to have the loan repaid was deferred by the committee, an arrestment having been placed on the loan at the instance of Henry Ogg & Co. Distillers at Strathdee distillery. Two years later when Alex Macdonald died there was a demand for the repayment of a loan of £90 belonging to his estate. These were substantial sums to have to be replaced and probably only the sympathetic indulgence of Alex Webster, advocate, kept the congregation from insolvency.

The problems confronting the treasurer were not all of one kind. In November 1842 a meeting was called 'to assist the treasurer in making the return anent the Income Tax. The clerk stated that the ledger and minute books are in the hands of the Presbytery since the first of July and still unattested, therefore it would put him to a good deal of inconvenience in making the said returns'.

What looked like being the final blow, fell on 17th April 1843 when the managers met to consider a letter to the treasurer from Alex Webster. It read, 'Sir, I have to remind you of the bill due by the managers of the Gaelic Chapel on the 23rd current for £124 16s. to which I request you will attend'. The managers instructed the treasurer to pay the interest on the bill (£4 16s) and £10 to account and to request of Mr Webster 'the favour to delay for some time as they find it inconvenient at present to answer the whole demand'. Mr Webster replied that payment must be made in full whereupon the managers 'finding that in consequence of the critical position of the Church at present they cannot meet with any person willing to advance money on the property they therefore feel themselves compelled to use every lawful steps to sell the property'.

In the fading light of a northern winter, Donald Sage was putting the finishing touches to his reminiscences of early youth. Discerning, from the vantage point of the Resolis manse, the signs of the times, he wrote, 'The sky of Providence is darkening down with more than ordinary gloom on the Church of my Fathers'.[4] Certainly the gloom that shrouded the Church in Gaelic Lane, was daily deepening.

Notes to Chapter 21

1. Parliamentary Papers. *Fifth Report of the Commissioners of Religious Instruction, Scotland* (1839), appendix, p 378.
2. For a brief account of the life of the Rev. Wm K Tweedie, see Rev. J A Wylie (ed.): *Disruption Worthies: a memoir of 1843* (Edinburgh, 1881), vol. 4, pp 481–488.
3. W K Tweedie: *The life of the Rev. John Macdonald AM* (Edinburgh, 1849).
4. D Sage: op. cit., p 144.

Chapter 22

*

Disruption and Demission

THE Disruption, the most cataclysmic event in the history of the Scottish Church since the Reformation, was triggered off in May 1843 by the resignation of 474 ministers from their livings in the Parishes of the Established Church. These men then commenced to minister in a church which adopted the name The Free Church of Scotland. The leaders of this movement, notably Dr Thomas Chalmers and Dr Wm Cunningham, were at pains to stress that this was not a new church. The ministers who signed the Act of Separation and the Deed of Demission, as the instrument of resignation was called, had no disagreement with the Church of Scotland. Their protest was not against the policies or the proceedings of that Church but against State interference in matters that involved the Church in what the protesters considered to be the exercise of its spiritual discretion. The Disruption was not envisaged as being, as is perhaps now commonly supposed, a disruption or division of the Church, but a disruption of the link that bound the Church to the State.[1] In the event, of course, the Church was not itself of one mind; and because it did not act as one body, it was inevitably rent in two. Even so, those who withdrew strongly denied the charge that they were secessionists.

The cause of disruption

Lay patronage – the appointment of ministers to Parishes by the heritors or landowners upon whom devolved the statutory duty of meeting the cost of providing Gospel ordinances in every parish – was the occasion, although not the cause, of the Disruption.[2] The Evangelical Party in the Church, although it repudiated the view that the patrons had always enjoyed an unfettered right to force their nominees into pastoral charges irrespective of the wishes of the congregations, did, nonetheless, recognise that, in the last analysis, the apportionment of the churches' temporalities lay outwith the jurisdiction of the Church. What the Evangelical Party refused to concede was that the Church was bound to defer to the wishes of the patron to the extent that a Presbytery was obligated to ordain to office presentees whom it judged to be unsuitable for a pastoral charge because they were unacceptable to the congregation. The Presbyteries, before proceeding to ordination, had a right to judge the qualifications for office of the presentee. The question at issue was whether these qualifications for office referred only to a candidate's life, literature and doctrine, or whether acceptability to the people had to be considered.[3] It was when the State in the shape of the Civil Courts including the House of Lords, acting at the behest of the patrons, insisted that the Church must ordain men irrespective of their acceptability to the people, that the Evangelicals protested that the spiritual liberties of the Church were being made subject to intolerable interference and that they had no alternative but to withdraw from the Establishment.

And so, in May 1843, the Church of Scotland, Free, came into being. It claimed to be the same Church as that which it had left, a Church adhering to the same Confession of Faith, loyal to the same principles, differing only inasmuch as in the discharge of its spiritual functions, it was to be subservient to no other authority than the will of God as understood by the collective mind of the Church. This noble manifesto proclaiming the spiritual independence of the Church was launched under the slogan 'The Crown Rights of the Redeemer', a slogan chosen by Dr R S Candlish.[4] It was heady stuff, guaranteed to excite the emotions of all those of an evangelical persuasion who saw the issue as one involving the honour of Christ. But the extent of support which the movement received was doubtless in part attributable to the political mood of the time.

The claims urged on behalf of the spiritual independence of the Church conveniently coincided with the demand for a more democratic society and a greater measure of liberty for the individual. The Reform Act of 1832, extending the franchise in the political sphere, encouraged the populace to expect equivalent concessions in the ecclesiastical sphere and those ministers who now championed the rights of the people in the choice of a minister, found a ready response especially among the emergent middle class.[5] But if many of the lay people adhering to the new denomination did so without fully understanding the theological issues at stake, the same must not be said of the ministers. The sermon preached by Dr Welsh, the retiring Moderator of Assembly, to the commissioners gathered in St Giles Church, Edinburgh, on 18th May 1843, was on the text, 'Let every man be fully persuaded in his own mind'. And these men were. They did not act precipitately under any kind of mass emotion.[6] Over many months and years they had pondered the issues at stake. When they took their decision to leave the security of the Establishment and joined themselves to the procession that 'honourably, humbly and hopefully' threaded its way to Tanfield Hall, there to constitute the Church of Scotland, Free, it was for conscience' sake that they went.

Aberdeen's ministers demit office

Aberdeen was unique among the cities of Scotland in that all 15 of its parish ministers adhered to the Free Church. In the other cities only about two-thirds of the ministers left the Establishment. Although it has been argued that it is an over-simplification to view the unanimity of action of the Aberdeen ministers as being solely the consequence of genuine conviction and respect for principle,[7] the men themselves saw it in these terms. Their resolve may to some extent have been strengthened by encouragement from within their congregations but those for whom congregational support would have been critical had they remained in the Establishment, ie those occupying the Parishes constituted by the Chapels Act of 1834 were those who, in any case, had been most forthright in their support of Non-intrusion principles. Any who resisted the popular movement would have had Principal Dewar for company; but whatever regrets some may have had over the need to quit the Establishment, all saw it as their duty to leave and did.

The attitude of the minister of the Gaelic Chapel was never in any doubt. He had allied himself with the Non-intrusion Party from its earliest days, especially with its local leaders such as Andrew Gray of Woodside. In 1830 Hugh Mackenzie sought and obtained approval from the South Parish Kirk Session to take up a collection in the Gaelic Chapel on behalf of the Anti-Patronage Society and anti-patronage lectures may have been a feature of the Gaelic Church calendar down the years.[8] When the parting of the ways came, Hugh Mackenzie appended his name to the Deed of Demission. His congregation shared his outlook and although the external managers, Alex Webster and David Chalmers, adhered to the Established Church, none of the congregational managers appear to have defected. Nor did there appear to be any break in the good relations that existed between the congregation and its external managers. In the minute of the 1843 annual general meeting, which was signed by Alex Webster himself, it is recorded that 'these gentlemen are still ready to advise and assist us in any affairs connected with this Church'.

The immediate problem that confronted congregations withdrawing from the Established Church was the question of accommodation. The former chapels-of-ease, although erected by congregational funds, were according to the terms of the constitution establishing their status as *quoad sacra* parish churches, the property of the Established Church. Consequently, in the immediate aftermath of the Disruption, the minister and office-bearers of many such churches felt themselves morally inhibited from continuing to occupy their buildings. Bon Accord Church on Union Terrace was a case in point. There, in the month of June, the Rev. Gavin Parker preached in the morning in the open-air in front of the church.[9] Similarly the congregation of Wood-side worshipped in the open-air for three Sundays before a temporary wooden building was erected.[10] A temporary building was, of course, a solution that allowed time for legal moves to take their leisurely course, which, in the case of Woodside, they did. But the Bon Accord congregation, lacking that amenity, reoccupied their building in July and, it would appear, did not thereafter come under serious pressure from the Presbytery to quit.

The Free Gaelic congregation

Information on the policy adopted by the Gaelic Chapel managers during this period is lacking, but the indications are that the congregation continued to meet in the Church on Gaelic Lane. The first meeting of the managers after the Disruption was on 6th June, that meeting being held, according to the minute, in 'Gaelic Church Session House'. Spring Garden Parish Church had passed into history. Eight of the ten congregational managers were present and John Mackay, tailor, took the chair. The clerk reported that 'the period of letting the seats is over and after attending for three weeks and two nights each week, the sum of £6 5s. 9d has been collected'. This figure was less than a fifth of the sum collected in each of the previous two six-monthly periods. Clearly the prospect that the building might be taken over by the Established Presbytery had a deterrent effect on letting. The meeting then instructed the treasurer to pay the gas account, to give the precentor and the church officer their salaries which fell due on the 20th of the month, to pay John Mackay (the chairman) interest on his loan of £20 and finally to pay 'the Rev. Mr. Mackenzie up to his time'.

The next meeting, convened by John Mackay on 19th June, was 'to receive a communication from the Rev. Mr. Paul, Presbytery Clerk, the tenor whereof follows ...':

> *Sir,*
> *I am directed by the Presbytery of Aberdeen to intimate through you to the managers of Spring Garden Church that said church became vacant on the 16 June curt., in consequence of the Rev. Mr. Mackenzie's having ceased to be a minister of the Established Church of Scotland.*
> *I am, Sir, your obedient servant*
> *Wm Paul Presbytery Clerk,*
> *Banchory Devenick 16 June 1843*

The managers agreed that John Mackay should reply as follows:

Rev Sir,

I received your letter of the 16 curt. and laid the same before the managers at a meeting held by them on the 19th inst. in the vestry of the Gaelic Church. They have only to state in reply that not only the Rev. Mr. Mackenzie but all the congregation (as far as known to them) have ceased their connection with the Church of Scotland as by law Established.

I am Rev. Sir,

Yours most respectfully,
John Mackay, preses.

There was to be only one more insertion in the minute book of the managers of the Gaelic Chapel. On the 4th of July 1843 a document entitled *Case for the managers of the Gaelic Chapel Aberdeen* had been drawn up by Alex Webster. The text of the document is inscribed in the minute book and reads as follows:

On the 27 May 1820 a constitution was granted by the General Assembly of the Church of Scotland for the said Gaelic Chapel a copy of which is herewith given in.

Agreeably to the first article thereof the feudal property of the chapel is vested in the Managers who stand infeft therein by Sasine dated the 21st September 1826 duly recorded, and which is also herewith given in.

There are debts presently due by the Managers affecting said chapel to the extent of £326. Two of the Managers who are infeft in the property viz., Alexander McDonald and George Dingwall are now dead. The surviving Managers are of opinion that under present circumstances it would be advisable and proper to sell the premises to enable them to pay off the debts affecting same, and they request the leave of the Presbytery to this being done, at the sight and under the direction of Messrs Alexander Webster, Advocate in Aberdeen and David Chalmers Printer there, who have kindly acted as honorary Managers for several years past. The only funds or property belonging to the chapel is the church.

The Managers elected on 7th May 1841 to continue in office for five years in terms of the fourth Article of the Constitution were

> *Alexander McDonald, Merchant Aberdeen*
> *Alexander Urquhart, Road Contractor Aberdeen*
> *John Stewart, Teacher Aberdeen*
> *Hugh Fraser, Merchant Aberdeen*
> *Alexander Millar, Road Inspector Aberdeen*
> *Alexander M. Stephen, Founder Aberdeen*
> *Alexander Mackenzie, Skinner Aberdeen*
> *William Gordon, Bookseller Aberdeen*

The Kirk of St Nicholas *circa*. 1795. The West Kirk (left) remains substantially unaltered, but the East Kirk (right of the central tower) was demolished and rebuilt in 1837. At the far right the undercroft, known as St Mary's Chapel, survived the demolition. *Courtesy Aberdeen City Library*.

The interior of St Mary's Chapel showing the 19th century furnishings.
Courtesy Aberdeen City Library.

An aerial view of the Denburn at its intersection with Union Street c. 1950. Railway tracks and Union Terrace Gardens occupy the valley of the Denburn. The corner of St Nicholas Churchyard with its granite screen fronting on to Union Street is visible in the lower right hand corner. The former Gaelic Chapel is encircled, its seven roof-lights indicating subsequent roof modification. On the far side of the Gaelic Chapel are the pinnacles of the former South Parish Church erected in 1830 on the site of the Belmont Chapel. © *Courtesy Aberdeen Journals.*

The south wall of the Gaelic Chapel virtually unaltered and showing original fenestration of 1795. A suspended floor now intersects with the windows. *Courtesy Aberdeen City Library.*

Looking east along Gaelic Lane from the corner of Belmont Street. The original north frontage of the Gaelic Chapel has been altered and the roof raised to allow insertion of two tiers of four windows. The door to the chapel, to the left of the downpipe, has a granite lintel with an ecclesiastical motif.
Photograph: J Livingston.

Above:
Rev. Donald Sage

Right:
John Ewen
(Principal Manager)

Below:
Rev. D M Connell

Above:
Rev. George Macdonald

Below:
Rev. Dr John Kennedy

All photographs: J Livingston (except Rev. D M Connell, photo: I R MacDonald.)

page 2   Minute 2 —

At the Gaelic Chapel in Aberdⁿ 5 August 1796 —
The Committee of the Gaelic congregation met in order to
examine the accounts, and Establish all manner
Of decent order & regulation relative to the temporal
Concerns Of the Congregation —— After the Accounts
Being balanced, It was declared by the Clerk, and
The Treasurer acknowledged himself a debtor to
The Congregation for £30-..-7 as balance of Cash
Remaining in his hand —— The Committee
have impowered the Treasurer & Preses, to settle
all accounts & debates with Peter Ross relating
The Pavement & extra work done to the
Congregation according to the Agreement made
with him for that Purpose — in case there Proposed
be objected by him, to refere the matter to the
Head managers —— The Committee have
Authorised the Treasurer at any Period when
first consulted with the President of the Committee
To borrow money in the name, & for the use of the
Congregation if necessity require it —— The
Committee Appointed — Ang^s M°Kay to regulate
The Clock, and have the Charge of the Sacramental
furniture & utensils, to draw, and sett the Communion
Tables occasionely, to see the Chapel always
Clean — and on compleating his Charge, the
Committee unanimously agreed to Pay him ten
Shillings a yearly — Lastly the Committee orders
the Clerk to buy Cloth for Book Case —

The said Ang^s M°Kay are bound in their
Charge, to see the Chapel Properly lighted
in time of Lecture; and windows drawn for
air when necessary — Also to observe that the walke
within the Parapet Dyk will be keept in
Clean & decent order —

                    Simon Fraser President

Front and south elevation of the former St Columba Free Church, Dee Street *c.* 1985.
Photograph: David Riley.

North side elevation of St Columba Free Church (Dee Street)
following demolition of adjoining buildings *c.* 1972. *Courtesy Aberdeen Town Planning Department.*

Rev. Donald Munro DD
Source: Norman Macleod

Principal Donald Maclean DD
Source: Rev. D K Macleod

Rev. Alexander Stewart DD
Source: J F M Macleod

Principal John Macleod DD
Source: J F M Macleod

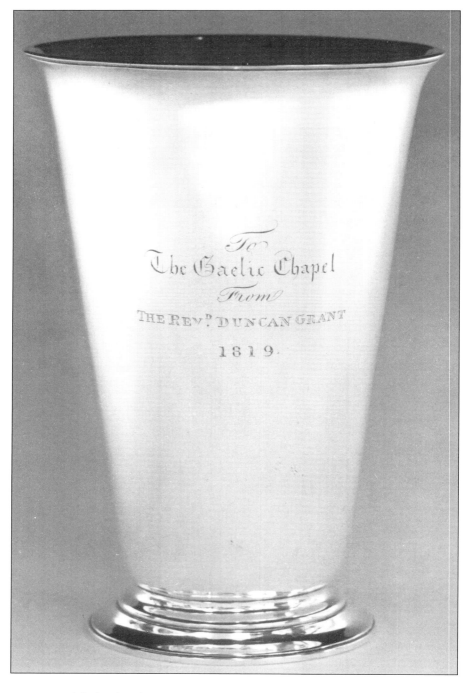

A beaker-shaped communion cup, one of two donated to the Gaelic Chapel
by the Rev. Duncan Grant, 1819. The silversmith was Wm Jamieson, Aberdeen.
Photograph: David Riley.

John Mackay, Tailor Aberdeen
Kenneth Dingwall, Quarrier Aberdeen

Mr Alexander McDonald is since dead. The Rev. Hugh Mackenzie having ceased to be a Minister of the Established Church of Scotland, the church became vacant on 16 June last by order of the Presbytery of Aberdeen and in terms of the Ninth Article of the Constitution the Managers have it in their power to apply to the Presbytery for getting the vacancy filled up within three months after the date thereof and in case the Managers fail to do so it is presumed that the Presbytery are not called on to interfere.

4th July 1843
Alex Webster for Managers.

Then follows the final entry:

Aberdeen 22nd July 1843

The foregoing case having been laid before a Meeting of the Managers of the Gaelic Chapel Aberdeen held this evening and deliberately considered was unanimously approved of and it was resolved that the same should be laid before the Presbytery of Aberdeen requesting that the terms thereof may be complied with.
Signed by

John Mackay
Alex McKenzie
Hugh Fraser
Alexr Urquhart
John Stewart
Alexander Millar
his
Kenneth X Dingwall
mark
William Gordon
John Stewart for Alexr M Stephen who is presently absent.

The smudged and finger-marked minute book bound in canvas sail-cloth which chronicled the fortunes of the Gaelic congregation in Aberdeen from 1796 was now discarded, the unused pages calling attention to the untimely disruption of its story.

The decision arrived at by the managers on 22nd July had in fact been anticipated by Alex Webster and the case, as drawn up by him on 4th July, was before the Established Presbytery when they met on 20th July. It was then referred to a committee anent chapels-of-ease along

165

with a case submitted by the Mariners' Chapel.[11] This committee reported to the Presbytery on 7th September when it was agreed to defer consideration until 3rd October.[12] The matter did not, in fact, come up again until 28th October when the report was ordered to lie on the table until next ordinary meeting.[13]

Gaelic in East St Nicholas

No further reference is to be found to the Gaelic Chapel in the minutes of the Established Presbytery and it would seem that the Presbytery at an early stage decided that the Established Church prospects in Gaelic Lane were hopeless. Wisely they decided to meet the need, or the challenge, by appointing a Gaelic minister to the now vacant East Church. They nominated the Rev. Simon MacKintosh of Inverness, persuading that Presbytery to release him on the grounds that 'it is a matter of great importance that a minister skilled in the Gaelic language should be settled in Aberdeen to dispose ordinances when necessary to any of the Gaelic population there who may require his services'.[14] To what extent his facility in Gaelic was made use of is unrevealed, but he proved to be a very popular minister. Born at Ardersier in 1815 he had been a student in King's College, Aberdeen, and may have attended the Gaelic Chapel from time to time.

In 1840, when he became a licentiate, Simon MacKintosh unwittingly found himself caught up in a celebrated Non-intrusion controversy which followed the death in 1839 of the parish minister of Daviot, Inverness-shire – the Rev. James MacPhail who had gone there from the Aberdeen Gaelic Chapel in 1800. Simon MacKintosh, perhaps because of his connection with the Clan Chattan whose ancestral territories encompassed that parish from time immemorial, was given the presentation. He was not, however, the people's choice.[15] Possibly they had already fixed their minds on Archibald Cook of the North Church, Inverness.[16] In any case, Simon MacKintosh's presentation was vetoed. His supporters carried the fight to the civil courts but the presentee himself resiled from the case and took a charge in Inverness. In Aberdeen Simon MacKintosh proved to be an effective preacher.[17] He gained the reputation of being evangelical and Calvinistic and this may well have helped him overcome the disability of being known as a 'Residuary'. Information is lacking as to the support, if any, that he received from those dissatisfied with the ministry in Gaelic Lane, but his early death in 1853, aged only 37, was widely regretted in the community and was a sore loss to the Established Church.

Gaelic Church redeemed

If the Established Presbytery reached a decision in response to the request from the managers of the Gaelic Chapel for permission to sell the property and repay the debt, it failed to be recorded in the minutes of the Presbytery. The Presbytery could see that there was very little it could do to thwart the implied intention of the managers which was to terminate the legal right of the Presbytery in the ownership of the mortgaged building by a sale and buy–back arrangement by the local trustees. It was certainly open to the Presbytery to enter a bid for the property, but it had neither funds to invest nor people to make use of the building if it was purchased. It could only be a liability and, in the depleted state in which the Established Church found itself, to add to its liabilities was not practical politics. Surprisingly, almost two years passed before this course of action was implemented by the managers and there is no obvious explanation for the long delay. Presumably during that time the congregation continued to occupy the Gaelic Chapel, but between 22nd July 1843 and 13th March 1845 there are no extant written records of its affairs. Perhaps the Gaelic Chapel minute book had been impounded by the Presbytery and, minutes, recorded *pro tem* on ephemeral folios, were never transcribed to a bound volume.

The strategy adopted by the Gaelic Church was, of course, being pursued by other churches. According to one account, Union Church on the Shiprow was vacated on 11th June 1843 and, with the agreement of the Presbytery, offered for sale to liquidate the debt of £1300. The building was then bought by the minister and congregation for £1795 and, within seven weeks of their leaving it, the congregation was back in undisputed possession of Union Free Church.[18] In Woodside Chapel there was a more serious contest between the Presbytery and congregation. Here the congregation vacated the building and occupied a temporary wooden structure. The chapel, which had been built in 1830, carried a debt of £1200 and in this case, it seems that the Presbytery claimed the church while repudiating the debt. The matter went to the Court of Session and 18 months passed before that court decided that church and debt had to go together, whereupon the building was again occupied by the congregation.[19] In Bon Accord Church the managers, having failed to obtain any information from the Presbytery as to its intentions, decided to force the issue and offered the building for sale on 6th March 1844 at an upset price of £1130. It was bought in at this price for the congregation by the trustees, no money passing hands in the deal.[20] The Mariners' Church, whose case was bracketed with that of the Gaelic Chapel by the Presbytery, was advertised for sale in November 1844 and purchased by the congregation on 6th December. Last of all the Gaelic Chapel came up for sale, the *Aberdeen*

Journal of Wednesday 9th April 1845 carrying the following notice.

GAELIC CHURCH FOR SALE

There will be exposed to sale by public roup within the writing chambers of Alex and John Webster, Advocates King St. Aberdeen upon Friday the 25 day of April 1845 at 2 pm in virtue of the powers contained in decrees of the Court of Session and in a Bond and Disposition in Security.

All and whole the chapel or place of worship in Gaelic Lane Aberdeen commonly called the Gaelic Church with the vestry and other buildings connected therewith and ground on which the same are built measuring 60 feet in front or thereby and 54 feet backward or thereby as particularly described in the Title Deeds.

All further information respecting the upset price and conditions of sale will be afforded by Messrs Webster.

Aberdeen 8 April 1845.

Three weeks later the *Journal* carried another notice.

NOTICE

The Gaelic Church having been lately purchased from the former managers by the Free Church congregation will be opened for public worship on Sabbath first the 4th of May when a collection will be made towards defraying the debt incurred. The services will be conducted by the Rev. Dr McDonald of Urquhart in the forenoon in Gaelic and in the afternoon and evening in English.

Free Gaelic inauguration

For at least thirty years John Macdonald of Ferintosh, the Apostle of the North, had regularly given assistance to the church in Aberdeen. The demands for his services had, if possible, increased since the Disruption, but ever since his student days Aberdeen had a secure place in his affections and he readily consented to the request of the managers that the lustre of his name and the magnetism of his preaching might be taken advantage of to make the official opening of the Aberdeen Free Gaelic Church, a memorable occasion. The outcome fully justified the expectations. Probably never again was the church as crowded as it was at the inaugural service. The devotion of the worshippers was reflected in the collection which amounted to £46 16s 4d, a very substantial sum in the context of the congregation's annual income, the collections for the previous twelve months having amounted in all to £63. The managers were duly gratified and assured the preacher of their appreciation of his charitable support. But charity, for the Aberdonians, not only began at home but ended there. The following month the Rev. Hugh Mackenzie reported that he had received a letter from the congregation of Ferintosh (Urquhart) requesting that a collection might be made in Aberdeen to aid them in their endeavours to build a manse for the evicted Apostle of the North. The clerk, summarising the subsequent discussion, wrote: 'The members present did not say much on the subject; it was left over till the next meeting.' If they said little, they did less. The matter was not referred to again.

The claim made by the Gaelic Deacons' Court in June 1843 that the whole of the congregation, so far as was known to them, had joined the Free Church, did not remain uncontested. It may be questioned if it was ever entirely justifiable since some of the managers appointed in 1841 do not figure in the immediate post-Disruption life of the congregation. Admittedly, all of the surviving managers signed the case which was submitted to the Presbytery on 22nd July 1843, but by 1845, when the records of the managers resume after a two-year gap, Alex Millar and John Stewart were no longer visibly involved. In the case of Alex Millar, a road inspector for the Buchan District who resided on King Street, there is no independent evidence that he survived in Aberdeen as his name disappeared from the Aberdeen Directory in 1840. But John Stewart, a teacher residing on the Shiprow, certainly did survive, for he continued to be listed in the Directory until the year 1874. At the time of the Disruption he had been acting as clerk to the managers. Three years previously he had been made an elder in the congregation. Yet from 1845, and possibly from 1843, he took no part in the affairs of the Gaelic Church.

The elders depart

Strangely, the first election of elders that took place after Spring Garden Parish Church had achieved its independent status added only very temporary strength to its Session. Of the six men ordained in 1841, all, with the exception of the illiterate quarrier Kenneth Dingwall, became disaffected and left. Between 1843 and 1848 John Stewart, teacher, John Mackay, tailor, Alex Mackenzie, skinner and congregational treasurer, Hector Mackay, roper, and Alex Ross, an overseer in the Banner Mill, all departed either sooner or later, most of them because of disaffection with the minister. All of the elders are credited with having signed the Act of Demission in 1843, but their names as they appear in the

Presbytery Record have been pencilled in rather than signed.[21] It is possible that their adherence was assumed. In 1845 Alex Ross, then residing on Frederick Street, was ordained an elder in St Clement's Parish Church where he remained in office until his decease in 1864. His case, along with that of John Stewart, gives some support to the view that not all of the worshippers in the Gaelic Chapel were happy to leave the Established Church. Another deserter, but on different grounds, was one of the deacons, Kenneth Ross, a blacksmith residing at Tanfield in 1841 and described in the 1842 Aberdeen Directory as a feuar of 26 Gaelic Lane, Woodside. In February 1846 he gave as the reasons for his resignation 'distance from the church and inconvenience'. Subsequently he was made an elder in Woodside Free Church, disappearing from the records in 1857, presumably on his decease.

It has been argued that Kirk Sessions of both the Established and the Free Churches in the mid-nineteenth century were controlled by the middle classes[22] and so it is of interest to note the socio-economic groupings of the elders elected to the Gaelic Kirk Session in 1840. Of the six men ordained, three – John Mackay, tailor, Hector Mackay, ropemaker, and Kenneth Dingwall, quarrier – would be classified as working class. The other three – Alex Ross, foreman in a textile mill, Alex Mackenzie, a self-employed skinner and John Stewart, teacher – fall into the lowest of the middle class groupings.[23] Probably the same could be said of the three Gaelic elders who formed part of the South Parish Session in 1834. From this it may be inferred that economic status was a less decisive consideration in the election of elders in the Gaelic Church than in some other churches. Absence of economic, or even educational, attainments was no barrier to the election of men who were considered to possess the requisite spiritual gifts. Traditionally in the Gaelic Chapel, and possibly in many chapels, as distinct from parish churches, the role of the Kirk Session was restricted to purely pastoral functions such as visitation, counselling, exhortation, prayer and the provision of spiritual leadership in general. The business affairs of the chapel remained in the hands of the managers and called for the exercise of different gifts. Elders were not then involved *ex officio* in the temporal concerns of the congregation. They were not appointed to the committee of management unless it was considered they had a contribution to make such as might arise out of the nature of their employment. This policy was eventually to be superceded by a more inclusivist one, but even in 1841 not all of the elders were appointed as managers. However a radical change occurred in 1843.

The pattern adopted by Thomas Chalmers with regard to the financial affairs of the Free Church of Scotland involved the formation of Deacons' Courts which embraced not just the minister and deacons – men elected for life and ordained to office – but all of the elders as well. Thereafter the elders occupied an increasingly dominant role in the business affairs of the Free Church congregations, a role similar to that of elders in *quoad omnia* Parishes of the Established Church where all the general financial concerns of the congregation came under the purview of the Kirk Session. This inclusivist policy had the effect of diminishing the spiritual role of the elders by altering, albeit unintentionally, the qualifications that were regarded as appropriate to the office of the eldership. Inevitably, since business capability was seen as necessary for the work of the Deacons' Court, men were appointed deacons on the basis of their commercial achievements and subsequently were advanced to the eldership with little regard being given to the possession of any additional gifts for the more spiritual office.

It seems unlikely that the socially eminent ever formed a distinct group within the Gaelic Church. Certainly there were some more prosperous and prominent in the community than the generality of the congregation; but they did not regard themselves as being thereby entitled to special recognition in the organisational hierarchy. Any having that outlook would betake themselves to more fashionable churches. The Gaelic Church was a more integrated congregation than most. Working class elders were no less welcome on pastoral visitation in middle class homes than middle class elders. In 1845 the congregation had six elders and it would appear that the most working class among them – Hector Mackay, roper, and Kenneth Dingwall, quarrier – were the most highly esteemed. In addition to six elders, seven deacons were ordained to the Gaelic Church. Within three years strife and dissension of one kind or another had reduced the staff of office-bearers to two elders and two deacons. For that exodus the Rev. Hugh Mackenzie bore much responsibility.

Notes to Chapter 22

1.   H Watt: *Thomas Chalmers and the Disruption* (Edinburgh, 1943), p 349.
2.   G D Henderson: *Heritage. A study of the Disruption* (Edinburgh, 1943), p 60.
3.   Ibid., p 70.
4.   T Brown: *Annals of the Disruption* (Edinburgh, 1884, new edition, 1893), p 5.
5.   A A MacLaren: *Religion and social class. The Disruption years in Aberdeen* (London, 1974), p 94.
6.   H Watt: op. cit., p 296.
7.   A A MacLaren: op. cit., p 58.
8.   *Minutes of the South St Nicholas Kirk Session*, vol 1, p 86 (4th March, 1830) (CH2-2-1).
9.   W Robbie: *Bon Accord Free Church, Aberdeen. A retrospect* (Aberdeen, 1887), p 33.
10. T Brown: op. cit., p 219.
11. *Records of the Presbytery of Aberdeen*, vol 13, p 363 (20th July, 1843) (CH2-1-15).
12. Ibid., p 382 (7th September, 1843).

13. Ibid., p 411 (28th October, 1843).
14. Ibid., p 375 (30th August, 1843).
15. For a somewhat partisan account, see 'The Presentation to Daviot' by Hugh Miller in *The Headship of Christ* (Edinburgh, 7th edition, 1873), pp 203-208.
16. See memoir of the Rev. Archibald Cook by Rev. Dr J R Mackay, reprinted in A MacPherson (ed.): *Sidelights on two notable ministries* (Inverness, 1970), p 35.
17. For a description of Simon MacKintosh's ministry, see J Martin: *Eminent divines in Aberdeen and the North* (Aberdeen, 1888), pp 234-238.
18. A Gammie: *The churches of Aberdeen* (Aberdeen, 1909), p 222.
19. P Morgan: *Annals of Woodside and Newhills* (Aberdeen, 1909), p 88.
20. W Robbie: op. cit., p 35.
21. *Records of the Free Presbytery of Aberdeen,* vol. 1, p 17 (CH3-2-5).
22. A A Maclaren: op. cit., p 121.
23. Ibid., pp 218-219.

Chapter 23

*

A ROOT OF BITTERNESS

THE official opening of the Free Gaelic Church by Dr Macdonald of Ferintosh in 1845 was a notable event in the life of the congregation but, as not infrequently happens, behind-the-scenes activity preparatory to the occasion was fruitful of much mischief. The minute of a Deacons' Court meeting held on 27th April 1847, written by the minister, refers to a bitter dispute that had its origin at the time of the inaugural services. Robert Maclennan, a communicant in the congregation and one of the twelve trustees of the Gaelic Church, had undertaken, presumably on his own suggestion, to decorate the pulpit and precentor's desk in honour of Dr Macdonald's visit. The green baize which he used for this purpose, he obtained from another of the trustees, Hugh Fraser, formerly tailor of Broadford but now owner of H Fraser & Co., clothiers and furnishing tailors of 24 Union Street. Perhaps Robert Maclennan expected his fellow trustee to donate the cloth, or more likely to loan the material and take it back into stock. Instead, Robert Maclennan received an account for 31s 4d (£1.56). Two years later Maclennan, being hard pressed by the supplier of the cloth, petitioned the Deacons' Court to the effect that he considered himself aggrieved by the actions of one of its members, Hugh Fraser, who had threatened him with prosecution for the payment of the account. Maclennan claimed that the account was not one which he was bound to pay and he craved redress from the Court. After the petition had being read, Hugh Fraser protested in the following terms:

I hereby protest against any subject of complaint against me, by Robert Maclennan, or any other person, being taken up or considered by this Deacons' Court inasmuch as it is beyond the minister's authority to summon a meeting of the Deacons' Court for the purpose of hearing complaints against the private character or conduct of an elder in the Church; and also inasmuch it does not belong to a Deacons' Court to hear or examine into any such complaints. And whereas by letter from the Rev. Mr. Mackenzie I am informed that such complaints were to be made against me at the meeting summoned for this day, I protest against the subject of certain repairs or alterations effected upon the church on the 5 May 1845 being now discussed except so far as concerns the propriety or impropriety of the Deacons' Court paying for these repairs out of the funds of the Church or otherwise.

The Court then divided on whether the treasurer, on behalf of the congregation, should settle the account and thereby sist further proceedings. John Macrae of Holburn Street, probably a brewer to trade, moved against payment and he was seconded by the treasurer, Alex Mackenzie, skinner or currier of 13 Denburn Terrace. An alternative motion in favour of payment was made by Alex Stephen. By far the most loyal supporter of the minister, Alex Stephen was in partnership in a brassfounding business when he first joined the congregation in 1835, but since 1841 he had conducted his own painting and decorating business. His motion was seconded, unconstitutionally, by the minister who was Moderator of the Court. A third motion by Wm Gordon, bookseller, that a decision be deferred, found no seconder and on a division the first motion carried. The Moderator recorded his dissent and his five reasons for dissent form a substantial part of the minute. The last of the reasons was to the effect that refusal by the Deacons' Court to meet the account would give those who were opposed to the distinctive principles of the Free Church opportunity to scoff saying, 'Here is an officebearer and a member of that Church who on the last communion Sabbath sat down at the Table of the Lord in the same Church and professed to be the disciples of the Lord Jesus Christ; to love the Saviour and to love one another as brethren and as children of the same family and yet but three or four days had elapsed when the one sends a letter to the other threatening to drag him to a court of law; here brother goeth to law with brother regardless of the authority and law of Him whom both profess to acknowledge as their own king and lawgiver'.

At the next meeting of the Deacons' Court, held on 4th May 1847, Hugh Fraser took the opportunity to supply 'answers' to the reasons for dissent given in by the minister at the previous meeting. This submission was ruled incompetent by the Moderator (the minister) on the grounds that the Court had not appointed Hugh Fraser, or anyone else, to answer the reasons for dissent. However, the matter having being raised, the Court proceeded to appoint their Clerk, Hugh Falconer, and John Macrae to answer the minister's reasons for dissenting.

A brother offended

The next meeting was held on 20th May 1847 and the minister's hand can again be discerned in the minute which reads:

A paper having been given in by Messrs Falconer and Macrae purporting to contain answers to the reasons of dissent recorded in the minutes of 27 April, the Moderator moved that said paper be not sustained by the Court inasmuch as instead of answering the reasons of dissent it deals in vague generalities

*and insinuations and imputes motives to the dissentient which he disclaims
and repudiates; which motion was seconded by Mr. Alex Stephen. It was
moved by Mr. Falconer and seconded by Mr. Urquhart that it be sustained.
The votes being called, Messrs Falconer, Urquhart and Macrae voted for the
second motion and Mr. Stephen for the first. Messrs Gordon and Dingwall
declined voting. The Court finds in terms of the second motion from which
finding the Moderator dissents for the reasons stated in his motion; to which
dissent Mr. Stephen adheres.*

Alex Stephen was the only one to offer unequivocal support to the
minister. Wm Gordon, bookseller, and Kenneth Dingwall, quarrier, both
well on in years and no doubt vexed by the contentious and unyielding
attitude displayed by the leading protagonists, declined to take sides.
Given such a belligerent spirit on the part of the Moderator, it is not to
be wondered at that the office-bearers now began to absent themselves
from further meetings. Kenneth Ross, the blacksmith from Woodside,
had sent in his resignation a year previously. Alex Urquhart, senior, a
road contractor of Skene Street who continued to be listed in the
Aberdeen Directory until 1856, did not attend the Deacons' Court after
September 1846. Hector Mackay, the most spiritually-minded of all
the office-bearers, made his last appearance at the Deacons' Court on
19th March 1847, no doubt anticipating by his absence the confronta-
tion that occurred between Fraser and Maclennan at the April meeting.
Hugh Fraser himself did not attend the Court after 4th May, the meeting at which his answers were refused. John Macrae made his final
appearance on 20th May, the meeting at which his answers were
sustained. Alex Urquhart, junior, a shoemaker to trade, Hugh Falconer,
the clerk, and John Mackay, tailor, were all to quit before the end of the
year. But despite the fact that the minister could count on none but
Alex Stephen for support, he resumed the offensive.

The next meeting of the Deacons' Court was held on 9th June. The
minute, bearing all the hallmarks of the minister's hand, reads:

*The minutes of the meeting of 20 May having been read, and also the paper
then handed in by Messrs John Macrae and Falconer containing the answers
to the reasons of dissent: seeing that said paper partly consists of the same
statements as were in the paper formerly tendered by Mr. Fraser and refused
by the court; seeing that it also professes to embody the letter sent by Mr.
Fraser to the Moderator on the 22 April last which is a garbled copy of said
letter and also that in addition to the insinuations and imputations alluded
to at the last meeting, it contains grave and serious charges which injuriously
affect the dissentients' character inasmuch as it more especially asserts that on
one occasion he, the dissentient, had spoken approvingly, if not anxiously, of
this Court having recourse to the civil law in order to compel the managers*

of the Poor's Fund in connection with this congregation to comply with our wishes; the Moderator having now put the question to the individual members present whether so far as they know there is any foundation for this charge or whether they ever heard him make such a proposal to this Court; and they having all answered in the negative, it was moved that the Clerk be required to explain why he appended his name to a statement which is now found to be a pure fabrication; whereupon the Clerk refused to give any explanation in the meantime.

A week later, on 17th June, the Clerk, Hugh Falconer, was given another opportunity to justify his remarks. Again the minute of the meeting was written, not by the Clerk but by the minister; and, in common with all of the minutes from 27th April onwards, it carries a forgery of the Clerk's signature. The minute reads as follows:

The minutes of last meeting having been read and approved off, the Moderator put the question again to the Clerk whether he had any explanation to give to the meeting in reference to the matter he refused to explain at last meeting. The Clerk said he had no explanation to give this night. The Moderator then made the following motion: that whereas the Clerk both at the last meeting and this evening refused to withdraw or explain a charge against the Moderator which this Court at its last meeting unanimously declared to be destitute of foundation; and whereas he appears to regard it as a heinous crime to lodge a complaint against an elder before a Deacons' Court, and that in reference to a matter which had no respect to his private character but to a mercantile transaction between him and a member of this church, while he seems to regard it as a meritorious act to bring false and calumnious charges against the minister before the same Deacons' Court; his conduct is highly censurable. Which motion was carried but from which the Clerk dissents.

The next meeting of the Deacons' Court was held on 12th July, an Annual General Meeting of the congregation having been held five days earlier. When the Deacons met on 12th July, the Clerk was asked if he had prepared a minute of the Annual General Meeting. When he had answered in the negative, the minister proceeded to read his own account of that meeting. There had been present in addition to the minister, four elders (John Mackay, tailor, Wm Gordon, bookseller, Alex Mackenzie, skinner, and Kenneth Dingwall, quarrier), three deacons (Hugh Falconer, Alex Stephen and Hugh Campbell) and about twelve members of the congregation. Also present were Hugh Fraser, clothier, and Hector Mackay, roper, both being described as 'late elders', and John Macrae, brewer and 'late deacon'. The only member of the congregation present who can be identified was the Gaelic precentor,

James Fraser, a candlemaker on Loch Street. He had been appointed precentor a year previously and he was to continue in that office until 1854 when he resigned on having 'obtained a situation in Glasgow'.

Congregational fracas

At the Annual General Meeting held on 7th July 1847 the minister presided and opened the meeting with prayer. He was about to intimate the evening's business when he was interrupted by Hugh Fraser 'who started up and questioned him as to his right to preside at that meeting'. It was unfortunate for Hugh Fraser that he was under the misapprehension that the rules that had been drawn up in 1796 for the regulation of congregational meetings were still in force. In these early days the minister did not usually attend a congregational business meeting, and even if he did the meeting elected its own chairman, usually the preses of the management committee. But now the minister informed Hugh Fraser 'that if he exercised but a very little share of patience he would know immediately' why the minister was in the chair. And so saying, he read from Act VII, section 4, article 1 (1846) which stipulated that in any meeting convened by the Deacons' Court (as was an Annual General Meeting), the minister if present would preside. Times had indeed changed with a decided shift in the balance of power from lay to clerical authority. Ministers of the Free Church were given powers by which, if they were so minded, they could act as despots.

The minute, having stated that the business for which the meeting was convened was concluded, continues:

> *It was then proposed by Messrs Hugh Fraser and James Fraser that a meeting should be held for the purpose of investigating the cause of the resignations among the officebearers, and the present state of the congregation. The Moderator observed that the sooner an investigation was made by the Presbytery the better; but as this meeting was called for a specific object and the congregation were not made aware that any other business would be introduced, they could not constitutionally enter upon that subject tonight. He then read the Act as to the disposal of the church and the right of upholding congregational meetings, and stated that if they were desirous to have a congregational meeting, it would be necessary to apply in the regular way to the Session or Deacons' Court. Mr. Fraser, late elder, then said 'The Moderator if he choses may go away, we can appoint another chairman'. And Mr. Macrae, late deacon, remarked 'If the Moderator won't call a congregational meeting, we can employ the auctioneer to call one at the church door'. The Minister, seeing it would be vain to argue the matter any longer with these men said he would now conclude the meeting – at the same time protesting against further proceedings that night and warned those present who were church members*

that if they persisted in the course proposed, they would subject themselves to the discipline of the church. He closed with prayer and dismissed the meeting. But before he left the desk, Mr. Fraser proposed that Mr. John Mackay, elder, take the chair and seeing Messrs Gordon and Dingwall retiring from the meeting he sneeringly exclaimed 'Aye Mr. Gordon, be you sure to follow the minister.'

Wm Gordon, bookseller, and Kenneth Dingwall, quarrier, withdrew, not so much because they were the minister's men but because they lacked sympathy with the confrontational policies of the Fraser faction. The real minister's man, Alex Stephen, painter and house decorator of Mitchell Place, King Street, remained behind to report proceedings.

Petition against overbearing minister

Sadly the conflict could not be confined within the walls of the Gaelic Chapel. That same month the Free Presbytery of Aberdeen was requested to investigate the situation in the Gaelic Church. A petition from five of the active office-bearers in the congregation was accompanied by another from five of the former office-bearers, and it was followed by one from 26 members of the congregation. All three urged the need for an inquiry into conditions in the Gaelic Church and, in the carefully chosen words of the Presbytery Clerk, 'the removal of obstacles to its prosperity'.[1] The substance of these petitions was elaborated more fully in a further document submitted some months later. This read, in part, as follows:[2]

'Being convinced that the present unfortunate condition of the Gaelic Church, is owing to the manner in which the ministerial duties are discharged in connection with it; your petitioners are constrained to complain before your Reverend Court of Mr. Hugh Mackenzie, minister of said Church, as they hereby do, and on the following grounds.

1   *Because his style of preaching is lifeless, and unsuited to the circumstances of his hearers.*
2   *Because he has almost wholly neglected the visitation of his people, throughout the whole course of his abode in Aberdeen, in numerous instances omitting to visit the sick; while he has persisted in this conduct, notwithstanding that the members of his Church Session have repeatedly urged him through many years, both privately and at the meetings of Session, to commence the visitation of his flock, offering to lend him every assistance in their power; and at one period they urged him for several successive meetings of Session, until he gave promises on the matter, which however, he entirely failed to fulfil.*

3   *Because he has manifested such a spirit of overbearing and rudeness in his Session and Deacons' Court, as to compel most of the office-bearers to resign.*

That your petitioners are prepared to bring forward full proofs of the truth of these charges, and of their other statements.

That they are therefore assured than an active minister is indispensable to the prosperity of the Gaelic Church.

That they are persuaded this would of itself lead to immediate exertions on the part of the members and friends of said Church, which would raise it to at least as flourishing a state as it ever existed in previously.

May it therefore please the Reverend the Presbytery to take the steps requisite for examining into these charges, and. to proceed further as they deem necessary for the welfare of the Church.

This petition was signed by 65 persons, about half of whom had left the congregation, thereby having been, as they averred, 'forced to make a sacrifice as regards the language'. The Presbytery recognised that the Gaelic dissidents would not be satisfied with anything less than an alternative ministry in the Gaelic language. Anxious to help both pastor and people, the Presbytery searched for a solution that would preserve intact the minister's reputation and his emoluments while at the same time making alternative provision for the satisfactory discharge of the preaching office. This, of course, was to attempt the impossible. The Presbytery took the easy way out and referred the matter to the General Assembly only to be told that the problem was one which the Presbytery must resolve.[3] Again the Presbytery attempted a reconciliation, urging the parties to come together in a spirit of mutual Christian forbearance and forgiveness. But, largely as a result of the minister's intransigence, the rift remained unbridgeable. The Presbytery took no further steps to impose a solution. The dissidents could do no other than go elsewhere but even in this, some were thwarted.

With malice aforethought

The former elder Hugh Fraser and former deacon John Macrae, both had to appeal to the Presbytery against the refusal of the Gaelic Church minister and Kirk Session to issue them with disjunction certificates. In defending his decision in this matter, Hugh Mackenzie supplied the Presbytery with extract minutes of the Kirk Session which referred to the estranged office-bearers in such excoriating terms that the Presbytery put on record 'their strong disapprobation of the language employed – language manifesting a spirit which the Presbytery do exceedingly regret to observe'.[4] This forthright censure of Hugh

Mackenzie's fondness for using the Session Minute Book to blacken and bludgeon his opponents, was supported by every member of Presbytery except the Rev. Wm L Mitchell, minister of Holburn Free Church. Since this Presbyter revelled in the reputation of being 'singularly rude and uncouth in his style of preaching',[5] he doubtless, regarded Hugh Mackenzie's stinging invective as the conventional language of the ministerial office. The Presbytery, however, saw it differently and ordered the Gaelic Kirk Session to 'expunge from their records all the proceedings in the case of Mr. Hugh Fraser'.[6] This minute book covering the Kirk Session deliberations for the period 1843-1869 is the only major gap in the congregational records of the Gaelic Church. It is a virtual certainty that the records remained in the custody of Hugh Mackenzie's family at least until 1910, possibly later; and why this volume should have become separated poses an interesting question.

Furnished with a disjunction certificate attesting his good standing in the church, Hugh Fraser joined the congregation of Bon Accord Free Church on 27th September 1848. Admitted at the same time were John Macrae, brewer, John Mackay, tailor, Hugh Falconer, the clerk, Kenneth Ross, Printfield, and Walter Ross, 57 Hadden Street, all with disjunction certificates signed by the Rev. Hugh Mackenzie.[7] Later arrivals in the same congregation included Hector Mackay, roper, Alex Mackenzie, skinner and John Campbell; the latter two having their disjunction certificates attested by Hugh Fraser and John Mackay in their capacity as elders in the Gaelic Church.

In 1847 a Gaelic-speaking Highlander from Sutherland, the Rev. Samuel Grant, had succeeded the deceased Gavin Parker as minister of Bon Accord Church. Grant's theological outlook reflected that of his Calvinistic predecessor and in most respects, the language only excepted, the refugees from Gaelic Lane would have felt at home in Bon Accord Church. The Kirk Session on Union Terrace also had its due share of strife and contention. In March 1848 the minister suspended one of his most prominent elders, Robert Ness, for disruptive behaviour and intemperate language.[8] Subsequently Ness, two other elders and three deacons, all resigned, but the former Gaelic office-bearers were not called on to make good the deficiency; only one was destined for office in Bon Accord. An election of ten additional elders held in 1851 saw Hector Mackay the roper top the poll.[9] Of about 400 voting-papers handed in on that occasion, there was not one that did not contain his name and, on almost every paper, his was the first name mentioned – surely a remarkable tribute to the reputation he rapidly acquired for piety and integrity. His death in 1860, aged 53, was greatly lamented.

Hugh Fraser never became an office-bearer in Bon Accord, but he remained in membership there. His business expanded from that of 'tailor' to 'clothier' and ultimately to 'clothier, hatter and outfitter', occupying premises at 24 and 30 Union Street. His residence migrated from George Street to Gerard Street and then to 8 Broadford Place. By 1863 he had retired from business and was living at 2 Black's Buildings. In 1866, 44 years after he had been admitted to the Gaelic Chapel by Donald Sage, his name disappeared from the Aberdeen Directory. The deacon John Macrae, the clerk Hugh Falconer, and the treasurer Alex Mackenzie, also remained in Bon Accord, but the elder, John Mackay, lifted his lines in 1855,[10] perhaps on departing from Aberdeen, his name not being listed in the Directory after 1853. Alex Mackenzie, skinner and currier of Denburn Terrace, a second generation member of the Gaelic Chapel who was deprived of his father's subscription rights because he did not understand the Gaelic language, but who nevertheless became a manager in 1819 and subsequently treasurer and elder, disappeared from the pages of the Directory in 1864 presumably on his decease. Kenneth Ross stayed only one year in Bon Accord before transferring his membership to Woodside Free Church where he became an elder. Possibly the only one to retrace his steps to Gaelic Lane was Walter Ross who was admitted to Bon Accord in 1848 with a membership certificate signed by Hugh Mackenzie. In 1856, the year after Hugh Mackenzie's retirement, Walter Ross lifted his lines from Bon Accord. In 1858, a Walter Ross was listed as being an elder in the Gaelic Church.

The losses that the Gaelic Church sustained in 1848 left the congregation seriously weakened. It was not long before the central committees of the Free Church began to question the need for, or the wisdom of, supporting a Gaelic congregation in Aberdeen.

Notes to Chapter 23

1. *Records of the Free Presbytery of Aberdeen,* vol. 1, p 247 (7th September, 1847) (CH3-2-5).
2. *Proceedings of the General Assembly of the Free Church of Scotland* (27th May, 1848). Reference from the Free Presbytery of Aberdeen relative to the Gaelic Church there.
3. *Proceedings of the General Assembly of the Free Church of Scotland* (27th May, 1848).
4. *Records of the Free Presbytery of Aberdeen,* op. cit., p 261 (4th January, 1848).
5. A Gammie: *The churches of Aberdeen* (Aberdeen, 1909), p 143.
6. *Records of the Free Presbytery of Aberdeen,* op. cit., p 268 (1st February, 1848).
7. *Kirk Session minutes of Bon Accord Free Church,* vol. 1 (1843-1870), p 92 (27th September, 1848) (CH3-874-1).
8. Ibid., p 29 (March 1848).
9. W Robbie: *Bon Accord Free Church, Aberdeen: a retrospect* (Aberdeen, 1887). For a fine tribute to the character of Hector Mackay, see pp 87-93.
10. This and other information concerning membership status in Bon Accord Church has been extracted from the Communion Roll of Bon Accord Free Church, 1843-1858 (CH3-874-17).

Chapter 24

*

An End in Sight

IT was the powerful Sustentation Fund Committee that threatened, in 1850, to pull the rug from beneath the Free Gaelic Church in Aberdeen. The Sustentation Fund was the central fund from which ministers of the Free Church were paid. Its original conception, one that was to persist down the years, was that Free Church ministers, having renounced the emoluments of the Established Church, would receive an 'equal dividend', or share, of the money subscribed by all Free Church congregations for the maintenance of the ministry. Dr Thomas Chalmers, who conceived the scheme, was quick to appreciate that while it possessed undoubted strengths, it also had serious weaknesses, and in 1845 he did his utmost to have the equal dividend replaced by a 'proportional dividend', a stipend which bore some relation to the liberality of the individual congregations. An equality of remuneration, he argued, implies an equality of effort. He urged that a minister should receive by way of stipend whatever sum his congregation remitted to the Sustentation Fund plus half as much again up to a maximum stipend of £150. For example, stipends based on congregational remittances of £50, £80 or £200 would be £75, £120 and £150 respectively.

The reason for amending the earlier scheme in which every minister received the same allowance (the equal dividend) was to provide an incentive to those congregations which were culpably remiss, sending niggardly contributions to the Fund not because of necessitous circumstances but because of the negligence of deacons and collectors, the stinginess of contributors or excessive spending on congregational items. In his concern to amend the Sustentation Fund Scheme Dr Chalmers failed to carry the Assembly with him. The ministers closed ranks to protect one another from becoming victims of defaulting congregations and the equal dividend remained the basis of clerical remuneration.[1] This however, had the effect of curtailing any expansion of the Fund and the stipend which was £122 in 1845 was only £119 in 1854.

The shortage of funds had a further, and potentially more damaging, effect. It meant that the church was unable to place ministers in poor, though populous, areas. For instance, for several years after the Disruption the Isle of Skye, where 20,000 persons adhered to the Free Church, had only one Free Church minister, Roderick Macleod of Snizort.

There was a considerable body of opinion in the Sustentation Committee that the Church would make better use of its resources by subsidising ministers in places such as Skye rather than in city congregations where Free Church people had a choice of ministers. Consequently in January 1850 the Sustentation Fund Committee met in Edinburgh to consider which congregations might be reduced to preaching stations, thus releasing resources for use elsewhere. By this time Dr Robert Buchanan of Glasgow had taken over the convenership of the Committee from the Rev. W K Tweedie who, when minister of the South Parish, had taken such a kindly interest in the Gaelic Chapel. Dr Buchanan was no sentimentalist. He took one look at the financial returns from the 24 congregations comprising the Free Presbytery of Aberdeen and concluded that three of them – the Gaelic Church, the Mariners' Church and Belhelvie – could be reduced to preaching stations.

Committee of Enquiry

The Presbytery of Aberdeen, asked to comment on the situation in the Gaelic Church, appointed a committee of enquiry which gave in the following report which the Presbytery adopted for transmission to the Sustentation Fund Committee.[2]

The Committee found

1   *That the average number of sitters on the Sabbath is about 300 and in the afternoon about 70.*
2   *That the attendance has decreased by about 30 during the last half year.*
3   *That in answer to the question what reasons could be assigned for the decrease? it was stated 'general dissatisfaction' but with what or with whom the office-bearers declined to say.*
4   *That the number of communicants in October last was about 114.*
5. *That the sum raised by the Association this year for the Sustentation Fund has been £15 and that £19 were added from Seat-Rents and church door collections making the amount remitted, or to be remitted, to the General Treasurer, £34.*
6   *That there is an increase this year of £6 on the amount raised by the Association for the Sustentation Fund, but a decrease of £5 from other sources.*
7   *That, to the question 'what reason can you assign for the low condition of the congregation as to numbers, and to the amount raised for the Sustentation Fund', the answer was 'unwillingness on the part of the people to give – two-thirds pay nothing to the Sustentation Fund and nothing for seat-rents' – the answer only applying to the latter part of the question.*

8   *That in the opinion of the office-bearers, the Gaelic-speaking population in Aberdeen exceeds 2000.*

9   *That to the question 'do you think that there is any prospect of the congregation increasing and becoming more vigorous under present arrangements' the answer was 'No'.*

10 *That the office-bearers having been asked if they could suggest any remedy for the presently depressed condition of the congregation or any plan whereby the Gaelic population could be brought more generally to attend ordinances in this church, stated that they thought the best remedy would be a popular assistant to Mr. Mackenzie; but that if this could not be accomplished, in their opinion the church should be, for a time at least, converted into a preaching station. They seemed to think that if a Gaelic Probationer of piety, active habits, and popular gifts were sent to them by the church, he would likely gather together again the Highlanders in this city. They appeared to be unanimously of opinion that the suppression of the congregation would be a great evil, as, from the attachment of the Gaelic people to their native tongue, they would either join themselves to some other body who might be willing to give them a Gaelic minister, or remain at home on the Sabbath rather than go to a church where only the English language was made use of. Your committee do not feel inclined to give any opinion in regard to this distressing case, but they are, however, convinced that some prudent and practical measures must be adopted speedily in order to prevent the Gaelic congregation from being entirely broken up by internal divisions.*

It can be seen from this report that the Presbytery were in favour of retaining the Gaelic congregation. It felt that the congregation could become self-supporting if another minister was appointed and so the Presbytery brought before the General Assembly in 1850 an application from the Gaelic congregation for permission to appoint 'an assistant and successor to the minister'. Perhaps surprisingly, the Assembly remitted the request to the Presbytery to dispose of in conjunction with the Commission of Assembly.[3]

Ministerial assistant proposed

The Presbytery then appointed a committee to handle the delicate matter of discussing the future role of the Rev. Hugh Mackenzie in the Gaelic congregation. This committee gave in a report on 16th July based on discussion with Hugh Mackenzie and four representatives of the congregation – Wm Gordon, bookseller and elder, Alex Stephen, decorator and deacon, James Fraser, candlemaker and Gaelic precentor, and Wm Stuart, a road surveyor who had come into prominence after the exodus of 1848. He must at that time have enjoyed the confidence of the minister, because in 1848 he joined Wm Gordon and Kenneth Dingwall on the Kirk Session bringing its strength up to three. At the same time he was appointed treasurer in succession to Alex Mackenzie who had gone to Bon Accord Church. When the Presbytery resumed discussion of the problem these men appeared for the congregation while, in the words of the Presbytery Clerk, 'Mr Duncan M Connell appeared for himself'.[4]

This is the first mention of one who was then emerging as a leader in the Gaelic congregation. Born in Argyllshire in 1823, his name made its first appearance in the Aberdeen Directory for 1849 where he is listed as a teacher in the Free North School. In these days it was not essential to have formal academic qualifications in order to teach. Anyone short of money, it was said, kept a school[5] and it was some time later, in 1853, that Duncan Connell graduated from Marischal College. Subsequently he studied divinity at Aberdeen Free Church College and in 1862 he was inducted as the first minister of Fortingall Free Church. In 1878 he transferred his allegiance to the Established Church and became minister of St Kiaran's Gaelic Church, Govan. A Gaelic scholar of some standing, he wrote what is still the only Gaelic text-book on astronomy.[6] Although described at his first appearance before the Presbytery as representing none but himself, it was not long before he became the spokesman for a substantial section of the congregation.

When, in the course of its enquiries, the Presbytery's Committee asked the Rev. Hugh Mackenzie if he was willing to have an assistant and successor appointed, he answered, 'I do, reserving my rights', by which he meant that he would not agree to a sharing of the Equal Dividend, then standing at £123, with the person to be appointed his assistant. Questioned by the same committee, the congregation's representatives, who already had the successor in mind, insisted that only an ordained assistant would be acceptable. When asked how much extra they were willing to contribute to the support of an ordained assistant, they promised £120-130. Invited to explain how a congregation with an annual income of about £150, of which only £35 was contributed to the Sustentation Fund, proposed to raise this extra money for the Fund, they replied that it was based on an anticipated increase in the attendance from the existing figure of about 300 persons to 800 persons, this latter figure being about 40 per cent of the Gaelic community in Aberdeen. Not surprisingly the Presbytery's Committee concluded that 'as the encouragement held out by the representatives of the congregation rests so much upon contingencies, they cannot advise the appointment of an ordained assistant but at the same time they are of the opinion that, from the present depressed condition of that congregation, it is very desirable that an unordained assistant should be speedily appointed in the hope that his labours among the Gaelic population of the city would bring the congregation into circumstances which would warrant the appointment of an ordained assistant and successor'.[7]

The Presbytery took a more hopeful view than did its committee. Encouraged by a written statement subscribed by 36 persons in the congregation promising to secure a salary of £130 to a colleague and successor, they urged the Sustentation Fund Committee to agree to the appointment of such. That Committee then gave its agreement on the understanding that the congregation would remit, in addition to the promised £130, the £50 that it had been in the habit of remitting to the Fund.[8] The congregation agreed and the way was now open to call an assistant minister or, as some insisted, 'a colleague and successor'. Twenty-eight years had passed since the congregation had last found itself in the happy position of being free to choose a minister. The fact that their ill-advised selection on that occasion was from Lawers on Lochtayside did not now discourage them from looking in the same direction. The man they had in view was the Rev. John Logan, minister of Lawers Free Church.

Logan of Lawers head-hunted

John Logan, born in Knockbain, Ross-shire in 1803, was well known to the Gaelic congregation as he had been a student at King's College. However his preference while there was for Gavin Parker's ministry and for a time he acted as assistant in Bon Accord Church.[9] In 1843 he was inducted to Lawers Free Church and he subsequently ministered in Dundee Gaelic Chapel, Duthil (Carrbridge), and lastly the Macdonald Memorial Church in Govan. He died in 1871. Dr Donald MacLean, one-time minister in Duthil, has left a vivid description of his predecessor who inspired so much enthusiasm in Aberdeen's Gaelic Lane: 'He was a fearless man, bold and impulsive but warm-hearted; vigorous and weighty as a preacher; capable as an organiser. However he was not long in the parish when he came into collision with 'the men'. Incidents which gave spiritual distress to Mr. Logan were accompanied by explosions of temper which were a source of personal danger to him.'[10] Given such a personality, it may be questioned how well he would have functioned in partnership with the Rev. Hugh Mackenzie, but the matter never came to the test.

The call was subscribed by all 100 members and 221 adherents present at the election meeting and the commissioners to the Presbytery of Breadalbane were armed with cogent reasons for John Logan's translation, not the least of which was 'there are many Gaelic-speaking students connected with the Free Church and it is of great importance in the present state of the Highlands that these students should be superintended by a Gaelic minister and encouraged to keep up their acquaintance with their native language to which an opportunity of hearing a popular Gaelic minister would greatly contribute'.[11] It was also claimed that 'the number who have signed the call is an indication that many who are at present remiss in their attendance on ordinances would wait regularly on his ministry and thus a strong and vigorous Gaelic congregation would exist here befitting the Capital of the North of Scotland'. The congregation appointed its own representatives to press their petition at the Presbytery of Breadalbane and an indication that this call had been effected by the rank and file of the congregation led by Duncan Connell rather than by the office-bearers, may be seen in the fact that the Deacons' Court decided that they also should be represented at the Presbytery and they appointed their clerk, Simon Mackenzie, to attend on their behalf. The meeting, held on 6th May 1851, left them sadly disappointed for 'Mr Logan read extracts from some correspondence which took place between himself and one of the elders of the Gaelic congregation from which it appeared that he had given every discouragement to any steps being taken to call him to Spring Garden. He said it was his conviction to decline the call'.[12] With great reluctance the congregation now yielded to pressure from the Presbytery to desist from further efforts to persuade John Logan to change his mind.

Candidate selection committee

In an attempt to achieve an early and harmonious appointment, the Presbytery nominated a vacancy committee to select suitable candidates from which a colleague and successor might be chosen.[13] Significantly, this committee included Duncan Connell, who acted as convener, and another backbencher, Alex Stuart, who was to play a prominent role for a few years. Two of the three members of Session – Wm. Gordon, bookseller and Wm. Stuart, road surveyor – were included, as was one of the deacons, Alex Stephen, decorator. James Fraser, candlemaker and Gaelic precentor, and Simon Mackenzie, the clerk, completed the selection committee, the last-named doubtless being appointed to represent the minister's interests. Despite the fact that he himself was not an office-bearer, it was this Simon F Mackenzie who had replaced Hugh Falconer as clerk both to the Deacons' Court and the Kirk Session in 1847. He was, in fact, the minister's eldest son and he continued to function as clerk until 1852, the year in which he enrolled as a divinity student in the Free Church College. He was licensed by the Free Presbytery of Aberdeen in 1856, and in 1857 he emigrated to Australia becoming a member of the Presbyterian Church of Eastern Australia and latterly the Presbyterian Church in New South Wales. He died in 1894 aged 66.[14]

The first candidate brought to Aberdeen was the Rev. Allan

MacIntyre of Strontian but he failed to give satisfaction. He was later to serve the Church in the Colonial field.[15] The next candidate – Mr Corbet, probably Charles Fraser Corbet born in Beauly in 1828, eventually ordained in Hopeman in 1856[16] – proved to be highly popular. He gave supply for at least six months during which he was supported by the congregational committee rather than the Deacons' Court. When he left, it was reported that the collectors at the Printfield registered their disappointment by refusing to continue as collectors. Corbet was followed by Alex Paterson, a probationer born at Culloden in 1824 and educated at King's College, Aberdeen and New College, Edinburgh.[17] After giving supply for three months, the congregation decided he would be a suitable colleague and successor. In September 1852 he received a call signed by 112 communicants and 463 adherents. Two months later it was reported that he had declined the call and in 1853 he was ordained to the Gaelic Church in Perth. Disappointed by their failure to enlist either Charles Corbet or Alex Paterson, the congregational committee felt the time had come for another approach to John Logan of Lawers.

When the Presbytery met on 1st March 1853 they had before them a petition from the congregation requesting the renewal of a call to John Logan, but this time it was to be conditional on the retirement of the Rev. Hugh Mackenzie.[18] Wm Gordon, Alex Stuart and Duncan Connell appeared in support of the petition. The Presbytery, impressed by the unanimity of the congregation and its willingness that Hugh Mackenzie should, although in retirement, retain the whole of the Equal Dividend, the additional stipend being subscribed by the congregation themselves, agreed to support their application for Assembly approval for this arrangement. They asked the Assembly to permit the Rev. Hugh Mackenzie to retire on health grounds and to receive the whole of the Equal Dividend or an equivalent sum arising from half the Equal Dividend and an equal amount from the Fund for Aged and Infirm Ministers.[19] The Assembly agreed to 'the appointment of a colleague and successor in the usual way in terms of the Act of Assembly but decline to concur in the proposal of the Presbytery that a sum should be allowed to Mr. Mackenzie from the Aged and Infirm Ministers Fund'.[20] The implication of that finding was that Hugh Mackenzie retained only the right to a proportion of the Equal Dividend as a retirement allowance. Urged by the congregational committee that a call now be sent to the Rev. John Logan, the Presbytery agreed 'on the understanding that Mr. Mackenzie is to receive the full Equal Dividend and his successor not less than £130 as guaranteed by the congregation'.[21] But it was evident, and not least to Hugh Mackenzie, that in the light of the Assembly finding he had only a right to half of the Equal Dividend. For the other half to be payable throughout his retirement, he was dependent on the goodwill of the congregation.

Call to Logan of Lawers

The call was signed without further delay and tabled at a meeting of the Free Presbytery of Breadalbane held on 9th July 1853, the Rev. John Logan declining at that stage of the proceedings to make any statement as to his intentions. However, at the next meeting of Presbytery – a meeting at which Wm Gordon, Wm Stuart and Duncan Connell were present as commissioners from the Aberdeen congregation – John Logan declared his acceptance of the call. Then to the consternation of the Aberdeen commissioners, the Presbytery of Breadalbane 'moved that it is inexpedient in present circumstances to translate Mr. Logan to the Gaelic Church which motion was unanimously agreed to'.[22] The Aberdeen delegation promptly intimated their intention of appealing to the Synod to reverse this finding – a move which, it may be assumed, had the support of John Logan. The Free Synod of Perth met on 18th October 1853 and Wm Gordon and Wm Stuart appeared on behalf of the Aberdeen congregation. Then 'Mr Logan being called upon to express his mind upon the subject, stated that his views had undergone a considerable change since the matter was before the Presbytery, in consequence of circumstances coming to his knowledge of which he was not then aware and that he now felt it to be his duty to decline the call'.[23]

The hopes of the Aberdeen congregation were finally shattered. What were the circumstances which had occasioned this change of heart? It was not that a more attractive offer had come to his notice. The next call he received was from Lochcarron and that he also declined. But it is evident that he declined the first call to Aberdeen signed in 1851 because he was to be colleague and assistant to Hugh Mackenzie. When the congregational committee again brought his name before the Presbytery in March 1853, it was 'on the condition of the retirement of the Rev. Hugh Mackenzie as an emeritus minister'. Hugh Mackenzie had agreed to this on condition of his continuing to enjoy the full equal dividend, but when, as a result of the Assembly decision, he was to be beholden to the congregation for half of his income, he had second thoughts regarding the course he had earlier assented to. This *volte-face* came to the notice of John Logan between the meeting of Presbytery in August and the meeting of Synod in October and effectively put paid to the consummation so greatly longed for in Aberdeen's Gaelic Lane.

The congregation was now thoroughly demoralised and this was reflected in the ingathering of its funds. In July 1854 'nothing was contributed to the Sustentation Fund with the exception of sixpence from Jessie Munro'; and three months later only one shilling (5 pence) was contributed with only one of the Sustentation Fund collectors,

Joseph Mackay, attending the quarterly meeting. In January 1855 not even Joseph Mackay turned up and nothing was contributed.

In April 1854 the congregational committee asked the Deacons' Court to approach the Gaelic Committee in Edinburgh to have a probationer allocated to the congregation, but Hugh Mackenzie warned them that 'unless there was an immediate change for the better it would be vain for them to expect that the ordinances of religion could be dispensed among them either by the ministrations of an ordained minister or a probationer'. They did, however, obtain the services of a probationer and he was paid by the congregational committee. Later in 1854 the congregational committee asked the Deacons' Court to take responsibility for supporting the probationer on the grounds that 'it was not for the good of the congregation to have two parties over the management of affairs and now that the services of a probationer were secured which were generally acceptable to the congregation the Deacons' Court be requested to take the responsibilities of his services into their own hands for thus alone they believe can the congregation be united in the promotion of the general good'. This the Deacons' Court declined to do 'in view of the fact that the congregation does not give the Deacons' Court funds sufficient for taking responsibility on themselves'.

Hugh Mackenzie's last stand

In July 1854 the congregational committee, 'having the good of the congregation at heart and supremely desirous to see its efficient working by the appointment of an adequate staff of office-bearers', urged the Deacons' Court through its Moderator to provide for the election of additional office-bearers. Why the request was transmitted through the Deacons' Court and not the Kirk Session may be gathered from the minute of the meeting of Deacons' Court which considered the request.

> *The Court while they see the propriety and the urgent necessity of having additional office-bearers appointed in the congregation find that they have no power in the matter as the Session is the proper Court to originate and carry this proposal into effect. The Moderator observed that during the last twelve months he had called several meetings of Session from the pulpit but that when he came to the Session House, he found but one elder present so that a Session could not be constituted, in consequence of which the Communion Roll had not been purged since March 1852; that for the reason mentioned only one meeting of Session was held this year, and that one nearly six months ago, at which he (the Moderator) proposed that a meeting of the congregation should be held on the following week for the purpose of electing*

additional elders and deacons, but that this proposal was negatived by both the elders whereupon he recorded his dissent.

Wm Gordon was present at the meeting of which the above is a minute and was probably not a guilty party. The loyal-hearted quarrier Kenneth Dingwall made his last recorded appearance at the Deacons' Court on 22nd July 1853 and had probably been deceased since that time. The third member of Session, whose support would have been essential for any positive decisions to be taken in the absence of Kenneth Dingwall, was Wm Stuart and he may well have been obstructive. If so it may have suited Hugh Mackenzie's purposes despite his protestations.

The state of affairs deplored by the congregational committee could not be left to continue, and in January 1855 the Presbytery, at the urging of the congregational committee, appointed Dr MacGilvray, minister of Gilcomston Free Church, to confer with the Gaelic Church office-bearers. The result was that the Deacons' Court 'agreed to take the responsibility of providing ordinances in the same way as they are maintained at present [by a probationer] the office-bearers taking along with them in this matter the minister on the one hand and the congregation on the other'. Another improvement followed from Dr MacGilvray's mediation. Alex Stephen, decorator, and Hugh Campbell, Printfield, both of whom had been deacons for ten years, were ordained elders together with the influential member of the congregational committee, Alex Stuart.

The old order was changing. Wm Stuart, road surveyor, elder and treasurer, now disappeared from the records. The last meeting that he attended was in January 1855. It seems that he was the elder who had been in correspondence with John Logan and who was most anxious to secure his services. Although he withdrew from office in the Gaelic Church, he did not leave Aberdeen, his name continuing to appear in the Aberdeen Directory until 1875. On 15th June 1855, Wm Gordon, bookseller, attended his last meeting. Admitted to the membership by Donald Sage in 1821, and who that same year baptised a son of Wm Gordon, the bookseller had given twenty years of service as an elder. The evidence suggests that he was one of the least partisan of the Gaelic Church supporters and probably only death itself severed his connection. On 29th June 1855 the minister, Hugh Mackenzie, was to make his last appearance at the Deacons' Court.

The probationer whose services at that time met with the general satisfaction of the congregation was a Mr John MacCallum. Because of Hugh Mackenzie's chronic ill-health, MacCallum had been sent to the congregation in October 1854 by the Gaelic Committee in Edinburgh. Apparently moves were afoot to have him go to Croick and Kincardine, Easter Ross and he reported to the Deacons' Court in March 1855 that he had put himself in the hands of the Gaelic Committee being willing to go to Croick or to stay in Aberdeen as they might instruct him. But he requested that the office-bearers write to the Gaelic Committee indicating his willingness to stay. The minister and Wm Gordon advised that such action be postponed until after the Presbytery had met with the congregation as they were soon to do. But 'Mr Alex Stephen insisted that they write immediately or he would resign this night'. A majority decided in favour of writing and the Gaelic Committee agreed to MacCallum remaining in Aberdeen for another three months. He left at the end of June and the following year he was ordained to Croick and Kincardine where he remained until his retirement in 1902.[24]

Hugh Mackenzie pensioned off

Early in 1855 the Presbytery, 'feeling that the Gaelic Congregation were in a very peculiar position in consequence of the age and delicate health of Mr. Mackenzie, the falling off of the congregation and other circumstances', appointed a committee to deal with the minister and people with a view to the matter being referred to the ensuing General Assembly.[25] The upshot was that Presbytery recommended to the Assembly 'that Mr. Mackenzie considering his long services to the Church, his age and infirm health should be placed on the Aged and Infirm Ministers Fund so that his income should continue equal to that derived from the Sustentation Fund'.[26] The Assembly agreed that he should be retired on £110 per annum, a figure only £9 short of the 1854 Equal Dividend.[27] On 3rd July 1855 he wrote to the Moderator of Presbytery as follows:[28]

> Sir,
>
> Having on a former occasion in a letter addressed to Rev. Mr. Spence, addressed an earnest desire to be relieved from the charge of the Free Gaelic Congregation provided that an arrangement could be made by which I might be enabled to retire with a reasonable provision for myself and family, and understanding that such a provision has been made by last General Assembly and being satisfied with the provision then made, I now beg leave to demit the charge of the congregation trusting that the Presbytery will take the over-sight thereof, counsel and direct them in their present weak and helpless state and that you and other members of Presbytery may be sustained and supported by the Head of the Church in all your endeavours to advance the interest of His Kingdom and promote his glory – is the earnest prayer of yours sincerely, Hugh Mackenzie.

Thus ended Hugh Mackenzie's 33 year ministry in the Aberdeen Gaelic Chapel. The congregation must have learned of his resignation with a feeling of thankfulness. His early life had been full of promise and later he was to be held in esteem as a Disruption minister. Yet it cannot be claimed that his ministry left fragrant memories in his congregation. 'Mr Mackenzie was a man of solid and varied acquirements. Although naturally of a reserved and unobtrusive disposition, yet those who knew him most intimately felt that they came in contact with a mind of superior calibre. In general scholarship he maintained a very high position. As a theologian he was surpassed by comparatively few.' So wrote his obituarist,[29] allowing himself that element of exaggeration that was thought appropriate to the occasion.

Hugh Mackenzie certainly had a good mind, but he was totally lacking in those pastoral gifts that endear a minister to his people. On the contrary his attitudes were such as gave rise to acute feelings of exasperation in those who shouldered the responsibility for maintaining the congregation's welfare. His own life was not free from difficulty and sorrow. Four of his children died in infancy. Two sons died, one aged 24, the other 21, in 1855 and 1859. He himself succumbed to his fourth heart attack on 31st January 1859 when aged 71. He was buried in St Nicholas Churchyard, almost in the shadow of the Gaelic Chapel. Later the congregation erected a handsome granite obelisk over his grave. It has been said that this was a mark of his congregation's affection,[30] but, as a posthumous gesture, it may have had more to do with the fact that his son was Session Clerk and his daughter was wife to the minister of the Gaelic Church when the stone was erected. Some of his descendants were quite distinguished. A great-grandson, George Edmond Crombie CMG entered the diplomatic service and became British High Commissioner to The Gambia in 1965.[31] He died in Aberdeen in 1973.

Notes to Chapter 24

1. For an outline of the historical events, see Rev. David Thorburn: *Historical review of the legislation of the Free Church of Scotland on the Sustentation Fund* (Edinburgh, 1855).
2. *Records of the Free Presbytery of Aberdeen,* vol. 1, p 393 (26th March, 1850) (CH3-2-5).
3. *Proceedings of the General Assembly of the Free Church of Scotland held at Edinburgh* (25th May, 1850) (Edinburgh, 1850), p 46 (CH3-984-4).
4. *Records of the Free Presbytery of Aberdeen,* vol. 1, p 419 (6th August, 1850).
5. G M Reith: *Dr Archibald Reith* (Aberdeen, 1898), p 4.
6. *Reul-eolas. Gaelic Astronomy.* Thomas M'Lauchlan remarks that this work is highly creditable both to the scientific and literary acquirements of the author and shows that Gaelic could very readily be converted into a vehicle for communicating the truths of science (*Celtic Gleanings*, Edinburgh 1857), p 141.
7. *Records of the Free Presbytery of Aberdeen,* vol. 1, p 413 (16th July, 1850).
8. Ibid., p. 438 (4th February, 1851).
9. W Robbie: *Bon Accord Free Church, Aberdeen: a retrospect* (Aberdeen, 1888), p 113.

10. D Maclean: *Duthil Past and present* (Inverness, 1910), pp 50 and 63.
11. *Records of the Free Presbytery of Aberdeen*, vol. 1, pp 452-453 (15th April, 1851).
12. Ibid., vol. 1, p 455 (6th May, 1851).
13. Ibid., vol. 1, p 458 (12th May, 1851).
14. For details of the ministry of the Rev. Simon F Mackenzie, see James Cameron: *Centenary History of the Presbyterian Church in New South Wales* (Sydney, 1905); and J Campbell Robinson: *The Free Presbyterian Church of Australia* (Melbourne, 1947).
15. W Ewing: *Annals of the Free Church of Scotland* (Edinburgh, 1907), vol. 1, p 232.
16. Ibid., vol. 1, p 125.
17. Ibid., vol. 1, p 287.
18. *Records of the Free Presbytery of Aberdeen*, vol. 1, p 538 (1st March, 1853).
19. Ibid., vol. 1, p 559 (10th May, 1853).
20. *Proceedings of the General Assembly of the Free Church of Scotland held at Edinburgh* (31st May, 1853), p 64 (Edinburgh, 1853) (CH3-984-6).
21. *Records of the Free Presbytery of Aberdeen*, vol. 2, p 2 (7th June, 1853).
22. *Records of the Free Presbytery of Breadalbane*, vol. 1, p 203 (4th August, 1853) (CH3-451).
23. *Records of the Free Synod of Perth*, vol. 1, p 174 (18th October, 1853) (CH3-259-2).
24. W Ewing: op. cit., p. 216.
25. *Records of the Free Presbytery of Aberdeen,* vol. 2, p 6 (March 1855).
26. Ibid., p 69 (1st May, 1855).
27. Ibid., p 72 (12th June, 1855).
28. Ibid., p 74 (3rd July, 1855).
29. *The Aberdeen Free Press and Buchan News* (11th February, 1859), p 5.
30. A Gammie: *The churches of Aberdeen* (Aberdeen, 1909), p 192.
31. *Aberdeen University Review,* vol. 45, p 226.

Chapter 25

*

HOPE REVIVED

HUGH Mackenzie resigned the charge of the Gaelic congregation in July 1855, but for several months prior to his resignation he had been incapacitated by a heart attack and the pulpit work had been carried on by probationers. Through the summer of 1855 the resident probationer was Thomas Grant who had been born in Cromdale in 1822. In later years, when he was minister of the Free Church in Tain, it was said of him that 'all over the Highlands his services were eagerly sought and greatly prized'.[1] It is uncertain how long he remained in Aberdeen or whether, if asked, he would have accepted a call to the Gaelic Church. But on Hugh Mackenzie's retirement the congregation was inhibited from calling a minister by a resolution of the 1855 General Assembly which deferred until 1856 a decision as to whether the congregation was to remain a sanctioned charge. The Sustentation Fund Committee continued to threaten it with having its status reduced to that of a preaching station, a fate that had already overtaken Saltcoats Gaelic Church in 1852 and Dundee Gaelic Church in 1854. But in 1856 the congregation, bolstered by a written guarantee from 18 members willing to subscribe a total of £70 annually to supplement the half Equal Dividend available for a new pastor, asked the Presbytery to bring its case before the General Assembly 'in the manner best calculated to secure the removal of the barrier in reference to the calling of a minister'.[2] The Presbytery must have been very persuasive for the Assembly agreed despite the fact that a few days earlier it had declined to receive a petition from the Dundee Gaelic Church for reinstatement as a sanctioned charge even although that congregation contributed a larger proportion of the Equal Dividend.[3] However, Assembly approval did not obviate the need for the Sustentation Fund Committee to sanction the financial arrangements for the calling of a minister and this the Committee declined to do 'in consequence of the inadequate sum proposed to be raised by the congregation'.[4] It seems that within the short space of six months the guarantee of £70 had been rescinded. The Sustentation Fund Committee now suggested a minimum of £50 from the congregation and, when this was agreed to, permission was granted.[5]

Free to call a minister, the congregation made choice of a probationer, Colin Sinclair, born in Melvich in 1828 and educated at Edinburgh University. The call was signed by 105 members and 238 adherents, evidence of a reasonable level of harmony within the congregation. The induction took place on 2nd April 1857 when the minister of Bon Accord Free Church, the Rev. Charles Ross, addressed the congregation in Gaelic. A new ministry usually results in a quickening of interest in a congregation and it would appear from the sums subscribed to the Sustentation Fund that the minister was enjoying more support that had been shown to his predecessor.

Revival in Aberdeen

It was during Colin Sinclair's ministry that the revival of 1859 and the early 1860s occurred. This movement had a marked effect on Aberdeen and the north-east, but there is no evidence that the Gaelic Church was noticeably affected. Colin Sinclair was himself associated with the revival movement,[6] as indeed were many other men who on occasion ministered in the Gaelic Church. Notable among these was John Emslie, afterwards Dr Emslie of Canterbury, New Zealand. Born at Keig in 1831, he studied divinity in the Aberdeen Free Church College from 1857-1861. During this time he occasionally preached in the Gaelic Chapel[7] while he acted as locum to the vacant charge of Free St Clements, a congregation which was so enthralled with his preaching that, even although he was not a candidate for the vacancy, he was elected over the official candidate, none other than Marcus Dods, a controversial scholar whose gifts eventually had him elected Principal of New College.

In the course of Colin Sinclair's ministry various improvements were carried out on the fabric of the Gaelic Chapel. In 1859 it was agreed to reslate the church, and that same year the Deacons' Court, on the casting vote of the chairman Alex Stephen, agreed that the church should be repainted. The contract was then awarded to Alex Stephen's firm of decorators. And it was not just the fabric that was given a face-lift. Shortly after Colin Sinclair's induction the Deacons' Court agreed to the purchase of twelve music books for the use of the choir. This is the first reference to the existence of a choir and the need for music books may be taken to indicate that it was a recent introduction. A new interest in the musical side of Psalm-singing had been initiated in Aberdeen in the mid-1850s. Largely as a consequence of the enthusiasm of Wm Carnie there was formed in 1855 the General Association for the Improvement of Psalmody[8] and echoes from this movement were clearly audible in the Gaelic Church.

In 1860 it was agreed that the building of a new vestry on the south side of the church should proceed without delay. The cost, inclusive of the provision of drainage into the Denburn, amounted to approximately £60. The following year the building programme continued with a decision 'to erect a meeting house for prayer and other church affairs at the east end of the church'. The Session House, as this building was termed, also cost £60 and, as 'it was found necessary to raise a loan of £20 in order to meet the expenditure, Mr. Cormack, Merchant in the Shiprow, kindly gave an interest-free loan'. When the building was complete, it was reported that 'a member of the Deacons' Court had presented the Church with a desk for the Session House which is henceforth to be considered the property of the Church'. It was at this same meeting that Alex Stephen intimated his resignation as congregational treasurer on the grounds of infirm health and it is possible that the desk was donated by him. He was thanked for the efficient manner in which he discharged the duties of treasurer over a period of seven years. Following his resignation he continued to attend meetings of the Deacons' Court for another six months, but thereafter his name is never included in the sederunt. It would seem that he also resigned from the Kirk Session to which he had been elected in 1854. Altogether he had played a prominent part in the affairs of the congregation for more than twenty years. Although his name disappears from the records in 1862, he continued to be listed in the Aberdeen Directory as living at 13 Devanha Terrace until 1874 and his widow resided there into the 1880s.

MacAlister of Tarbert

Following Alex Stephen's resignation, the name of Donald MacAlister was suggested as treasurer. Arriving late at the meeting at which his name had been proposed, he asked for time to consider the matter and a week later, intimated his willingness to accept the post. Donald MacAlister, a native of Tarbert, Loch Fyne, was employed as an agent for the publishing firm of Wm Mackenzie. His literary ability in Gaelic was made use of by John Francis Campbell of Islay who, unable to write Gaelic himself, enlisted MacAlister's help in producing his celebrated work *Popular Tales of the West Highlands*.[9] After working in Glasgow and Perth he was transferred to Aberdeen in 1858, taking his wife and three sons to a house at 220 George Street. His eldest son, Donald, a brilliant child, attended the Free Church school in Charlotte Street where he had as one of his teachers another prominent member of the Gaelic congregation – Duncan Connell. Later in life this lad was to achieve many distinctions, among them Senior Wrangler at Cambridge, President for 27 years of the General Medical Council, and Principal of Glasgow University from 1907-1929. The memory of his childhood years in Aberdeen remained with him in later life. In 1906 he looked for, but did not find, the church in Gaelic Lane that held so many memories for him.[10] His mother was a woman whose knowledge of Scripture had astonished 'Rabbi' Duncan,[11] and likewise his father was a deeply spiritual man who would have been most useful in any capacity in the Gaelic Church and not least, given his business acumen, as treasurer. However, his tenure of the office was brief for in 1864 he was transferred to Liverpool as agent for Blackie & Son, publishers. He died there in 1881 aged 56 years.

Hugh Mackenzie junior, takes office

During Colin Sinclair's ministry there were two elections of office-bearers. When Sinclair was inducted in 1856 there were only three elders, but in his first year he ordained another five, one of whom lasted only one year. In 1860 a further seven were elected to the eldership making 14 in all. Neither before nor after was the Session so numerous. Among those elected in 1860 was Donald MacAlister, who had previously been an elder in Perth Gaelic Church; and Hugh Mackenzie, the 25-year-old son of the former minister. Hugh Mackenzie was destined to be by far the longest-serving office-bearer in the history of the congregation, his tenure of the office extending to 49 years. For most of his life he was employed by the North of Scotland Bank, latterly as first teller at that bank's head office in Castle Street. Hugh Mackenzie married a daughter of a prominent Town Councillor, Dean of Guild David Macdonald (1819-1901). This highly successful accountant, although a native of Woodside, was closely identified with the Highland community, both his father and his grandfather having served in the Black Watch. Likewise he was a prominent Free Churchman. An elder in Free St Clement's, he was returned as a representative of the Presbytery of Lewis to the General Assembly for 15 successive years.[12]

In the late 1850s, following the death of the Rev. David Carment, latterly minister of Rosskeen Free Church, steps were taken to erect a new Free Church in the town of Invergordon. This resulted in the severing of Colin Sinclair's connection with the Aberdeen Gaelic congregation. The General Assembly of 1861 sanctioned the new charge and the building was opened for worship later that year. In the Spring of 1862 Colin Sinclair preached as a candidate for the Invergordon Church. On his return to Aberdeen he sent back to the Invergordon treasurer, £5 of the £10 which he had been given 'to cover his expenses etc'.[13] A sum equivalent to one month's stipend certainly seems generous as expenses; but, perhaps, it was the custom to err on the side of generosity. He had received (and retained) the same amount from the Aberdeen congregational treasurer to meet his expenses as a commissioner to the previous General Assembly. Whether it was his preaching or his gesture of indifference to material interests that impressed the Vacancy Committee, Colin Sinclair received a call to be the first minister of Invergordon Free Church.

When the Aberdeen congregation heard of this proposal they drew up a memorial urging him to decline the call. However, Alex Stephen, decorator and former treasurer, and three other office-bearers, declined to sign the memorial. Nevertheless, despite their refusal, they announced perversely that 'it was their wish that Mr. Sinclair should decline the call and still remain with them, although they could not see their way clear to sign the memorial now before them'. When the call came before the Presbytery on 30th September 1862, Colin Sinclair intimated his conviction that he ought to accept it, and the Presbytery gave their approval by a vote of 17 to 6. His furniture was sent by sea from Aberdeen to Invergordon and by November he had commenced his second and last pastorate which was to continue for 38 years. He retired from the charge in 1899, entered the Union in 1900, and died aged 76 while attending the General Assembly of 1905. He had one son and ten daughters, five of whom were married to Free Church ministers. A grandson, the Rev. Francis J L MacLauchlan, was for a time minister of Rosemount Church, Aberdeen (1938-41), and, following distinguished chaplaincy service, minister of the Old High Church, Inverness (1950-62).

Notes to Chapter 25

1. W Ewing: *Annals of the Free Church of Scotland* (Edinburgh, 1907), vol. 1, p 175.
2. *Records of the Free Presbytery of Aberdeen,* vol. 2, p 97 (6th May, 1856) (CH3-2-6).
3. *Proceedings of the General Assembly of the Free Church of Scotland held at Edinburgh* (24th May, 1856) (Edinburgh, 1856), p 27.
4. *Records of the Free Presbytery of Aberdeen*, vol. 2, p 116 (December, 1856) (CH3-2-6).
5. Ibid., vol. 2, p. 124 (3rd February, 1857).
6. Anon: *Reminiscences of the Revival of fifty-nine and the sixties* (Aberdeen, 1910), pp xv and 87.
7. J G Emslie: *John Emslie 1831-1907. He came from Bennachie* (Christchurch, New Zealand, 1963), p 24.
8. Wm Carnie: *Reporting Reminiscences* (Aberdeen, 1902), vol. 1, p 122.
9. E F B MacAlister: *Sir Donald MacAlister of Tarbert* (London, 1935), p 8.
10. Ibid., p 169.
11. R Cowan: *Reminiscences* (Blairgowrie, 1924), p 105.
12. *In Memoriam* (Aberdeen, 1901), pp 81-85.
13. D Fraser: *The Story of Invergordon Church* (Inverness, 1946), p 23.

Chapter 26

*

AGITATORS AND TALEBEARERS

WITHIN a month of Colin Sinclair's induction to Invergordon, the Session of the Gaelic congregation reported to the Presbytery that they wished to give a call to a Murdoch Macdonald, probationer. The Presbytery appointed a committee to consider the financial strength of the congregation. In the meantime another probationer named D C Macdonald was appointed to supply the Gaelic congregation for £7 per month. When the committee gave in its report, the Presbytery agreed to sanction the congregation's Sustentation Fund schedule on the basis of a commitment to contribute £80 to the Fund, 'the minimum in the circumstances of the congregation and having in view its previous history'.[1] The amount which the congregation had been asked for to clear the way for Colin Sinclair's induction in 1857 was £50 and the Presbytery felt that a commitment to give £80 (the sum actually contributed by the congregation in 1862) would win a sympathetic response from the Equal Dividend Platform Committee. In the event it did not. That committee informed the Presbytery that 'it seemed doubtful whether this was a congregation which ought to be continued on the Platform of the Equal Dividend'.[2] In reply the Presbytery affirmed that the *per capita* givings of the Aberdeen congregation compared favourably with that of Gaelic congregations in Glasgow and Edinburgh and that Assembly support for Gaelic congregations in the south justified similar treatment for the Aberdeen congregation.

The Equal Dividend Platform Committee remained obdurate. They based their refusal to sanction an appointment on the 1861 Act of Assembly which instituted the Equal Dividend Platform Committee and laid down guidelines by which that committee was to judge a congregation's entitlement to support. The particular requirement which the Committee felt was not satisfied was with regard to the number of people adhering to the congregation, or in this case the number of Gaelic speakers in Aberdeen. They went on to say: 'In the opinion of the Committee, the case of a Gaelic-speaking population in a town by no means presents so strong a claim as that of a rural Highland parish where the distance from other Free Churches, the amount of the population, and the poverty of the people, form a strong claim for its being continued or placed on the Platform of the Equal Dividend.' On receipt of this report, the Gaelic congregation sent a deputation to urge the Presbytery to 'protect their interests' which the Presbytery agreed to do. The issue finally went to the 1863 General Assembly and among the documents laid before it was an 'Extract Minute of the Deacons' Court of the Gaelic Church of date the 9th of April current bearing that the office-bearers of the congregation had gone through the whole town and neighbourhood, and had ascertained that the number of the Gaelic-speaking population was considerably above 2,000, and not 1,000 as stated in the papers formerly before the Committee'.

If the Deacons' Court had indeed met on the date stated, the Clerk omitted to enter a record of it in the minute book which lacks any reference to a census of Gaelic speakers in 'the whole town and neighbourhood'. The revised figure was, however decisive in determining the Assembly's finding. When the matter came before the Assembly, the Equal Dividend Platform Committee, in accordance with the terms of its remit, proposed that the Aberdeen Gaelic Church be taken off the Equal Dividend Platform and the congregation of Tarbert, Harris be substituted in place of it. The claims of Tarbert rested on the fact that the Parish of Harris, which had a population of 4000, almost all of whom were connected with the Free Church, had only one Free Church minister and he resided in Manish, twelve miles from Tarbert. There could not, affirmed the Committee, be a stronger case for admission on the Platform of the Equal Dividend.

Prior to the meeting of the General Assembly, the Deacons' Court of the Gaelic congregation had agreed that they should offer to contribute £100 annually to the Sustentation Fund should this be necessary to retain Equal Dividend Platform status. But, in the event, that bid did not need to be tendered. The General Assembly disregarded the advice of its Committee and the Aberdeen congregation was given permission to call another minister on the basis of a promised contribution of £80. As it happened, Tarbert was happily provided for in the person of Dr MacKintosh Mackay who, after a life-time of service in Dunoon and Australia retired to Tarbert where he laboured for another ten years until failing strength compelled his resignation.[3]

Call to Murdoch Macdonald thwarted

On Colin Sinclair's departure to Invergordon, Dr Walter MacGilvray, the able and scholarly minister of Gilcomston Free Church, had been appointed Interim-Moderator of the Gaelic congregation. The choice was an appropriate one for Dr MacGilvray was both a Gaelic speaker and a high Calvinist; but the congregation's right to call a minister having been secured, he now relinquished the interim-moderatorship and the Rev. John Adam, minister of the Free South Church, was appointed in his place. No doubt this was a popular appointment with the congregation, for it was the Rev. John Adam, together with Donald MacAlister the treasurer, who had successfully defended the congregation's claim on the floor of the Assembly. In the administrative work of the Church Dr Adam was in his element and he ultimately found full range for his gifts as Secretary of the Free Church Home Missions Committee. As Interim-Moderator he moved to fill the vacancy without further delay.

The congregation restated their wish to call Murdoch Macdonald, probationer, a scholarly man born 30 years earlier in Lochbroom and a graduate of the University of Glasgow and New College, Edinburgh. In July 1863 a call to Murdoch Macdonald was signed by 152 members and 127 adherents. Unfortunately Innellan Free Church had earlier voted to give a call to the same man.[4] Their call was signed by 64 members and 26 adherents which no doubt reflected the strength of that congregation relative to the Aberdeen one. But, although smaller, that call had no dissentients, whereas there were 19 dissentients to the Aberdeen call, among them Wm Forbes, one of the elders.

At the meeting of 9th July at which the call had been signed, the Presbytery following the normal practice called for objections, where-upon 'Mr Wm. Forbes, elder, said that Mr. Macdonald in his preaching did not give to the Holy Spirit his proper place in the conversion of the sinner so far as he could judge'.[5] Probably Wm Forbes did not, at the time, fully appreciate the seriousness of the charge he was making, or the fact that, if he failed to substantiate it, he exposed himself to the discipline of the Church. Someone, however, enlightened him and at the next meeting of Presbytery, when called upon to justify his state-ment, a somewhat chastened Wm Forbes 'craved leave to explain that he did not mean to charge Mr. Macdonald with unsoundness of doctrine with reference to the work of the Holy Spirit in the conversion of sinners, but merely that Mr. Macdonald did not make the Spirit's work in conversion the leading topic of all his discourses'.[6] After delibera-tion, the Presbytery agreed to receive the explanation and to allow the objection in its altered form to stand as the basis of Wm Forbes' oppo-sition, at the same time warning the objector 'of the impropriety and sinfulness of rashly making charges against the doctrine or character of a probationer'. Having delivered this rebuke, the Presbytery then proceeded to dismiss the objection as 'insufficient to warrant any delay and not sufficiently definite to be investigated'.

The Presbytery likewise set aside, as being incompetent at this stage, a petition 'bearing to be from certain members and adherents of the Gaelic Church praying the Presbytery not to sustain the call'. The call was sustained but the damage had been done. Two days later Murdoch Macdonald accepted the call from the congregation of Innellan. His scholarly gifts would have been used to better advantage in the university town and it was, doubtless, the dissension in the Aberdeen congregation that discouraged him from going there. He was not happy in Innellan and left within twelve months to go to Nairn Free Church where he indulged his interest in church history by writing *The Covenanters in Moray and Ross*. In 1875 he was appointed to the chair of church history in Ormond College, Melbourne. From that position he was responsible for promulgating the Declaratory Act of 1882 which delineated the sense in which certain problematical statements in the Westminster Confession of Faith (*eg* the salvation of infants or the six day creation of the world) were understood by the Presbyterian Church in Victoria.[7]

Call to A C Fullerton sabotaged

Thwarted in their ambition to secure Murdoch Macdonald, the vacancy committee furnished the Presbytery with a new list of candidates which included the names of some who afterwards became well-known in Ross-shire church circles. Those named were John MacCallum, minister of Kincardine in Ross; Donald Gordon of Edderton who had figured on a previous list; Alex Urquhart, minister of Tarbat, Easter Ross; and Thomas Grant minister of Tain Free Church who had given supply during Hugh Mackenzie's illness. But when December came and the people met to sign a call, the name before them was not on the list of candidates. It was that of A C Fullerton, a native of Arran and a graduate of Glasgow University who, at the time, was aged 43 years.[8] The Deacons' Court had agreed two months earlier that he should be invited to preach on the occasion of a special collection being uplifted for the work of the Highlands and Islands Committee (originally known as the Gaelic Committee). He must have discharged this duty in such a manner as to persuade a section of the congregation to send him a call.

The Presbytery met with the congregation for the purpose of signing the call on 22nd December 1863 and it was then subscribed by 84 members and 60 adherents. But when dissents were called for, 'there was given in and read a petition bearing to be signed by 59 members and 83 adherents praying the Presbytery for various reasons to stay further proceedings'. There was also a second objection lodged on the grounds that the objectors (four in all) did not understand Fullerton's Gaelic. And lastly, one bold spirit, James Macdonald to name, lodged an objection on theological grounds. He averred that when Fullerton had preached in the Gaelic Church on Christ in Gethsemane, he had stated that 'the sorrows of Christ's soul at that awful hour were so great that they were like to rend the soul away from the tabernacle of clay and cause his death, and probably they would have done so but for a circumstance recorded by the Evangelist Luke, *viz.,* that an angel appeared unto him from heaven strengthening him'.

When the Presbytery met on the 5th January to consider these objections, they noted that the call had been signed by 125 members (inclusive of eight elders and six deacons) and 97 adherents – 222 persons in all. James Macdonald's objection that Fullerton's exegesis was erroneous 'inasmuch as there could be no probability of Christ's dying before completing the plan of redemption' was rejected with more gentleness than that accorded to the earlier critic, Wm Forbes. A carefully worded motion that 'the objection be repelled insofar as it implies any unsoundness of doctrine on the part of Mr. Fullerton or any opinion that should bar his entrance into the ministry' was agreed without a vote.

The objection grounded on Fullerton's incomprehensible Gaelic was considered ill-founded inasmuch as the call was signed 'by a large proportion of the strictly Gaelic-speaking part of the congregation and it is not for a moment to be supposed that they would have united in calling one who was unable to speak the language to which they are so devotedly attached'. In addition it was noted that the objectors on the language question were in fact those who were prominent in getting up the primary petition which, although allegedly signed by 142 persons, proved after careful investigation to be 'a compound of fiction and forgery'. Names had been appended to it without the knowledge of the parties themselves and against their consent. Other names were on it which had no connection with the congregational roll. Others were minors who could not subscribe such a document. In a word, it was a fraudulent document, got up by two of the elders, Wm Forbes and Donald Macbean, to thwart the candidacy of A C Fullerton. In this they succeeded, for although the Presbytery urged his acceptance of the call and arranged a conference with him on his first declining it, he adhered to his decision. Another three years were to pass before he was ordained to his first charge, that of Strathdon. Subsequently he held charges in Grantown and Glasgow. Although a married man, he died childless and bequeathed a legacy of £400, in those days a very substantial sum, to the congregation of Strathdon, a cause that in its day had struggled valiantly against anti-Free Church attitudes on the part of the landowners.

When Fullerton decided against accepting a call to the divided congregation, a section of the Gaelic Church now turned against those who, in their determination to have Fullerton's election annulled, resorted to discreditable methods. At a meeting of Presbytery on 2nd February 1864 at which the subscribed petition against proceeding with a call had been dismissed on the grounds of its fraudulent character, action was urged within the Presbytery against the elders who had submitted it; but the Presbytery agreed by a majority of 11 to 5 to take no further proceedings. Professor Lumsden dissented and appealed to the Synod on the grounds that 'it is not expedient to refuse to investigate charges against the moral character of office-bearers' and that 'it is unjust to all parties concerned to refuse to make such investigation'.[9] Lumsden's view was shared by a section of the congregation and at the meeting of Presbytery held on 29th March, there was submitted a petition from 101 members and 75 adherents of the Gaelic Church craving that the Kirk Session should 'interdict two members of Session from officiating at the ensuing Communion on account of charges against them'.[10] The Presbytery advised against further action pending the decision of Synod.

Two weeks later Professor Lumsden's appeal came before the Synod.[11] The first motion revealed a marked predilection for sitting on the fence. It was moved that 'the Synod dismiss the dissent and complaint and reaffirm the judgment of the Presbytery but at the same time instruct the Presbytery to consider whether some further steps should not be taken for bringing the parties to a proper sense of the conduct complained of'. Others viewed this stance as a form of pious ambivalence and urged that 'the Synod sustain the dissent and complaint and reverse the finding of the Presbytery and further direct that the Presbytery shall investigate the whole case and do in the matter according to the laws of the Church'. The first motion carried by 11 votes to 10. In the light of the Synod's finding it fell to the Presbytery to 'consider whether some further steps should not be taken'. Some wished to continue consideration of the matter, but a motion that 'the Presbytery having taken into consideration the remit from the Synod into the Gaelic case and having heard a statement from the Moderator of the Gaelic Session in regard to the present state of the congregation, deem it inexpedient to take any further steps in the case', was carried by the casting vote of the Moderator, the Rev. Dr David Brown.[12]

Call to George Macdonald succeeds

Faced with Alex Fullerton's unshakeable refusal to reconsider a call, the Gaelic congregation had turned their attention to another candidate and the Moderator of Presbytery obviously felt that the abandonment of further action against the office-bearers who had opposed Fullerton's candidature might promote greater harmony within the congregation and lead to a settlement. On 17th June the Presbytery, having been informed that 'the congregation by a very large majority had made choice of Mr. George Macdonald, preacher of the Gospel, to be their minister', agreed to moderate in a call in favour of Mr Macdonald. When the Presbytery met with the congregation for this purpose, the call was subscribed by 103 members and 53 adherents. When dissents were called for, Donald Macbean, elder, and five others, entered their dissent. Eventually the call was signed by 137 members (inclusive of seven elders and six deacons) and 97 adherents — 234 persons in all.

The induction of George Macdonald took place on 5th August 1864 when the Moderator of Presbytery, the Rev. Wm Anderson preached and addressed the people. This was the first induction to the Aberdeen Gaelic Church at which the people were addressed in English. After the induction, ripples from the earlier controversy continued to be felt. Two of the elders had declined to sign the call and they were doubtless behind a petition that was brought before the Presbytery on 27th September 1864 from 'certain parties professing to have been connected with the Gaelic Church'. The thrust of the petition may be gleaned from the terms of the Presbytery's finding which was that they could not 'entertain the said memorial, it being wholly informal and further-more inasmuch as the memorial contains a proposal that steps should be taken for the formation of a second Gaelic congregation in Aberdeen, the Presbytery resolve that they give no countenance to such an idea as being wholly inadmissable in the circumstances'.[13] From this motion, which was agreed to without a vote, one minister dissented, because in his view the petition was contumacious and the petitioners ought to have been disciplined. It is not clear whether the petitioners were those who had opposed the earlier majority decision or those who urged that stronger measures ought to have been taken against the dissidents. The likelihood is that it was the former party who had now withdrawn. By the end of the year the two offending elders were no longer listed in the Kirk Session sederunt and George Macdonald had settled into his first and only pastorate. His ministry there was to last 34 years, almost exactly the same duration as that of the unlamented Hugh Mackenzie whose daughter George Macdonald married in 1869 following the death of his first wife whom he had married in the year of his induction.

Notes to Chapter 26

1. *Records of the Free Presbytery of Aberdeen*, vol. 2, p 343 (6th January, 1863) (CH3-2-6).
2. *Proceedings of the General Assembly of the Free Church of Scotland: Report of the Committee on the Platform of the Equal Dividend* (Edinburgh, 1863), appendix, p 8.
3. J Graham: *Disruption Worthies of the Highlands* (Edinburgh, 1877), pp 79-88. Biographical sketch of Mackintosh Mackay by John Kennedy.
4. *Records of the Free Presbytery of Dunoon*, vol. 2, p 330 (7th July, 1863) (CH3-100-2).
5. *Records of the Free Presbytery of Aberdeen*, vol. 2, p 369 (9th July, 1863) (CH3-2-6). The deficiency that Wm Forbes here complained of was the lack of a proper emphasis on the need for Divine intervention in relation to the new birth, a deficiency which, ten years later, Dr Kennedy, in his onslaught against the hyper-

evangelism of D L Moody, characterised as being the soft centre of the new evangelicalism.

6. Ibid., vol. 2, p 371 (4th August, 1863).

7. A Macdonald: *One hundred years of Presbyterianism in Victoria* (Melbourne, 1937), p 130.

8. For a portrait and account of A C Fullerton's gifts and achievements, see J J Rae (ed.): *The Ministers of Glasgow* (Glasgow, n.d.), pp 263-270.

9. *Records of the Free Presbytery of Aberdeen*, vol. 2, p 388 (2nd February, 1864).

10. Ibid., vol. 2, p 392 (29th March, 1864).

11. *Records of the Free Synod of Aberdeen*, vol. 2, p 271 (12th April, 1864) (CH3-1-2).

12. *Records of the Free Presbytery of Aberdeen*, vol. 2, p 397 (11th May, 1864) (CH3-2-6).

13. Ibid., vol. 2, p 408 (27th September, 1864).

Chapter 27

*

ENTERTAINING INNOVATIONS

GEORGE Macdonald was born on 26th October 1832 at Forse on the boundary between the Parishes of Halkirk and Reay in Caithness where his forbears had farmed for 14 generations. His father was regarded as one of 'the men' of Caithness and a close relative – the Rev. Alexander Macdonald of Glenurquhart – was a noted Highland minister. George Macdonald was reared in an atmosphere of Gaelic piety and, having overcome some early deficiencies in his education, he matriculated at the University of Edinburgh. In April 1864 he completed his divinity training at New College and by August he was settled in Aberdeen as minister of the Gaelic Chapel. There is no doubt that he was devoted to the Gaelic language and its literature. While in Edinburgh he had been secretary of the Celtic Society[1] and in Aberdeen his enthusiasm for promoting the Gaelic language found an outlet in Gaelic classes which he conducted for the benefit of students in his congregation. Indeed his ministry seemed to be largely directed at the welfare of Highland students. While he was noted for his endeavours on behalf of the Highland and Islands Committee of the Free Church his pulpit gifts evoked few compliments. Three eye-witness accounts are available.

Peculiar preacher

A daughter of Dr John Kennedy of Dingwall recalled her father's regular visits to the Gaelic congregation, but her recollection of George Macdonald's pulpit abilities was more romantic than factual. Referring to her father being in Aberdeen she wrote, 'Once a year he went to assist Mr. Macdonald of the Free Gaelic Church. Mr. Macdonald kindly repaid that assistance by coming now and again to preach in Dingwall. He was an able preacher, a true friend and a guest always welcome to the Dingwall manse'.[2]

Another woman had a different, if no less romantic, assessment. Mrs Jean Watson, who wrote under the pen-name of Deas Cromarty, remembered his preaching as conveying an impression of sombre melancholy, unfulfilled promise, a Gaelic voice crying to the Gaelic soul with 'a strange recurrent cry amid the low guttural of the Highland tones. The sermon is long and ideas flitter through it like shadows over a wide hill-side when the autumn day goes down. Suddenly, as it were the fling of the pipes, comes a wail charged with keen force and weird entreaty. You may forget what has been said but you will never forget this cry'.[3]

For an honest matter-of-fact estimate of his pulpit gifts we can take the words of Dr Alexander Stewart, also an eye-witness, but, unlike the others, writing thirty years after his death. He wrote, 'Mr Macdonald was a scholarly man and was especially an authority on Celtic matters, but he was a poor preacher. He had an unpleasant voice, and his faults of elocution were not helped by the facial contortions which accompanied the delivery of his message'.[4] Deas Cromarty of course was saying the same thing, but in a coded form of words, as George Macdonald was still alive when she was writing.

Benevolent provision

Insufficient income was a recurrent problem in most Gaelic congregations and Aberdeen was no exception. Only congregations with a highly-rated preacher could avoid the need to resort to special fund-raising schemes. Although novel methods were soon to be introduced, the Gaelic church in the mid-nineteenth century still adhered to the long established practices, *ie* personal doorstep collecting from the faithful, or engaging popular preachers to occupy the pulpit for special services. By February 1865, a mere six months after George Macdonald's induction, the Deacons' Court minuted their concern to arrange for Sunday evening lectures with outside preachers to raise funds. It was left to the minister and the treasurer to make the arrangements.

The treasurer was David Macpherson, a flesher in the New Market. He had been appointed a year earlier following the resignation of MacAlister, the book agent for the publishers Blackie. Sadly his tenure as treasurer was brief in the extreme. In 1866 he took ill and died in April leaving a widow and young family. Macpherson was held in high esteem as an elder and the impoverished circumstances of his family evoked the sympathy of his fellow office-bearers. In December 1867 the Deacons' Court resolved that a collection be taken on behalf of the widow and family. When this became known some murmuring must have arisen that other widows were being neglected, for the Court reconvened two weeks later and adjusted their finding to read that the collections would be 'in behalf of all the deserving poor of the congregation'. The collection was taken on 15th January at all three services and after deducting the cost of printing and advertising it yielded £3.52. It was agreed that 30 shillings (£1.50) be given to the Macpherson family. Twelve individuals received 2s 6d and two received 5 shillings (25 pence). The Macphersons would seem to have had a special place in the affections of the congregation, but they are not referred to again.

No further collection for those 'in very destitute circumstances' is minuted until November 1876 when £1.30 was gathered and disbursed to three people. However, in December 1877 the Deacons' Court agreed that a special collection be taken on behalf of Hector Munro, an office-bearer in the congregation, 'laid aside for sometime back through ill health'. The sum of £2.60 was raised and handed over to him. Living at 11 Shuttle Street, he had been appointed a deacon in 1855 and he played an active role in congregational affairs for twenty years. In June 1866, following the death of David Macpherson, he was appointed congregational treasurer and continued in that office until March 1875 when his resignation was accepted. His last appearance at the Deacons' Court was on 16th February 1876 and he died on 4th May 1878 when he was living at 11 North St Andrew Street.

Lament for the beadle

The beadle Robert Mackay was another who gave faithful service over a long period. That he was held in high esteem was evident enough on Sunday 8th February 1874 when it was seen that he was absent from his accustomed place, his whereabouts unknown. His mysterious disappearance certainly had the effect of uniting the two factions in the congregation in a common concern for one who, for more than thirty years, had been synonymous with the Gaelic Church. In its first issue after the weekend, the *Aberdeen Daily Free Press* carried the following advertisement on its front page:

MAN AMISSING

Robert Mackay, Beadle of Free Gaelic Church has been missing from his home since Saturday evening. He was last seen about 5 o'clock on said evening in Skene St. Had a parcel of pew notices in one hand and a walking staff in the other. He is an aged man of low stature, had on a brown top coat and dress hat; wore a Macduff tartan scarf with yellow and mauve worsted cuffs. Had in his possession a pocket book bearing his name with about ten shillings in silver. Any information regarding him will be gratefully received by Miss Mackay, 6 Black's Buildings or by Rev. Mr. Macdonald, 18 Bon Accord Terrace.

It seems that in the late afternoon of that fateful first Saturday in February 1874 the beadle, in the course of his duties, had been at the manse on Bon Accord Terrace. Wending his way through Summer

Street en route to his home in Black's Buildings (located approximately where the Denburn Health Centre now stands) he had been spotted on Skene Street at 5 pm, about one hour after he had left the manse. On Skene Street he was in a direct line to his home but he failed to appear. The daughter with whom he stayed raised the alarm and a fruitless search ensued. That Saturday the mild weather with which the month had opened gave way to more wintry conditions and over the weekend a keen frost set in. From the time of his disappearance nothing was heard of the beadle until 2 pm on Monday when two men came on him lying in a field at Mains of Cults farm almost five miles from his home. He was taken to a nearby house and a cab was sent for, to take him home, but on reaching Holburn Street he died in the cab. Mackay was an old man who was known to be in poor health and in the words of the *Daily Press,* 'was becoming rather dottled'. It was assumed that on reaching Skene Street he had become disorientated and headed westward, walking on until forced by exhaustion to lie down. If he walked westward into Cults along Craigton Road (then a mere cart track) he would have reached Mains of Cults, where Cults Academy now stands, before collapsing. As the *Daily Press* remarked, 'How he could have lived during Saturday night and the whole of Sunday, Sunday night and the greater part of Monday, in the midst of cold and stormy weather, is a mystery to all who knew his weak and ailing condition'. With the benefit of modern medicine, we now know that the beadle was probably a victim of Alzheimer's Disease of which an early symptom is disorientation on a familiar route.

The Deacons' Court at their next meeting minuted 'their heartfelt sorrow at the melancholy circumstances connected with his death and deep sympathy with his daughter in her sore bereavement. He filled the position of church officer in the congregation for upwards of thirty years and he always conducted himself with the greatest prudence and propriety. He was a native of Strathnaver, Sutherlandshire. He possessed natural endowments far above the average of men in his position in life. In his feelings and deportment he was always most gentlemanly; and as a Christian he was warm, sincere, humble and unobtrusive'. Such an extensive tribute engrossed in the Deacons' Court minute book was quite exceptional and testified to the high esteem in which he was held. His friendly greeting, whether in Gaelic or English, was sorely missed.

Diminishing returns

The financial condition of the congregation was a never-ending prob-lem. When the General Assembly of 1863 agreed to place the Gaelic congregation on the Equal Dividend Platform in response to an under-taking to contribute a minimum of £80, the Deacons' Court, unknown to the Assembly, had in fact been willing to increase that figure to £100 should that have been necessary to ensure acceptance. Perhaps they had anticipated that a new ministry would bring new life to the congregation but if so they were to be disappointed. In 1871 the Deacons' Court felt it necessary to petition the Sustentation Fund Committee to have the congregation's contribution reduced from £80 to £60. They pointed out that comparing the year 1862-63 (the last year of Colin Sinclair's ministry) with 1864-65 (the first year of George Macdonald's), Sustentation Fund contributions, seat rents and church door collections had dropped from £50, £60 and £65 respectively to £35, £47 and £42, *ie* the total income had declined almost 30 per cent from £175 to £124. This decline they attributed to:

1   *the aftermath of the dispute and division during the vacancy.*
2   *death and infirmity among the old and loyal members of the congregation.*
3   *the unwillingness of the young to contribute as generously as their elders.*
4   *'the severity of the last two seasons on working people of which the Gaelic congregation is entirely made up'.*

Lest any should be disposed to attribute the decline to ministerial shortcomings, they added reassuringly, 'the members and adherents of the congregation are as numerous at present as at any previous period during these last seven or eight years'. However the decrease from £65 to £42 in church door collections would seem to indicate that attendances had declined over the period. Both the Presbytery and the Sustentation Fund Committee, noting that 'the membership was small and the people almost all of the labouring classes', agreed that £80 seemed beyond reach of attainment and consented to accept a reduced sum of £70. However they urged the need to appoint additional deacons and to step up the visitation of the people for the collection of funds. Additional office-bearers were appointed in December 1871, but three months later further enquiry from Presbytery elicited the response that 'districts had been partially visited but owing to the present state of the town with the existence of smallpox and the state of feeling prevalent, the Court unanimously agreed to postpone any further visitation for the present'. For the remainder of George Macdonald's long ministry the three main sources of income tended to decrease. The minutes regularly report arrears of seat rents and in 1882 only £26 was subscribed under that heading together with £31 under sustentation fund and £34 for church door collections, exclusive of communion collections which amounted to £12. That year only £42 was remitted to the Sustentation Fund Committee. The basic income of the congregation, excluding exceptional and miscellaneous items, hovered around the £100 per annum figure for the remainder of the century. Most years

£60 was remitted to Edinburgh for the Sustentation Fund although only about half of that figure was subscribed locally.

Social meetings

In January 1868 the Deacons' Court 'resumed consideration of having a social meeting in connection with the congregation'. Earlier minutes do not record the matter as being under discussion, but now a committee consisting of the minister, four elders, two deacons and four additional persons from the congregation was formed. The committee got to work immediately and only four days later they reported to the Deacons' Court that they had made arrangements for holding a social meeting on Monday 10th February in 'the schoolroom in connection with Belmont Congregational Chapel'. On the evening following this event the Court again met to 'return their most cordial thanks to the Committee appointed to make arrangements for the social meeting of the congregation which was held last night in Belmont Church school-room and was evidently a very successful one, the place being quite crowded and everyone present expressing the desire that a similar meeting should be annually held'. And so it was that a new feature of congregational life came into being.

The next social gathering was held in early December of the same year. On the earlier occasion musical entertainment had been provided by the choir of Longacre Methodist Chapel. Perhaps it was on that account that it had been deemed prudent to hold the event outside the Gaelic Church. But when the Court came to discuss arrangements for the next social, the committee suggested that it could be held in the Gaelic Church itself rather than in the less hallowed precincts of the nearby Belmont Street Church. From this decision, Alex Hendry, Skene Street, one of the elders on the social committee, dissented. The meeting was duly held and judged to be a great success, the church being quite filled. Thanks were recorded to 'clergymen and other gentlemen who addressed the meeting and who thus contributed so much to the enjoyment of the evening'. A highlight of the evening was the presentation of an elegant pulpit gown, cassock and bands to the minister.

After their first social gathering, the Deacons' Court outlined the remit of the Committee as having to do with 'what repairs the church requires, the probable expense of such repairs and what plan might be adapted to meet such expense and also to take steps toward the improvement of the Psalmody of the congregation'. Perhaps the congregation's uninhibited enthusiasm for the new style get-together gave rise to inflated notions as to what could be achieved from the proceeds. The social gathering held in November 1872 brought in £10 9s, but as expenses amounted to £9 18s 6d the balance was only 10s 6d, and on the suggestion of the minister it was agreed to use it to purchase a map of Palestine for the benefit of the Bible Class.

In December 1874 it was decided to install some form of heating in the church and a hot air stove to be situated in the centre of the church was approved. The estimated cost of £25 payable after six months was to be defrayed by special efforts. Whereupon, and doubtless to nobody's surprise, the minister's wife undertook 'to get up a concert' for the purpose. Catherine Macdonald was a daughter of the former minister and sister to Hugh Mackenzie, clerk to the Deacons' Court and one of the most influential men in the congregation. In 1864, the year of his induction in the Gaelic Church, George Macdonald had married Elizabeth Helen Elder, a daughter of John Elder, minister in Walls, Shetland. She died after giving birth to twin sons and he remarried in 1869. Catherine Macdonald was a lady who got things done and within three months she presented the Deacons' Court in person with receipted accounts for the entire cost of the heating apparatus. In addition she handed over 'the sum of 2s. 6d. being the balance from the concert together with subscriptions from a few private friends'. The Court thanked her warmly for her interest in the matter and allocated the surplus of 2s 6d to the Sunday School.

Manse project

In October 1875 the Deacons' Court, perhaps encouraged by Mrs Macdonald's fund-raising abilities, appointed a committee to purchase a manse. This undertaking, because of the demands it would make on the congregation's financial resources, and the likely effect of that on its remittances to central funds, required the approval of Presbytery. Presbytery, it should be said, had urged congregations as early as 1866 to inaugurate a Manse Fund and was therefore predisposed to grant approval. The Deacons' Court appointed its clerk, Hugh Mackenzie, to commend the project at Presbytery. This he did, successfully, arguing 'the importance of the Gaelic Church in Aberdeen is not to be estimated so much by the numbers or resources of its members as by its position and work in a university and commercial city'. He claimed there were nearly thirty students connected with the congregation and that it was in the interests of the Free Church in the Highlands that there should be in Aberdeen a minister who would 'be able to assist them in their Gaelic studies'. The Highlanders attracted to the herring fishing industry also claimed the attention of a minister and 'as this branch of industry is only in its infancy in Aberdeen there is reasonable ground to expect that the number of them, will greatly increase. Besides these,' he continued, 'other reasons could be adduced to show that the work done by the Gaelic congregation is increasing in interest and importance'.

Although he did not expand on what these reasons were or might be, the congregation were given authority to set about acquiring a manse in Aberdeen on condition that £200 towards the cost of purchase would be subscribed by the congregation itself. Robert Lumsden, manager of the North of Scotland Bank, was appointed treasurer of the Manse Fund. He was not connected with the congregation but he had strong links with the Aberdeen Free Presbytery, his brother James being Principal of the Free Church College in Aberdeen. The Presbytery also appointed a number of influential men as assessors to the Manse Committee.

In February 1877 this committee recommended that the most southerly house under construction on the eastward side of Albury Road be purchased at a cost of £1135. Contributions amounting to almost £600, none of which had come from the congregation, were in the Fund and a further £100 was looked for from the denominational Manse Building Fund. The Presbytery agreed to the purchase on condition that at least £150 of the £200 which the congregation had undertaken to raise would be forthcoming. However there must have been some doubt as to the availability of congregational or other contributions because it was further agreed that the sum of £500 could be borrowed from the North of Scotland Bank to complete the purchase. Happily Francis Edmond, a director of the North of Scotland Bank, was the congregation's Law Agent. Since both he and Robert Lumsden, the Bank's General Manager, were on the Manse Fund Committee, a loan was soon negotiated on favourable terms. But the congregation still had the responsibility to repay that loan and it may not have been entirely coincidental that at the meeting of the Deacons' Court at which this decision was taken, the congregational treasurer, Alex Macdonald, intimated his desire to be relieved of the treasurership.

Bazaar proposal

In taking the initiative to purchase a manse the Aberdeen congregation were not far behind their Gaelic counterparts in the other cities, the first Glasgow Gaelic manse having been purchased in 1872. But what was bought had to be paid for and the congregation's commitment was not easily attainable especially at a time (October 1877) when the Deacons' Court recorded a marked decrease in district collections for the Sustentation Fund and the congregational treasurer again sought to be relieved of the treasurership. However in March 1878 the Court minuted what it saw to be a way out of its financial difficulty: 'A proposition to hold a Bazaar for the liquidating of the debt remaining on the manse was tabled and regarded in a favourable light by the Court, but it was resolved to postpone the fixing of the time when such will be held until the matter became more matured.'

Although the deacons met fortnightly there was no further reference to the bazaar until 28th October when it was reported that 'the Moderator made a statement to the effect that the arrangements for the Bazaar are being matured and he hoped to be able to give a fuller report at an early date'. That report was given in November when the Moderator stated that the Ladies' Committee had agreed to hold it on the first Friday and Saturday of February 1879. That was the first intimation that such a committee existed. Clearly the entire project was in the capable hands of the minister's wife and when the Court met after the event they recorded 'their hearty thanks to the Moderator and Mrs Macdonald for their untiring zeal and arduous labours in connection with the whole matter'. And so well they might for the treasurer reported that the event had raised over £430 which, when put against expenses and the debt due on the manse, yielded a surplus of £4. The bazaar had raised an amount equivalent to the ordinary income for the congregation for at least three years and the debt was liquidated. That was no ordinary achievement. The Presbytery at its meeting that month noted that the titles to the manse were now in its possession. Possessing a manse not only relieved the congregation of the need to make rent allowances to the minister, but gave a more settled aspect to the minister's residence. Down the years the minister seemed to be for ever on the move. In 1874 he resided at 18 Bon Accord Terrace, but the following year he was living at 2 Devanha Terrace. Albury Road, although a new development, was still conveniently situated for walking to Gaelic Lane.

The innovative fund-raising events did not give rise to any improvement in the regular weekly givings of the congregation and balancing income with expenditure continued to test the ingenuity of the Deacons' Court. The social meetings committee which had been formed in 1868 and given a remit that encompassed everything from the improvement of the fabric to the improvement of Psalmody was still in existence and continued to arrange social gatherings usually in mid Winter. Tickets were issued and given to the deacons for distribution in their respective districts but the organisation was dilatory and casual. A social meeting held in December 1877 prompted sales of 285 tickets at 6d each; a further 24 persons paid on entry and 69 gratis tickets were issued to Sunday School children. But the sales income of £7 14s 9d had to be set against expenses of £7 10s and so the balance was a mere 4s 9d. Another social gathering held four years later in January 1882 produced an income of just over £5, but expenses in this instance were lower and the balance slightly over £2 from which it was agreed to give £1 to the Sunday School superintendent 'to help give a treat to the

Sunday School'. This congregational activity now seemed to have lost contact with its original remit, the novelty had gone and enthusiasm was shifting to a different form of entertainment.

Concert group

In February 1882, six weeks before the end of the financial year, the Deacons' Court viewed with dismay the projected deficit and decided to have recourse to the one proven method of fund-raising. They appointed a committee 'to confer with Mrs Macdonald with a view to get up a concert in order to obtain funds to match up the deficiency in the church accounts'. This committee was known as the Concert Committee. In addition to the Moderator it consisted of Alex Macdonald, elder and Clerk to the Deacons' Court, together with two others, one of whom, George Polson, was listed in the sederunt of the Deacons' Court but as a committee member and not as a deacon.

The decision to have unordained men attend the Deacons' Court had been approved by a congregational meeting in March 1880 when nine named individuals were appointed 'to assist the Deacons' Court in carrying on their work in the congregation'. The attendance of the persons referred to as committee members was extremely spasmodic; several of them are not recorded as having attended any meeting and usually no more than one attended. As it happened George Polson, the one most often in attendance, was not one of those appointed at the congregational meeting. Neither was the other member of the concert committee, William Ross, who had been convener of the moribund social meetings committee. At a later meeting of the Deacons' Court, and on the nomination of the minister, he too was appointed a committee member of the Court 'as he bore an excellent character and was accustomed to secondary school teaching and could speak Gaelic' – qualifications that represented a fine blend of the ethical, the professional and the cultural.

The concert committee set to work with a will and within two weeks reported that Mrs Macdonald had obtained Miss Lucas' consent to give an amateur concert. Miss Lucas was a local impresario, an accomplished musician and organist at Rubislaw Parish Church. It was agreed the concert be held in the Music Hall on or about 18th March 1882, admission one shilling for reserved seats and sixpence for the rest. There is no doubt it lived up to the hopes of its promoters who reported to the Deacons' Court a week later that as far as could be ascertained the sum realised amounted to £45 13s 6d. This was the largest single entry in the annual congregational accounts, comparing favourably with church door collections amounting to £34, sustentation fund contributions of £31 and seat rents of £26. The concert kept the church solvent.

Notes to Chapter 27

1. J M MacPhail: *Kenneth S Macdonald DD* (Edinburgh, 1905), p 34.
2. *Free Church of Scotland Monthly Record* (January 1938, p 10).
3. Deas Cromarty (Mrs Jean Watson): *Scottish Ministerial Miniatures* (London, 1892), pp 172-175.
4. *Free Church of Scotland Monthly Record* (November, 1929), p 284.

Chapter 28

*

LEAVING GAELIC LANE

IN March 1882 Alex Macdonald, Clerk to the Deacons' Court, submitted a memorial 'from students from the Highlands studying at Aberdeen anent the state of the church and the privileges which they themselves enjoyed in connection. They expressed themselves in favour of a building more worthy of the cause of the Highlanders'. This memorial had been presented on behalf of the students by Walter Calder, a native of Bonar Bridge who, at the time, was aged about thirty and was in process of completing his training in divinity. He had been connected with the congregation for at least eight years and was active in evangelism through the congregational branch of the YMCA. He was also involved in outreach to Highland fishermen. But 'the state of the church' to which the memorial referred had to do with its fabric rather than its spiritual life; and the cause they had in mind was that of the Highlanders rather than the Gospel. Perhaps the students felt that the condition of the Gaelic Chapel was a disincentive to attendance. This view was certainly shared by the Deacons' Court which a year earlier had unanimously agreed to sell the Gaelic church and relocate in a newly constructed building. Subsequently the Presbytery had appointed a committee to consider a petition from the congregation requesting authority to erect a church on Jasmine Terrace, off King Street. In May 1882, James Iverach, minister of Ferryhill Free Church, a close friend of the Gaelic Church minister, moved that the Gaelic Church be permitted to relocate to the Jasmine Terrace neighbourhood. This move was opposed by the office-bearers (but not the minister who was on the point of moving to Edinburgh) of the North Free Church; but the petition carried by twelve votes to three.

The church on Dee Street

On 18th July 1882 the Deacons' Court held a special meeting at which it was reported that a church on Dee Street occupied by the Free Methodist congregation was to be sold; whereupon 'the meeting taking into account the very unsatisfactory state of their present church, being quite unfit to worship in any longer, and being unwilling to face another winter in it, were unanimous in their opinion that the purchase by the congregation of the church on Dee Street, would be a wise and prudent thing and they unanimously resolved with the permission of Presbytery to make the purchase'. The Presbytery were due to meet on lst August but on 25th July a hastily convened meeting of the Deacons' Court was informed that the sale of the Dee Street property was to take place the following day. The Deacons' Court now resolved to disregard the need for Presbytery approval and agreed to purchase the property if it sold for less than £1500. In the event they were able to purchase it for the upset price of £1200. The congregation now moved quickly to sell the old chapel in Gaelic Lane and concluded a private bargain with the adjoining proprietors at the corner of Belmont Street, G & W Fraser, printers, who had been in business for ten years. The agreed price was £1100. When the Presbytery met on 5th September it agreed 'in the peculiar circumstances of the case to approve of the action taken so far as the acquisition of new buildings and the disposal of the old Gaelic Church are concerned'. It subsequently allocated to the congregation as its territorial area the back streets known as Gordon Lane and Gordon Street. Dee Street, with better quality housing, remained the territory of the Free West Church on Union Street, despite being distal to Gordon Street.

The church on Dee Street had been erected in 1857 by Congregationalists from Frederick Street, a disputed settlement having given rise to a division of that congregation. One section opened a church on Blackfriars Street and the other section moved to Dee Street. In 1870, the Dee Street church having been 'preached empty by its last minister' (a Mr Wallace), the two sections came together again and eventually built the Skene Street Congregational church (a building last used as a place of worship by the Free Presbyterian Church in the 1970s). Before the Dee Street building was sold, an attempt was made to resuscitate the Congregational cause there by two Aberdeen-born students who were to become very distinguished churchmen, *viz* John Hunter DD and Peter T Forsyth DD. They held afternoon services which drew large congregations[1] but in 1871 the building was sold for £850 to a society of Free Methodists who had separated from the Wesleyan Longacre Chapel. In 1881 that society disbanded and the building became the home of the Gaelic Church.

The new Gaelic Church had as its local trustees the minister, George Macdonald; his brother-in-law, the Session Clerk Hugh Mackenzie of 16 Silver Street; Alex Macdonald of 20 Broad Street, Clerk to the Deacons' Court; and John Urquhart, contractor, Banchory Park, a deacon since 1871. The minute of the final meeting in Gaelic Lane held on 25th October 1882 then reads: 'In recognition of the valuable services rendered to the congregation by Messrs Hugh Mackenzie and Alex Macdonald, the Deacons' Court offer them respectively their choice of the seats in the Dee Street Church which may best suit them there and their families'. The minister and Alex Macdonald were charged with selecting what things were to be retained from Gaelic Lane, but only the clock is mentioned – it to be 'repaired so as to fit it for the Church in Dee Street'. The hot air stove that had been installed at a cost of £25 in 1875 was sold for £9.

The purchase of the church on Dee Street also included an adjoining residential property at 15 Gordon Street to which considerable repairs were judged to be necessary before it could be made habitable. To effect this and also to carry out various improvements to, and redecoration of, the church building, the Deacons' Court agreed to raise a loan of £300 from the General Trustees of the Free Church of Scotland. The terms of the loan required that it be repaid not later than May 1888 and the Court readily agreed to meet the conditions. The church was occupied for worship at the end of October 1882 and a social meeting was held on Tuesday 7th November. Problems that only occupancy and use could reveal then demanded attention and the following winter the Deacons' Court received many complaints about a downward-flowing draught of cold air in the building. The Court appointed a 'committee anent the cold currents of wind in the church' which from time to time 'gave in a provisional report', but no solution was ever minuted and the problem was never resolved.

St Columba offends

Apart from the period 1834-43 when it was termed Spring Garden Parish Church, the congregation had been known as the Gaelic Church since its inception. This was now considered to be a disadvantage as many people imagined that the preaching was always in Gaelic. With the move uptown and upmarket it was decided to assert its new image with a new name and a congregational meeting on 28th August agreed 'to change the name of their church from Spring Garden to St Columba'. The Presbytery considered the request on 5th September 1882 and although some members of Presbytery moved that 'the present name be retained' the ministers of John Knox Gerrard Street Free Church and Ruthrieston Free Church moved that the congregation be named 'Columba Free Church'. This, of course, was not precisely the name that the congregation had selected and they chose to ignore the abbreviated form. Naturally this gave rise to some difficulties and at the meeting of Presbytery on 7th May 1883 George Macdonald's friend, Iverach, moved 'that the Presbytery in response to the petition of the Free Gaelic congregation, now resolve that the name of the congregation shall be St Columba'. This found no favour with the most conservatively-minded member of Presbytery, the Rev. A M Bannatyne of Union Free Church. He moved that 'nothing has occurred to warrant

the Presbytery to change the new name given to the Gaelic Congregation by the Presbytery on 5th September 1882'. When he found no
seconder to support him and Iverach's motion became the finding of
the Presbytery, Bannatyne dissented for the following reasons:

1   *it is unusual for the Presbytery to alter a solution so recently arrived at.*
2   *no inconvenience or injury has been caused to the congregation.*
3   *the original reason for a change was to get rid of the Gaelic appellation.*
4   *the congregation have been opposing Presbytery by using a wrong name.*

However the real reason for his opposition – the conviction that
dedicating Presbyterian churches to saints was a reversal to popish
superstition – was not engrossed in the minute. The revival of this
practice occurred in the late eighteenth century and there was already
in Aberdeen one Free Church (St Clement's) with the objectionable
prefix. 'We have one saint too many in Aberdeen already,' Bannatyne is
reported to have said. Thus the congregation got its new church and
new name both of which were to give service for 94 years, six years
longer than the Gaelic Chapel in Gaelic Lane. With high hopes and
renewed enthusiasm the congregation now faced the future. But the
glory of the second temple was not the glory of the first. A new mood
was abroad in the congregation.

Opposing move

The move from Gaelic Lane to Dee Street did not meet with universal
approval. In such circumstances there will always be those who say 'the
old is better'. But if there was any significant level of protest within the
congregation there is no hint of it in the minutes. The projected move
when it was first mooted in May 1882 did, however, give rise to
correspondence in the *Aberdeen Journal* in which an opponent of the
move, writing under the pseudonym 'A Highlander', set out various
arguments against vacating Gaelic Lane. He was answered by another
correspondent using the pseudonym 'A Highland Student'. The
protagonists doubtless knew each other's identity. 'A Highland Student'
was almost certainly Walter Calder who, earlier that year, had acted as
spokesman for the student group urging the need for a new church. 'A
Highlander', in all likelihood, was John Noble, the future minister of
Lairg and author of *Religious Life in Ross*. At the time he and Walter
Calder were fellow students in the final year of divinity at the Aberdeen
Free Church College.

'A Highlander', alias John Noble, in his letter to the *Aberdeen Journal*,
made his points tellingly and in keeping with his obituarist's description
of him as 'an ardent and unflinching defender of personal convictions'.[2]

He was, he said, a regular worshipper in the Gaelic Church and he claimed that the proposal to move came not from the congregation as a whole, but from a small section; the original petition having been drawn up by 'a few members and signed by one or two students and a number of school-boys'. Arguing from the ample sufficiency of accommodation in the existing church, its advantageous central location, the scarcity of financial resources and the impracticability of achieving 'even comparative unanimity in the management of affairs' in a congregation representative of so many different parts of the Highlands, he urged that the church in Gaelic Lane should be retained, being 'hallowed by memories that ought not lightly to be disturbed'.

'A Highland Student' replied that the petition, or memorial as he more accurately described it, had been signed by no fewer than 42 students and to say that the chapel could accommodate ten times the number who attended was a gross exaggeration. 'A Highlander' retorted that the average attendance at the Gaelic service was about thirty and at the English service fifty to sixty; but, he continued, even though it should be double that estimate, 'did a congregation averaging about one hundred, and which, after twenty years labour by the present minister, could not meet its ordinary outlay without the secular aid of public concerts, warrant the building of a new church?' No attempt was made to counter that thrust. The maximum strength of the congregation at that time may be gauged from its annual statistical schedule which listed 129 members on the communion roll (23 of them on parish relief), plus 100 adherents.

The musical programme continued to feature in the church's calendar and a notice in the *Aberdeen Journal* of 18th May 1885, refers to a performance of the cantata 'Eva' given by the church choir in the church the previous Saturday. The minister presided and the choir was under the leadership of the church precentor, John Cummings, a clerk living at 109 Menzies Road. He had been appointed English precentor a year earlier at a salary of £10 per annum, but in November 1885 it was reduced to £6 per annum 'considering the general depression which prevails'. This failed to diminish John Cummings' enthusiasm for the work and he continued as precentor until the Deacons' Court in 1904 requested him to demit office on account of his age. The next year he was ordained a deacon in the congregation. He was succeeded as precentor and choirmaster by Wm Ironside who was a teacher of music and lectured to divinity students at the Free Church College. After only one year in office, and perhaps as a consequence of the uncertain future for St Columba United Free as it then was, Wm Ironside resigned to become choirmaster at St James's Episcopal church. He died in 1909 aged 39.

Hall construction

In 1888 the Deacons' Court agreed to erect a hall at the rear of the church with access from Gordon Street. It was to be an extension of the existing Session House which could accommodate no more than forty persons. The want of a proper hall was felt to hamper congregational work and the new hall was designed to hold about 150 persons. As such it would serve as a 'religious centre' for all Aberdeen Highlanders. Estimates for the new hall came to £110. It was agreed to hold a two day bazaar in the Music Hall on 16th and 17th March 1889, the proceeds to be used to meet the cost of the new building and also to repay the outstanding £300 loan from the General Trustees which the Deacons' Court had undertaken to repay by 1888. In the light of the fact that the1879 bazaar had raised £430 this would have seemed well within reach. Arrangements were made to involve the Free Church public at large in provisioning eight stalls identified as a flower stall, a dairy stall, a refreshment stall, a students' stall, a congregational stall, a workmans' stall, a Free Church stall, and a Cults stall. The Deacons' Court appealed to the public for help on the grounds that 'the congregation is a poor one, and while being consistently recruited from all parts of the Highlands is also subject to a continual drain of members and adherents leaving the city for employment elsewhere'.

Many from outside the congregation did indeed volunteer their assistance and most of the Free Church dignitaries in the city appeared on the platform or sent an apology. The bazaar was opened on both days by men of commanding stature in the community. On the first day it was Dr Wm Ferguson of Kinmundy, a prominent landowner in Aberdeenshire and a great grandson of the leader of the secession in the north, the Rev. Wm Brown of Craigdam. On the second day the opening fell to Lord Provost (later Sir) Wm Henderson, another pillar of the Free Church on the national level. A local shipping magnate he was married to a granddaughter of Dr Kidd of Gilcomston. Despite such notable patronage the bazaar raised only £240, about half of the anticipated amount. The hall was built but the congregation remained in debt. The loan from the General Trustees was not repaid until 1912.

Although there was a rear door entrance from Gordon Street, access to the new hall was effectively through the south aisle of the church in the same way as access to the vestry was via the north aisle. The two ends of the enlarged building were separated by a folding partition which could be opened to maximise the seating area. The fitting of double cloth-covered doors at the end of each aisle was a later improvement designed to increase the sound-proofing so as to allow services to be held simultaneously in both church and hall. Another modification was the elevation of the three rearmost pews by nine, six and three inches respectively. The back rows in any church are always the most popular and the enhancement of all-round visibility which this alteration secured, served only to heighten the attraction of the rear pews. A few years later, when there was an influx of students unaware of, or indifferent to, the time-honoured rights of long-established worshippers, the attention of the Deacons' Court was drawn 'to the matter of the sittings occupied by the students who were flocking in a body to certain seats and so excluding whole families from the seats rented by them'. It was agreed to point out to the students 'such seats in the church as the students might most conveniently occupy'. However this direction was of little effect for in 1899 the Court again noted numerous complaints by seatholders that they were continually being crowded out of the seats let to them by the students attending the services. The solution then come to was to direct the students to the gallery.

Centenary celebration

The year 1895 was the year chosen by the congregation to commemorate the centenary of the Gaelic Church. It was certainly the centenary of the building of the Gaelic Chapel, although the centenary of the commencement of Gaelic worship in Aberdeen, or the founding of the Highland Congregation, pre-dated it by a decade. In September 1895 the Deacons' Court agreed to a suggestion from the minister that Professor George Adam Smith, formerly minister of Queen's Cross Free Church and at the time Professor of Old Testament in Trinity College, Glasgow, be invited to the celebration. He must have declined for the Moderator subsequently reported that Dr J Calder Macphail of Pilrig Free Church, Edinburgh, formerly of the Free East Church, Aberdeen and a distinguished Gaelic scholar, would be the preacher at the centenary celebration on 10 November. A social evening was held on 12th November at which the speakers were Professor Iverach and the minister of Rutherford Free Church, the Rev. James Stewart, both speakers being North countrymen from Halkirk and Edderton respectively. Fitting tribute was paid to the interest shown by the Rev. George Macdonald in the welfare of Gaelic students over a period of almost thirty years.

Notes to Chapter 28

1.   L S Hunter: *John Hunter DD. A Life* (London, 1921), p 12.
2.   See biographical sketch of John Noble prefacing *Religious Life in Ross,* p xlii.

*

Chapter 29

MISSIONS TO THE HIGHLANDERS

T HE contribution of the Gaelic congregation to general evangelism in Aberdeen was more limited under George Macdonald than was the case under his predecessor, Colin Sinclair, who is mentioned along with other Aberdeen ministers – including the Gaelic-speaking A C Fullerton who was closely associated with the Gaelic church – as being prominent in evangelistic work during the revival of the early 1860s[1] George Macdonald and his associates had a more insular outlook. In March 1873 the Kirk Session, invited to assist in the work of the Aberdeen City Mission, an outreach conducted under the auspices of the Free Presbytery of Aberdeen, responded that 'as the congregation under their care is a working-class congregation, all the primary efforts which they could possibly put forth must be directed toward the gathering together of Highlanders in and around Aberdeen, and in endeavouring to secure the attendance upon ordinances of such as come to town from time to time, and on this account they cannot undertake mission work in any particular district'. They claimed that 'their ordinary operation extends on the one side to Bucksburn and on the other side to the Bridge of Dee, and further that during two months of the summer herring fishing season, between 200 and 300 Highlanders are present in Aberdeen whose spiritual wants the Session have to super-intend'. To assist in this outreach the congregation had, at the time (1873), the services of a catechist – effectively an assistant minister – appointed and financed by the denominational Highlands and Islands Committee of which George Macdonald was a member.

Discontented catechist

The catechist appointed was Duncan Cameron who previously had been catechist at Ardnamurchan. While he was employed at Ardnamurchan a petition was sent to the Highlands and Islands Committee requesting his removal. The Committee agreed to this in 1871, but on his appealing not to be moved in the Winter on account of his age and infirmity, the Committee delayed his settlement in Aberdeen until 1872. He stayed little more than one year, for in July 1873 he wrote to the Committee 'setting forth that the climate in Aberdeen is much too severe for him and earnestly praying the Committee to give him a more suitable appointment before the Winter weather set in'. They offered him a post in Gigha and although it was not the practice of the Committee to meet the expenses of catechists (or indeed ministers) moving from one place to another, when he said he was unable to go unless his expenses, which he estimated to be between £8 and £9, were met, the Committee 'having taken all the circumstances into consideration resolved to give him £9 for the purpose'. However, when he got to Gigha he was still dissatisfied, complaining that his accommodation was 'devoid of all the ordinary comforts of a dwelling house' and he asked to be returned to Glasgow. When Walter Calder first went to Aberdeen as a student he lodged with Duncan Cameron and later described him as a 'man of more than ordinary intelligence and Christian experience'.[2]

Another attempt at evangelising lapsed Highlanders in Aberdeen was made in September 1884 when the minister reported to his Session that he had arranged with Dr John Adam, convener of the Home Mission Committee, for a missioner to be sent to Aberdeen for an evangelistic campaign. When he was minister of the Free South Church in Aberdeen, Dr Adam had enlisted his considerable influence to persuade the Assembly to retain the Gaelic Church on the Equal Dividend Platform and he was obviously sympathetic to the needs of the Gaelic congregation. The mission ran for two weeks and was conducted by the Rev. George Campbell who, earlier in the year by a decision of the General Assembly, had been suspended from the pastorate of Argyle Free Gaelic Church, Glasgow, on a charge of immorality. Although removed from his own pulpit, the Church was concerned not to destroy his usefulness and he continued to be employed by the Highlands and Islands Committee before he was eventually re-settled at Shawbost in 1895.[3]

Herring industry outreach

In the summer of 1873 the Deacons' Court agreed that the church should be opened on Sunday afternoons at 4.15 pm for use by the fishermen during the fishing season. It was difficult to persuade the office-bearers of the congregation to support this work, but David Mackay, a deacon, volunteered to take charge. It seems likely that this form of outreach was undertaken each summer during the fishing season, but it is rarely mentioned in the minutes. However in June 1898 the clerk to the Deacons' Court reported that he had consulted the East Coast Mission with a view to procuring accommodation at Point Law in which to carry on services for the Highland fishermen during the season and that he had been offered the use of the Seaman's Rest, Point Law, for one service each Sunday. They agreed to run an evening service to be taken by the missioner appointed by the Highlands and Islands Committee. That year the missioner was the Rev. Kenneth Macrae who later in the year was ordained at Glenshiel where he remained until his translation to Lochalsh in 1915. The work among the Highland fishermen and herring lassies was of the type where it was possible to do much and achieve little and those who engaged in it were easily discouraged. When the congregation of Free St Clements, Footdee, opened a new church in 1883, Sir Wm Henderson purchased the old church on Prince Regent Street for the use of Gaelic-speaking fishermen who came to Aberdeen. Why this should have been thought necessary is perhaps a commentary on the attitude of the Gaelic church then in process of establishing itself in Dee Street. Sadly this imaginative scheme did not prove to be the success which had been anticipated and it was ultimately abandoned.[4]

Walter Calder, in keeping with his status as an aspiring minister, was also actively involved in outreach work and was president of the congregational branch of the YMCA. After being licensed in 1882 he received a call to Bourtreebush (Newtonhill) Free Church. When the call came before the Presbytery for approval, George Macdonald objected to the settlement and dissented on the grounds that Walter Calder was a Gaelic-speaking preacher. Perhaps he felt that a Gaelic-speaking minister should go to a congregation that needed a Gaelic minister. Four years later when Calder received a call to Strathy Free Church, George Macdonald moved that the call be acceded to. After being in Strathy, Calder went to the High Church in Stornoway in 1903. His last charge was at Lawers.

Clannishness deplored

It is unlikely that George Macdonald would have envisaged any threat to his own position as a Gaelic minister when Walter Calder was ordained at Newtonhill, but the language problem that first confronted the congregation under Duncan Grant in 1818 was still there in 1882. Effectively there were two congregations under one roof. At the commencement of George Macdonald's ministry in 1866 the main morning service at 11 am was in Gaelic and an English service was held in the afternoon at 3 pm. An English Bible Class was held on a Sunday evening. There was a Gaelic prayer meeting on a Monday evening and an English prayer meeting on a Wednesday evening. At communion time the services in the church were in Gaelic and separate English communion services were held in the Belmont Street school. The minister himself must have been conscious of the lines of division within the congregation and he sensed the need to have the main morning service as an English service. In November 1873, in conformity with the original articles of association of the Gaelic congregation, he held a meeting of male members and adherents to confer on the question of changing the Gaelic service from the morning to the afternoon and the English service from the afternoon to the morning while retaining the evening English service. A statistical survey had revealed that there were 160 bilingual persons above 13 years of age connected with the congregation, 219 persons who were monolingual English speakers above 13 years of age and only nine who understood only Gaelic. After the Moderator gave a full report of the statistics of the congregation and explained the nature and reasons for the proposed changes, discussion followed, and on a vote being taken the proposals were agreed to by 26 votes to 4 – a small sample on which to base a decision if it may be assumed that there were about 190 men associated with the congregation.

In order to conciliate parties who might have had a difficulty in connection with the change, it was agreed to run it on a trial basis for twelve months and to delay the introduction of the proposed arrangements for six months. Communion services were to remain unaltered. When in January 1874 the result of this meeting was put to the office-bearers for ratification, of the eight elders on the Session, John Ross, Hugh Mackenzie, H Forbes and John Duff supported the change; R Fraser and Rod MacCulloch were opposed and John Mackenzie and R Cumming were absent. Of the four deacons present, three – H Munro, D Mackay and A Mackay – were in favour and John Macdonald was opposed. In due course the changes were instituted and the Kirk Session records contain no reference to any reconsideration at the end of the trial period. These changes of course did not win universal favour and the minister, feeling that not everyone was giving wholehearted support, called a special meeting of office-bearers on 1st September 1874 to consider how best to advance the religious interests of the congregation. This meeting was attended by four of the eight elders, *viz* Hugh Mackenzie, John Duff, Rod MacCulloch and H Forbes; two of the five deacons, *viz* A Mackay and D Mackay; plus Walter Calder as president of the congregational YMCA; and the Sunday school superintendent, Alex Macdonald who was to be elected an elder in 1882. That the problem was largely one of achieving a spirit of brotherliness and corporate unity may be deduced from the resolution minuted, *viz* 'that the Gaelic-speaking elders give their attendance as much as possible at the English prayer meetings in order to foster a spirit of unity between the two congregations'. It seems the Gaelic elders took little to do with the non-Gaelic worshippers.

Five years later, in January 1879, the minister called another meeting of office-bearers. By this time the two elders who had been absent from the January 1874 meeting were no longer in office having been judged to have lapsed from membership of the congregation in August 1875. Three others had been ordained in 1877 and of the nine elders in office, four – Hugh Mackenzie, Rod MacCulloch, John Duff and D Mackay – were present along with four of the eight deacons plus two students. The Moderator, in opening the conference, stated that while it was the duty of the members of the church to ask that they be directed to a right decision in connection with the critical questions which were then being discussed,[5] what was of most concern to them was the state of religion among themselves and the distress which prevailed owing to the commercial crisis in the country. Each of those present contributed to the discussion of which it was recorded 'there was a strong feeling that something should be done to increase the attendance at the congregational prayer meetings, and that measures should be taken to lead the office-bearers to cherish a deeper interest in one another and also in members of the congregation'.

The meeting then adjourned the discussion for a week to allow members to consider what practical steps would be advisable in order to promote the spiritual life of the congregation. When they reconvened, three decisions were noted:

1 *to use means to increase the attendance at the Gaelic weekly prayer meeting.*

2 *that with regard to the English weekly prayer meeting, the Session earnestly impress upon the English-speaking office-bearers their duty to attend and to take part in the meeting. It was further suggested that the English-speaking elders along with the minister and divinity students should conduct the meetings in turn. This suggestion was strongly recommended.*

3 *that the Session hold a prayer meeting on the last Tuesday of every month at 7.30 p.m. at which all office-bearers are enjoined to be present and also that a meeting of Session should be held the same evening immediately after the prayer meeting with the deacons present, to afford the office-bearers present an opportunity to confer together, how best to advance the Lord's cause in the congregation.*

The first of these special prayer meetings was held a week later, six persons, three elders and three deacons out of a possible nine elders and eight deacons, being present. Only one other such meeting is mentioned and thereafter the resignation of one elder and two deacons was noted. The minutes fail to reveal any improvement in the spiritual tone of the congregation or of its office-bearers, but in so saying it has to be remembered that it is of the nature of minutes to highlight problem areas. Problems continued to be in evidence, for in 1890 the Moderator stated that 'complaints were made by communicants that tickets were delivered sometimes at their doors, the elder declining to come in though invited, and at other times at the church door, and urged that advantage should be taken of the opportunity for prayer and godly conference and that this perfunctory way of discharging solemn duty should end'. Although communion cards were being issued, the use of communion tokens had not been discontinued. Communicants were expected to obtain a token at the preparatory service in exchange for the card which then served as an indication of who intended to communicate. The chief purpose behind the use of cards was to put pressure on the elders to visit the communicants, but in this it was only partially successful and the people were not slow to register their displeasure.

The rapid turnover among the office-bearers sometimes made it difficult to maintain continuity of operations within the congregation. By 1890 George Macdonald had completed his semi-jubilee in the Gaelic Church. Of the nine elders in office on his arrival, now only his brother-in-law, Hugh Mackenzie, remained. And from among twenty men ordained to the eldership during his ministry, only five remained in office. The turnover in deacons was even greater.

George Macdonald deceased

George Macdonald's constitution was not the most robust and in May 1881 he was given three month's leave of absence on health grounds. This was subsequently extended to six months, the Presbytery accepting responsibility for the English services and the minister having to make provision for the afternoon Gaelic service. The Rev. John Tainsh, minister of John Knox Gerrard Street Free Church, was appointed Interim-Moderator during the minister's illness, on the face of it a surprising appointment since he was not a Gaelic speaker; whereas James Iverach, minister of Ferryhill Free Church and a close friend of George Macdonald, was a Gaelic speaker. Possibly the Presbytery in making the appointment were following the convention of nominating the most recently inducted minister in the Presbytery

In the Spring of 1896 the Kirk Session met under the chairmanship of the visiting communion preacher, Rev. Alex Macdonald, a Stornoway man who was minister of Ardclach in Nairnshire. The minute refers to the absence of George Macdonald due to serious illness. He resumed his place at the Kirk Session in September 1896 and made his last appearance on 2nd January 1898. He died on 4th March aged 66 years and was buried in Allenvale cemetery where the congregation erected a memorial stone in the shape of an Iona Cross. His widow lived into her 93rd year and died in October 1934. They had four daughters, two of whom, Catherine Frances and Charlotte Balfour, were unmarried.

George Macdonald also had twin sons by his first wife Elizabeth Elder. One of his sons, John George Macdonald predeceased his father. Aged 29 years, he died suddenly on 1st August 1895 in Dublin where he was resident secretary for a major insurance company. His twin brother, A Neil Macdonald, qualified as a solicitor and practised in Aberdeen until 1914 when he moved to Thurso. John George Macdonald, although not a member of the Deacons' Court, was co-opted as clerk (but with no minute of his appointment) in January 1883 and continued to act as clerk until the North British & Mercantile Insurance Company transferred him to Bradford in August 1889. He was followed in the clerkship by his twin brother who clerked the Court until he too left town in the course of his employment. Once again the clerkship was put in the hands of a non-member of the Deacons' Court, in this case John B Banks, the son of an elder, Wm Banks. His was the most legible script of any of the Gaelic congregation clerks, but A Neil Macdonald's move out of town was not permanent and in 1897 John Banks resigned in favour of his predecessor who had returned to the congregation. Neil Macdonald became a communicant member in October 1896 and six months later he was ordained an elder. At the first Kirk Session meeting following his ordination he deputised as Session Clerk in the place of his step-uncle Hugh Mackenzie. He married Susanna a daughter of this step-uncle (there was no blood relationship between them) thus further securing the family control exercised since the Rev. Hugh Mackenzie's induction in 1823. A son of this marriage, George Francis Alexander Macdonald, born in 1903, also qualified in law, but the clerical genes deriving from his grandfather and great grandfather eventually exerted their dominance and in 1927 he commenced training for the priesthood of the Episcopal Church in Scotland. Sadly in 1934, shortly after being inducted to St Columba's Episcopal Church at Newton in Lanarkshire, he died aged 31.

Notes to Chapter 29

1. Anon: *Reminiscences of the Revival of fifty-nine and the sixties* (Aberdeen, 1910), p xv.
2. *Memorials of the Rev. Christopher Macrae Munro* (Edinburgh, 1890), p 29.
3. I R MacDonald: *Glasgow's Gaelic Churches* (Edinburgh 1995), p 41.
4. A Gammie: *The Churches of Aberdeen* (Aberdeen, 1909), p 186.
5. A reference to Wm Robertson Smith and Higher Criticism.

Chapter 30

*

THE CHANGING SCENE

IN 1898 the Gaelic pulpit was vacant for the first time in 34 years. Aberdeen was now a very different place to that which met the eyes of George Macdonald in 1864. On his arrival there was no motorised transport of any kind, not even bicycles (these made their first appearance in Aberdeen in 1869),[1] but by the end of the century the city had taken on a modern appearance with motors and tramcars. Moreover it had been expanding westward from the Denburn. Land to the north and west of Queen's Cross, which in 1860 had been occupied by the occasional isolated cottage, now paraded streets of solid residences or impressive rows of granite terraces. It was no longer the compact society that had given shelter to the infant Gaelic congregation and even the ecclesiastical community was more diffuse and less supportive.

On his arrival in Aberdeen George Macdonald enjoyed the companionship of several Gaelic-speaking ministers. There was Walter MacGilvray, a native of Islay, who had already been two years in Gilcomston and had previously been minister of Hope Street Free Gaelic Church in Glasgow. Charles Ross, who had been ordained as minister in Bon Accord Free Church in the year of Walter MacGilvray's induction to Gilcomston, was also a Gaelic speaker who had been nurtured in the faith by the Fathers in Ross-shire. He was married to Isabella Flyter of Alness, a grand-daughter of Ronald Bayne. In 1869 he had left Bon Accord for the Gaelic congregation in Tobermory, his loyalty to the traditions of the fathers undiminished. There was also J Calder Macphail, not just a Gaelic speaker but also a Gaelic scholar from Speyside, who was minister in the Free East Church from 1849 to 1868. These men all gave valuable support to the Gaelic Church as did George Macdonald's fellow-countryman from Halkirk, James Iverach minister at Ferryhill Free Church from 1874. Another with whom George Macdonald would have had some rapport because of his Highland connections, was the Rev. Donald M MacAlister, ordained to Old Machar Free Church, Old Aberdeen in 1878. From 1886 he was minister of Free Greyfriars in Edinburgh where he played a leading role in the contendings of the continuing Free Church after the Union of 1900.

Constitutionalists and Unionists

The changing scene was not confined to ministerial translations or to the architectural landscape. Religious attitudes were also undergoing significant revision in the city. In 1881 William Robertson Smith had been removed from his Old Testament Chair in Aberdeen's Free Church College because of the unsettling effect of his 'Higher Critical' teaching; but that did not arrest the movement in favour of a lowering of the Free Church's confessional standards. The driving force behind this movement was the prospect of a union between the Free Church and its sister denomination, the United Presbyterian Church. With that end in view, the Free Church in 1892 passed a Declaratory Act which had the effect of giving ministers liberty of opinion concerning much of the theology of the Westminster Confession. The passage of this Act divided the Free Church into opposing parties: Unionists who favoured the proposed changes, and Constitutionalists who opposed them. When an attempt to rescind the 1892 Act failed, two ministers from the Constitutionalist Party seceded in 1893 and formed the Free Presbyterian Church. However the majority of constitutionalist sympathisers postponed making a stand until the Union was consummated. Consequently there was no secession in Aberdeen until after 1900. Even so, during the last decade of the nineteenth century, church members who took an interest in theological matters, rallied to the support of one party or the other. Highland students, particularly the Highland divinity students, were prominent in supporting the Constitutionalist Party. But the Aberdeen minister who was the standard bearer for the constitutionalists, was not George Macdonald of the Gaelic Church, but A M Bannatyne of Union Free Church.

A M Bannatyne

Alexander Mackinlay Bannatyne, a native of the Island of Bute, was inducted to Union Free Church in 1858, remaining there until 1890 when, in utter despair at the liberalising tendencies of the Free Presbytery of Aberdeen, he retired to Rothesay where he ministered to an independent congregation of his own gathering. Always a loyal friend of the Highland church, he was the most colourful of its representatives in Aberdeen. Although of a sternly uncompromising outlook he was said by his contemporaries to be an outstanding man in every way. 'Even among the handsome men of his time, he was conspicuous by the height of his figure, the nobility of his walk, and the grand proportions of his head with its snow-white hair. It was no unhappy inspiration that styled him the John Knox of Aberdeen, so uncompromising was he in all matters of principle'.[2] Bannatyne would not brook any change in the arrangements for worship in his congregation, even retaining the after-noon hour of worship when most churches had switched to the evening. Needless to say, hymns and even paraphrases were rigidly excluded as was instrumental music.

These matters of course had been the subject of discussion in the Presbytery since 1866, and in these and other controversial issues, such as the demand for the dis-establishment of the national church or the drive for union of non-established churches, Bannatyne's opposition was guaranteed. When he resigned from Union Church, the Presbytery minute stated that 'the reasons, while valid to him, are not such as the Presbytery are called to investigate'.[3] What these reasons were is not stated, but earlier in the year he had had a major disagreement with Presbytery. This arose over its refusal to take issue with Free Trinity Kirk Session over the introduction of instrumental music; and also with the same Session for restoring to fellowship without compearance those guilty of ante-nuptial fornication. When Bannatyne left Union Free Church his Session Clerk, and one other elder, also resigned, their reasons being 'identical with those on the ground of which the Moderator resigned the pastorate'.[4] For the most part his congregation did not share his views, but towards the close of his pastorate he attracted support from the constitutionalist students.

The Highland Host

The closing years of the nineteenth century witnessed the arrival in Aberdeen of a group of exceptionally gifted Highland students who were to play a significant leadership role in the Highland church in the next century. These men, prior to taking an Arts course at King's College, were all bursars at the Grammar School of Old Aberdeen. Donald Munro, a native of Brora and latterly minister at Ferintosh and Rogart, entered the Old Aberdeen Grammar School in 1882, the year that John Noble of Lairg finished at the Free Church College in Aberdeen. Munro remained in Aberdeen for six years and for all of that time he matched the image of the legendary Highland student living off oatmeal and herring. In his first Session he lived in an old fishing boat beached on the Dee.[5] There he survived on oatmeal brought from his father's croft, and fish bought for next to nothing in the local fish market. In 1885 he was followed at the Grammar School, and later at the University, by John Macleod from Fort William, subsequently Principal of the Free Church College. Likewise in 1886, Munro and Macleod were followed at the Grammar School and the University by Donald MacLean from Lochcarron, John MacLeod's future colleague in the Edinburgh Free Church College. Munro, MacLeod and Maclean were all to receive an honorary DD from their *alma mater*. Alex Stewart from Glen Glass, a future Moderator of the Free Church General Assembly and a distinguished editor of its *Monthly Record,* who was to receive his DD from Glasgow University in 1927, enrolled in the Old Aberdeen Grammar School in 1888. So did Kenneth Macrae from Lochalsh, one of the 27 ministers who declined to enter the Union of 1900.

These men were all of the Constitutionalist persuasion, but although they were all Gaelic speakers (indeed Gaelic scholars), they were not all in membership of the Gaelic congregation. From among the group, only the names of Donald Maclean and Kenneth Macrae are to be found on the roll of St Columba Free Church. There were, of course, at that time several other divinity students attending the Free Church College who were in membership in St Columba's. These proved to be Unionists and they included Allan MacKillop from North Uist (latterly Professor of Divinity in Queensland, Australia), Dr Alex F MacInnes from Duirinish (latterly United Free minister at Kirkliston), Farquhar Kennedy from Lochalsh (latterly minister in Harris), Angus Macfarlane from Duirinish (latterly minister at Dores and Bona) and George Mackay from Thurso (latterly minister at Croy and Dalcross).

The absence from the roll of the Gaelic congregation of the names of Donald Munro, John Macleod and Alex Stewart is an indication that these men did not find the ministry of George Macdonald to be to their liking. That conclusion is confirmed in respect of Alex Stewart by the recollections of Allan Macdonald MacKillop, Stewart's friend and contemporary Macphail bursar at the Old Aberdeen Grammar School (known locally as 'the Barn'). Stewart, MacKillop and another Macphail bursar, Murdo Beaton, who was also of the Constitutionalist persuasion, were in the habit of receiving their monthly bursary instalments from George Macdonald, the Fund's Aberdeen agent. In his autobiography MacKillop recalls one occasion when the bursars presented themselves for receipt of their maintenance allowance.

This function took place at the end of the mid-week prayer meeting. Both Stewart and Beaton attended to collect their bursary, but neither of them worshipped on Sundays in St Columba's. They were attending the congregation over which the Rev Mr Bannatyne was minister. To settle this matter [ie their church attendance] *Mr Macdonald summoned the three bursars at the 'Barn' – Beaton, Stewart and MacKillop – to go to his house for an interview. He was with a scythe cutting the grass on his lawn when we arrived. It looked like an unfriendly act. I was not liable to censure.*

Mr Macdonald came promptly to the point, as he leaned on the handle of the scythe. He put the first question: 'Mr Stewart, why do you not come to hear me preach?' Stewart, then about 18 years of age, gave his answer Luther-like 'without horns or teeth'. It was: 'Mr Macdonald, I have a conscientious objection to listening to you.' The rejoinder came quick and scathing

– 'Yes you have a conscientious objection; yet you constitutionalists would take money although the devil spewed it. Still, I don't blame you but that older man, the pig-headed owl, Willie Sabhail.' The interview was over.[6]

John Macleod's biographer states that, having a predilection for the old school orthodoxy, Macleod was 'usually to be found sitting at the feet of George Macdonald in St Columba's or, as occasionally happened, waiting upon the ministry of Rev A M Bannatyne'.[7] In so saying, he misjudged the situation regarding Macleod's preference. As for Dr Donald Munro's preference for church attendance, John Macleod himself, writing a biographical sketch of his friend, stated that 'as already an ardent defender of the constitution of the Free Church, he laid himself out for enlisting comrades of like mind as a Purity of Worship Association in which he was the leading spirit'.[8] That spirit would certainly have found its kindred more in Bannatyne than in Macdonald.

The House of Rimmon

MacKillop's recollections also illustrate how innocent these Highland students were of any encounter with the new forms of worship and of how apprehensive they were of being contaminated by the experience. He refers to an occasion when a distinguished Congregational minister in Aberdeen advertised a Sunday evening lecture intended to refute the heresies of Dr Marcus Dods, a leading Free Church liberal. The minister, Dr Alex Stewart of John Street Congregational Church, was an able controversialist and his vow to demolish his adversary in public attracted the Free Church Constitutionalists. Recalling the occasion MacKillop wrote:

I heard that my Highland friends were going to hear Dr Stewart. I resolved to go with them. We were at his church as soon as it was open. Not one of us before that had ever heard an organ or a hymn in public worship. The first thing that upset us was that at the door we were handed a hymn book. More or less reverently we placed them on a nearby table. We were welcomed cordially and courteously led up almost to the front seat.

A little before the preacher was to enter the pulpit the organist began to play a voluntary. This was carrying the matter further than my friends could bear. Nearly all of them stood up and grasped their hats and made for the door before they should be found guilty of having bent the knee in the house of Rimmon. My friends Alexander Stewart and Murdo Beaton who were my classmates at the Grammar School went with the rest. I felt like the character in the Gaelic song:

> 'Thòisich mi air fàs lapach
> Eadar seòrsa nàir is gealtachd'

> *I could not move. As I had been only a fortnight in the city I was not likely to find my way home. One of the older students named William Sabhail (from the name of his father's farm), seeing the difficulty I was in, very kindly resolved to stay with me and abide by the consequences. His kindness I never forgot. Next year he died as he had been for some time in ill health.*[9]

This was the same Willie Sabhail that George Macdonald blamed for taking the Macphail bursars away from St Columba's to Bannatyne's Church. Although Bannatyne would permit no deviation from the traditions of the fathers, he failed to convince his people that his was a better way. In little more than a year after he had left Aberdeen, all the changes which he had identified with ecclesiastical and spiritual decadence, had been introduced to Union Church. The afternoon service was changed to an evening service, the congregation were sitting for prayer and standing to sing, and hymns were in use. The Gaelic church in Dee Street continued to shun these innovations for another seven years; but the next pastorate was to see them all in place.

When the congregation became vacant following the death of George Macdonald, the Highland Committee became responsible for supplying the pulpit with probationers who nominally were appointed to preach for four Sundays. Little time was wasted in filling the vacancy and a congregational meeting for the purpose of electing a minister was held on 3rd May 1898. Prior to that meeting it had been suggested to the Interim-Moderator that he approach the Rev. Andrew Grant, Free Church minister in Helmsdale since 1889, to ascertain his willingness to give favourable consideration to a call. He declined to be considered, having recourse to the standard plea that he 'could not consider a call in the present circumstances of his own congregation'. A native of Rothiemurchus, he was aged forty at that time and he remained in Helmsdale until 1902 when he accepted a call to Queen Street church in Inverness where he died in 1911. The Aberdeen office-bearers only learned of his decision when they met prior to the congregational meeting. They then had to come up with an alternative name, preferably, as was pointed out to them by the Interim-Moderator, one which would meet with unanimity both among the office-bearers and the congregation. Consequently 'after deliberation and consultation on various names' (and all in the space of 15 minutes!) it was agreed to recommend to the congregation the name of A F Campbell which name duly carried at the congregational meeting.

A F Campbell inducted

Archibald F Campbell was one of two probationers sent to supply the congregation at the time of George Macdonald's death. He was born in Glenorchy, Argyllshire, in 1868 and had been licensed in 1897 after training in the Free Church College in Glasgow. When he came to Aberdeen to supply the pulpit he was a young energetic bachelor. The congregation, which according to its annual statistical return, consisted of 155 communicant members and an equal number of adherents above 14 years of age, was said to be unanimous in calling him, but the call was signed by only 56 members and 77 adherents together with seven elders and nine deacons – 149 persons in all. One of the eight elders omitted to sign the call, possibly Rod MacCulloch. With the exception of Hugh Mackenzie, MacCulloch, an employee with the Northern Agricultural Company, was the longest-serving office-bearer having been ordained an elder in 1871 and a deacon six years earlier. He was one of the elders who had opposed transferring the Gaelic service from the forenoon to the afternoon. The ordination and induction took place on 21st July 1898 when the preacher was Wm Mackintosh Mackay, minister of the South Free Church (now St Mark's). It was an appropriate choice for he was a grandson (on his mother's side) of the most notable of the congregation's ministers, the Rev. Donald Sage. Under Campbell's ministry there was some evidence of growth in the congregation, the roll having risen to 180 communicants inclusive of eleven elders and 14 deacons, but he did not excel as a Gaelic preacher. A contemporary claimed that he had only six Gaelic sermons which he used in rotation.[10]

Innovations in worship

The new minister clearly felt that in 1898 it was time to bring the congregation's worship into line with the 20th century and he set about modernising it. The practice of standing for prayer was discontinued and replaced by standing for praise, the style which by now had been adopted by the majority of city congregations. In 1898 the Deacons' Court approved the purchase for use in the Sunday School of 48 copies of the Joint Hymnary. This was the new Church Hymnary issued that year and jointly authorised for public worship by the Church of Scotland, the Free Church of Scotland, the United Presbyterian Church and the Presbyterian Church in Ireland. However when the English precentor submitted an application to the Deacons' Court a year later for the purchase of copies of the Joint Hymnary for use by the choir, he was told the purchase would be superfluous 'seeing there is no present prospect of the hymns being introduced in congregational worship'.

Perhaps not surprisingly what seemed inconceivable in 1899 had become a reality by 1903 when hymns formed part of the congregation's praise. If a decision in favour of the introduction of hymns had been taken by the Kirk Session, it is not recorded in the minutes. Nor did it need to be, for strictly speaking the conduct of public worship is the responsibility of the minister alone. In December 1904 the Kirk Session minutes reported that 'the Session had under consideration the conduct of public worship in relation to the recent introduction of hymns and after discussion resolved to give no further direction on the matter than this, "that they felt that not more than two hymns should be sung at either the forenoon or evening services"'. However, the Kirk Session, while free to offer an opinion on the relative proportions of hymns and Psalms, had no authority to direct what should be done, the conduct of public worship being the exclusive responsibility of the minister, subject only to the Presbytery.[11]

Another of A M Bannatyne's marks of a congregation resistant to modernism disappeared when, in 1901, the afternoon was freed from religious exercises by rescheduling the Gaelic service to follow the forenoon English service. By the end of the century the congregation was determined to conform to modern ideas of public worship and the Gaelic church in its worship and emphasis was tending increasingly to imbibe the spirit and copy the example of the contemporary church. In April 1901 the Kirk Session decided that 'during the Rev. Mr. Campbell's intended absence for the sake of his health, the weekly prayer meeting be discontinued'. It was October before Mr Campbell returned, but no indication is given that the prayer meeting was resumed. The fact that in the absence of the minister continuance of the weekly prayer meeting was considered to be impracticable, or a matter of no consequence, is an indication of the quality of spiritual leadership in the Kirk Session. Yet they were not wholly indifferent to the old standards and in 1902, after a discussion initiated by Hugh Mackenzie (the minister again being absent), the Session agreed to convey to the Town Council their disapproval of Sunday operation of tramcars. That year the average attendance at Kirk Session meetings was usually three. At one meeting only two elders, Hugh Mackenzie and A Neil Macdonald, were present. These of course were the men in whose hands the effective leadership of the congregation rested.

Hugh Mackenzie, whose father had been inducted as minister of the congregation in 1823, had been in office forty years, 38 of them as Session Clerk. When, in his 65th year, he asked to be relieved of the whole or part of the duties of the clerkship on account of advancing years, his son-in-law and step-nephew, A Neil Macdonald, a son of the former minister, was appointed Joint Session Clerk. The minute of 12th September 1900 includes a tribute to Hugh Mackenzie's clerkship, acknowledging that he possessed 'in the highest degree the tact and ability which such a post requires; that he has kept the books entrusted to his charge in an admirable manner and attended to the meetings with unfailing regularity while his insight and wisdom, combined with long experience of business matters, have often rendered invaluable service to the Session when it had to deal with any matters which required careful handling'. The minute concluded with the hope that their meetings would continue to be favoured 'with his genial and helpful presence for many years to come'. Thereafter although some of the minutes are signed by Hugh Mackenzie, none was written by his hand but uncle and nephew remained together to preside over the exequies of the Gaelic congregation during its brief autonomous existence in the United Free Church.

Notes to Chapter 30

1. *A record of events in Aberdeen and the North 1801-1927* (Aberdeen, 1928).
2. A Gammie: *The Churches of Aberdeen* (Aberdeen, 1909), p 223.
3. *Records of the Free Presbytery of Aberdeen* (2nd December, 1890), p 521 (CH3-2-8).
4. *Union Free Church Kirk Session Minutes* (29th December, 1890), p 157 (CH3-851-1).
5. *Aberdeen University Review*, vol. 25, p 45 (1937-8). Lord Boyd Orr: *As I Recall* (London, 1966), p 41. For a biographical sketch, see J Macleod: *Donald Munro of Ferintosh and Rogart* (Inverness, 1939).
6. A M MacKillop: *A Goodly Heritage* (North Kessock, Inverness, 1998), pp 84-85.
7. G N M Collins: *John Macleod DD* (Edinburgh, 1951), p 29.
8. J Macleod: *Donald Munro of Ferintosh and Rogart* (Inverness, 1939), p 10.
9. A M MacKillop, op. cit., p 83-84.
10. Donald Murray Manuscript. I am indebted to Mrs Harriet Macleod of Port of Ness, Isle of Lewis, for a copy of her father's manuscript. Mr Murray was for a time Session Clerk of the post-1900 Free St Columba congregation.
11. W Mair: *Digest of Church Law* (2nd edition) (Edinburgh, 1985), p 109.

Chapter 31

*

LOST PROPERTY

A T the end of the 19th century there were three major Presbyterian
churches in Scotland: the Church of Scotland, the Free Church of
Scotland and the United Presbyterian Church, a church which had its
roots in the secessions from the Church of Scotland in 1733 and 1761.
In 1896 new momentum was given to earlier talks on the possibility
of uniting the non-established churches. They had much in common
and mutual co-operation in a campaign to bring about the dis-establishment of the Church of Scotland served to cement the bonds.
Consequently, after fairly protracted negotiations, the Free Church and
the United Presbyterian Church agreed to consummate a union on
30th October 1900. All 593 congregations in the United Presbyterian
Church entered a Union with 1068 congregations from the Free
Church of Scotland to form the United Free Church of Scotland.
Although there was unanimity in the United Presbyterian Church
regarding union, there was a section of the Free Church implacably
opposed to the union. At the Union Assembly of 1900 this constitutionalist minority registered 27 votes against union as against 643 votes
in favour of union. Few though the opponents of union were, they
were determined to challenge the Assembly's decision. They did so on
the grounds that the Free Church was irrevocably tied to the Establishment Principle, while the basis of union treated that, and other matters
in the Confession of Faith, as open questions. Because of that, the
United Church, in the view of the minority, had departed from the
church's historic confessional position. In passing the Act of Union, the
majority of the Free Church had acted beyond their powers and having
departed from the church's constitution they were no longer entitled to
the name or the property of the Free Church.

The aftermath of Union

The Constitutionalists had asserted this view throughout the years of
Union negotiations and warned that in loyalty to the church of 1843
they would be forced to seek restitution through the courts. When they
sought redress in the Scottish courts, their claim, to nobody's surprise,
was dismissed. But when they took their case to the House of Lords,
that body, in an historic judgment given in 1904, ruled that the

majority had indeed departed from the church's constitution while lacking the power to do so. Consequently the minority, the Lords decreed, were entitled to retain the name of the Free Church of Scotland and all the property and funds vested in it. Notwithstanding this vindication of the minority, it was evident to both sides that there would have to be a division of the assets between the two parties, for the victors had neither ministers nor congregations to make use of the buildings which were legally theirs. Consequently an Executive Commission was appointed by Act of Parliament to allocate the church's property between the contending parties. The basis of allocation was that the Free Church should be awarded those properties where it could be established that one third of the members and adherents belonging to the congregation in 1900 were opposed to the Union. In 1900 there were 25 Free Churches in Aberdeen and all of them elected to enter the Union.

The question of whether or not the congregation of St Columba Free Church should enter the Union appears not to have been discussed within the congregation. There is no minuted reference to a decision having been taken either by the Deacons' Court or by the Kirk Session. But if a congregational meeting had been held, its decision would not have been in doubt. The Communion Roll of St Columba Church in 1901 listed 165 names. Only a handful of these eventually transferred their membership to the reconstituted Free Church. Although the group did include one or two families from the St Columba roll, there was no way in which the continuing Free Church could successfully claim the property of St Columba or any other Free Church in Aberdeen on the basis of allocation and none was allocated. When the Free Church in 1906 assembled statistics supporting their claim to have a working congregation in Aberdeen, they produced a register with 134 names of which it was said that 72 had been associated with one or other of 13 Free Church congregations in Aberdeen in 1900. Of these congregations by far the largest transfer was said to be from St Columba which supplied 18 members and 17 adherents. On the other hand, the United Free Church authorities disputed the accuracy of these statistics and would concede only 24 of the 72 persons listed in the Free Church submission as having any connection with Aberdeen Free Church congregations in 1900.

In many areas, especially in the north and west, Free Church congregations continued virtually unaffected by the events of 1900. In other places, displaced and sundered congregations endeavoured to carry on in temporary premises. Where local leadership was lacking, the Church at an earlier stage sought to organise Free Church worship services in strategic locations, but Aberdeen was too remote from the Free Church heartland to be given immediate attention. In February

1903 an anonymous correspondent wrote to the *Free Church Monthly Record* urging that services be commenced in Aberdeen where he found the brief and bright services then on offer and interspersed with 'solos, chants, hallelujahs, anthems, organs, hymns and seven-fold Amens', far from satisfying. However Aberdeen had to wait until 1905 before an attempt was made to resuscitate the Free Church cause in the city. As in other places, the favourable decision of the House of Lords in 1904 encouraged some underground sympathisers to come to the surface.

Minority challenge

An inaugural service re-constituting the Aberdeen congregation of the Free Church of Scotland was held in the Square Room of the Music Hall on Sunday 5th March 1905 when the preacher was the Rev. S Hamilton who was on the teaching staff of the Free Church College which at that time was meeting in New College. The *Evening Express* reporter who kept the Aberdeen public informed with the kind of enthusiasm normally reserved for ecclesiastical scandal, which indeed, on account of the effrontery of its sponsors, it was presented as being, went so far as to say, 'judging from remarks one hears, some courage will be needed to put in an appearance'. Even so, some 124 persons, with or without courage, attended the morning service and 110 attended the evening service. The *Daily Journal* reporter claimed that many worshippers belonged to the ranks of the curious rather than the committed, 'their true affiliation being betrayed by the hymn-books they carried'. But in a generally unsympathetic report he commented on the heartiness of the singing led by Mr A Smith, a gifted precentor who was to serve the congregation until 1923.

The following Sunday there were 200 worshippers present, the majority of which in the view of the *Daily Journal* reporter were elderly people. The preacher was the Rev. J C Robertson, formerly of Rayne United Free Church, a late convert to the Free Church cause. The vicissitudes of the embryonic congregation were a matter of considerable interest in the city and every Monday the *Aberdeen Daily Journal* carried news of the Sunday services in addition to rumoured developments. On 11th June the company of worshippers, which numbered fewer than fifty, were formally constituted a congregation by the ordination of office-bearers, three elders and three deacons. Of the elders only John Still who acted as Session Clerk and had previously been in membership in St Columba, gave extended service. Similarly of the deacons, only Wm Joyner, a tram conductor who became an elder in 1922, was destined to give long service.

It was not until 1907 that the renascent Free Church congregation was given a building in which to worship. For more than two years the newspaper columns were agog with speculation as to which, if any, of the former Free Churches might be allocated to the despised 'Wee Frees', as the Constitutionalists were derisorily named. Much indignation accompanied each and every rumoured suggestion regarding possible transference of property, the columnists choosing to ignore the fact that, as Lord Robertson said in his 1904 judgment, 'justice is done by giving people not what fits them, but what belongs to them'. On 13th August 1904 the *Evening Express* reported that 'the Wee Frees are entirely unrepresented in Aberdeen', adding illogically, 'A Wee Free congregation here it is to be feared would be very wee indeed'. On 4th March 1905 the *Evening Express* reported that the rumour-mill was working overtime. The West Church, Bon Accord, John Knox, Ferryhill and Woodside had all been identified as realistic targets with the Free West said to be the favourite of the predators because of its prime location on Union Street, its stately style and its ample endowments. However, the St Columba congregation on Dee Street always felt that it was the most likely to be thrown to the wolves.

In October 1906 the Executive Commission gave out decisions on a number of contested properties claimed by the Free Church in various parts of the country, but Aberdeen did not feature among them. Thus it was under a false sense of security that the St Columba Sunday School Superintendent at their annual rally later that month 'gave expression to the thankfulness of the congregation that all anxiety as to the possibility of losing their congregational property had been removed'. Their thankfulness was short-lived.

St Columba relinquished

At the close of the forenoon service in St Columba Church on 21th April 1907, A Neil Macdonald rose up to make a statement to the congregation regarding their property. He began by saying that some months previously the Executive Commission had allocated all the Free Church buildings in Aberdeen to the United Free Church but had subsequently come to the view that some provision should be made for the Free Church. He then went on to say:

Now it happens that our congregation has contributed to the members and adherents of the Free Church congregation a number, which although comparatively insignificant and very much less than that which they credit themselves with having received from us, is still in excess of that they have received from any other of the UF churches in the city. They have, too, been recruited to some extent from Highlanders who, whether recent arrivals in Aberdeen or not, have never had any connection with this congregation. And still further they have, in a memorandum setting out their claim to a church here, transmitted to the Commission in November last, made representations which can only mean that they recognised that their chief work for the future must lie among the Highlanders permanently or temporarily resident in Aberdeen.

He then explained that the Presbytery which was to meet the next day would have to consider which building from among the 25 former Free Churches in Aberdeen should be surrendered to comply with the altered view of the Commission. He knew that the resuscitated Free Church congregation was essentially a Highland congregation, that it, more than any other body, adhered to the traditional ethos of the Highland church and that its appeal would be directed at Highland people. He warned the St Columba congregation that the common perception that the Free Church was a Highland body could result in the buildings belonging to the former Gaelic congregation being allocated to the protesters.

The Presbytery met in private and made no statement, but it was known that different views as to which building should be relinquished had been aired but no decision reached. The Executive Commission then issued their finding on 23rd May. It was reported under the headline 'The Fate of St Columba Church. The Frees Declared Possessors.' Apparently the final selection by the Commission had been between St Columba on Dee Street and Bon Accord on Rosemount Viaduct. Bon Accord was an imposing new building less than ten years old. The Commission felt that the claims of equity would be better met and the demands of justice better served with the new building, but the old building on Dee Street better fitted the historical associations on the one hand and the meagre future prospects on the other. Since the Presbytery showed no inclination to act generously, the Commission decreed that St Columba be surrendered. This came as no surprise to the Free Church authorities. It was the fulfilment of their fears rather than their hopes, for it was the least of all the Free Church buildings in Aberdeen. But in that respect it matched the prospective congregation.

Regrettably the Rev. J C Robertson, formerly of Rayne, who in May 1905 had been appointed Interim-Moderator at the request of the congregation, chose to disparage the award, claiming that the building was a liability which threatened the continued viability of the congregation. He and the dispossessed St Columba UF Session Clerk, A Neil Macdonald, conducted an extremely acrimonious correspondence in the pages of the *Evening Express* in which Robertson claimed that the building was oppressed with debt of £550, the debt exceeding the market value of the property which he estimated to be £400. A Neil Macdonald countered by saying that they had recently turned down an offer of £3000 for the church on Dee Street together with the adjoining tenement property on Gordon Street and that they had been accustomed to value the congregation's heritable property (including the manse) at £3500. Naturally, given his and his family's long connection with the congregation, he felt particularly aggrieved to think that its long history was, as it seemed to him, about to end. After all, that congregation had the longest history of any of the former Free Church congregations in Aberdeen and as he himself wrote, 'to the pang of parting we shall have to add the further pain of seeing St Columba rot and decay unoccupied'. He claimed that the victors in the dispute, with an average attendance of 35, had already reached the 'likely limits of expansion locally'.

Another correspondent to the *Evening Express* (June 15th, 1907) claiming to be a member of St Columba UF, berated the Presbytery for sacrificing St Columba 'in favour of others strong in number and rich in pocket'. He claimed that Presbytery had arranged alternative worship premises for the St Columba UF congregation 'for four months in order that Presbytery may have time to provide a suitable church but behind this is the expectation of the legal Frees throwing up our church within that time'. Perhaps some genuinely believed that the Free Church congregation in Aberdeen would be a short-lived institution that, having sprung up in a night, would wither in a night. Some certainly assumed that the Free Church had no intention of maintaining a struggling congregation in Aberdeen and would dispose of the property at the first opportunity. But that was never the intention of the Free Church leadership, many of whom had themselves been students in Aberdeen and who passionately believed that the Free Church had a duty to Highland students which it had at all cost to discharge. Some Free Church sympathisers in Aberdeen, dismayed alike by the thankless and derogatory remarks of the Free Church spokesman J C Robertson and the bitter self-centred denunciation of A Neil Macdonald, sent the correspondence to Archibald MacNeilage, the editor of the *Free Church Monthly Record*, who replied with a characteristically balanced letter to the Aberdeen Press. He wrote:

> *I know nothing about the financial position of the St Columba buildings in Dee Street, and say nothing about that. Whatever that position may be I cannot substantiate the view that St Columba Church and manse will spell ruin to the Free Church cause in Aberdeen. Possession of any church and manse in your city by the Free Church would always be better than possession of no church or manse; and possession of the church which has the Gaelic tradition in Aberdeen must, to a church like ours, which draws so much of its strength from the Highlands, be beneficial. I for one, therefore, am glad that the allocation of St Columba has been made to the Free Church. On sentimental grounds, that is because of its association with the ministry*

of Dr Walter McGillivray, I personally would like to have obtained Gilcom-
ston, but I do not therefore despise what has been allocated, and I trust bright
days are in store for the Free Church in St Columba, Dee Street.

While writing this, I do not wish it to be supposed that I am devoid of
sympathy for those who, like Mr. Macdonald, take another view of ecclesias-
tical questions, and have spent and been spent in connection with the Dee
Street property. I hope it is possible for one to wish his own cause and
denomination well, without wishing ill to his neighbours; and it is one of the
sad features of the situation created by the disastrous 'union' of 1900 that it
has separated very friends, and in the very nature of the case made it impos-
sible for men to be loyal to their own convictions and yet do by others as they
would like. I do not labour that point now. No fair-minded man will say that
it is an outrage to give the Free Church one church and manse in Aberdeen.

In your city there are year by year many young people from the north and
north-west Highlands and as a considerable proportion of these come out of
Free Church homes, the Free Church has a duty to them which she seeks to
discharge. The exact number of such persons resident in Aberdeen during the
past winter is unknown to me. I am, however, aware that it was considerable,
and it would be sinful on the part of the Free Church not to do the best she
could for them. Many fishermen are also to be found in your city at certain
seasons, and among them are a large proportion of Gaelic-speaking Free
Churchmen. In the city there are persons who believe the Free Church has a
right to exist in Scotland, who prefer the simplicity of her worship, which is
that universally practised throughout the Church in the Disruption era, and
I venture to assert that such persons, wherever they may be found, are gener-
ally good-living, law-abiding members of the community.

In accordance with the principles on which the Executive Commission operated, not only the building but its contents were allocated to
the Free Church congregation. Normally that would include moveable
furniture (although there was little enough of that in Dee Street), the
communion vessels, tokens, linen and records. Alex Gammie, the
Evening Express religious correspondent, states that an exception was
made in respect of the records which were retained by the UF Church.
But, if so, the bulk of these were subsequently transferred to the Free
Church congregation.

A last farewell

The farewell service for the UF congregation took place on Sunday
evening 23rd June 1907 when the minister, the Rev. A F Campbell,
preached from 1 Corinthians 15:58: 'Beloved brethren be ye steadfast,
unmoveable, always abounding in the work of the Lord, forasmuch as
you know that your labour is not in vain in the Lord.' At the end of his

sermon he made reference to their departure from a building hallowed by many sacred associations. The indefatigable reporter for the *Evening Express* was present and wrote, 'Nothing was said or done to which any member of the Free Church could have taken the slightest exception; everything was in keeping with the spirit of Christian charity'. That was an honourable conclusion to their stewardship. After singing the second paraphrase to the tune St Paul, acknowledging the God of their fathers to be their God still, and seeking His guidance for their wandering footsteps, they filed out into an uncertain future.

The Presbytery had agreed that for the next four months the dispossessed congregation should meet in Union Hall. Even so it was inevitable that some of the UF congregation would retrace their steps to Dee Street. That process may have been accelerated when the Rev. A F Campbell received a call to Grant Street UF Church in Glasgow where he was inducted on 11th October 1907 and where he remained until he died on 1st July 1930. His departure confirmed the Presbytery in its resolve to terminate the independent existence of the demoralised congregation – a congregation without a church and without a minister. The decision was taken to unite the remnant with the High UF which worshipped in one of the triple kirks on Belmont Street and which had as its minister another Highlander, the Rev. Duncan M Munro, a native of Cromarty. And so on 10th October 1907, that section of the old Gaelic congregation led by Hugh Mackenzie and A Neil Macdonald was formally united with Aberdeen High United Free. One of the conditions of union was that provision would be made in the form of a student assistant for a weekly Gaelic service and on the Sunday following the union, a Gaelic service was held at 2.30 pm, the preacher being a divinity student A J Morrison who latterly was minister at Logie-Easter and who received an honorary DD from his *alma mater* in 1955. In 1935 the High Church in Belmont Street was sold and the congregation moved to Hilton where it entered a new phase of life as High Hilton. At some stage the Gaelic service was transferred to Trinity Church on Crown Street. By then the old Highland component of High Hilton had disappeared without trace.

Chapter 32

*

SOCIAL ASPECTS
OF THE GAELIC CHURCH

PRESENT day interest in the social history of religion has given rise to a variety of studies of urban religion in which the role of class-based relationships in the formation of community structures has been explored by recourse to church and congregational records. Topics that have been investigated include class and social segregation in city congregations, the problems encountered by migrant or ethnic minorities in maintaining their religious distinctives in an alien culture, the role of elitism in urban communities and class conflict as a motivating factor in church attachment. In all of these areas the records of the Aberdeen Gaelic Chapel provide pertinent data.

More recently, in a detailed study of urban Gaelic culture, Charles Withers viewed Lowland Gaelic chapels as 'institutions dealing not with a coherent migrant identity based on shared birthplace and language, but with social difference, diversity and ambivalence within the urban highland populations'.[1] Some features of the Aberdeen Gaelic Chapel may be taken as supportive of this deemed diversity. The congregation was certainly fluid in its composition, being made and re-made as newcomers arrived, replacing those leaving the city or moving to the suburbs. Over the years, economic inequalities emerged among the long-stay worshippers and within the congregation there would be coteries determined by language, kinship, locality or affluence. But while there was a diversity of circumstances among the chapel-goers, there was not the same diversity with regard to their religious aspirations. Whatever the congregation may have lacked in terms of 'a coherent migrant appearance', it nevertheless possessed a shared purpose which was to worship in a style which linked the people with their past. In the opening decades of the 19th century that style was expressed in Gaelic-language worship. In the closing decades Gaelic waned, becoming the language of worship of a minority. Yet even English-language worship in the chapel had its distinctive Highland overtones which were not to be found in other city congregations. Whether in Gaelic or in English, the urban expression of Highland religion in Lowland Gaelic chapels was one and the same with that practised in the homeland churches. The chapel therefore, while admittedly heterogeneous in some respects, nevertheless embodied a unity of religious outlook which was truly characteristic of the migrant culture. Of course, many urban Highlanders had little or no interest in participating in regular Sunday worship. Yet even these had recourse to the Highland church for marriages, funerals and even baptism. These rites of passage are key indicators of cultural identity which further affirm the coherence of the migrant culture in its religious mode.

Social class and Chapel management

The first appeals in the *Aberdeen Journal* in 1788 and 1789 for funds to provide gospel ordinances for the Highlanders – 'this little society of strangers', as John Ewen termed them – made no reference to their economic condition. This may have been because some prominent Highlanders like Ronald Bayne and Colquhoun MacGrigor, were known to be in comfortable circumstances. However, when the Trustees (Colquhoun MacGrigor, James Chalmers and John Ewen) petitioned the Magistrates for the use of St Mary's Chapel, they stressed the indigent circumstances of the Highlanders; and the public appeal launched in 1795 for subscriptions to the Gaelic Chapel referred to them as 'among the lower ranks of the community'. Throughout the nineteenth century, when representatives of the congregation appeared before Presbytery or the Sustenation Fund Committee to defend the need for a substantial subsidy from central funds, the plea was invariably advanced that the people 'were almost all of the labouring classes'. Reporting to the Parliamentary Commissioners of Religious Instruction in 1837, the Gaelic Church minister affirmed that 'the whole congregation with the exception of about twelve individuals are of the poor and working class'. It was, of course, in the interests of the case to emphasise the indigence of the people, but even if overstated there was a large measure of truth in the description.

In the post-Disruption years the general level of affluence enjoyed by the Gaelic Chapel worshippers may well have been below that of the opening decades of the 19th century, for it is evident that in Aberdeen, as in Glasgow, many of the Highlanders who prospered in their careers soon forsook the Gaelic Chapel for other congregations, if only for the sake of the religious welfare of their monolingual families. This was in fact stated in the appeal placed in the *Aberdeen Journal* of 24th May 1837. 'A large proportion of the original members of the congregation have been removed by death and those who still survive are aged and few in number. Their offspring being brought up in this place are more conversant in the English than in the Gaelic. Hence they worship in other churches of the city.' Consequently the chapel played host to a continual influx of new arrivals, people with minimal financial resources, labourers, quarriers and unskilled workers who, on achieving better employment and a higher standard of living, found one of the newer congregations then being established in the city more to their liking. Those with an urge to evangelise their fellow Highlanders no doubt felt compelled to retain their membership of the Gaelic Chapel, as did those for whom Gaelic was the decisive factor in meaningful worship. But these would be a minority of the newcomers and the unending exodus of worshippers sapped the vitality of the chapel and prevented the Highland Congregation in Aberdeen from achieving a prosperity equivalent to that enjoyed by the Highland community, the more affluent members of which rapidly integrated with Aberdeen society.

The occupations and social status of the nine elders ordained prior to 1805 are unknown, except for Alex Murray who resided in the Green. He was a woolcomber and, although one of the original feu assignees, he was illiterate, as was Donald Chrystie. When the last of the irregular ordinations to the Kirk Session took place in 1805, one of the three new appointments was Ebenezer Murray, another of the original chapel feuars. He resided at 27 Gordon Street and had a merchant's business at the foot of Broad Street. The other men ordained were Duncan MacGregor, a man of unknown occupation but an excellent scribe residing on George Street, and Alex Macdonald, a merchant of East North Street with a home address on King Street. With the exception of Alex Macdonald we know very little about the twelve elders chosen by the minister of the day 'with concurrence of the elders then in office and approbation of the congregation, to join with him in the government of the church, and exercise of discipline and watch over the manners of the people'. But what we know of the ministers who appointed these elders, and of the duties assigned to them, indicates that it was on account of their spiritual discernment and pastoral usefulness, and not on account of their social status, that they were chosen. Collectively it was their duty to exercise discipline as a court of the church, overseeing the moral condition of the people and judging the fitness of applicants for communicant membership, while, individually, 'as the minister should sow the seed, they should seek the fruit'. But the elders did not have any responsibility for, or jurisdiction in, the building or its finance. That was the province of the managers who were appointed by a different procedure and from a separate constituency.

Under the original chapel constitution, management of the material or temporal assets of the congregation – its property and finance – was kept separate from the spiritual oversight of the congregation. In 1796 the chapel management committee consisted of three or four invited external managers whose function it was to give advice and assistance in legal and commercial matters, in association with eight or ten under-managers who were elected annually, the power of election being restricted to those who had subscribed to the amount of five shillings and upwards to the chapel's building fund. The franchise for voting on matters of a spiritual nature did not involve the 'subscribers' *per se*. Such matters were determined by the vote of those who qualified to take part in the election of a minister, *ie* heads of families and unmarried men who had paid for seats in the chapel and had been regular hearers for a minimum of twelve months prior to an election and who understood the Gaelic language. It is evident that the qualifications necessary for voting in connection with the spiritual concerns of the congregation were more demanding than that required for influencing its temporal affairs. In the case of the latter, simply having contributed a minimum of five shillings to the building fund entitled the contributor to vote in the annual election. Only one elder, Alex Murray, was elected to the first management committee. Although illiterate, he was appointed preses.

The new constitution imposed on the chapel by the General Assembly of 1820 made some significant changes in the election of the managers. Restricting the election to the subscribers was abolished and the franchise was altered so that election was now in the hands of those authorised to vote at the election of a minister, *ie* heads of families, unmarried men who were paid-up seat-holders and had been communicants at least once each year for two years preceding an election and who understood the Gaelic language. The term of office was increased to five years, so dispensing with the need for annual elections. At the same time the right of the congregation to appoint its own elders was withdrawn. Under these new arrangements there was still a complete separation in the oversight of the secular and the spiritual concerns of the congregation, but that changed with the Act of the Free Assembly of 1846 which gave to the elders an influential, if not decisive, role in the business affairs of the congregation. Prior to that Act which accorded the elders an automatic place on the Deacons' Court, the elders, *qua elders*, were not involved in the management of a congregation's temporal assets.

Although the original constitution confined the election of the chapel management committee to the subscribers, arguably the more affluent section of the congregation (cf Ingram Street Chapel, Glasgow),[2] there is no evidence that a hegemonic elite dominated the chapel management in the manner said to have occurred in Glasgow's Gaelic Chapels where men who claimed to represent and speak for the Gaelic community insinuated their way into the chapels' self-electing management and then wielded their status as a means of social advancement in the local urban society.[3] Although in Aberdeen men of standing in the community – men such as the local politician John Ewen, the editor James Chalmers or the lawyer Alex Webster – were invited to assist the elected managers with advice and by undertaking correspondence on behalf of the chapel, they were not themselves Highlanders. From all accounts their involvement was wholly philanthropic. Perhaps Aberdeen did not offer the same opportunities for social climbers to achieve civic recognition, as did the chapels in Ingram Street or Duke Street. In any case there is nothing in the lore of the church in Gaelic Lane to suggest that the management had any motives beyond that of providing spiritual and charitable assistance to Highland incomers.

Seat rents as a deterrent to church attendance

Seat rents are frequently cited as a device for excluding the working classes from church attendance and for achieving greater social homogeneity in a congregation.[4] Although such a mechanism could obviously be effective in the more opulent west end congregations in Edinburgh and Glasgow, its significance in the Gaelic congregations in Scottish cities is more questionable. As often happens with new ventures, when the Aberdeen Chapel first opened its doors there was an enthusiasm among the people to pay seat rents to ensure their place at the services. A differential price scale was drawn up; the 'briest' (front) pews in the gallery were priced at 10s 6d and subscribers to the building fund were given preference in the allocation. The equivalent seats on the ground floor together with the 'table seats' were charged at 5s 3d per sitter. Although not stated it seems the minimum rent was set at one shilling, for in 1805, when there was an across-the-board reduction in seat rents, the basic charge was set at 6d. The front pews and the table seats then carried a price tag of 3s 6d, while the front gallery seats were offered at four shillings to subscribers and at five shillings to non-subscribers.

At the first allocation of seats, a recommendation from the elders to the managers that seats be allocated to the poor gratis, was rejected, partly out of a concern that those identified as being poor 'may be recommended by members of the Session more for partiality than charity'. The committee then expressed their willingness 'to acquiesce with the Session in these charitable acts on this condition that a private gift will be given to the Clerk at every time of sitting of those that are needy objects of that charity – and not to give public intimation to increase the poor among us and burden the cause'. That is to say, at the twice yearly collection of seat rents a donation to the funds in lieu of seat rent would be expected from the sponsor of the pauper. It is doubtful if this happened in practice.

The Highlanders may well have been averse to paying seat rents, a reluctance which according to Dr Norman Macleod – *Caraid nan Gaidheal* – resulted from the seat rent system being a novelty to them – 'They never heard of it till they came to Glasgow'.[5] In many Highland churches all the sittings were free. Residence in the parish, especially the *quoad civilia* Parishes, gave a right of occupancy. Although the Parliamentary churches (built as a consequence of the 1824 Act of Parliament to improve the provision of churches in Highland Parishes) were allowed to raise revenue from seat rents, it was stipulated that one-third of the seats should be free. Despite that requirement, in places where there was a strong demand for seats, the proportion was sometimes reduced to one quarter as happened at Shieldaig.[6] The minister of Shieldaig, in making his return to the Commissioners of Religious Instruction, added plaintively, 'Although the people eagerly take sittings, a number do not pay'. He also reported that 'the attendance is even greater than the number of sittings, as the people crowd together'.

Inability or unwillingness to pay seat rents did not automatically exclude that section of the community from church attendance. Many newcomers to the city would have assumed that in a church catering for Highlanders, they had a common right to admission. When the Presbytery sent a committee of inquiry to the Aberdeen Gaelic Church in 1850, it was to discover that two-thirds of those attached to the congregation paid nothing either to the Sustentation Fund or for seat rents. Probably neither the level at which the managers set the seat rents, nor the moral pressure which they exerted for payment to be made, had as seriously a deterrent effect on church attendance as is sometimes represented. The people simply ignored the demands.

For the most part, church attendance was a function of the popularity of the preacher and it is evident that during the ministry of Duncan Grant, or that of Donald Sage, the people crowded into the church; as indeed they did when there was a celebrated visiting preacher such as Macdonald of Ferintosh. Then boards were put across the aisles to increase the sitting capacity. On the other hand, a dull preacher provided little incentive for crowded attendances. As early as 1801, during Macphail's pastorate, the managers were complaining about the 'backwardness' of the people in paying their dues and they reacted by threatening that ...

none was to receive any benefits in this chapel except the hearing of the Word only, none to receive the privilege of the communion nor a line to the Infirmary or to the Work-House except their seat be paid or their name be recorded in the seats set apart for those not able to pay seats; they are desired to get a line from the elder in the quarter they reside in for that purpose.

When the chapel was not crowded, even the managers conceded that non-payers were not to be denied 'the hearing of the Word'. The pass-keepers or pew-openers were not bouncers; indeed their efficiency in ensuring that seat-holders would get access to their seats when the chapel was crowded was often called into question. The claim advanced by the Rev. Hugh Mackenzie in 1837, to the effect that 'many are deprived of the means of public worship and religious instruction in consequence of their inability to pay high seat rents', was primarily a convenient excuse to account for the poor attendances consequent to his unpopularity as a preacher. Inability, or more likely unwillingness to pay seat-rents, did not deprive would-be worshippers of admission. If admission was refused it would not have been because of lack of space, but simply to enforce a principle. Such a course was threatened in 1836 when the reluctance to pay had become so widespread that the committee toughened their previous stance towards hearers and instructed the pew-openers that 'no hearers may be accommodated with seats who do not pay for the same with the exception of strangers or occasional hearers'. Nonetheless, it is extremely unlikely that any were turned away in Aberdeen and the suggestion that poverty prevented the great majority of Gaelic Highlanders from attendance on public worship in Glasgow[7] or elsewhere may need to be qualified in the absence of evidence that the chapel in question was crowded with seat-holders.

Elitism and the eldership

The homogeneity of the primary Highland community in Aberdeen, as in other centres of population, would in time have given place to a diversity in which some individuals possessing superior skills or gifts came to occupy more responsible or influential positions in society. It has been argued that the elite that emerged in this way from the migrant community often exerted a leading or dominant role on their compatriots in other spheres of community life by means of which they sought to achieve civic recognition in the host community. Evidence for this form of social climbing in the late eighteenth century has been adduced in respect of Glasgow's Gaelic community where some prominent individuals in the city's Highland clubs provided charitable assistance, educational training and employment opportunities for their fellow countrymen thereby achieving a more prestigious place in the community.[8] The projection of this scenario to include the Gaelic church as an occasion or opportunity for asserting an elitist cultural hegemony has been suggested, but on more slender evidence. Even in Glasgow, where there was more opportunity for employers to achieve a dominant position in all aspects of society, there are few instances where it can be argued that the worshipping community looked to the materially successful for spiritual leadership. And where plausible instances of such a class-based relationship within the chapel can be demonstrated, it would not have been on the grounds of a leader's elevated social status that deference would have been paid, but on account of his acknowledged superiority in spiritual stature.

Role reversal was commonplace in the Highland church. As Donald Macleod has said, in Gaelic communities men could occupy positions of menial drudgery through the week, 'but on Sunday they were aristocrats, dressed in their finest and rising to the full height of human dignity in intelligent enraptured worship of their Maker'. Worshipping in the same congregation would be men who though 'giants in the world of commerce, were dwarfs in the world of the spirit'.[9] The Gaelic congregations in Glasgow, Aberdeen or elsewhere, did not concede the right to spiritual leadership solely on the grounds of worldly attainment. It could happen, of course, that those who were achievers in the secular world were also endowed with spiritual excellence. But Gaelic congregations were not blind to the gifts of the Spirit. They acknowledged the leadership of those who gave evidence of living close to God and in making that acknowledgement they were quite capable of acting independently of any elite, whether managers, manufacturers or ministers. The suggestion that the Aberdeen Chapel managers sought to guide the Highlanders into an English way of life by introducing English into the Gaelic Chapel[10] is to misconstrue their action. In Aberdeen, as in Glasgow and elsewhere, bilingualism was introduced in an attempt to keep families within the same congregation. That this transition was resisted by a militant section of the congregation was not because of their opposition to an English way of life or to any unwillingness to be incorporated into Aberdeen society. It was solely on the grounds of their preference for worship in the Gaelic mode. To quote Donald Macleod again, 'The lure of the language and its distinctive liturgy triumphed over all else'. Of course when the Gaelic community reached the stage of becoming completely assimilated into the urban society, Caledonian or Highland societies were formed with a view to preserving the Gaelic language and its traditions. But the purpose of the Gaelic Church was not the maintenance of the migrant culture. It was to bring the Gospel to those who could not, or would not, otherwise hear it.

Class conflict and church affiliation

In a study of the social standing and personal attributes of men elected to the eldership in pre- and post-Disruption churches in Aberdeen, it was concluded[11] that a significant level of support for the Free Church came from the emerging middle classes who saw their efforts to climb the social ladder obstructed at the ecclesiastical level by the established landed and merchant families. Detailed analysis of the membership of Kirk Sessions before and after the Disruption, led to the conclusion that in Aberdeen the growth of the Free Church was attributable to young entrepreneurs who switched their support from the Established Church to the Free Church where they were promptly made elders because of their ability to furnish capital for the church's building programme. According to this view, suitability for the eldership rested not in an appointee's spiritual qualities, but in his socio-economic status.

While it is true that a new place was given to elders in the management of the Free Church's temporal affairs by the Act anent the Duties of Elders and Deacons (Act VII, 1846), that Act was also careful to stipulate 'the peculiar duties of elders'. These duties included the requirement 'that they superintend and promote the formation of meetings within their districts for prayer, reading the Scriptures, and Christian fellowship, among the members of the Church'. In other words, elders were expected to be able to understudy the pastoral office of the minister, a function which is sometimes overlooked by social historians studying Scottish church life.

The thesis that the Free Church enjoyed the support of men from the urban middle classes, who in turn achieved recognition by ordination to the eldership, was based on an apparent correlation between election to office and middle class social mobility as revealed by changing residential addresses in the Aberdeen Directory. In the nature of this exercise, there was, of necessity, an element of guesswork in deciding if a named individual on a Kirk Session roll was one and the same with a corresponding name in the pages of the Aberdeen Directory. Taking the Gaelic Church as an identity-check, the success rate in determining the identity of the elders, would appear to be poor. Alex Macdonald, merchant of East North Street, who represented the Gaelic Church firstly on the General Kirk Session and latterly on the South Parish Kirk Session, is incorrectly identified with an MD attached to the Royal Artillery. Robert Sutherland, plasterer of George Street and Broad Street, whose membership of the General Kirk Session and the South Parish Kirk Session paralleled that of Alex Macdonald, is taken to be a glazier and painter of King Street and Union Street. Of the other two Gaelic elders on the South Parish Kirk Session, Hugh Fraser, tailor and clothier, latterly of Union Street, is omitted altogether and William Gordon has not been identified as a bookseller on Summer Street. Nor has either of the other elders of the Free Gaelic Church – Kenneth Dingwall, an illiterate quarrier of Gilcomston, and William Stuart, road surveyor of North Broadford – been identified.

A survey of the office-bearers (managers and elders) in the Gaelic Church shows no correlation between the eldership and social standing or financial resources. In the pre-Disruption Gaelic Church, there were several businessmen who loaned money to the church, only one of whom, Alex Macdonald, East North Street, was an elder. Others who loaned money – such as James Dingwall, vintner, Woodside; John Macdonald, tailor, Queen Street; Duncan Mackenzie, shoemaker, Skene Square; and Ebenezer Murray, merchant, Broad Street – served on the management committee for longer or shorter periods but were never ordained as elders. In that respect the membership of the management committee shows a better correlation with business skills, but the

possession of such skills, or even literacy, was not an absolute requirement for membership. It was, however, the norm, and the great majority
had some skill. People involved in road-making – contractors, inspectors
or surveyors – were well represented.

It may be questioned to what extent social mobility should be taken
as indicating aspirations after social status. Many citizens moved house
as a matter of routine. It was a way of life even for those whose station
in life was secure and not itself subject to change. For instance, Hugh
Mackenzie, when minister of the Gaelic Church, made no fewer than
eleven changes of residence between 1825 and 1854. At four of the
addresses he stayed for only one year.

Another area in which attitudes prevalent in the Gaelic Chapel
differed from those assumed to operate in terms of the 'social climbing
middle classes' thesis, has to do with the qualifications deemed appropriate for the office of the eldership. Regardless of the many changes in
civic life and religious outlook that occurred throughout the 19th
century, election to the office of the eldership in the Gaelic church
stipulated in principle, and expected in practice, the exercise of spiritual
gifts. Men to be ordained to the eldership were expected to possess
more or less of all the qualifications referred to in the New Testament
as necessary for men exercising spiritual oversight in the church (see
Titus 1:7-9; 1 Peter 5:2-4). Far from there being 'a necessary social
status' from which to advance to the eldership, there is no evidence that
social discrimination was practised in the appointment of elders. Social
standing was no hindrance, provided the man in question gave evidence
of possessing the requisite spiritual gifts. While there were some men of
the small merchant class among the founding fathers of the Gaelic
Chapel, none of that class (as far as is known) was appointed to the
eldership. Of the first nine appointed, two were illiterate. Fifty years
later another illiterate member, the quarrier Kenneth Dingwall, was
elected an elder. Neither social status or defective education was a
barrier to office. Spiritual gifts were what was looked for and not infrequently the congregation found these qualities to be more in evidence
at the lower end of the social scale. The roper Hector Mackay was
another from the working classes ordained alongside the quarrier
Kenneth Dingwall. The esteem in which Hector Mackay was held was
well-nigh universal. That he achieved the same esteem when he left the
Gaelic Church for Bon Accord Church, indicates that the estimation of
personal sanctity arrived at in Gaelic Lane was not confined to the
Gaelic Church.

The elder in his office

In a brief biography of Hector Mackay, William Robbie, author of

Aberdeen: Its Traditions and History, gives an insight into the lifestyle of an elder from the Highland tradition.[12]

> *Morning and evening, his household met around the family altar; and he spent much time in private meditation and prayer. In the social circle he never engaged in frivolous conversation. His manner was quiet and words weighty; but, at the same time, far removed from gloom or asceticism. On the contrary his high-toned piety was beautifully blended with a subdued cheerfulness which made his company always pleasant and attractive.*

Putting that into contemporary language, Hector Mackay was a well-balanced family man who took a lively interest in every wholesome aspect of life; a man who enjoyed company and who was ready to offer advice and counsel as occasion demanded. Morning and evening he would conduct family worship in his own home, and when visiting the homes of the congregation he would be invited to 'take the Book'. He would begin with a short opening prayer invoking a blessing on the act of worship. Then several verses of a Psalm would be sung by those present. The Scripture reading which followed would be chosen to suit the occasion of the visit, whether one of joy or sorrow, of trial or difficulty; or if family worship was a daily practice in the home being visited, he might take up the reading where it had ended on the day previous. In his own home he almost certainly followed the tradition of reading through the Old Testament, chapter by chapter in the morning, and similarly through the New Testament in the evening. The Scripture having been read, Hector Mackay would conclude the worship by leading in prayer, he and all present kneeling for that closing act of worship. In the course of his prayer he would commend the visited family, individually or collectively, with their particular needs as known to him, to the gracious interposition of an omnipotent God. Their circumstances having thus been consciously brought to the notice of a divine saviour and heavenly father, the occupants would feel their hearts comforted and their spirits uplifted as the elder took his homeward journey.

In his report to the Parliamentary Commissioners in 1837, the Rev. Hugh Mackenzie stated that in addition to the prayer meetings held in the church, prayer meetings were also held in the districts of the city and suburbs for the benefit of the Highland population. These gatherings would have been held in the homes of the more established people. An elder would conduct the meeting, calling on several of the men present to lead in prayer and interspersing the prayers with Psalm singing and Scripture reading. Probably the majority of these meetings would have been in Gaelic and it is possible that those attending would have been representative not so much of the district (*eg* the Gallowgate or Gilcomston) as of a Highland locality such as Sutherland, Skye or Inverness. In its own way, the district meeting played an important cultural role in the life of the chapel-goers providing a more saintly version of the household ceilidh.[13] At such a gathering the highly popular spiritual songs of Gaelic poets such as Dugald Buchanan could, and did, figure largely in the repertoire, despite their rigid exclusion from the formal church services as being non-canonical.

The district meeting also provided an opportunity for the exchange of news from the homeland and the benefits or otherwise of emigration would have been a regular topic of conversation. The Gaelic Church had a significant transient component with people moving to and from Aberdeen, and some going abroad to New York or Canada or South America. Minutes of the Gaelic Church include references to some who returned from America. From the manse two sons of the Rev. Hugh Mackenzie emigrated to Australia, Simon in 1857 and William in 1869, both taking up pastorates in the Presbyterian Church of New South Wales.

The home life of chapel-goers in the early years of the 19th century would certainly have respected the traditions of the Highland church as regards Sabbath observance. After the toil and drudgery of six wearisome days, the Sabbath was a delight, a day on which to think of other things; a day to rest weary limbs and refresh jaded minds. Domestic work was minimised but not debarred and the pulpit was looked to for mental stimulation. Bacchanalian pursuits were severely discountenanced at all times, but alcoholic spirits were not generally excluded from the home and many regarded whisky as the kindly provision of a beneficent creator, a commodity for which thanks was to be offered no less fervently than that for daily bread.

In no home influenced by Highland religion would food be eaten without grace being said; and in the more conscientious homes it was the practice not just to 'give thanks' before eating, but to 'return thanks' at the end. The words of thanksgiving would not always be audible, especially from the lips of those less practiced or more self-conscious about 'giving thanks'. But sight could serve where hearing failed, for the demeanour of the officiant was as predictable as the words themselves and gave due notice of the beginning and the end of the invocation. This trait is brilliantly recalled by Neil Gunn who was raised in a community where some characteristics of Highland religion lingered into the twentieth century. In a Highland home when the meal was brought to the table it was the mother who gave the starting signal as in Gunn's novel *Morning Tide* where the wife bade her husband, 'Ask the blessing, John .... Her husband lifted his left hand to his brow, which he smoothed for a moment. Then he pronounced the Grace that was in the Shorter Catechism. There was a living note of intercession, and his open hand kept moving over his forehead and his closed eyes'. When he lowered his hand the grace had ended. There was a brief pause, an involuntary silence, 'for personal indulgence after communion with God was not seemly. Yet the momentary silence was never obtrusive, and the mother always broke it naturally and cheerfully'.[14] Only then did they begin to eat. That ritual gave a dignity to life even at the plainest of tables. And at a poor man's table 'the grace becomes exceedingly graceful'.[15]

Notes to Chapter 32

1. C W J Withers, *Urban Highlanders* (East Linton, 1998) p. 238.
2. C W J Withers: 'Highland Clubs and Chapels: Glasgow's Gaelic Community in the Eighteenth Century' in *Scottish Geographical Magazine,* vol 101, p 23 (1984).
3. C W J Withers: 'Class, culture and migrant identity: Gaelic Highlanders in urban Scotland'. See pp 74-75 in G Kearns and C W J Withers (eds): *Urbanising Britain* (Cambridge, 1991), pp 55-79.
4. C G Brown: *The Social History of Religion in Scotland since 1730* (London, 1987).
5. *Second Report of the Commissioners of Religious Instruction, Scotland*, quoted by C W J Withers (1991), op. cit., p 75.
6. *Fourth Report of the Commissioners of Religious Instruction, Scotland.* Parliamentary Papers (1837-38) (122), xxxiii, p 201.
7. C W J Withers: (1991), op. cit., p 75.
8. C W J Withers: (1984), op. cit.
9. D Macleod: 'Foreword to Glasgow's Gaelic Churches' by I R MacDonald (Edinburgh, 1995), p v.
10. C W J Withers: 'Kirk, club and culture change: Gaelic chapels, Highland societies and the urban Gaelic subculture in eighteenth-century Scotland' in *Social History,* vol. 10, pp 171-192 (1985).
11. A A MacLaren: *Religion and social class. The Disruption years in Aberdeen* (London, 1974).
12. Wm Robbie: *Bon Accord Free Church, Aberdeen. A retrospect* (Aberdeen, 1887), p 92.
13. D E Meek: 'Saints and Scarecrows: The Churches and Gaelic Culture in the Highlands since 1560' in *Scottish Bulletin of Evangelical Theology*, vol. 14, pp 3-22 (Edinburgh, 1996), p 10.
14. N M Gunn: *Morning Tide* (Edinburgh, 1931), pp 43-44.
15. C Lamb: *Elia. Grace Before Meat* (London, 1823).

Chapter 33

*

THE GAELIC CHAPEL
AND HIGHLAND RELIGION

BY the end of the eighteenth century Gaelic congregations had been established in all the major Scottish cities – Glasgow, Edinburgh, Perth, Dundee, Greenock, Paisley and Aberdeen.[1] The last of these to erect a building was Aberdeen in 1795. Fifty years later, its status was not considered to be of the highest importance in Gaelic church circles. David Carment, the one-time minister of Glasgow's Duke Street Gaelic Church, considered that 'next to Glasgow, the Greenock Gaelic Chapel was, in point of numbers, in point of piety and in point of respectability, the next most important Gaelic congregation in Scotland'.[2] The verdict of history, however, may yet accord to Aberdeen a more influential role in the story of the Highland church.

It is a matter of no little interest that from the very beginning of the spiritual awakening in the Highland church in the early eighteenth century and right through into the twentieth century, many of the church's most influential ministers had been trained in Aberdeen. Among these may be mentioned Lachlan Mackenzie of Lochcarron, Angus Mackintosh of Tain, David Carment of Rosskeen, John Kennedy of Killearnan, his son John Kennedy of Dingwall, Norman Macleod of Assynt, John Macdonald of Ferintosh, Alexander Macleod of Uig, Roderick Macrae of Knockbain, Alexander Stewart of Cromarty, Roderick Macleod of Bracadale and Donald Sage of Resolis, as also his father and grandfather before him. These and many other ministers referred to in the pages of this book received some part of their vocational training in Aberdeen. The extent to which the years spent in the city influenced the subsequent ministries of these men is still unexamined by church historians but the shared experience of life and learning in Aberdeen must have made some impression on their outlook and ministry. College classes, whether at Marischal or King's, would be the primary influence in conditioning their mental outlook but it would be wrong to exclude the role of the Gaelic Chapel in shaping impressionable hearts and minds.

Leaving aside its part in the training of future Highland ministers, the story of the Gaelic Chapel is a unique account of the association of Gaelic-speaking Highlanders for their mutual support and improvement from their first appearance in Aberdeen in any significant numbers in the late eighteenth century to the time of their virtual assimilation

263

into the local community at the beginning of the twentieth century.[3]

While the genesis of the Highland community in the North-East is to be traced to économic forces – the hardships prevalent in the northern counties and the opportunities for work in Aberdeen's emergent granite industry – it was the isolation experienced by monolingual Gaelic speakers which first gave rise to a concern for their welfare. That concern found its most distinctive and visible embodiment in the Gaelic Chapel, founded primarily to minister to spiritual needs which were not otherwise being catered to in the community. In addition, concern for the material or social welfare of the chapel-goers, although given less emphasis, was not altogether lacking, and many had reason to be grateful for the support which the chapel afforded in things temporal and spiritual. It was the only Gaelic congregation in Aberdeen although there was some Gaelic preaching in the independent Cotton Chapel in the Printfield between 1822 and 1838, and in East St Nicholas in the early years following the Disruption. In 1815 Aberdeen is reported to have had two Gaelic schools, one in the Printfield and the other in the town itself.[4]

Gaelic rules

The development of the Aberdeen Chapel was highly unusual. This arose from its remoteness from the territorial Highland church and also because, at its formation, the ecclesiastical authorities in Aberdeen regarded it as an insignificant and ephemeral gathering. Later as the congregation became established, the fact that it had not been officially approved was overlooked. Consequently, in its formative years from 1790 to 1820, it possessed a freedom of action that was quite exceptional. It enjoyed the relative independence of a chapel-of-ease, but without the restrictions that normally were attached to such places. Since chapel pulpits offered alternative ministries to that of the parish church where the incumbent was often unacceptable to the people, presbyteries were generally very reluctant to permit their establishment; and when approval was given, the presbytery usually retained control of the calling of a minister. In Edinburgh, authority to call a minister to the Gaelic Chapel was vested with the SSPCK, but the Presbytery retained *jus devolutum*. By contrast the Aberdeen congregation enjoyed complete liberty of action in the calling of a minister. Furthermore, a minister inducted to a chapel-of-ease was not permitted to have his own Kirk Session. The congregation was under the parish church's Kirk Session from which the chapel minister was excluded. But the Gaelic congregation had its own Kirk Session and four separate elections to the eldership took place prior to 1819, when the presbytery finally woke up to the fact that the chapel had not been officially recognised.

By that time, and indeed from 1798, authority to license a chapel had been transferred to the General Assembly and in 1820 that body ensured that the Aberdeen Gaelic Chapel was operating on a regular basis.

With the passing of the years, Gaelic preaching, originally the *raison d'être* for the chapel's existence, had of necessity to be supplemented with English preaching, if only for the benefit of children whose first, and in many cases, only language, was English. Even before the end of the eighteenth century, the established congregation was becoming more and more bilingual and regular worshippers were increasingly content to listen to English preachers such as Dr Kidd. Moreover English services tended to attract larger congregations and better collections, thereby increasing the all-round benefit. A census taken in 1863 gave attendances at the forenoon Gaelic service as 250-300, whereas 400-450 attended the afternoon English service.[5] And so, from the early years of the nineteenth century, Gaelic preaching, while still a cardinal feature of the chapel's programme, was no longer the be-all and end-all of its life. The trend to bilingual preaching soon gained momentum.

It was at this point that Gaelic took on a divisive rather than a unifying role. During the Rev. Duncan Grant's pastorate the Gaelic lobby sought to restrict the use of English and strongly opposed any attempt to introduce it into the main Sunday services. In this the lobbyists were aided by the chapel's constitution, a last minute amendment to which ensured that only those who understood the Gaelic language should have a vote in major policy decisions. Under these circumstances the Gaelic Chapel's original role of outreach to a spiritually needy and deprived community was, in time, modified to indulge the understandable concern of those Gaels for whom worship had to be in Gaelic in order to be truly meaningful.

This commitment to the Gaelic language eventually gave the Gaelic church a role in supporting the language which had formed no part of its original aims and objects. The view that Gaelic has suffered less neglect at the hands of the church than at the hands of educators, businessmen or government officials, and that its abandonment in religious worship marked the final stages of its demise,[6] can certainly be supported from the annals of the Aberdeen Gaelic Church. A century after its foundation, appreciative comment on the life and ministry of the Rev. George Macdonald, minister of the congregation from 1864 to 1898, referred almost exclusively to his interest in, and support for, the Gaelic language. Seemingly oblivious to the paradox of trying on the one hand to distance the congregation from the image of a special-interest, Gaelic-only minority group by re-naming the Free Gaelic Church as St Columba's Free Church, and on the other hand of making a particular pitch at Gaelic speakers, the Rev. George Macdonald did all he could to promote the Gaelic language among Highlanders in Aberdeen. That had not been a concern of the founders of the Gaelic Church. Their concern was for the moral and spiritual welfare of Highlanders unacquainted with the English language.

Highland ways

It is not without interest that the congregation, when first constituted, was known and advertised as 'The Highland Congregation' and this designation proved to be more enduring than its variant 'The Gaelic Church'. Although Gaelic preaching was the *raison d'être* for its formation, the congregation eventually catered for a wider constituency embracing Gaelic speakers and others whose preference was for worship in accordance with the Highland tradition. That of course raises the question of what is meant by Highland religion and what are its features? The language and liturgy of Gaelic worship has its own uniqueness, but the religion of the Highlands encompasses a broader base, one not confined to, or especially identified with, the Gaelic language. Donald Macleod draws a distinction between Highland Presbyterianism on the one hand, and on the other hand Highland churches of Episcopal, Baptist or Pentecostal tradition. Congregations of the second group he views as being simply replicas of their counterparts elsewhere, whereas he considers Presbyterianism in the Gaidhealtachd to be a distinct variant of Scottish Presbyterianism.[7]

Donald Meek[8] identifies among the distinctives of Highland religion in general, a profound reverence in worship, the centrality of scripture, a veneration of preaching, Sabbath observance and a heightened awareness of Divine sovereignty. But he also adds that these features have in time past been characteristic of Christian spirituality in places outwith the Highlands. While there are some unique features attaching to the past practice of Highland Presbyterianism – the Friday Question Meeting of the communion season being a good example – a case can be made for the view that religious practice in the Highland church through the nineteenth century simply preserved to a later period and in a more thorough-going way what had once been the common heritage and practice of the reformed church in Scotland.

To the popular mind Presbyterianism is the feature most closely identified with the Highland church, in much the same way as crofting is identified with Highland land–use. These cultural features (Presbyterianism and crofting) often serve as markers for imagining the sociology or anthropology of the Highlands.[9] While it must be conceded that the church in the Highlands is seen today as possessing its own unique style of religious worship and personal piety, it is important to remember that Highland evangelicalism is but one manifestation of a continental spiritual movement that spread across large parts of Europe and America. The religion now identified with the Highlands is not indigenous to it. It was imported to the Highlands following the Revolution Settlement of 1688 and the re-establishment of Presbyterianism in 1690. Thereafter the church, more than any other civic force, unified what were disparate, if not indeed distinct races, bringing one system of church law and administration to bear on Gaels and non-Gaels alike.

The features that are commonly associated with the practice of religion in the Highlands and islands – a liturgy devoid of visual colour and a life-style devoted to austerity and self-denial – were common-place in the lowlands of Scotland in the eighteenth and early nineteenth centuries. Indeed it is hard to think of any aspect of the life and doctrine of Highland Presbyterianism, or the mood or manner of its adherents, that did not have its counterpart in the religious life of the lowland peasantry at the beginning of the nineteenth century.[10] Recently Kenneth Ross, in a discussion of the distinctive characteristics of High-land religion, quotes the biographer of Dr Moody Stuart to the effect that 'in the experimental, subjective and searching character of his preaching he was more allied to the Highland divines such as Dr Kennedy'; from which Ross goes on to say that this trait 'was gradually being displaced in the lowland Free Church',[11] thereby indicating that at one time a typically Highland style of preaching was widespread in the lowland church.

In his book, *The Days of the Fathers in Ross-shire*, his enduring memorial to Highland religion published in 1861, Dr Kennedy made a lengthy comparison between the idealised religious practice of his Ross-shire parishioners and that of their co-religionists in the South. He had little difficulty in finding the former to be superior to the latter. But in 1875, in the course of his passage of arms with Dr Horatius Bonar over Moody-style evangelism, Kennedy was to argue that in earlier times the church in the lowlands had, in its ministry, men of the type of Dr Love (a native of Paisley) who, in his doctrine and practice, was indistinguishable from his brethren in the Highlands. Furthermore, in Kennedy's opinion, there were other lowland preachers whose ministry was of a pattern with that of the Highland church, even to the extent of manifesting the gift of prophetic discernment ('the secret of the Lord') so greatly esteemed by the leaders in the North in the days of the Fathers.[12] Possibly he had in mind men like the Covenanting preacher Alexander Peden (1626-86), often referred to as Peden the Prophet, and others similarly gifted.

The lowland church that Kennedy criticised was not the church it had once been. At one time it had been as orthodox as Kennedy's church. But the changes it was experiencing, which Kennedy viewed in terms of deterioration and degeneracy, were to come to the Highland church in later days, just as the gospel itself had come later. In its best days, as Kennedy himself conceded, the church in the South differed in no significant respect from the church in the Highlands. Inevitably the decline of the former would be followed by the decline of the latter. Despite the extraordinary success which accompanied the preaching of the gospel in the Highlands, the ebb had commenced in Kennedy's own time and the signs were to be seen in the Highland church in its lowland outposts in Aberdeen and Glasgow.

Theological diversions

The Highland church was also to experience tensions induced by a rapidly changing society. The intermingling of the population consequent to improved communications and increased accessibility had its effect, hastening the importation and adoption of more liberal opinions and less temperate behaviour. This was especially noticeable with regard to the secularising of the Lord's Day during the latter part of the nineteenth century. City churches were the first to feel constrained to come to terms with the spirit of the age and the Gaelic congregations were not immune to this pressure. In Aberdeen Hugh Mackenzie was such an autocratic Calvinist that no hint of change occurred during his life-time, but throughout George Macdonald's pastorate there was a growing readiness to follow the mood of contemporary society.

It was this tendency across the denomination that alarmed those of an ultra-conservative outlook and brought about a polarisation within the Free Church. The church in the Highlands tended to a more rigid conservatism, while the church elsewhere was adopting a somewhat *laissez-faire* theological standpoint. In that widening polarisation, the conservative party, led by Begg of Newington and Kennedy of Dingwall, became identified with a mood of intolerance to change. While it was entirely proper for the conservatives to take a stand against a theological rationalism that threatened the foundation truths of Christianity, it was unfortunate that the camp-followers of this movement appeared to regard the ability to detect error, and denounce opponents, as the hallmark of the enlightened Christian, so giving the impression that finding fault was as much a part of the Christian life as faith and charity. But theological change was not all on one side. The practical theology of the conservatives was also undergoing revision. Emphasis was being placed not just on the objective truths of Scripture in respect of salvation, but also on the subjective experience of the believer and in such a way as to demand a higher level of Christian attainment from prospective communicants than that previously sought.

It may be recalled that John Kennedy had already enrolled at Aberdeen University as a student for the ministry in his pre-conversion days. His father, the minister of Killearnan, is not recorded as having had any misgivings concerning this decision taken at a time when, according to Dr Kennedy's biographer, the son's 'religion – if such it can be called – seemed to consist of little more than a strong dislike to a cold and heartless moderatism, a high admiration and peculiarly warm affection for his venerated father, and great confidence in the efficacy of that father's prayers'.[13] But some thirty years later Dr Kennedy was seeking, not from prospective applicants for the ministry but from prospective applicants for admission to the Lord's Table, what he termed 'an accredited profession' – by which he meant not a precipitate decision to join the church, but a sustained level of commitment such as had stood the test of time and the scrutiny of friend and foe. Of course, on occasion, Kennedy was capable of giving the most affectionate and spontaneous welcome to some nerve-racked applicant seeking admission to the Lord's Table.[14] But his practice did not always reflect his strongly-held opinions, and the stress which he laid on self-examination, in both his preaching and his writing, conveyed to the church at large the impression that if many were called, few were chosen. Where this critical attitude on the part of ministers and Kirk Sessions prevailed, it had the effect of diminishing additions to the communion roll. Communicant membership in the church in the Highlands began to be seen as appropriate only to those who had attained to an advanced level of godliness.

Although George Macdonald was one of Kennedy's circle, he and his Kirk Session took a fairly relaxed approach to applicants for admission to the Lord's Table. In the opening years of his ministry it was the practice for the Kirk Session to interview applicants for membership. But in the early 1870s it became the practice for the minister to inform the Session of the names of applicants, adding that he had examined and conferred with the parties and, having done so, recommended that they be admitted into membership. The Session, 'after deliberation', gave their consent, the individuals concerned being formally admitted at the close of a pre-communion service.

In this and other ways, it is evident that attitudes in Gaelic Lane had been modified with the passing of the years. With the changed outlook, there was a greater openness to the introduction of para-church activities. Social events were increasingly in evidence and even before the move to Dee Street took place a bazaar and an amateur concert in the Music Hall had been staged with great enthusiasm. Despite these concessions to the spirit of the age and their fondness for quasi-religious soirees which he regarded as 'an unmitigated nuisance',[15] Kennedy did not turn away from helping the congregation which he had supported since his student days. He was no extremist on the conservative wing of the church, and those who were regarded him as a weak and unsatisfactory Calvinist. Admirers of Jonathan Ranken Anderson (condemned by the

General Assembly of the Free Church for making false accusations against his brethren) had a profound antipathy to Kennedy who voiced his criticisms in a more gracious and less personal manner. Whatever reservations he may have had regarding 'the present cast and tendency of religious thought and feeling in Scotland', he did not indulge in the degree of segregation practised by some of those who have since claimed him as their standard-bearer. The biographer of Professor A H Charteris, a contemporary conservative theologian in the Established Church, credits Kennedy with having affirmed his willingness to put off his own mid-week meeting in the Free Church to allow his people attend a meeting in Dingwall Parish Church at which Charteris was the speaker.[16] Kennedy himself, left free to preach the gospel of sovereign grace, was unlikely to decline an opportunity on the grounds that by associating with those who took a different theological viewpoint, he was compromising the truth. According to Alex Macrae (the biographer of Dr Aird of Creich), Kennedy preached at a preparatory service held in Thurso in 1874 in connection with D L Moody's visit to the town[17] and in October 1882 he would have opened the Gaelic congregation's new church on Dee Street had it not been for a previous engagement, an engagement which, as it happened, he was unable to fulfil because of illness.

However tarnished the image of Gaelic Lane may have become in respect of conformity to sound practice, Kennedy showed no reluctance to be associated with its worship. There is no evidence that George Macdonald introduced paraphrases into public worship, despite his being at liberty to include these as 'inspired materials of praise'. But had he done so, it should have caused Dr Kennedy no embarrassment. He himself included the singing of a paraphrase during public worship at the opening of his new church in Dingwall in 1870.[18] And in the Aberdeen church, whatever its shortcomings, he remained a regular preacher. In a tribute read from the Dee Street pulpit following the death of Dr Kennedy on 28th April 1884, George Macdonald said, 'He preached his greatest sermons in the old church in Gaelic Lane'; by which he may, or may not, have meant that Kennedy's greatest preaching had been in Gaelic Lane.

There were many who first heard Dr Kennedy in the unprepossessing surroundings of the Gaelic Church. One such was William Robertson Nicoll, the future editor of *The British Weekly*. He was struck by the contrast between the dilapidation of the place and the freshness of the preacher's style. Today Kennedy is perceived as being an old-style preacher; yet to his contemporaries he conveyed the opposite impression. At a time 'when fresh forms of speech had not yet found their way into the northern pulpit, and when language twice dead and withered' was the preacher's hallmark, 'the spring-like newness' of Kennedy's

English was what gripped Robertson Nicoll. Many years later he recalled how on a week-day summer evening, when Kennedy appeared in the grim, old Gaelic Chapel, 'the grave subdued air of the worshippers who filled the church brightened into obvious expectancy'.[19] Just as Robert Finlayson's preaching was like a breath of fresh air to an earlier generation accustomed to the dry, dull scholarly sermons of the Moderates,[20] so Kennedy's preaching in Gaelic Lane came across to his contemporaries as stylish and thrilling. In his presentation of the Gospel which, as Wm R Nicoll remarked, contained no hint of a 'jaunty, superficial easy-going religion', Kennedy nevertheless succeeded in being a modern preacher.

Cultural pursuits

In the mid-nineteenth century, some churches sought to counter social delinquency through Temperance Societies, Penny Banks, social meetings and popular lectures, activities viewed by many at that time as dangerous innovations.[21] The church in Gaelic Lane did not appear to share that narrow view of the church's task. In its endorsement of para-church activities, the Gaelic congregation distanced itself from the ultra-conservative element in the Free Church, represented by A M Bannatyne of Union Free Church. These activities took account not only of Gaelic culture (George Macdonald's Gaelic classes for students), but also embraced musical renditions such as the cantata 'Eva'. A reference in 1871 in the satirical Aberdeen periodical, *The Chameleon*, to a 'deputation from the Gaelic Church, whose performances on the much-admired and sensational Scotch fiddle were the theme of universal admiration' raises the question whether the satire (if anything more than a double entendre on 'Scotch fiddle') was dependent for effect on the incongruity of the idea, or whether it was intended as an exaggeration of a suspected, if undeveloped, enthusiasm.[22]

Whether or not fiddle music had any part in the life of the Gaelic congregation, the question of the legitimacy of cultural associations under the aegis of the church is one which has given rise to heated controversy within the Highland church. From the time, towards the end of the nineteenth century, when the development of modern amenities widened the opportunities for social gatherings in the church, conservative elements opposed the formation of cultural societies of any kind. Perhaps it was felt that these extraneous or peripheral interests offered a more visible target for attack or demonising than did heterodoxy, and that their eradication would serve to prevent a congregation from being infiltrated by church-goers lacking genuine Christian conviction. It has been asserted that the post-1900 Free Church, like the pre-1900 Free Church, permitted 'practices to which discriminating

Christians could legitimately take exception'.[23] This certainly was the view of the ultra-conservative lobby largely staffed by Free Presbyterian recruits to the Free Church. Social meetings they viewed with especial disfavour. In 1913, when Professor John Macleod (a former Free Presbyterian) was called to the Free North Church in Inverness, he made it a condition of his acceptance of the call that the social events which had been so notable a feature of the life of that congregation under his predecessor, the Rev. Murdo Mackenzie, would be discontinued. Out went the Gaelic class, together with the Women's Literary Society and the Men's Mutual Improvement Society. In the opinion of many discerning, if not 'discriminating' Christians, both members and office-bearers of that congregation, it was a retrograde step which not only had a debilitating effect on the life of the congregation, but also did nothing to strengthen its spiritual vitality.

A century ago, in rural congregations in straths and glens, the need for congregational life to embrace community interests, although by no means absent, was much less urgent than in the cities of Scotland where there was a real need to provide opportunities for participation in character-building and mind-broadening activities within a Christian environment. If kept in proper perspective, involvement in cultural pursuits could serve both to educate the people and to christianize the culture. The church both in Gaelic Lane and Dee Street seemed willing to make the attempt, but whether it succeeded in achieving a proper balance between the interests of the cultural heritage and the imperatives of the Christian faith, is not easily answered. It certainly was in a position to influence those of its members who were concerned with the interaction between the past and the present, between heritage and destiny. George Macdonald's involvement with Gaelic interests in the city was comprehensive. His family's association with musical circles was likewise intimate. It may be assumed that Gaelic song also enjoyed their patronage. But the death of George Macdonald, together with his successor's limited acquaintance with the language, brought to an end congregational support for Gaelic culture. Thereafter members of the congregation interested in Gaelic culture espoused *An Comunn Gàidhealach*. Many who took a prominent part in the life of the congregation after 1900 had a no less prominent part in *An Comunn* well into the twentieth century.

After 1900 the witness to the Highland church heritage in Aberdeen was to continue, but under different, and some might say narrower, auspices Following the allocation of the Dee Street building to the continuing Free Church, the resultant linkage of the St Columba United Free congregation with the former Free High congregation, effectively terminated the Highland character of the united congregation and its links with the Highland church. Dispossessed St Columba worshippers wandered hither and thither, some drifting back to Dee Street despite the bitter aftermath of 1900. With the passage of time, the former hurts were to be forgotten, so much so that in 1934 the minister of the post-1900 Free Church congregation in Dee Street, the Rev. Duncan Leitch, was invited to officiate at the Aberdeen funeral of George Macdonald's widow, 111 years after her father's induction to the Gaelic Chapel.

Today Gaelic Lane and Dee Street are both desolate as far as Gospel ministry is concerned. The buildings still stand, mute testimony to a former age and a past concern. But the church that relinquished the buildings has not forsaken its mission or lost its power to attract the spiritually hungry. The sound of plaintive psalms and ancient melodies, impressive and moving as it rises and falls in solemn cadence and sacred harmony, still charms the Highland ear; the fervent prayer from caring lips still soothes the aching heart; the quickening power of Gospel truth still lifts the drooping spirit and calms the anxious soul. The church is where the people of God assemble for worship and Highland people are still drawn together by a desire to meet for worship 'in the manner to which they have been accustomed from their infancy'.

Notes to Chapter 33

1. I R MacDonald: 'The beginning of Gaelic preaching in Scotland's cities' in *Northern Scotland,* vol 9, pp 45-52 (1989).
2. *Proceedings of the General Assembly of the Free Church of Scotland held at Edinburgh* (22nd May, 1848), p 67.
3. For a detailed account see C W J Withers: 'Highland Migration to Aberdeen, c.1649-1891' in *Northern Scotland,* vol 9, pp 21-44 (1989).
4. C W J Withers: *Gaelic in Scotland 1698-1981* (Edinburgh, 1984), p 197.
5. *Proceedings of the General Assembly of the Free Church of Scotland* (1863). Report of the Equal Dividend Platform Committee, p 5.
6. C W J Withers: op. cit., p 261.
7. D Macleod: 'The Highland Churches Today' in J Kirk (ed): *The Church in the Highlands* (Edinburgh, 1999), p 146.
8. D E Meek: *The Scottish Highlands* (Geneva, 1996), p 35.
9. S Macdonald: *Reimagining Culture: Histories, Identities and the Gaelic Renaissance* (Oxford, 1997).
10. A Kennedy: *Memories of Scottish Scenes and Sabbaths more than Eighty years ago* (Edinburgh, 1902).
11. K R Ross: *Church and Creed in Scotland* (Edinburgh, 1988), p 238.
12. J Kennedy: *A Reply to Dr H Bonar's Defence of Hyper-Evangelism* (1875). Reprinted as *Evangelism: a Reformed Debate* (Portdinorwic, North Wales, 1997), p 120.
13. A Auld: *Life of John Kennedy DD* (Edinburgh, 1887), p 5.
14. N C Macfarlane: *Apostles of the North* (Stornoway, 1926), p 242.
15. J Kennedy: *The present cast and tendency of religious thought and feeling in Scotland* (Inverness, 1955), p 53.
16. A Gordon: *The life of Archibald Hamilton Charteris* (London, 1912), p 302.

17. Alex Macrae: *Revivals in the Highlands and islands in the 19th century* (Stirling, n.d.), pp 171-172. A P F Sell in *Defending & Declaring the Faith* (Exeter, 1987) insists that Kennedy 'had stood entirely aloof from Moody's meetings'. Macrae, as if to counter denials of his statement regarding Kennedy's support, gives Kennedy's text on the occasion as John 6: 35.

18. I M Macrae: *Dingwall Free Church. The Story of 100 Years and More* (Dingwall, 1970).

19. W R Nicoll (ed.): *The British Weekly*, vol. 4, p 77 (1st June, 1888).

20. R Macleod: *The John Bunyan of the Highlands*. Transactions of the Gaelic Society of Inverness, vol. LIV, pp 240-268 (1984-86).

21. J B Allan: *Rev. John Duncan* (London, 1909), p 155.

22. *The Chameleon* (Aberdeen, 1871), no. XX, p 1.

23. M Grant in C Graham (ed.): *Crown Him Lord of All* (Edinburgh, 1993), p 35.

*

Appendix

RECORDS OF THE HIGHLAND CONGREGATION
FOUNDED IN ABERDEEN IN 1785

A: One bound manuscript volume comprising:

1. *The Origin of the Gaelic Congregation in Aberdeen*, a historical account probably drawn up in 1792 by the Rev. John Mackenzie and continued until October 1823, giving information on the appointment of ministers and elders and sundry other items of information appropriate to the business of the Kirk Session.
2. A list of 330 hearers attached to the congregation in 1795.
3. A list of communicants from 1820 to 1843.
4. A copy of the Chapel constitution approved by the 1820 General Assembly.
5. A baptismal roll kept by the Rev. Donald Sage from 1819 to 1822.

B: One bound manuscript volume comprising:

1. Minutes of the Gaelic Chapel managers from July 1796 to July 1843.
2. The original constitution of 1796 loosely inserted as a single sheet.
3. A copy of the feu disposition for the site in Gaelic Lane.
4. Subscription lists recording donations to the Chapel Building Fund from:
    (a) The Town's Inhabitants.
    (b) The Women of the Congregation.
    (c) Members of the Congregation.

C: Minutes of the Deacons' Court of the Free Gaelic Church:

1. Volume 1 with Minutes from 13th March 1845 to 27th March 1876
2. Volume 2 with Minutes from 1st May 1876 to 20th January 1904.

D: Minutes of the Kirk Session:

Minutes of the Kirk Session from 1790 until 1823 are included in the narrative of events recorded in the volume entitled *The Origin of the Gaelic Congregation in Aberdeen*.
   The Chapel had no separate Kirk Session from 1823 until the congregation was given *quod sacra* status as Spring Garden Parish Church in 1834. The volume (or volumes) containing Kirk Session Minutes from 1834 until 1869 is missing.
   There is one volume of Kirk Session Minutes of the Free Gaelic Church (latterly St Columba Free Church) from 19th April 1869 to 8th February 1906.

*

BIBLIOGRAPHY

MANUSCRIPT SOURCES

Church of Scotland Records:

Records of the Presbytery of Aberdeen	CH2-1-10
	CH2-1-11
	CH2-1-12
	CH2-1-13
Records of the Presbytery of Chanonry	CH2-66-5
	CH2-66-6
Records of the Presbytery of Inverness	CH2-553-7
Records of the Presbytery of Lochcarron	CH2-567-3
Records of the Presbytery of Nairn	CH2-554-1
Records of the Presbytery of Selkirk	CH2-337-8
Records of the Presbytery of Tongue	CH2-508-2
Register of the Synod of Aberdeen	CH2-840-5
Minutes of the St Nicholas Kirk Session	CH2-448-48
Minutes of the South St Nicholas Kirk Session	CH2-2-1

Free Church of Scotland Records:

Records of the Free Presbytery of Aberdeen	CH3-2-5
	CH3-2-6
Records of the Free Presbytery of Breadalbane	CH3-45-1
Records of the Free Synod of Aberdeen	CH3-1-2
Records of the Free Synod of Perth	CH3-259-2
Minutes of Bon Accord Free Church Kirk Session (1848)	CH3-874-1
Communion Roll of Bon Accord Free Church (1843-58)	CH3-874-17
Minutes of Union (Aberdeen) Free Church Kirk Session	CH3-851-1

Royal Bounty Committee Records:

Minutes of the Royal Bounty Committee	CH1-5-59
	CH1-5-60

276

Society in Scotland for the Propagation of Christian Knowledge (SSPCK):

Minutes of Committee Meetings   GD95-2-12
                                                       GD95-2-13
                                                       GD95-2-14

Other Manuscript Material:

Anderson, J: *A fragment of history* (1885). Preface to Assembly Papers on Woodside Chapel-of-Ease (1831). MS in Aberdeen Central Library.

PRINTED PAPERS AND OFFICIAL REPORTS

Aberdeen Town Council Register, volume 64.
Acts of the General Assembly of the Church of Scotland:
     Assembly Papers: CH1-2-137, CH1-2-143.
     Assembly Papers: 'Cause of the Chapel-of-Ease Woodside' (1831).
Free Church of Scotland, Proceedings of the General Assembly.
Parliamentary Papers: Fourth Report of the Commissioners of Religious Instruction, Scotland (1838).
Parliamentary Papers: Fifth Report of the Commissioners of Religious Instruction, Scotland (1839).
Society for the Support of Gaelic Schools (Edinburgh Gaelic Schools Society).

Newspapers and Journals:

Aberdeen Free Press and Buchan News.
Aberdeen Journal.
Aberdeen University Review.
Forres Elgin and Nairn Gazette.
Free Church of Scotland Monthly Record.
The British Weekly.
The Chameleon.

Works of Reference:

A Record of Events in Aberdeen and the North 1801-1927 (Aberdeen, 1928).
Aberdeen Almanack.
Aberdeen Directory.
Annals of the Free Church of Scotland.
Fasti ecclesiae Scoticanae (Church of Scotland).
In Memoriam (Aberdeen, 1901).
The Black Kalendar of Aberdeen (1878).

PRINTED BOOKS AND ARTICLES

Allan, J B: *Rev. John Duncan* (London, 1909).
Anderson, P J (ed.): *Aurora Borealis Academica* (Aberdeen, 1899).
Anderson, P J (ed.): *Records of Marischal College and University* (Aberdeen, 1898).
Anderson, T A: *Inverness before Railways* (Inverness, 1885).
Angus, R: *Sermons by the late Rev. Henry Angus with a Memoir of his Life* (Aberdeen, 1861).
Auld, Rev. A: *Ministers and Men in the Far North* (Wick, 1869; reprinted Glasgow, 1956).
Auld, Rev. A: *Life of John Kennedy, DD* (Edinburgh, 1887).
Bannerman, W: *The Aberdeen worthies* (Aberdeen, 1840).
Barron, J: *The Northern Highlands in the Nineteenth Century* (Inverness, 1903).
Bayne, P: *Life and letters of Hugh Miller* (London, 1871).
Brown, C G: *The Social History of Religion in Scotland since 1730* (London, 1987).
Brown, D: *Memoir of the life of Dr John Duncan* (London, 1872).
Brown, T: *Annals of the Disruption* (Edinburgh, 1884, new edition, 1893).
Bruce, J: *Lives of Eminent Men of Aberdeen* (Aberdeen, 1841).
Buchanan, R: *The ten years' conflict* (Glasgow, new edition 1852).
Bulloch, J: *Centenary Memorials of the First Congregational Church in Aberdeen* (Aberdeen, 1898).
Burleigh, J A: *Church History of Scotland* (London, 1960).
Burns, T: *Old Scottish communion plate* (Edinburgh, 1892).
Cameron, J: *Centenary History of the Presbyterian Church in New South Wales* (Sydney, 1905).
Candlish, R S: *Sermons and memoir of the Rev. Andrew Gray* (Edinburgh, 1862).
Carnie, Wm: Reporting Reminiscences, (Aberdeen, 1902), volume 1.
Collins, G N M: *John Macleod, DD* (Edinburgh, 1951).
Connell, D M: *Reul-eolas* (Edinburgh, no date).
Cooper, J: *Cartularium ecclesiae Sancti Nicholai Aberdonensis* (Aberdeen, 1892).
Cowan, R: *Reminiscences* (Blairgowrie, 1924).
Cowan, R: *Our church fathers* (Elgin, 1899).
Cunningham, J: *The church history of Scotland* (Edinburgh, 2nd edition, 1882).
Dingwall-Fordyce, *A Family record of the name of Dingwall Fordyce in Aberdeenshire* (Fergus, Ontario, Canada, 1885 and 1888).
Dow, A C: *Ministers to the soldiers of Scotland* (Edinburgh, 1962).
Drummond, A L and J Bulloch: *The Church in Victorian Scotland 1843-1874* (Edinburgh, 1975).
Duff, D in *The New Statistical Account of Scotland* (Edinburgh, 1845), volume 10.
Dundonnell Cause: *Report of the Trial by Jury, Thomas Mackenzie, Esq. against Robert Roy, Esq. W.S.* Reported by Simon MacGregor, May 11th 1830 (Edinburgh).
Duthie, R: *Records of the first church in Woodside (Independent or Congregational) 1818-1945* (Banff, 1946).
Emslie, J G: *John Emslie 1831-1907. He came from Bennachie* (Christchurch, New Zealand, 1963).
Ewing, W: *Annals of the Free Church of Scotland* (Edinburgh, 1907).
Findlater, W: *Memoir of the Rev. Robert Findlater* (Glasgow, 1840).
Fraser, D: *The Story of Invergordon Church* (Inverness, 1946).
Fraser, G M: *Historical Aberdeen* (Aberdeen, 1905).
Fraser, G M: *Aberdeen Street Names* (Aberdeen, 1911).
Galt, J: *Annals of the Parish* (Foulis edition, London, 1911).
Gammie, A: *The Churches of Aberdeen* (Aberdeen, 1909).
Gibson, A J H: *Stipend in the Church of Scotland* (Edinburgh, 1961).
Gillies, W A: *In famed Breadalbane* (Perth, 1938).
Gordon, A: *The life of Archibald Hamilton Charteris* (London, 1912).

Graham, C (ed.): *Crown Him Lord of All* (Edinburgh, 1993).

Graham, J (ed.): *Disruption worthies of the Highlands* (Edinburgh, 1877).

Gray, A (ed.): *The progress of the chapel question from its first discussion in 1825 to its settlement in 1834 by the elevation of the ministers of chapels to the rank of the parochial clergy* (Aberdeen, 1836).

Gregg, W: *A short history of the Presbyterian Church in the Dominion of Canada* (Toronto, 1892).

Gunn, N M: *Morning Tide* (Edinburgh, 1931).

Haldane, A R B: *Three centuries of Scottish posts* (Edinburgh, 1971).

Hamilton, H: *An economic history of Scotland in the eighteenth century* (Oxford, 1963).

Henderson, G D: *The Burning Bush. Studies in Scottish Church History* (Edinburgh, 1957).

Henderson, G D: 'The Divinity Chair of King's College' in *Aberdeen University Review* (Aberdeen, 1928), volume 25, pp 120-131.

Henderson, G D: *Heritage. A study of the Disruption* (Edinburgh, 1943).

Hewat, E G K: *Vision and achievement 1796-1956* (Edinburgh, 1960).

Hunter, L S: *John Hunter DD. A Life* (London, 1921).

Innes, C (ed.): *Extracts from the council register of the burgh of Aberdeen 1570-1625* (Aberdeen, 1848).

Kay, J: *A series of original portraits with biographical sketches* (Edinburgh, 1877).

Keith, A: *A thousand years of Aberdeen* (Aberdeen, 1972).

Kennedy, A: *Memories of Scottish scenes and Sabbaths more than eighty years ago* (Edinburgh, 1902).

Kennedy, J: *The apostle of the North* (Inverness, 1886; new edition, 1932).

Kennedy, J: *The days of the fathers in Ross-shire* (Edinburgh, 1861; new edition, Inverness, 1927).

Kennedy, J: *The present cast and tendency of religious thought and feeling in Scotland* (Inverness, 1955).

Kennedy, J A: *Reply to Dr H Bonar's Defence of Hyper-Evangelism* (1875). Reprinted as *Evangelism: A Reformed Debate* (Portdinorwic, North Wales, 1997).

Kennedy, W: *Annals of Aberdeen* (London, 1818).

Kirk, J (ed): *The Church in the Highlands* (Edinburgh, 1999).

Knight, W: *Colloquia peripatetica* (Edinburgh, 1879).

Lamb, C: *The Essays and the Last Essays of Elia* (London, 1952).

Lyall, F: *Of Presbyters and Kings. Church and State in the Law of Scotland* (Aberdeen, 1980).

MacAlister, E F B: *Sir Donald MacAlister of Tarbert* (London 1935).

McBride, P (ed.): *Sermons and letters of Dr John Love of Anderston Chapel* (Glasgow, 1838).

Macdonald, A: *One hundred years of Presbyterianism in Victoria* (Melbourne, 1937).

Macdonald, G: *The Highlanders of Waipu* (Dunedin, 1928).

MacDonald, I R: *Glasgow's Gaelic Churches* (Edinburgh 1995).

MacDonald, I R: 'The beginning of Gaelic preaching in Scotland's cities in *Northern Scotland* (1989), volume 9.

MacDonald, I R: 'Aberdeen's Churches in the Late Eighteenth Century' in *Northern Scotland* (1999), volume 19.

Macdonald, J: *Isobel Hood's memoirs and manuscript* (Aberdeen, 1843).

Macdonald, S: *Reimagining Culture. Histories, Identities and the Gaelic Renaissssance* (Oxford, 1997).

Macfarlane, N C: *Apostles of the North* (Stornoway, 1926).

MacGregor, D: *Campbell of Kiltearn* (Edinburgh, 1874).

MacGregor, D: *The Shepherd of Israel* (London, 1869).

McGrigor, J: *Autobiography of Sir James McGrigor* (London, 1861).

MacInnes, J: *The evangelical movement in the Highlands of Scotland 1688 to 1800* (Aberdeen, 1951).

MacKillop, A M: *A goodly heritage* (North Kessock, Inverness, 1998).

Mackinnon, L: *Recollections of an old lawyer* (Aberdeen, 1935).

MacLaren, A A: *Religion and social class. The Disruption years in Aberdeen* (London,1974).

M'Lauchlan, T: *Celtic Gleanings* (Edinburgh, 1857).

Maclean, D: *Duthil Past and Present* (Inverness, 1910).

Macleod, J: *Scottish Theology* (Edinburgh, 1943).

Macleod, J: *By-paths of Highland church history* (Edinburgh, 1965).

Macleod, J: *Donald Munro of Ferintosh and Rogart* (Inverness, 1939).

Macleod, R: 'The John Bunyan of the Highlands' in *Transactions of the Gaelic Society of Inverness* (1984-86), volume liv.

McNaughton, W D: *The Scottish Congregational Ministry 1794-1993* (Glasgow, 1993).

MacPhail, J M: *Kenneth S Macdonald DD* (Edinburgh, 1905).

MacPherson, A: *Sidelights on two notable ministries* (Inverness, 1970).

MacPherson, J: *Cunntas Aithghearr mu Bheatha 'n Urramaich Raibeart Fiunlason* (Lochalsh, 1870).

Macrae, A: *Revivals in the Highlands and Islands in the 19th century* (Stirling, 1905).

Macrae, I M: *Dingwall Free Church. The Story of 100 Years and More* (Dingwall, 1970).

Macrae, N: *The romance of a royal burgh: Dingwall's story of a thousand years* (Dingwall, 1923; reprinted 1974).

Mair, Wm: *Digest of Church Law* (Edinburgh, 1895).

Martin, J: *Eminent divines in Aberdeen and the North* (Aberdeen, 1888).

Maxwell, A S: *Monumental inscriptions St Nicholas Aberdeen* (Aberdeen, 1972).

Meek, D E: 'Saints and Scarecrows: The Churches and Gaelic Culture in the Highlands since 1560' in *Scottish Bulletin of Evangelical Theology,* volume 14 (Edinburgh, 1996).

Meek, D E: *The Scottish Highlands* (Geneva, 1996).

Miller, Hugh: *Leading Articles* (Edinburgh, 1890).

Miller, Hugh: *My schools and schoolmasters* (Edinburgh, 1854, reprinted 1886).

Miller, Hugh: *The Headship of Christ* (Edinburgh, 1873).

Milne, J: *Aberdeen: topographical, antiquarian and historical papers on the city of Aberdeen* (Aberdeen, 1911).

Morgan, P: *Annals of Woodside and Newhills* (Aberdeen, 1909).

Munro, A M: *Memorials of the aldermen, provosts and lord provosts of Aberdeen 1272-1895* (Aberdeen, 1897).

Munro, C: *Memorials of the Rev. Christopher Macrae* (Edinburgh, 1890).

Munro, D: *Records of Grace in Sutherland* (Edinburgh, 1953).

Noble, J: *Religious life in Ross* (Inverness, 1909)

Orr, J Boyd: *As I Recall* (London, 1966).

Parker, G: *Selected portions from the diary and manuscripts of the Rev. Gavin Parker* (Aberdeen, 1848).

Rae, J J (ed.): *The Ministers of Glasgow* (Glasgow, no date).

Reith, G M: *Dr Archibald Reith* (Aberdeen, 1898).

Reminiscences of the Revival of fifty-nine and the sixties (Aberdeen, 1910).

Rettie, J: *Aberdeen fifty years ago* (Aberdeen, 1868).

Robbie, W: *Aberdeen: its traditions and history* (Aberdeen, 1893).

Robbie, W: *Bon Accord Free Church, Aberdeen. A retrospect* (Aberdeen, 1887).

Robertson, J: *The book of Bon-Accord* (Aberdeen. 1839).

Robinson, J C: *The Free Presbyterian Church of Australia* (Melbourne, 1947).

Rodger, E H B: *Aberdeen doctors at home and abroad* (Edinburgh, 1893).

Roger, C: *A week at Bridge of Allan* (Edinburgh, 1851).

Ross, A: *John Philip (1775-1851)* (Aberdeen, 1986).

Ross, J: *A Record of municipal affairs in Aberdeen* (Aberdeen, 1889).

Ross, K R: *Church and Creed in Scotland* (Edinburgh, 1988).

Sage, D: *Memorabilia Domestica* (Wick, 1889, reprinted 1975).

Scott, Hew: *Fasti ecclesiae Scoticanae* (Edinburgh, first edition, 1871).

Sell, A P F: *Defending & Declaring the Faith* (Exeter, 1987).

Sinclair, J (ed.): *The Statistical Account of Scotland* (Edinburgh, 1797), volume 19.

Small, R: *History of the Congregations of the United Presbyterian Church 1733-1900* (Edinburgh, 1904).

Smith, R M: *The history of Greenock* (Greenock, 1921).

Stark, J: *Dr Kidd of Aberdeen* (Aberdeen, third edition, 1898).

Thom, W: *The history of Aberdeen* (Aberdeen, 1811).

Thomson, D P: *Women of the Scottish Church* (Perth, 1975).

Thorburn, Rev. D: *Historical review of the legislation of the Free Church of Scotland on the Sustentation Fund* (Edinburgh, 1855).

Tullibardine, The Marchioness of: *A military history of Perthshire* (Perth, 1908).

Tweedie, W K: *The life of the Rev. John Macdonald AM* (Edinburgh, 1849).

Walker, G: *Aberdeen Awa'* (Aberdeen, 1897).

Walker, R S (ed.): *James Beattie's day-book 1773-1798* (Aberdeen, 1948).

Walker, Wm: *The bards of Bon-Accord* (Aberdeen, 1887).

Walls, A F: *Some Personalities of Aberdeen Methodism 1760-1970* (Aberdeen, 1973).

Warner, G T and C H K Marten: *The groundwork of British history* (London, 1936).

Watson, Mrs Jean (Deas Cromarty): *Scottish Ministerial Miniatures* (London, 1892).

Watt, H Thomas: *Chalmers and the Disruption* (Edinburgh, 1943).

Wilson, J: *A memoir of Mrs Margaret Wilson* (Edinburgh, second edition, 1838).

Wilson, J H: *The Bon-Accord repository* (Aberdeen, 1842).

Wilson, R: *An historical account and delineation of Aberdeen* (Aberdeen, 1822).

Withers, C W J: 'Highland Clubs and Chapels: Glasgow's Community in the Eighteenth Century' in *Scottish Geographical Magazine*, volume 101 (1984).

Withers, C W J: *Gaelic in Scotland 1698-1981* (Edinburgh, 1984).

Withers, C W J: 'Highland Migration to Aberdeen, c. 1649-1891' in *Northern Scotland,* volume 9 (1989).

Withers, C W J: 'Kirk, club and culture change: Gaelic chapels, Highland societies and the uban Gaelic subculture in eighteenth-century Scotland' in *Social History*, volume 10 (1985).

Withers, C W J: 'Class, culture and migrant identity: Gaelic Highlanders in urban Scotland' in G Kearns and C W J Withers (eds): *Urbanising Britain* (Cambridge, 1991).

Withers, C W J: *Urban Highlanders* (East Linton, 1998).

Wylie, Rev. J A: *Disruption Worthies: A Memorial of 1843* (Edinburgh 1881).

Wyness, F: *City by the grey North Sea* (Aberdeen, 1965).

INDEX OF MINISTERS

[NB: Most of those listed served in a number of charges. The location shown is that which is commonly identified with each minister. Ministers in Aberdeen are identified by their parish.]

*

INDEX OF PERSONS
(OTHER THAN ORDAINED MINISTERS)

INDEX OF AUTHORS

[NB: The page numbers refer to literature citations in the end notes.]

INDEX OF PLACES

INDEX OF SUBJECTS